ACTIVEX

No experience required.

ACTIVEX™

No experience required.™

Joseph Schmuller

SYBEX®

San Francisco • Paris • Düsseldorf • Soest

Associate Publisher: Gary Masters
Acquisitions Manager: Kristine Plachy
Acquisitions & Developmental Editor: Suzanne Rotondo
Editor: Kim Wimpsett
Technical Editor: David Shank
Book Designers: Patrick Dintino, Catalin Dulfu
Graphic Illustrator: Patrick Dintino
Electronic Publishing Specialist: Deborah A. Bevilacqua
Production Coordinator: Anton Reut
Proofreaders: Theresa Gonzalez, Charlie Matthews
Indexer: Lynnzee Spence
Cover Designer: Ingalls + Associates

Screen reproductions produced with Collage Complete.

Collage Complete is a trademark of Inner Media Inc.

SYBEX is a registered trademark of SYBEX Inc.
No experience required. is a trademark of SYBEX Inc.

TRADEMARKS: SYBEX has attempted throughout this book to distinguish proprietary trademarks from descriptive terms by following the capitalization style used by the manufacturer.

The author and publisher have made their best efforts to prepare this book, and the content is based upon final release software whenever possible. Portions of the manuscript may be based upon pre-release versions supplied by software manufacturer(s). The author and the publisher make no representation or warranties of any kind with regard to the completeness or accuracy of the contents herein and accept no liability of any kind including but not limited to performance, merchantability, fitness for any particular purpose, or any losses or damages of any kind caused or alleged to be caused directly or indirectly from this book.

Photographs and illustrations used in this book have been downloaded from publicly accessible file archives and are used in this book for news reportage purposes only to demonstrate the variety of graphics resources available via electronic access. Text and images available over the Internet may be subject to copyright and other rights owned by third parties. Online availability of text and images does not imply that they may be reused without the permission of rights holders, although the Copyright Act does permit certain unauthorized reuse as fair use under 17 U.S.C. Section 107.

Library of Congress Card Number: 97-67410
ISBN: 0-7821-2114-4

Manufactured in the United States of America

10 9 8 7 6 5 4 3 2 1

*To my wonderful mother, Sara Riba Schmuller
Who taught me how to read the first book I ever read,
I dedicate the first book I'll ever write.*

Acknowledgments

Any book is a team effort. While the author may be the most visible player, the contributions of the author's teammates make the book possible. It's a pleasure to acknowledge those contributions and to thank the Sybex team I was privileged to work with.

Acquisitions & Developmental Editor Suzanne Rotondo had the faith and confidence that this dyed-in-the-wool magazine writer could make the grade as a rookie book author. Suzanne helped me crystallize my thoughts on organization and catalyze the beginning of the book.

Editor Kim Wimpsett did a remarkable job of keeping my ideas comprehensible and my words readable. Every author should have the good fortune to work with an editor as cooperative, knowledgeable, and supportive as Kim.

Technical Editor David Shank of Microsoft patiently worked through the manuscript and all the code examples, providing constructive comments, incisive questions, and valuable insights. Thanks to his tireless efforts, the book you're reading is a much stronger one.

Suzanne, Kim, and David did world-class work in every way. Any errors or inconsistencies that remain are, alas, the fault of the author.

Thanks also to the Sybex production team, particularly Electronic Publishing Specialist Debi Bevilacqua and Production Coordinator Anton Reut, who worked diligently page after page to turn my writing into the book you see before you.

Others contributed to this effort in significant ways. David Fugate of Waterside Productions put the process in motion that resulted in this book. My friends and colleagues at PathTech Software Solutions offered support and valuable information. A special note of thanks goes to PathTech CEO Bob Touchton for laying out the seven critical business functions that appear in Skill 18.

For the past six years, I've had the pleasure to be the Editor in Chief of *PC AI* magazine. I thank my colleagues at *PC AI*—Publisher Terry Hengl, Vice President of Marketing Robin Okun, and Managing Editor Elizabeth Olson—for their cooperation and understanding as I completed this book.

I express my deepest thanks to my mother and my brother David for their love, support, and patience throughout this project…and my love and gratitude to GOMD for absolutely everything, and for much more than one man could ever hope.

Contents at a Glance

skills

skills

skills

Table of Contents

Introduction

Some Imagination Required

The last several years have seen the Internet assume a primary place in almost everything we do with computers. Through the World Wide Web, the Internet's newly acquired starring role has spawned competing visions of how the future of PC-Internet interaction should unfold. One vision is to provide Web browser capabilities that put your desktop on the Internet. Give your browser some tools to display eye-catching graphics and animation from World Wide Web sites, along with a few rudimentary capabilities to communicate with the computers that host those Web sites, and you'll happily surf the Net. You might think of this as the "Web of Dreams" vision: build the Web and they will come.

Microsoft, however, has moved in the opposite direction. Instead of putting your desktop on the Internet, their vision is to put the Internet on your desktop. If your browser can make a Web site look and act like any other Windows application, you'll be able to use it intuitively and productively. Then, the wealth of information that the Web provides will seemingly (and seamlessly) be at your fingertips as you actively seek it out. A great idea, but how do you make it happen?

Microsoft's ActiveX technology is the answer. It provides developers with the tools and techniques to build the kind of user interface into a Web page that you'd find in a commercial Windows package. Command buttons, text boxes, list boxes, and more are available for use via ActiveX. Referred to as ActiveX *controls*, these onscreen devices enable users to exploit the many capabilities of the World Wide Web.

The Objective

This book shows you how to incorporate ActiveX controls in the Web pages you develop. I assume you're starting out with a working knowledge of computers and Windows 95, a desire to learn about a technology that will help you build exciting Web pages, and the imagination to use that technology in new and productive ways. My objective is to give you extensive experience with ActiveX controls and with what they can do, and then let your imagination do the rest.

When I thought about the quickest path to this objective, I drew upon my work as a teacher. I've found that the best way to present a technical subject is often to start by leading students step-by-step through hands-on exercises, and then use the knowledge they've gained as a framework to impart the subject's foundational concepts in a more formal way. Too many books, I've discovered, follow the reverse path: They present the formal concepts first, and then the experience. While the flow typically seems logical and natural to the author, it's often not as natural for the reader.

ActiveX presents an added challenge to anyone who would teach it. The technology is changing at a breathtaking pace. Developers are expanding ActiveX every day—partly because of the constant demand for innovation in Web page development and partly because it's an easy technology to expand, once you understand it.

So the idea is to quickly give you a lot of hands-on experience with ActiveX, an insight into the formal aspects of the technology, and some way of getting a handle on how it's growing.

The Organization of the Book

To give you the experience, the insight, and the vision, I've laid out the book in three parts. Part I, "Diving In," immediately gets you acquainted with ActiveX controls. You'll embed a variety of ActiveX controls into HTML documents, learn to script them in Visual Basic Scripting Edition (VBS), and make them interact with one another and with users. Along the way, you'll learn some HTML (Hypertext Markup Language, the basis for most of what you see on the Web) and some important VBS concepts.

After Part I develops your experience base and your skill set, Part II, "Exploring the Tools," changes direction a bit. Now that you've worked first-hand with ActiveX technology, you're ready to understand the foundations of the technology and its tools. In this part you'll closely examine the technology, its underlying models, and the tools you've used. The knowledge you acquired in Part I provides the backdrop for understanding.

Part III, "Building the Technology," shows you how to move ahead on your own. You'll acquire a strategy for learning about new controls, you'll learn how to create new controls, and you'll get a picture of where ActiveX is headed.

Each part consists of a set of Skills designed to make you a seasoned ActiveX technologist. Let's take a look at the Skills in each part of *ActiveX: No experience required.*

Part I

Part I consists of Skills 1 through 9. Skill 1, "Embedding ActiveX Controls: Buttons and Labels," starts you off by introducing you to the development tools you'll have to acquire to follow along with the book. (They're all free and downloadable from Microsoft Web sites.) You'll set up an environment that organizes and facilitates your work, and you'll use the development tools to embed two ActiveX controls into a Web page. You'll learn some HTML, you'll get your first look at the ActiveX Control Pad, and you'll use three of the Control Pad's four components: the Text Editor, the Object Editor, and the HTML Layout Control. You'll use Internet Explorer (IE) to open the Web pages you've created.

Skill 2, "Creating Scripts," gets you involved with the fourth ActiveX Control Pad component, the Script Wizard. You'll use it to write programs in VBS for the controls you embedded in Web pages in Skill 1, and you'll progress to some new controls. By the end of Skills 1 and 2, you'll know all about how to put a control into a Web page and how to write programs that work with mouse-clicks and keystrokes. Skill 3, "Examining ActiveX Objects," shows you how to dissect the controls you worked with in the first two skills. You'll learn how and where they reside on your machine, and how they got there in the first place.

Skill 4, "Working with Graphics," is your entry into the world of Web-based graphics. You'll work with an ActiveX control that allows you to put graphic images into your Web pages and another control that makes those images respond to mouse events. You'll finish Skill 4 with a look at simple animation, a concept that carries over into Skill 5, "Introducing Interactivity: The TextBox Control," and Skill 6, "Building Interactivity: ListBoxes, ComboBoxes, Option Buttons, and PopUp Menus." In those Skills, you'll learn how to program ActiveX controls that draw users into meaningful interactions with Web pages.

Skill 7, "Displaying Data, Documents, and Ideas: Chart, First Impression, Acrobat Reader, and InterAct," goes beyond text and graphics and introduces you to controls that visualize complex information and concepts. In Skill 8, "Multiplying the Media: Music, Sound, and Video," you'll work with multimedia-oriented ActiveX controls. You'll learn how to build Web pages that incorporate music, audio, and movies.

You'll finish Part I by learning about the fascinating technology of Agents, intelligent little creations that will astound you with what they can do. Skill 9, "Working with Agents," shows you how to program the Microsoft Agent control, an animated onscreen character that has capabilities for animation, speech production, and speech recognition.

Part II

Skills 10 through 14 constitute Part II. In contrast to the Skills in Part I, the Skills in Part II take you through the tools and the technology of ActiveX. Skill 10, "Getting Into VBScript," is an inside look at the statements, functions, and other constructs built into VBS. Skill 11, "Putting VBS and HTML Together," builds on your knowledge of VBS. You'll learn how to directly combine VBS with some of the constructs built into HTML.

Skill 12, "Dissecting the ActiveX Control Pad," puts the ActiveX Control Pad under the microscope. You'll find out about all its nooks and crannies and you'll pick up some tips that will speed up your development efforts. Skill 13, "Digging Up the Roots of ActiveX," gives you an understanding of ActiveX's history. You'll learn where ActiveX came from, and you'll learn the model that forms its foundation.

Skill 14, "Dissecting Internet Explorer," shows you the ins and outs of IE. You'll use VBS to manipulate IE's appearance, and as you do so, you'll gain insight into the model that underlies IE.

Part III

Skills 15 through 18 round out the book. Because no single book can cover all the existing ActiveX controls (and because new ones are appearing all the time), Skill 15, Learning New Controls," gives you a strategy for working with new controls and understanding how they operate.

Skill 16, "Introducing Visual Basic 5 Control Creation Edition," familiarizes you with the Visual Basic 5 Control Creation Edition (VB5 CCE), a development environment that enables you to create new ActiveX controls of your own. Skill 17, "Creating and Using Controls," continues your work with VB5 CCE, showing you how to build a control that you can embed in a Web page.

Skill 18, "Scoping Out the Future of ActiveX," finishes things up with a look at where ActiveX is headed. You'll see how the technology might make its presence felt in a variety of areas.

Code Examples

The code for the hands-on exercises in the pages that follow appears on the Sybex Web site. Instead of having to type in each code listing, you can save time and energy by downloading certain listings. Each code file that's on the site is noted in the book with its name in parentheses along with this icon:

Downloading the Code

You can download the code examples from `http://www.sybex.com`. Click on the No Experienced Required icon to get to the series page. Once you're there, click on ActiveX to access the code files.

Listings

One more word about the code. When you're learning a new language and a new technology, it's often helpful to see the whole listing for a programming exercise. You might not always download the code from the Web, but you'll still want to see the code so that you can check your own work. In most cases, the book presents the entire listing for a particular exercise.

Notation Conventions

Throughout the book, our discussion will take various forms. Sometimes, I'll ask you to type something. Sometimes, I'll direct your attention to features of your display or your keyboard. At other times, I'll bring new terminology into the fray.

To help keep things comprehensible, here are some conventions for our notation:

- When I ask you to type a word or a phrase, I'll put the word or phrase in **bold** font.

- I'll use `monospaced` font to indicate a word or phrase that is in a code listing. I'll also use this font for names of files and folders.

- When I refer to onscreen items—like titles of windows, folders, buttons, elements in lists, items in dialog boxes, menus, or menu choices—I'll put those items in Headline Style (Regardless of How They Appear Onscreen).

- When I refer to named keys on your keyboard, I'll put those in Initial Capital Letters, too (for example, Alt, Tab, Esc, Ctrl).

- To indicate keystroke combinations, I'll put a plus sign (+) between a pair of keys. For example, Alt+Tab means "hold down the Alt key while you press the Tab key."

- To indicate a menu choice, I'll use this symbol: ➢. Thus, "File ➢ Save" refers to the Save choice from the File menu.

- New terminology can sometimes be confusing—particularly when you don't know that it's new. For this reason, I'll use *italics* to signal the first appearance of an important word or phrase.

- Sometimes a line of code is too long to fit on a line of text, and I'll have to continue it on the following line. When that happens, I'll start the continuation line with ➡.

Here are some other items that you'll see along the way:

NOTE   This is a Note. It provides a piece of additional information about a topic.

THIS IS A SIDEBAR

Occasionally, I'll discuss a topic that requires more space than a Note. If putting the discussion into the main body of the text would disrupt the flow, I'll present it to you in a sidebar that looks like this.

TIP   This is a Tip, which is intended to be a shortcut or a trick that helps you be more productive.

WARNING   This is a Warning. It indicates a condition or an action that could be potentially harmful to your work or your computer.

Ready, Set...

So...no experience is required, but some imagination is. A lot of information awaits you in the pages to come—information designed to make you think, create, and develop insights of your own.

Take a deep breath, turn to Skill 1, and let's get started....

PART I

Diving In

The Skills in Part I will quickly give you firsthand experience with a variety of ActiveX controls. You'll embed these controls into Web pages, and you'll make them interact with each other and with users. You'll start with Command Buttons and Labels and work all the way up to multimedia and Agents. In this Part, you'll also learn how to use the ActiveX Control Pad's tools: the Text Editor, Object Editor, HTML Layout Control, and Script Wizard.

S K I L L

one

1

Embedding ActiveX Controls: Buttons and Labels

- ❑ Setting up a work environment

- ❑ Introducing HTML

- ❑ Working with the Object Editor

- ❑ Embedding Command Buttons and Labels into HTML

- ❑ Working with the HTML Layout Control

Welcome to ActiveX—Microsoft's hot new tool set for adding sizzle to Web pages. Follow along with this book, and you'll learn how to use the tools.

This book will focus on the specific skills that you'll need. You'll learn how to make your pages interactive by adding some well-known (and some exciting new) User Interface gadgets—such as Command Buttons, ListBoxes, ComboBoxes, multimedia controls, and more. And you'll learn how to make these controls interact with each other, as well as with end users.

Why is it important to learn about ActiveX? As Microsoft Internet Explorer becomes an increasingly popular Web browser, you'll see more and more Web sites incorporating ActiveX technology. This means that Web site builders and Webmasters will use the technology as part and parcel of their design and development process. So whether you're a Web designer, a Webmaster, or a Web consumer, ActiveX will soon be an integral part of your life—if it isn't already.

ActiveX evolved from earlier Microsoft technology, and its increasing popularity stems, in part, from its connection to a programming language that many people have worked with in one form or another—BASIC. With ActiveX, you use a subset of Microsoft's popular Visual Basic—Visual Basic Scripting Edition—to bring Web pages to life. With this scripting language (VBScript for short, VBS for shorter), the requisite programming knowledge is minimal. In the development tools you'll work with in this book, a wizard helps you along.

ActiveX's popularity is on the rise for another reason. This technology makes it easy and fun to develop a sophisticated presence on the World Wide Web. ActiveX has the greatest potential for making Web sites interactive: Put a few building blocks together, add a script that directs them, and you have a Web site that captures people's attention, sticks in their minds, and keeps them coming back.

Tools of the Trade

In order to use this book and become experienced with ActiveX, you'll need several tools (and I'm assuming that you'll work in Windows 95).

Internet Explorer

First, you have to have Microsoft Internet Explorer to view the Web pages that you create. You can download Internet Explorer 3.01 (we'll refer to it as IE) from Microsoft's Web site at `http://www.microsoft.com/ie/download/`.

> **NOTE** In your travels around the Web, you may have seen numerous sites (other than Microsoft's) that allow you to link up to the Microsoft Web area for downloading IE. When you use IE to hit many of those sites, you'll probably experience ActiveX firsthand.

The ActiveX Control Pad

Another tool figures prominently in what you'll do: the ActiveX Control Pad. As you'll see, this little package is a big asset: It enables you to quickly and easily put ready-made ActiveX objects (called *controls*) into your Web pages. Download the setup file for the ActiveX Control Pad (the setup file is called `setuppad.exe`) from `http://www.microsoft.com/workshop/author/cpad/`.

The ActiveX Control Pad has four major components:

- The Text Editor for creating pages in HyperText Markup Language (HTML)

- The Object Editor for working with ActiveX objects

- The HTML Layout Control for using a two-dimensional visual tool to edit HTML files in WYSIWYG ("What You See Is What You Get") fashion

- The Script Wizard to guide you as you build VBScript

By the way, it's a good idea to create a shortcut icon for the Control Pad. An important tool, it will play an important role in everything you do.

Visual Basic 5 Control Creation Edition

One more tool completes our bag of tricks. After you've worked with a number of ActiveX controls, you might want to build a few of your own. You might even create a world-class control. Microsoft has put together Visual Basic 5 Control Creation Edition (VB5 CCE), a new version of Visual Basic to help you turn your inspiration into reality. You can download the latest version from `http://www.microsoft.com/vbasic/controls`. VB5 CCE is different from VBScript, although they share a common ancestry: VBScript adds functionality to ActiveX controls, and VB5 CCE enables you to create ActiveX controls.

Setting Up a Work Environment

Before we get started using the tools we just learned about, let's agree on a work environment that makes our efforts as smooth and efficient as possible. We'll develop our Web pages in the ActiveX Control Pad and examine them in Internet Explorer (IE), so let's enable ourselves to quickly move back and forth between the two.

A Directory Structure

First, let's set up a directory structure to store our work:

1. Create a new folder called ActiveX No Exp Req, and open this folder.

2. Within this folder, create a separate folder for the work we'll do in each Skill (skill 1, skill 2, and so on).

As you follow the discussion for a Skill, keep its folder open; for instance, while following along with this Skill, keep the skill 1 folder open.

I keep this file structure on my E: drive. Obviously, if you keep yours on C: or D:, your path names won't look exactly like mine.

 NOTE   When a filename in parentheses and a code icon precede a code listing, use that filename to download the code. You can download this book's source code from the Sybex Web site at http://www.sybex.com/. Click on the No Experience Required icon, and then click on the ActiveX icon. You'll find loads of utilities and tools to download and check out, as well.

IE: Your Default Web Browser

Whenever you develop a Web page, the first thing you should do is give it a file-name and save it (in the appropriate folder for the skill you're working in at the time). As you go through the development steps, you'll sometimes want to stop and examine your work. You'll want to be able to double-click on the icon that represents the page you created and have it open in IE.

To do this, make sure that IE is your default Web browser and that it's designated to open Internet Documents. If IE is your only Web browser, you're all set. If it's not, follow these steps:

1. Go to the Windows 95 Control Panel and double-click on the Internet icon. The Internet Properties dialog box will open.

2. Click on the Programs tab. On the page that appears, click on File Types....

3. In the scrollable Registered file types list, find Internet Document (HTML) and click on it.

If the File type details box shows that files with the extensions HTM or HTML open with IEXPLORE, everything's fine. If not, click on the Edit button and follow these steps:

1. In the Edit Type dialog box, scroll through the Actions pane until you see Open.

2. Select Open.

3. Click on the Edit... button.

4. The Editing Action for Type: Internet Document (HTML) dialog box appears.

5. Click on Browse... and you'll see still another dialog box, Open With.

6. This dialog box presents folders and files. Search through it until you find `Iexplore.exe`, select it, and click Open.

7. Click OK to get back to the Edit File Type dialog box.

8. If you want to change the icon associated with Internet Documents, click the Change Icon... button.

9. In the Change Icon dialog box that opens, scroll through the pane of icons until you find one you like. Select that icon and click OK. (You can also click Browse... and look for other icons in folders throughout your computer.)

10. Close all the dialog boxes, and close the Control Panel.

Skill 1

Control Pad to IE, and Back Again

The first time you open your Web page, you'll double-click on the icon that represents it. How do you get to that icon? Remember that you've opened the folder that stores your work, and that you've left it open. To quickly get to that folder from the ActiveX Control Pad, you'll use a keystroke combination: Alt+Tab. Keep pressing the Tab key (while holding down Alt) until you select the icon that represents the folder you want to see. Then, take your fingers off both keys.

When you finish looking at your handiwork, *do not close IE*. Use Alt+Tab to return to the ActiveX Control Pad and start editing again. When you want to reexamine your work in IE, *do not close* the ActiveX Control Pad. Use Alt+Tab to return to IE. On your second visit (and all subsequent visits) to IE, click on the Refresh button (it's on the toolbar near the top of IE) to see your updated Web page. If you don't click on this button, you'll see the previous version of your Web page.

 NOTE   As you become more experienced with switching back and forth between the ActiveX Control Pad and IE, you'll find a particular key very helpful: F5. Clicking on that key is the same as clicking the Refresh button on the IE toolbar. This is useful for two reasons. First, you'll save a couple of seconds. Second, sometimes you'll hide the IE toolbar to give yourself more room on the Web page.

The Alt+Tab combination is apparently one of the best-kept secrets about working in Windows. A substantial majority of Windows 3.1 users were unaware of this capability for moving back and forth among applications. It's a good bet that this lack of awareness has carried over into Windows 95.

 TIP   Here's another useful keystroke combination: Ctrl+Esc. This one displays the Windows 95 Start menu. We won't use it in this book, but you might find it handy to know.

Getting Started: Introducing HTML

Let's get going. We're going to create a simple Web page. We'll use the Control Pad to build it, and IE to examine what we've built.

NOTE   I'll assume that you've installed Internet Explorer and the ActiveX Control Pad. If not, see "Tools of the Trade" earlier in this Skill for more information.

When it's done, your Web page will look like Figure 1.1. It will have a line of text that is centered, large, and displayed in bold font. More importantly, it will have two ActiveX controls: a Command Button and a Label. Each one is centered on the page. Six lines separate the text line from the first control, and six more separate the first control from the second.

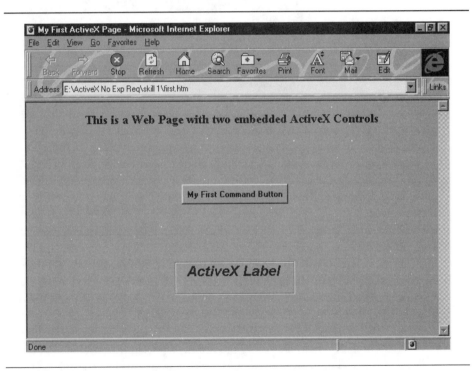

FIGURE 1.1: Follow along with this Skill, and this is what your first ActiveX Web page will look like when you're done.

 NOTE   Depending on your computer's setup, your Command Button may look slightly different from that shown in the figure. For example, screens with resolutions above 800/600 may truncate the button's caption.

To get started creating this Web page, open the ActiveX Control Pad. Start it from the Programs menu that pops up when you click on the Windows 95 Start button or from a shortcut icon on your desktop.

After the introductory screen, the ActiveX Control Pad will open and you'll see a screen that looks like Figure 1.2.

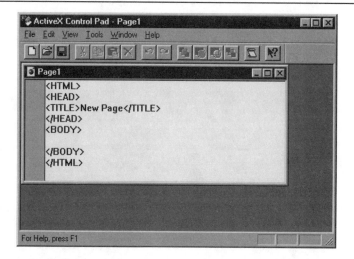

FIGURE 1.2: This is the screen you see when you open the ActiveX Control Pad.

As you can see, the ActiveX Control Pad is ready for you to start creating *Hyper-Text Markup Language* (HTML). HTML is more or less the universal language for creating Internet documents, and you can use any text editor to create HTML code.

The ActiveX Control Pad Text Editor appears when you open the application. Each word inside angle-brackets (<>) in the Text Editor is called a *tag*. When a Web browser such as IE or Netscape Navigator opens an HTML file, it uses the tags to interpret the document's structure and to show it on the screen as the developer intended.

UNDERSTANDING HTML TAGS

Tags are the "markups" in Hypertext Markup Language. Most come in pairs. The first member of the pair (<HEAD>, for example, in Figure 1.2) is called a *start tag*. It indicates the beginning of the area that the tag-pair applies to. The second member of the pair, the *stop tag* (or *end tag*), always has a slash (/) as its first character (</HEAD>) and indicates the end of the area that the tag-pair applies to.

Some tags are universal; you'll find these in almost every HTML document:

- <HTML> and </HTML> indicate the beginning and the end of an HTML document.

- <HEAD> and </HEAD> identify the properties of the entire HTML document.

- <TITLE> and </TITLE> are at the beginning and end of the title that appears in the browser's title bar. They appear between the two members of the HEAD tag-pair.

- <BODY> and </BODY> form the boundaries of the document's main body.

To make your HTML code comprehensible to others, you can enclose comments in angle-brackets. The left angle-bracket precedes an exclamation point and two hyphens. Two hyphens precede the right angle-bracket. It looks like this:

<!-- Comments go in here -->

When your Web-browser sees this kind of angle-bracket structure, it doesn't try to interpret what's between the brackets. That makes it a good device for enclosing comments in HTML. Your browser will ignore your comments, but your fellow humans will find them extremely helpful. You should make it a habit to use comments frequently throughout your Web page coding.

Before going any further, save the file that you just opened in the ActiveX Control Pad. Give it the name first.htm and save it in your skill 1 folder. In the Text Editor, delete the text New Page. Type **My First ActiveX Page** and make sure it sits between <TITLE> and </TITLE>.

Now we'll start to create the body of the page. After <BODY> and before </BODY>, type **This is a Web Page with two embedded ActiveX Controls**.

Let's now take a look at the page in a browser to see where we stand. Save the file. Use Alt+Tab to go to the skill 1 folder, and find the icon that represents first.htm. Double-click on the icon. IE opens, and then after a few moments, your page appears. At this point it should look like Figure 1.3.

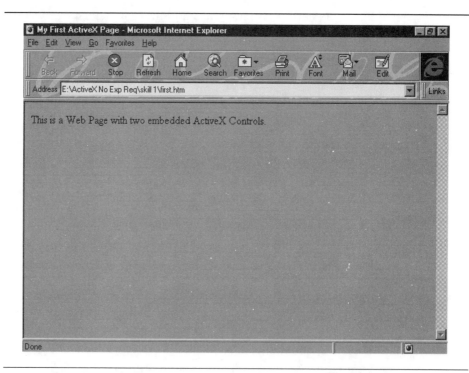

FIGURE 1.3: The initial stage of developing your first ActiveX Web page

Pretty plain, isn't it? In order to make the text appear as in Figure 1.1, we have to make it big, bold, and centered:

1. Alt+Tab back to the ActiveX Control Pad window.

2. Maximize the ActiveX Control Pad application window and then maximize the Text Editor window.

3. We'll use three HTML tag-pairs to adjust the text. Just before the line of text between the BODY tags, type **<B> <BIG> <CENTER>**. (Don't type the period.)

    As you might imagine, the first tag indicates bold font, the second makes the font larger, and the third centers the line on the page.

4. Just after the line of text, type **</CENTER> </BIG> </B>** to complete the tag-pairs.

    Your ActiveX Text Editor should hold these lines of HTML code:

    ```
    <HTML>
    <HEAD>
    <TITLE>My First ActiveX Page</TITLE>
    </HEAD>
    <BODY> <!-- These tags adjust the text line -->
    <B> <BIG> <CENTER>
    <!-- This is the text line -->
    This is a Web Page with two embedded ActiveX Controls
    </CENTER> </BIG> </B>

    </BODY>
    </HTML>
    ```

5. Select File ➢ Save to save your work, and return to IE.

Your screen should now look as it did before. To see the new formatting, click the Refresh button (or press the F5 key on your keyboard). IE loads the new version of your Web page, and your screen should now look like Figure 1.4.

Adding the Sizzle: Embedding Buttons and Labels with the Object Editor

Now it's time to add two ActiveX controls to your HTML code. A Web site developer would say that when you add a control, you *embed* it in an HTML document.

In the Text Editor, insert a blank line just before </BODY>. Position the cursor at the beginning of this line. Select Edit ➢ Insert ActiveX Control….

You'll see the dialog box that appears in Figure 1.5.

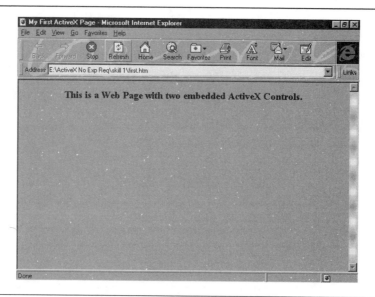

FIGURE 1.4: Your first Web page after you've adjusted the text. This is how Internet Explorer (IE) interprets the HTML code you've entered so far.

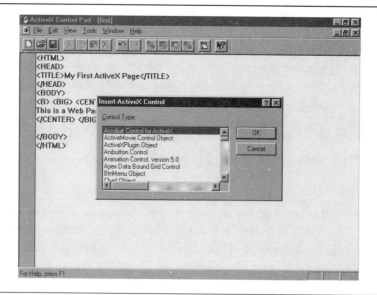

FIGURE 1.5: The dialog box that appears when you select Insert ActiveX Control... from the Control Pad's Edit menu

The Insert ActiveX Control dialog box shows a list box containing the ActiveX controls that are available on your machine. Take a moment to scroll through the list to give you a general idea of what the ActiveX world is all about. Although this list is already fairly long, the world of ActiveX controls is expanding every day, and developers have created more than a thousand of them. When you select controls to embed in your Web pages, you'll select them from this list.

Embedding a Command Button

From the Control Type list, select Microsoft Forms 2.0 Command Button and click OK. Your screen should look like Figure 1.6. You are now in the ActiveX Control Pad's Object Editor.

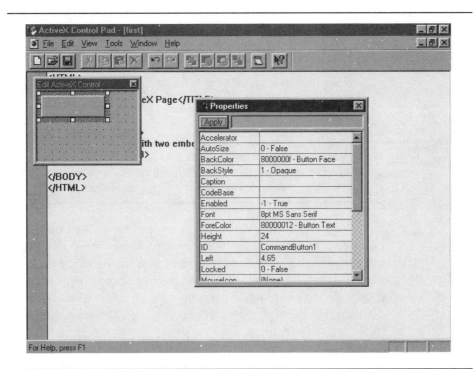

FIGURE 1.6: The Object Editor appears when you select an ActiveX control from the scrollable list of available ActiveX controls.

With the Object Editor, you modify the appearance (and other properties) of the control you selected. It is shown in the window on the left (Edit ActiveX Control). You use the window to visually change aspects of the control's appearance. The scrollable window on the right is the *Properties sheet.* In the Properties sheet, you enter values for the control's properties.

NOTE   Because the Edit ActiveX Control window's background is a set of regularly spaced dots that make up a grid, it looks like this window might be designed to help you position the control on the Web page. That's not its purpose. It just enables you to quickly modify the appearance of the control.

Our goal, remember, is to construct a Web page that looks like Figure 1.1. Let's start by putting a caption on the Command Button. In the Properties sheet, click on the row labeled Caption. Now position your cursor in the rectangular area at the top of the Properties sheet. Called the *Setting Box,* it's the area just to the right of the Apply button. In the Setting Box, type **My First Command Button**. Then click on Apply. In general, this is how you modify a control's properties:

1. Select a property in the Properties sheet.

2. Enter information in the Setting Box.

3. Click the Apply button to modify the property.

TIP   The way you enter information into the Setting Box depends on the type of property you've selected. For some properties, you type information. For some, you choose from a drop-down list. For others, you select an item from a dialog box.

At this point, only part of the caption appears on the Command Button in the Edit ActiveX Control window. In order to make the entire caption appear, you'll use one of the eight little white squares that surround the Command Button. These squares are called *sizing handles.* Hover your cursor over the middle sizing handle along the right-side boundary. When it becomes a two-headed arrow, double-click. This automatically expands the Command Button to a size that shows the entire caption.

Next, make the font bold. In the Properties sheet, select the Font property. The Properties sheet changes a bit. A new button appears to the right of the Setting Box. The new button has three dots (a structure referred to as an *ellipsis*). This indicates that clicking on the button brings up a display of further information (much as clicking on Insert ActiveX Control… brought up the Object Editor). In this case, clicking the ellipsis brings up the Font dialog box (see Figure 1.7).

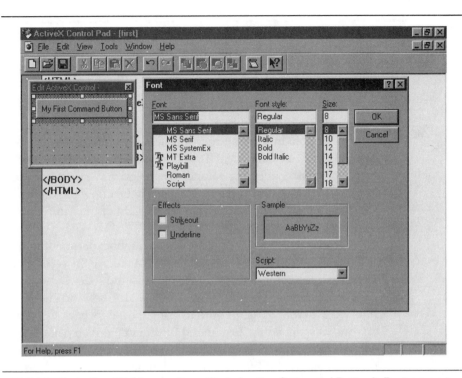

FIGURE 1.7: Clicking on the ellipsis for the Command Button's Font property brings up the Font dialog box.

The Font dialog box presents you with a set of choices about the caption's font, its font style, and its size. From the Font Style list, select Bold. You'll see what the bold text looks like in the box labeled Sample. Click OK. Once again, the Command Button is too small for its caption, as bolding expands the thickness of the letters. Adjust the button's size by double-clicking on the appropriate sizing handle. The Edit ActiveX Control window may be too small to show the whole button. To adjust the window's size, position the cursor on any side. When a double-arrow appears, drag the side to expand the button.

It's a good idea to give the Command Button an *identifier*. The default identifier is CommandButton1. To find this default identifier, look through the Properties sheet until you see ID. Change the default ID by clicking on ID and typing **cmdbtnFirst** in the Setting Box. (Later, I'll explain why we chose that particular identifier.) Click Apply.

TIP   Beginners sometimes confuse the ID property with the Caption property. The ID identifies a control to the other controls in the HTML document. It doesn't appear in the displayed Web page. The Caption appears on the control.

Let's modify one more property of the Command Button. When we view the page in IE, we can have the cursor's appearance change when the mouse moves over the button. In some applications this is useful, as it indicates the functionality available in a particular area. If you've ever worked with a word-processor, you've seen the cursor change appearance when you move it around the screen. Click on the MousePointer property. The Setting Box now has a list of options. Click on the down-arrow that now appears to the right of the Setting Box to see the list. Select the I-Beam option.

While you're in the Object Editor, you might experiment with some of the Command Button's other properties—particularly the color of the caption (Fore-Color) and the color of the button's background (BackColor). Note how the colors change when you select from the Colors dialog box and click OK. When you're finished experimenting, be sure to bring the colors back to their original values.

Now, let's embed the Command Button in the Web page. Close the Edit ActiveX Control window and the Properties sheet. Notice that the HTML document in your Text Editor has changed. It now looks like Figure 1.8.

One new feature in the HTML document is the OBJECT tag-pair. Between <OBJECT> and </OBJECT>, several new lines of code tell your browser that a Command Button is now embedded in the document. The first member of the tag-pair holds four pieces of information between the word OBJECT and the closing angle-bracket (>): the Command Button's ID, its width, its height, and its ClassID. The first three are values that you entered in the Object Editor. The fourth one comes up for discussion in Skill 3.

You'll also see a number of lines that start with <PARAM NAME = . Like the ID, width, and height, the values after the "=" sign reflect information that you entered into the Object Editor. This is one way that the ActiveX Control Pad speeds up development: It writes significant parts of the code so that you don't have to.

Another new feature is the symbol that appears to the left of the newly inserted code. Clicking on this symbol brings back the Object Editor and allows you to edit the Command Button's properties once again.

```
ActiveX Control Pad - [first]                                    _ 8 X
File  Edit  View  Tools  Window  Help                            _ 8 X

<HTML>
<HEAD>
<TITLE>My First ActiveX Page</TITLE>
</HEAD>
<BODY>
<B> <BIG> <CENTER>
This is a Web Page with two embedded ActiveX Controls.
</CENTER> </BIG> <B>

<OBJECT ID="cmdbtnFirst" WIDTH=160 HEIGHT=29
 CLASSID="CLSID:D7053240-CE69-11CD-A777-00DD01143C57">
   <PARAM NAME="Caption" VALUE="My First Command Button">
   <PARAM NAME="Size" VALUE="4234;767">
   <PARAM NAME="MousePointer" VALUE="3">
   <PARAM NAME="FontEffects" VALUE="1073741825">
   <PARAM NAME="FontCharSet" VALUE="0">
   <PARAM NAME="FontPitchAndFamily" VALUE="2">
   <PARAM NAME="ParagraphAlign" VALUE="3">
   <PARAM NAME="FontWeight" VALUE="700">
</OBJECT>

</BODY>
</HTML>

For Help, press F1
```

FIGURE 1.8: After you close the Object Editor windows, your HTML document has changed.

Notice that none of the information in the new code about the Command Button specifies the button's location within the Web page. What effect does this lack of information have? To see for yourself, save your work, return to IE, and click on the IE Refresh button. Your Web page appears as in Figure 1.9. (As you move the cursor around the page, you'll see its appearance change to an I-beam as it moves over the Command Button.)

Today's version of HTML has no way to set exact positions (in terms of x-y coordinates) for objects that you embed in HTML code. Just as we used HTML tags to modify the text line, we have to use HTML tags to do the job here— although later in this Skill (see "Laying Out the Sizzle: Positioning Buttons and Labels with the Object Editor") we examine an ActiveX Control Pad tool that makes things a lot easier.

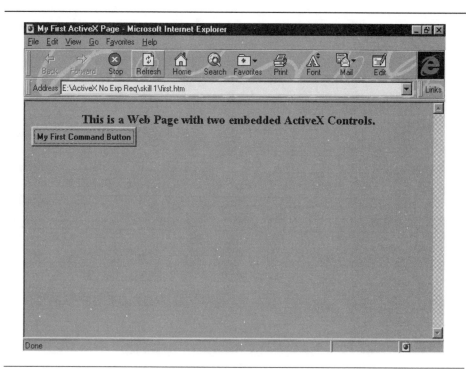

FIGURE 1.9: The Web page with the text and the Command Buttons

In the meantime, let's add the tags to do the job now:

1. Alt+Tab back to the Control Pad.

2. Before the first <OBJECT> tag, type **<CENTER>**.

3. After </OBJECT> type **</CENTER>**. This centers the Command Button, just below the text.

4. Next, save your work, Alt+Tab to IE, and click Refresh to see the changes you just made.

    To get the page to look more like Figure 1.1, we have to use another HTML tag to move the button down the page. HTML's line-break tag, <BR>, does the trick.

5. Return to the ActiveX Control Pad. Right after </B> (the tag that indicates that we've finished bolding the text line), type **
** six times.

This drops the Command Button six lines down the page. The HTML code in your Text Editor should look like this:

```
<HTML>
<HEAD>
<TITLE>My First ActiveX Page</TITLE>
</HEAD>
<BODY>
<!-- These tags adjust the text line -->
<B> <BIG> <CENTER>
<!-- This is the text line -->
This is a Web Page with two embedded ActiveX Controls
</CENTER> </BIG> </B>
<!-- These tags add six line breaks -->
<BR> <BR> <BR> <BR> <BR> <BR>
<!-- This tag centers the object which follows -->
<CENTER>
<!-- This is an embedded Command Button -->
<OBJECT ID="cmdbtnFirst" WIDTH=160 HEIGHT=29
 CLASSID="CLSID:D7053240-CE69-11CD-A777-00DD01143C57">
  <PARAM NAME="Caption" VALUE="My First Command Button">
  <PARAM NAME="Size" VALUE="4234;767">
  <PARAM NAME="MousePointer" VALUE="3">
  <PARAM NAME="FontEffects" VALUE="1073741825">
  <PARAM NAME="FontCharSet" VALUE="0">
  <PARAM NAME="FontPitchAndFamily" VALUE="2">
  <PARAM NAME="ParagraphAlign" VALUE="3">
  <PARAM NAME="FontWeight" VALUE="700">
</OBJECT>
</CENTER>
</BODY>
</HTML>
```

6. Finally, save your work, go back to IE, click on Refresh, and you'll see a screen that looks like Figure 1.10.

Embedding a Label

We're now missing only one element of the Web page shown in Figure 1.1—the Label. Embedding a Label is similar to embedding a Command Button: Alt+Tab back to the ActiveX Control Pad and position the cursor after </CENTER> and before </BODY>. Select Edit ➤ Insert ActiveX Control… . Select Microsoft Forms 2.0 Label and click OK. In the Properties sheet, click on ID, type **lblFirst** in the Setting Box, and click Apply.

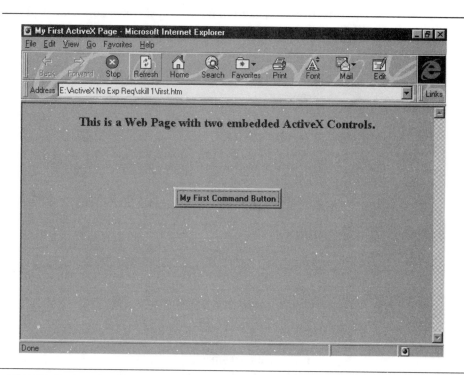

FIGURE 1.10: The Web page with the Command Button centered and lowered

Now select Caption. In the Setting Box, type **ActiveX Label** and click Apply.

Let's change the caption's appearance. Select Font from the Properties sheet. Click on the ellipsis button to the right of the Setting Box. In the dialog box that appears, move to the list of fonts and select Arial. From the list of font styles select Bold Italic. From the list of sizes, select 16 Pt. Click OK.

All these modifications leave the caption larger than the Label. Go to the Edit ActiveX Object window and drag a sizing handle until you can see the whole caption. The caption, however, is left-justified. To center it, select Text Align from the Properties sheet. Click on the down-arrow to the right of the Setting Box and then select Center from the drop-down list.

To make the Label look a bit snazzier, select the Special Effect property, and choose Etched from the drop-down list in the Setting Box.

Close both windows of the Object Editor. You're now back in the Text Editor. Our edits in the Object Editor resulted in additional lines of HTML code. Specifically, we have another <OBJECT> tag-pair. This pair, of course, gives the specifications for the ActiveX Label control we just inserted.

Once again, we use HTML tags to center the new control on the Web page. Insert a blank line before the <OBJECT> tag that specifies the Label. Position the cursor at the beginning of that line. Type **
** six times and then type **<CEN-TER>**. Position the cursor just after the second </OBJECT> and type **</CENTER>**.

The HTML code in your Text Editor should look like the listing that follows (first.htm). As you may recall from the HTML code I showed you before, I've added a few comments. It's a good idea for you to add them, too. When you dragged the sizing handle for the Label, you may have dragged it slightly more (or less) than I did. As a result, your values for WIDTH and HEIGHT may vary from the ones in the listing. If you like, you can change them directly in the Text Editor. Just type the new values in the appropriate place (they represent numbers of pixels):

first.htm

```
<HTML>
<HEAD>
<TITLE>My First ActiveX Page</TITLE>
</HEAD>
<BODY>
<!-- These tags adjust the text line -->
<B> <BIG> <CENTER>
<!-- This is the text line -->
This is a Web Page with two embedded ActiveX Controls
</CENTER> </BIG> </B>
<!-- These tags add six line breaks -->
<BR> <BR> <BR> <BR> <BR> <BR>
<!-- This tag centers the object which follows -->
<CENTER>
<!-- This is an embedded Command Button -->
<OBJECT ID="cmdbtnFirst" WIDTH=160 HEIGHT=29
 CLASSID="CLSID:D7053240-CE69-11CD-A777-00DD01143C57">
  <PARAM NAME="Caption" VALUE="My First Command Button">
  <PARAM NAME="Size" VALUE="4234;767">
  <PARAM NAME="MousePointer" VALUE="3">
  <PARAM NAME="FontEffects" VALUE="1073741825">
  <PARAM NAME="FontCharSet" VALUE="0">
  <PARAM NAME="FontPitchAndFamily" VALUE="2">
  <PARAM NAME="ParagraphAlign" VALUE="3">
  <PARAM NAME="FontWeight" VALUE="700">
</OBJECT>
</CENTER>
<!-- These tags add six line-breaks -->
<BR> <BR> <BR> <BR> <BR> <BR>
<!-- This tag centers the object that follows -->
<CENTER>
```

```
<!-- This is an embedded Label -->
<OBJECT ID="lblFirst" WIDTH=181 HEIGHT=48
 CLASSID="CLSID:978C9E23-D4B0-11CE-BF2D-00AA003F40D0">
  <PARAM NAME="Caption" VALUE="ActiveX Label">
  <PARAM NAME="Size" VALUE="4784;1270">
  <PARAM NAME="SpecialEffect" VALUE="3">
  <PARAM NAME="FontName" VALUE="Arial">
  <PARAM NAME="FontEffects" VALUE="1073741827">
  <PARAM NAME="FontHeight" VALUE="320">
  <PARAM NAME="FontCharSet" VALUE="0">
  <PARAM NAME="FontPitchAndFamily" VALUE="2">
  <PARAM NAME="ParagraphAlign" VALUE="3">
  <PARAM NAME="FontWeight" VALUE="700">
</OBJECT>
</CENTER>
</BODY>
</HTML>
```

Save the file. Alt+Tab back to IE, and click the Refresh button. Your screen now looks like Figure 1.1.

Laying Out the Sizzle: Positioning Buttons and Labels with the HTML Layout Control

The Object Editor makes it easy to embed ActiveX controls into HTML documents. What it doesn't do, as you've seen, is make it easy to position those controls. HTML, at the moment, just doesn't have the capability to handle exact positional information.

What we need is a tool that lets us lay out our ActiveX controls on a grid, size them any way we like, modify their properties to our heart's content, and then drag them around until we're happy with where they are on the page and in relation to one another. As long as we're dreaming, let's imagine that we could also store our layout in a file and then embed this file (rather than just embed individual controls) into an HTML file. We could even embed this layout file in more than one Web page, if we wanted to.

What I've just described is more than a wish list. It's Microsoft's HTML Layout Control, and it's part of the ActiveX Control Pad application. In this section, we'll use the HTML Layout Control to set up a Web page like the one in the preceding section, with a few changes just for variety.

The HTML Part

In the ActiveX Control Pad, close first.htm. Use File ➢ New HTML to create a new file. Name the new file second and store it in ActiveX No Exp Req\skill 1. In the Text Editor, delete New Page and type **My Second ActiveX Web Page** between <TITLE> and </TITLE>. Between <BODY> and </BODY> type **I used the HTML Layout Control for this one**. As in the preceding section, use the <B>, <BIG>, and <CENTER> tags to format the line you just typed.

The Layout

Now it's time to lay out the controls. Select Edit ➤ Insert HTML Layout.... The ActiveX Control Pad responds by asking you for the name of a file—a file with an .ALX extension. This extension stands for "ActiveX Layout." Since you've requested that the Control Pad insert a layout, it wants to know which layout to insert.

One problem: We haven't laid anything out yet. In the dialog box that's now on your screen, type **layout for second** in the File Name text box. (Make sure that this filename goes into the skill 1 folder.) Click Open.

The Confirm dialog box appears and tells you that the file does not exist. It asks if you want to create it. Click Yes.

Now you're back in the Text Editor, and your screen resembles Figure 1.11. A new object, the layout file, is now part of your HTML document. Examining this document in IE would show no change from our previous version, of course, since we've put nothing in the layout.

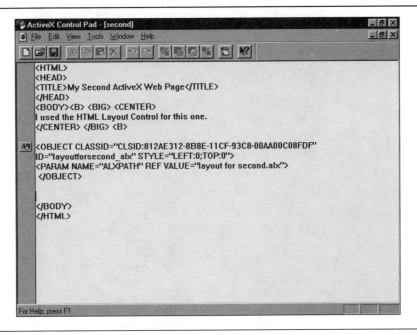

FIGURE 1.11: The Text Editor with a new object inserted into the HTML document. This object specifies a layout file. The symbol to the left of the object is a push button that takes you back to the Layout Control.

Let's remedy that. Another item has just appeared in the Text Editor: the symbol to the left of the code that specifies the layout file. This symbol is not the same as the symbol we saw in the previous section—and with good reason. The symbol we saw earlier is a button that takes you the Object Editor. This symbol is a button that takes you to the HTML Layout Control. Click on it, and your screen should look like Figure 1.12.

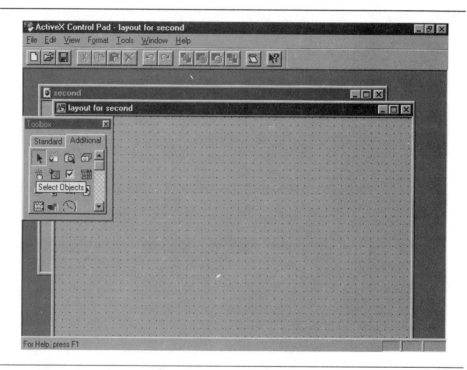

FIGURE 1.12: The Layout Control presents a grid and a Toolbox.

Now you have a grid that enables you to position objects on your Web page and a Toolbox that contains objects you can insert on your page. The Toolbox has two tabbed pages, Standard and Additional. They give you access to ActiveX Controls. If you hover the cursor over an icon in the Toolbox, a Tool Tip balloon tells you which ActiveX control the icon represents. The Toolbox does not contain all the ActiveX controls available on your machine. Later, we will learn how to add additional controls to the toolbar. For the moment we'll concentrate on using the Toolbox to build a Web page.

On the Standard page, find the icon that represents the Command Button. Click on it and move the cursor (don't drag it) to the grid. The mouse cursor becomes a cross and a small rectangle. Position the cross where you want to place the Command Button's upper-left corner. Don't spend a lot of time deciding—you can easily change your mind about the location. When you click on that spot a resizable Command Button opens.

The sizing handles that appear are a visual clue that you can change the Command Button's height and width. You can also drag the Command Button anywhere on the grid. Unlike the grid in the Object Editor, when you place a control in the HTML Layout Control grid it affects how the control will appear in the Web page.

Let's move the Command Button to where we'd like it to appear on our Web page. Maximize the Layout Control window. Position the cursor on the Command Button, click, and hold the mouse down. Drag the Command Button so that it's centered, about one-third of the way down the page. (This is easier than using HTML tags, isn't it?)

Now we'll work with the Command Button's properties. You can get to the Properties sheet in any of three ways. One way is to right-click on the Command Button and select Properties from the pop-up menu. The other way is to select Properties from the View menu. Still another way is to hover the cursor over the boundary of the control. When the cursor becomes a four-headed arrow, double-click the boundary. (The third way is a toggle. If you do it when the Properties sheet is open, double-clicking closes it. By the way, exercise a little caution: If you double-click when the cursor is a two-headed arrow, you might change the size of the control, as I described earlier.)

Open the Command Button's Properties sheet and set these properties:

- Set the ID property to **cmdbtnSecond**.

- Set the caption to **My Second Command Button**. Use the sizing handles to adjust the button's height and width so that you can see the full caption.

- Set the Font property to Wingdings.

- Using the Font dialog box, set the font style to Bold and the font size to 16 Pt. Click the checkbox to the left of Strikeout and click the checkbox to the left of Underline. Click OK. To see all the bizarre symbols on the Command Button, resize it and drag it to the left.

- In the preceding section, we made the cursor change to an I-Beam when it makes contact with the Command Button. This time, you select the shape that you want the cursor to take.

Close the Properties sheet. Your screen now looks like Figure 1.13.

Now let's add the Label control. Unlike the Object Editor, you don't have to close the HTML Layout Control and open it again for each new object. Select the Label control from the Standard page of the Toolbox. Move the cursor to position the Label, and open the Label's Properties sheet when you reach the appropriate position (centered, about two-thirds of the way down the page).

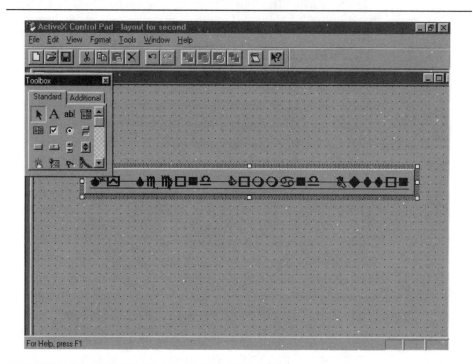

FIGURE 1.13: The Layout Control after you've modified the properties of the Command Button

Set these properties:

- Set the Label's ID property to **lblSecond**.

- Set the Caption property to **ActiveX Label**.

- Set Font to Terminal, the font-style to Bold Italic, and the font size to 14 Pt. Make sure the Label is big enough to show the entire caption.

- Set the TextAlign property to Center.

- Set the SpecialEffect property to Bump.

- Set the Backcolor property to white.

Close the Properties sheet. Figure 1.14 shows what the HTML Layout Control display looks like when you've finished.

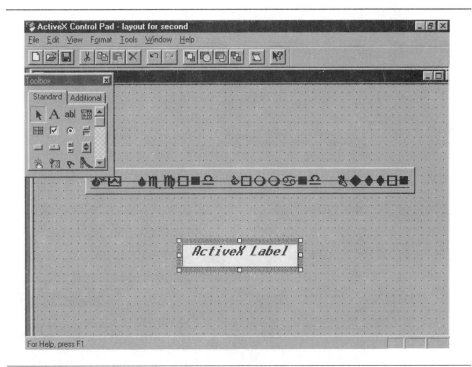

FIGURE 1.14: The HTML Layout Control after you've modified the properties of the Command Button and the properties of the Label

Close the Toolbox and the grid and save your changes when prompted. In the Text Editor, save your work and Alt+Tab to IE. In the Address field, change first.htm to **second.htm** and press Enter, and you'll see a Web page that looks like Figure 1.15.

Here's the HTML code—with my comments—for what we've done (second.htm):

Second.htm

```
<HTML>
<HEAD>
<TITLE>My Second ActiveX Web Page</TITLE>
```

```
</HEAD>
<BODY>
<!-- These tags adjust the text line -->
<B> <BIG> <CENTER>
<!-- This is the text line -->
I Used the HTML Layout Control for this one
</CENTER> </BIG> </BIG>
<!-- This object is the layout -->
<OBJECT CLASSID="CLSID:812AE312-8B8E-11CF-93C8-00AA00C08FDF"
ID="layoutforsecond_alx" STYLE="LEFT:0;TOP:0">
<PARAM NAME="ALXPATH" REF VALUE="layout for second.alx">
</OBJECT>
</BODY>
</HTML>
```

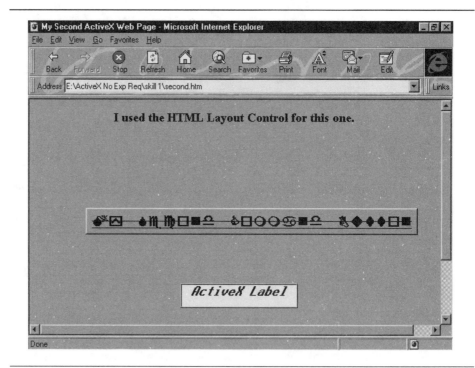

FIGURE 1.15: Your second Web page. It's similar to the page in Figure 1.1, but we've made a few changes.

Taking Stock

You've now used two essential tools of ActiveX Web site construction: the ActiveX Object Editor and the HTML Layout Control. The Object Editor allows you to directly embed ActiveX controls into an HTML document. Although you can change a control's properties by editing the HTML code, you can't set precise positions with the Object Editor. You have to use HTML tags to position the objects you embed.

The HTML Layout Control, on the other hand, allows you to easily set exact locations for objects, but you can't directly edit their properties in the HTML code. The object that the HTML Layout Control embeds isn't an ActiveX control —it's a layout. One advantage that the HTML Layout Control has is reusability. Once you've saved a layout, you can embed it in many other HTML documents. The HTML Layout Control also has other useful capabilities that we'll examine as we progress.

You may have noticed that although the Command Buttons you embedded look good, they don't do anything when you click them. How do you add functionality to your ActiveX controls?

Skill 2 will show you.

Are You Experienced?

Now you can...

- ☑ build a work environment for efficiently using the ActiveX Control Pad in conjunction with Microsoft Internet Explorer

- ☑ use the ActiveX Control Pad's Text Editor to write HTML code

- ☑ use the ActiveX Object Editor to embed ActiveX controls into your HTML code

- ☑ work with Properties sheets to specify the properties of a control

- ☑ use the HTML Layout Control to position, size, and embed ActiveX controls

- ☑ build Web pages that feature Command Buttons and Labels

S K I L L

2

two

Creating Scripts

When we embed ActiveX controls in Web pages, we want them to *do* things—not to just look good. We want them to interact with each other and with users. In effect, we want to create *behaviors* for the objects we embed.

The way we create behaviors is to write *scripts* for ActiveX controls to follow. A script is a set of instructions that resides inside an HTML document. Writing a script is not as demanding as writing a full-blown computer program, although programming is involved any time you write a sequence of steps for a computer to follow.

We'll write our scripts in Visual Basic Scripting Edition (VBScript, or VBS). Although another language, JavaScript, is available, we'll confine our discussion to VBS: It's easy to learn, and because it's derived from BASIC, you might be familiar with some of its concepts already. (If not, you soon will be.) VBS, a subset of Microsoft's popular Visual Basic language, enables you to tell ActiveX controls exactly what you want them to do.

Juicing Up Your Web Page

Figure 2.1 shows the Web page we'll build in this section. We'll base it on the first Web page we created in Skill 1; in order to explore some new concepts and get into scripts, however, we'll make a few changes. We'll begin by adding some flair to the text line. Next, we'll surround the text line with a couple of classy-looking horizontal lines. After that, we'll insert another line of text and embed an additional ActiveX Command Button.

Changing the Text

In the ActiveX Control Pad, open the file `first.htm` that you created in Skill 1. Since you'll change it, select File ➤ Save As... and save it as `first script` in the `skill 2` subdirectory.

To get started, modify the HTML code at the beginning of the file:

1. Change the text between the <TITLE> tags to **My First Scripted ActiveX Page**.

2. Then change the first line of text to read "This is a Web Page with three embedded ActiveX Controls."

3. Next, delete the <B>, <BIG>, </B>, and </BIG> tags. In their place type **<H2>** before the text line and **</H2>** after the text line.

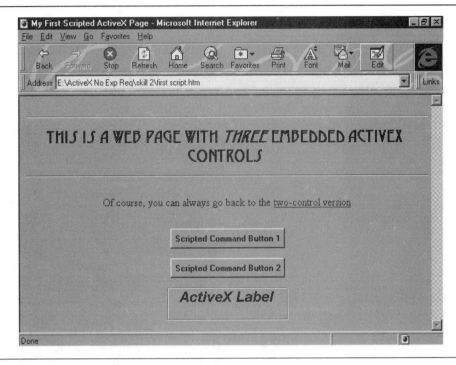

FIGURE 2.1: We'll alter our first Web page in preparation for script creation.

This pair of HTML tags tells the Web browser that the text the tags enclose is a *second-level* heading. As you might imagine, <H1> and </H1> indicate a first-level heading, <H3> and </H3> a third-level heading, and so forth up to the sixth level. The higher the number, the smaller the font.

Modifying the Look of the Text

We'll now use HTML <FONT> tags to change the look of the text. Before the text line type **<FONT FACE = Desdemona>**. After the text line type **</FONT>**. This tells the browser to render the text in Desdemona font.

TIP

The word "render" often appears in connection with a Web browser. It's a shorthand way of saying "process something and show it onscreen." Different Web browsers often render the same file in different ways.

Just to see what some other fonts look like, you might try Braggadocio and Haettenschweiler. (I'm not particularly fond of either one; I just like the names "Braggadocio" and "Haettenschweiler.") If your computer doesn't recognize these fonts, your browser renders a default font.

Like many HTML tags, <FONT> has a set of *attributes*—parameters that provide the browser with information on exactly how to implement the tag. Table 2.1 shows all of the <FONT> tag's attributes.

TABLE 2.1: Attributes of the HTML *<FONT>* Tag

Attribute	What It Does
COLOR	Sets the font color. The value can be a hexadecimal, an RGB (red-green-blue) color value, or a color name that you predefined
FACE	Specifies the name of the font face. If you provide a list of font faces, your browser tries each one from left to right until it finds one it can render. If all the fonts you listed are unavailable on the client computer, the browser uses a default
SIZE	Defines the font size (a number between 1 and 7; 7 is the largest)

For emphasis, italicize "three" by typing **<EM>** just before `three` and **</EM>** right after `three`. Set off the text line with two etched horizontal lines: type **<HR>** before <FONT FACE = Desdemona> and **<HR>** after </FONT>.

To have a look at what you've done so far, save your work (File ➤ Save) and double-click on the `first script` icon. When you're finished with IE, remember to leave IE open and then Alt+Tab back to the ActiveX Control Pad.

Adding a Hypertext Link

Next we'll add a text line that includes an important feature: a hypertext link. After the ending </CENTER> tag that centers the first text line (and before the line breaks), type **<CENTER>** and then type **Of course, you can always go back to the two-control version.** After this, type **</CENTER>**.

Let's enable the end user to click on `two-control version` to make the `first .htm` file appear. To do this, we use the HTML *anchor* tags, represented by <A> and </A>. Type the first tag just to the left of `two-control version`; type the second just after it. Now we must tell the anchor tags that they anchor `first.htm`. In the first anchor tag, in between A and >, type a space and then type **Href = "E:\ Active X No Exp Req\skill 1\first.htm"**. Make sure you type the close quote in the `Href` attribute. If you don't, the Script Wizard (which we're about to use) won't see the ActiveX controls you've embedded.

NOTE

Hypertext, the ability to click on a word, phrase, or area to move from one file to another is the "HT" in HTML. It's one of the major features of the World Wide Web. In the anchor tag, if we specify the location of a Web page on another computer (instead of a local file path), we jump to that page when we click on the hypertexted phrase.

We've now coded the two text lines in the Web page shown in Figure 2.1. The Text Editor should now have these lines of HTML:

```
<HTML>
<HEAD>
<TITLE>My First Scripted ActiveX Page</TITLE>
</HEAD>
<BODY> <!-- These tags adjust the text line -->
<CENTER>
<H2>
<!-- This is the text line -->
<HR> <FONT FACE = Desdemona>
This is a Web Page with <EM>three</EM> embedded ActiveX Controls
</FONT> <HR>
</H2>
</CENTER>
<CENTER>Of course, you can always go back to
➥the <A Href = "E:\ActiveX No Exp Req\skill 1\first.htm">
➥two-control version</A> </CENTER>
<!-- These commands add six line-breaks -->
<BR> <BR> <BR> <BR> <BR> <BR>
<CENTER>
<!-- This is an embedded Command Button -->
<OBJECT ID="cmdbtnFirst" WIDTH=160 HEIGHT=29
  CLASSID="CLSID:D7053240-CE69-11CD-A777-00DD01143C57">
    <PARAM NAME="Caption" VALUE="My First Command Button">
    <PARAM NAME="Size" VALUE="4234;767">
    <PARAM NAME="MousePointer" VALUE="3">
    <PARAM NAME="FontEffects" VALUE="1073741825">
    <PARAM NAME="FontCharSet" VALUE="0">
    <PARAM NAME="FontPitchAndFamily" VALUE="2">
    <PARAM NAME="ParagraphAlign" VALUE="3">
    <PARAM NAME="FontWeight" VALUE="700">
</OBJECT>
</CENTER>
<!-- These commands add six line-breaks -->
<BR> <BR> <BR> <BR> <BR> <BR>
<!-- Center the object which follows -->
<CENTER>
```

```
<!-- This is an embedded label -->
<OBJECT ID="lblFirst" WIDTH=181 HEIGHT=48
 CLASSID="CLSID:978C9E23-D4B0-11CE-BF2D-00AA003F40D0">
    <PARAM NAME="Caption" VALUE="ActiveX Label">
    <PARAM NAME="Size" VALUE="4784;1270">
    <PARAM NAME="SpecialEffect" VALUE="3">
    <PARAM NAME="FontName" VALUE="Arial">
    <PARAM NAME="FontEffects" VALUE="1073741827">
    <PARAM NAME="FontHeight" VALUE="320">
    <PARAM NAME="FontCharSet" VALUE="0">
    <PARAM NAME="FontPitchAndFamily" VALUE="2">
    <PARAM NAME="ParagraphAlign" VALUE="3">
    <PARAM NAME="FontWeight" VALUE="700">
</OBJECT>
</CENTER>
</BODY>
</HTML>
```

Text-Editing ActiveX Controls

In this section, we're going to use the Text Editor to make changes to controls we've embedded, without using the Object Editor.

Just as Href is an attribute of the anchor tag <A> and FACE is an attribute of the font tag <FONT>, in the same way ID, WIDTH, HEIGHT, and CLASSID are attributes of the object tag <OBJECT>. Just as we worked with the Text Editor to handle Href and FACE attributes, we work with the Text Editor to modify the <OBJECT> attributes. We'll also use the Text Editor to modify a PARAM NAME. We could use the Object Editor to make these changes, but it's easier to stay in the Text Editor. Here's what to do in the Text Editor:

1. Change cmdbtnFirst to cmdbtnScript1.

2. In <PARAM NAME="Caption" VALUE ="My First Command Button">, change the value to "**Scripted Command Button 1**".

3. The longer caption requires a longer Command Button, so change the Width from 160 to 171.

Delete four of the line breaks before the Command Button and five of the line breaks after the Command Button. If you commented your code in Skill 1, remember to change the comment statements appropriately.

Now we can be clever about creating the HTML code for the second Command Button. With your mouse, select all the HTML code that represents the Command Button. The Command Button's code is:

```
<OBJECT ID="cmdbtnScript1" WIDTH=171 HEIGHT=29
 CLASSID="CLSID:D7053240-CE69-11CD-A777-00DD01143C57">
    <PARAM NAME="Caption" VALUE="Scripted Command Button 1">
    <PARAM NAME="Size" VALUE="4234;767">
    <PARAM NAME="MousePointer" VALUE="3">
    <PARAM NAME="FontEffects" VALUE="1073741825">
    <PARAM NAME="FontCharSet" VALUE="0">
    <PARAM NAME="FontPitchAndFamily" VALUE="2">
    <PARAM NAME="ParagraphAlign" VALUE="3">
    <PARAM NAME="FontWeight" VALUE="700">
</OBJECT>
```

Then use the keystroke combination Ctrl+C to copy this code. Position the cursor after the Command Button's code (and before the Label's code), and use Ctrl+V (or Shift+Ins) to paste the code you copied.

Voila! You've created the code for another object, and you didn't have to use the Object Editor to do it. To make this second Command Button unique, change its ID to cmdbtnScript2 and change its Caption to Scripted Command Button 2. Use <CENTER> before the <OBJECT> tag and </CENTER> after the </OBJECT> tag to make sure this new Command Button is centered, and place one line-break <BR> between the new button and the Label.

The HTML code should now look like the lines that follow. IE renders this code to look like Figure 2.1:

```
<HTML>
<HEAD>
<TITLE>My First Scripted ActiveX Page</TITLE>
</HEAD>
<BODY>
<!-- These tags adjust the text line -->
<HR>
<!-- This is the text line -->
<FONT  FACE = Desdemona> <CENTER> <H2>
This is a Web Page with <EM> three </EM> embedded ActiveX Controls
</CENTER>
</H2>
</FONT>
<HR>
<CENTER> Of course, you can always go back to
➡the <A Href = "E:\ActiveX No Exp Req\chapter 1\first.htm">
➡two-control version </A> </CENTER>
<CENTER>
```

```
<BR> <BR> <CENTER>
<!-- This is an embedded Command Button -->
 <OBJECT ID="cmdbtnScript1" WIDTH=171 HEIGHT=29
 CLASSID="CLSID:D7053240-CE69-11CD-A777-00DD01143C57">
    <PARAM NAME="Caption" VALUE="Scripted Command Button 1">
    <PARAM NAME="Size" VALUE="4516;776">
    <PARAM NAME="MousePointer" VALUE="3">
    <PARAM NAME="FontEffects" VALUE="1073741825">
    <PARAM NAME="FontCharSet" VALUE="0">
    <PARAM NAME="FontPitchAndFamily" VALUE="2">
    <PARAM NAME="ParagraphAlign" VALUE="3">
    <PARAM NAME="FontWeight" VALUE="700">
</OBJECT>
</CENTER>
<!-- This commands adds one line-break -->
<BR>
<CENTER>
<!-- This is an embedded Command Button -->

<OBJECT ID="cmdbtnScript2" WIDTH=171 HEIGHT=29
 CLASSID="CLSID:D7053240-CE69-11CD-A777-00DD01143C57">
    <PARAM NAME="Caption" VALUE="Scripted Command Button 2">
    <PARAM NAME="Size" VALUE="4516;776">
    <PARAM NAME="MousePointer" VALUE="10">
    <PARAM NAME="FontEffects" VALUE="1073741825">
    <PARAM NAME="FontCharSet" VALUE="0">
    <PARAM NAME="FontPitchAndFamily" VALUE="2">
    <PARAM NAME="ParagraphAlign" VALUE="3">
    <PARAM NAME="FontWeight" VALUE="700">
</OBJECT>
</CENTER>

<!-- This command adds one line-break -->
<BR>
<!-- Center the object which follows -->
<CENTER>
<!-- This is an embedded label -->
    <OBJECT ID="lblFirst" WIDTH=181 HEIGHT=48
     CLASSID="CLSID:978C9E23-D4B0-11CE-BF2D-00AA003F40D0">
        <PARAM NAME="Caption" VALUE="ActiveX Label">
        <PARAM NAME="Size" VALUE="4784;1270">
        <PARAM NAME="SpecialEffect" VALUE="3">
        <PARAM NAME="FontName" VALUE="Arial">
        <PARAM NAME="FontEffects" VALUE="1073741827">
        <PARAM NAME="FontHeight" VALUE="320">
        <PARAM NAME="FontCharSet" VALUE="0">
        <PARAM NAME="FontPitchAndFamily" VALUE="2">
```

```
            <PARAM NAME="ParagraphAlign" VALUE="3">
            <PARAM NAME="FontWeight" VALUE="700">
        </OBJECT>
    </CENTER>
    </BODY>
    </HTML>
```

It's a good idea to add some comments, as I've done here.

Working with the Script Wizard

We're finally ready to start adding behaviors to our buttons. Let's start with something simple. When we click on the first Command Button, we'll have it change the Label's caption. To follow a time-honored tradition, the button-click will change the caption to "Hello World!" Clicking on the second button will change the caption back to "ActiveX Label."

 NOTE   The "time-honored" tradition I mentioned comes from the original book on C (a very popular programming language). In that book, the authors (the inventors of C) had their first program print the message "Hello World!" Ever since then, it seems that the first program in almost every computer-related book duplicates this in some way.

Setting Up the Wizard

We'll use the ActiveX Control Pad's Script Wizard to help us write the script. First, let's make sure it's set up properly. In the ActiveX Control Pad, select Tools ➢ Options ➢ Script…. The Script Options window appears.

This window presents two sets of options that specify how the Script Wizard looks when you open it in the future. In the Script Pane View box, select List View (if it isn't already selected). In the Default Script Language box, select Visual Basic Scripting Edition (if it isn't already selected). Click OK to close the Script Options window and your Script Wizard is ready to go.

Components of the Wizard

Select Tools ➢ Script Wizard…. Figure 2.2 shows the Script Wizard window that's now on your screen. Two of the panes show the identifiers for the ActiveX controls you've embedded. The left pane asks you to Select an Event, the right pane asks you to Insert Actions. We'll refer to the first as the Event pane, and to the second as the Actions pane. The choices we make in these two panes affect what happens in the third—the Script pane.

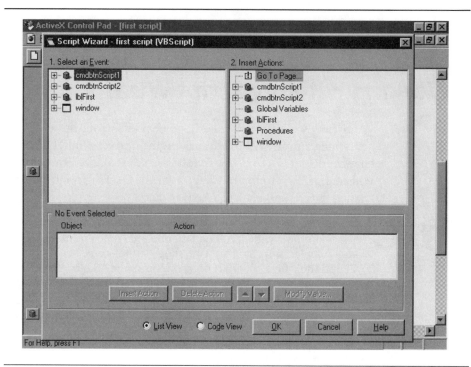

FIGURE 2.2: The Script Wizard window consists of an Event pane, an Actions pane, and a Script pane. Choices you make in the first two panes affect what happens in the third.

Connecting Events to Actions

Each ActiveX control is associated with a number of *events*. Think of an event as a signal that a control sends. A Command Button, for example, has a Click event (among others). The Click event is a signal that the user has clicked the Command Button.

At the moment, nothing happens when we click either of our Command Buttons. This is because we haven't associated either button's Click event with an action.

Here's where we change all that. In the Event pane, click the plus sign (+) directly to the left of cmdbtnScript1. The plus becomes a minus sign (-) and you'll see the dialog box in Figure 2.3. The items that have opened directly beneath cmdbtnScript1 are the events associated with this Command Button. As you can see in Figure 2.3, Click is one of those events.

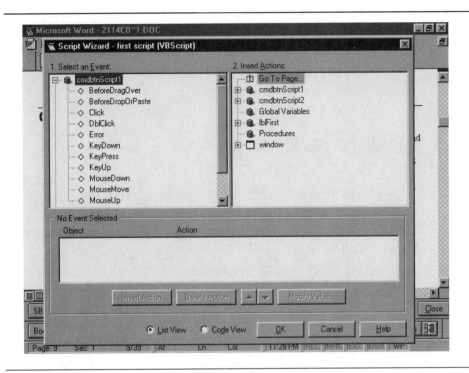

FIGURE 2.3: When you click on a control's ID in the Event pane, the events associated with that control appear.

To associate it with an action, select the Click event. This highlights the first row of the Script pane, and the title of the Script pane changes. Its title is now On cmdbtnScript1. Click the Perform the Following Actions: option.

What action do we want our button's Click event to generate? At the beginning of this section, we said that the button-click would change the Label from "ActiveX Label" to "Hello World!" Translated into script jargon, this means that the button-click changes the value of the Caption of lblFirst.

Let's get it done. In the Actions pane, click on the + to the left of lblFirst. The Actions pane now shows all the properties of lblFirst. If the property names seem familiar, it's because you've seen them before in the control's Properties sheet.

Select the Caption property of lblFirst. Then click on the Insert Action button (just below the Script pane). The dialog box that opens (entitled lblFirst Caption) prompts you to enter a text string. Type **Hello World!** and then click OK. (Don't type quotation marks around the string. The Wizard inserts them for you.)

The Script pane shows the result of your typing and clicking. The Label's ID, lblFirst, is in the Script pane's Object column. The phrase Change Caption to "Hello World!" is in the Action column. Taken along with the Script pane's title, this tells your computer "When cmdbtnScript1's Click event occurs, change the Label's caption to 'Hello World!'"

Congratulations! You've just written your first script.

The Wizard's Effects

Return to the Text Editor by clicking OK. Your Text Editor has some new lines of code—your script. These lines appear in Figure 2.4.

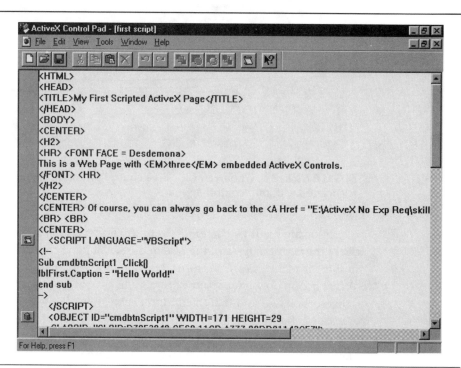

FIGURE 2.4: The script you created via the Script Wizard

The script is easy to understand when you break it down:

- The first thing to notice about the added code is the pair of new tags. `<SCRIPT LANGUAGE = "VBScript">` is the first member of the tag-pair; `</SCRIPT>` is the second.

- The `LANGUAGE` attribute tells you (and IE) that the code enclosed in the tags is VBS.

- A set of angle-brackets with an exclamation point and hyphens surrounds the code.

- The title of the code, `Sub cmdbtnScript1_Click()`, tells you that the code pertains to the Click event of the first Command Button.

- The next line, `lblFirst.Caption = "Hello World!"`, reflects your work in the Script Wizard, and the line after that ends the code.

Note also the new symbol to the left of the code. Similar to symbols that the other tools create when you embed their code into the Text Editor, the Script Wizard creates a push button that takes you back to the Script Wizard for editing.

Take a look at the page in action. Save your work, Alt+Tab to the `skill 2` folder, and double-click on the icon for `first script`. When the page comes up in IE, click on the first button. The Label's caption does indeed change to "Hello World!"

Let's assign similar functionality to the second Command Button. Follow the steps we just went through to make a button-click on the second Command Button return the Label to its original caption. In the Text Editor, right-click the mouse. This pops up a menu that combines choices from the Edit menu and the Tools menu. Use this menu to get to the Script Wizard.

Once you're in the Script Wizard, follow these steps:

1. In the Script Wizard's Event pane, select cmdbtnScript2 and then select its Click event.

2. In the Actions pane, select lblFirst and then select its Caption property. Either click the Insert Action button as we did before, or double-click on Caption.

3. In the lblFirst Caption dialog box that appears, type **ActiveX Label**.

4. Click OK to close the lblFirst Caption dialog box.

5. Click OK again to return to the Text Editor.

Test the page in IE. Save your work, return to IE, and click Refresh. You'll find that you can switch back and forth from the original Label caption to the new one by alternately clicking the two Command Buttons.

NOTE   By the way, if you haven't tried the hypertext link yet, click on the text at the end of the second text line and watch IE bring up `first.htm`. Be sure to click the Back button to return to `first script` before you leave IE.

Scripting Double-Clicks, Keyboard Events, and Mouse Events

Now that you've written a couple of scripts, let's explore the Command Buttons and the Label a bit more.

Clicking and Double-Clicking

In addition to the Click event, we'll work with the Double-Click event. Here are the behaviors we'll script for the first Command Button:

- Clicking the first Command Button changes the Label's caption and changes its background color.

- Double-clicking the first Command Button changes the caption's font from italic to non-italic and underlines the caption.

The behaviors we'll script for the second Command Button undo the actions of the first Command Button:

- Clicking the second Command Button changes the Label's caption back to its original text and changes its background color to its original color.

- Double-clicking the second Command Button changes the caption's font back to italic and removes the underline.

To script the first Command Button's capabilities, follow this sequence:

1. In the Text Editor, right-click and select Script Wizard....

2. In the Event pane, select cmdbtnScript1 and open its events.

3. Select the Click event.

4. In the Actions pane, select lblFirst and open its properties.

5. Double-click on BackColor. Because you have to supply a color, the Script Wizard helps you by opening a dialog box full of colors.

6. Select any color you like and click OK. (I picked white.)

7. Now go back to the Event pane. This time select cmdbtnScript1's DblClick event.

8. In the Actions pane, find Font under lblFirst and click on the + sign next to it.

9. Double-click on Italic. In the dialog box that opens, select False and click OK.

10. Double-click on Underline. In the dialog box, select True and click OK.

Back in the Text Editor, note the additions to the script for the first Command Button. You now have lines of VBS code that pertain to the Double-Click event as well as for the Click event. The script for the first Command Button now looks like this:

```
<SCRIPT LANGUAGE="VBScript">
<!--
Sub cmdbtnScript1_DblClick(Cancel)
lblFirst.Font.Italic = False
lblFirst.Font.Underline = True
end sub
Sub cmdbtnScript1_Click()
lblFirst.BackColor = &H00FFFFFF
lblFirst.Caption = "Hello World!"
end sub
-->
    </SCRIPT>
```

Now script the second Command Button to undo the actions of the first.

1. In the Text Editor, click on the Script Wizard symbol to the left of the script for the second Command Button. The Script Wizard is now ready for you to edit the second Command Button's script. In fact, it's ready for you to work on the Click event.

2. In the Actions pane, select lblFirst and click on the + to its left.

3. Double-click on BackColor and select the original gray as the color.

4. Back in the Event pane, select cmdbtnScript2's DblClick event.

5.   In the Actions pane click on the + next to Font.

6.   Double-click on Italic, and in the dialog box that opens, choose True, and then click OK.

7.   Also in the Actions pane, under Font double-click on Underline and go through the steps to make its value False.

8.   Click on OK to return to the Text Editor.

The VBS code for the second Command Button's script should look like the code for the first, except for the values on the right of the equal signs (=) :

```
<SCRIPT LANGUAGE="VBScript">
<!--
Sub cmdbtnScript2_DblClick(Cancel)
lblFirst.Font.Italic = True
lblFirst.Font.Underline = False
end sub
Sub cmdbtnScript2_Click()
lblFirst.BackColor = &H00C0C0C0
lblFirst.Caption = "ActiveX Label"
end sub
-->
    </SCRIPT>
```

TIP   I directed you to follow the steps in the Script Wizard to give you more experience with this tool. Now that you've worked with the ActiveX Control Pad, however, you can use a shortcut. In the Text Editor, copying and pasting the relevant code from the first Command Button script into the code for the second Command Button does most of the work. You'd complete the effort by making the necessary changes to property values.

As always, save your work, Alt+Tab to IE, click on Refresh, and examine what you've done. You should be able to click on the first Command Button and change what the Label says from "ActiveX Label" to "Hello World!" and at the same time change the color of the Label from gray to white (or to whatever color you chose). Double-clicking on the first Command Button should change the font from italic to non-italic and underline the caption. Figure 2.5 shows what the Web page looks like after the first Command Button's Click event and Double-Click event.

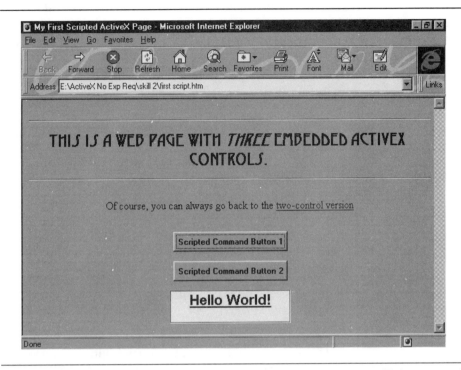

FIGURE 2.5: Your Web page after the first Command Button's Click event and its Double-Click event

Clicking on the second Command Button should change the caption back to "ActiveX Label" and the Label's color back to gray. Double-clicking on the second Command Button should change the caption back to italics and remove the underline. After the second Command Button's Click event and its Double-Click event, the Web page should appear as it did in Figure 2.1.

TIP   If these Click and Double-Click actions don't occur, you may have forgotten to hit the Refresh button.

The Keys to Success

Let's do a little more exploring. Go back to the Script Wizard to make some additions to the script for cmdbtnScript1. (We'll make similar additions to the script for cmdbtnScript2.)

In the Event pane, you'll see events other than Click and DblClick. Let's examine these four: KeyDown, KeyUp, MouseDown, and MouseUp. We'll work with the KeyDown and KeyUp events of the Command Buttons, and we'll work with the MouseDown and MouseUp events of the Label.

The two Key-related events result from actions on your keyboard. When you push down on a key you activate KeyDown. When you let up on the key you activate KeyUp. These events occur only if their associated control has the *focus*. Focus specifies which onscreen element is capable of providing input to the system at any particular time. The focus can move from element to element. One way to give the focus to a control is to click on it. When something has the focus, its appearance changes slightly. In Windows applications, when a Command Button has the focus, a dotted line surrounds its caption.

A control's KeyDown event occurs when the control has the focus and the user pushes down on any key on the keyboard. The control's KeyUp event occurs when the control has the focus and the user lets the key up.

We'll script these behaviors for KeyDown and KeyUp:

- With the focus on the first Command Button, KeyDown moves the Label's caption to the left, and KeyUp moves the Label's caption back to the center of the Label.

- With the focus on the second Command Button, KeyDown moves the Label's caption to the right, and KeyUp moves the Label's caption back to the center of the Label.

To experiment with these events, get back to the Script Wizard and go through these steps:

1. Select cmdbtnScript1's KeyDown event (in the Event pane) and lblFirst's Text Align property (in the Actions pane).

2. Double-click on Text Align.

3. In the dialog box that opens, select Left and click OK.

4. In the Event pane, select cmdbtnScript1's KeyUp event.

5. In the Actions pane, double-click on lblFirst's Text Align property.

6. In the dialog box, select Center and click OK.

Now go through similar steps for cmdbtnScript2:

1. Select cmdbtnScript2's KeyDown event (in the Event pane) and lblFirst's Text Align property (in the Actions pane).

2. Double-click on Text Align.

3. In the dialog box that opens, select Right and click OK.

4. In the Event pane, select cmdbtnScript2's KeyUp event.

5. In the Actions pane, double-click on lblFirst's Text Align property.

6. In the dialog box, select Center and click OK.

Moving with the Mouse

Now let's work with the MouseDown and MouseUp events. These events fire when the mouse is clicked in the specified control. The MouseDown event occurs when the user pushes the left mouse button down. The MouseUp event occurs when the user lets the left mouse button up.

The behaviors we'll script change the Label's color. They occur when the mouse is clicked in the Label control:

- Pushing the mouse button down changes the Label's color to light blue.

- Letting the mouse button up changes the Label's color to gray.

In the Event pane of the Script Editor, open the events for lblFirst. Select MouseDown. In the Actions pane, select the BackColor property of lblFirst and double-click on it. In the colors dialog box that opens, choose light blue (or some other color if you prefer). Follow the same steps for lblFirst's MouseUp event, except choose the original gray as the value of BackColor.

 TIP   I'll leave it to you to try out the MouseMove event. That one fires when you move the mouse across a specified control with neither mouse button pressed. You can also try the KeyPress event, which is a bit different from KeyDown (we'll examine this event in the next Skill).

Examining Your Work

When you open the Web page (after saving your work, and clicking Refresh when you're in IE), you should see a number of things. The Command Buttons work as before, and after you click the first one, pressing any key on your keyboard moves the caption to the left of the Label control, and letting up on the key moves the caption back to the center. After you click the second Command

Button, pressing a key moves the caption to the right of the Label control, and letting the key up moves it back to the center.

Move the mouse-cursor into the Label. Pressing down on the left mouse button changes the Label's color to light blue (or whatever color you selected). Letting up on the button changes the caption's color back to gray.

The HTML code in `first script` should look like the listing that follows (`first script.htm`).

 first script.htm

```
<HTML>
<HEAD>
<TITLE>My First Scripted ActiveX Page</TITLE>
</HEAD>
<BODY>
<!-- These tags adjust the text line -->
<CENTER>
<H2>
<!-- This is the text line -->
<HR> <FONT FACE = Desdemona>
This is a Web Page with <EM>three</EM> embedded ActiveX Controls
</FONT> <HR>
</H2>
</CENTER>
<CENTER>Of course, you can always go back to
Âthe <A Href = "E:\ActiveX No Exp Req\skill 1\first.htm">
Âtwo-control version</A> </CENTER>
<!-- These commands add two line-breaks -->
<BR> <BR>
<CENTER>
<!-- This is an embedded Command Button -->
    <SCRIPT LANGUAGE="VBScript">
<!--
Sub cmdbtnScript1_KeyDown(KeyCode, Shift)
lblFirst.TextAlign = 1
end sub
Sub cmdbtnScript1_KeyUp(KeyCode, Shift)
lblFirst.TextAlign = 2
end sub
Sub cmdbtnScript1_DblClick(Cancel)
lblFirst.Font.Italic = False
lblFirst.Font.Underline = True
end sub
Sub cmdbtnScript1_Click()
lblFirst.BackColor = &H00FFFFFF
lblFirst.Caption = "Hello World!"
end sub
-->
```

```
    </SCRIPT>
    <OBJECT ID="cmdbtnScript1" WIDTH=171 HEIGHT=29
     CLASSID="CLSID:D7053240-CE69-11CD-A777-00DD01143C57">
        <PARAM NAME="Caption" VALUE="Scripted Command Button 1">
        <PARAM NAME="Size" VALUE="4234;767">
        <PARAM NAME="MousePointer" VALUE="3">
        <PARAM NAME="FontEffects" VALUE="1073741825">
        <PARAM NAME="FontCharSet" VALUE="0">
        <PARAM NAME="FontPitchAndFamily" VALUE="2">
        <PARAM NAME="ParagraphAlign" VALUE="3">
        <PARAM NAME="FontWeight" VALUE="700">
    </OBJECT>
</CENTER>
<!-- This command adds a line-break -->
<BR>
<CENTER>
<!-- This is an embedded Command Button -->
    <SCRIPT LANGUAGE="VBScript">
<!--
Sub cmdbtnScript2_KeyDown(KeyCode, Shift)
lblFirst.TextAlign = 3
end sub
Sub cmdbtnScript2_KeyUp(KeyCode, Shift)
lblFirst.TextAlign = 2
end sub
Sub cmdbtnScript2_DblClick(Cancel)
lblFirst.Font.Italic = True
lblFirst.Font.Underline = False
end sub
Sub cmdbtnScript2_Click()
lblFirst.BackColor = &H00C0C0C0
lblFirst.Caption = "ActiveX Label"
end sub
-->
    </SCRIPT>
    <OBJECT ID="cmdbtnScript2" WIDTH=171 HEIGHT=29
     CLASSID="CLSID:D7053240-CE69-11CD-A777-00DD01143C57">
        <PARAM NAME="Caption" VALUE="Scripted Command Button 2">
        <PARAM NAME="Size" VALUE="4234;767">
        <PARAM NAME="MousePointer" VALUE="3">
        <PARAM NAME="FontEffects" VALUE="1073741825">
        <PARAM NAME="FontCharSet" VALUE="0">
        <PARAM NAME="FontPitchAndFamily" VALUE="2">
        <PARAM NAME="ParagraphAlign" VALUE="3">
        <PARAM NAME="FontWeight" VALUE="700">
    </OBJECT>
</CENTER>
 <BR>
<!-- Center the object which follows -->
```

```
<CENTER>
<!-- This is an embedded label -->
    <SCRIPT LANGUAGE="VBScript">
<!--
Sub lblFirst_MouseDown(Button, Shift, X, Y)
lblFirst.BackColor = &H00FFFF80
end sub
Sub lblFirst_MouseUp(Button, Shift, X, Y)
lblFirst.BackColor = &H00C0C0C0
end sub
-->
    </SCRIPT>
    <OBJECT ID="lblFirst" WIDTH=181 HEIGHT=48
     CLASSID="CLSID:978C9E23-D4B0-11CE-BF2D-00AA003F40D0">
        <PARAM NAME="Caption" VALUE="ActiveX Label">
        <PARAM NAME="Size" VALUE="4798;1270">
        <PARAM NAME="SpecialEffect" VALUE="3">
        <PARAM NAME="FontName" VALUE="Arial">
        <PARAM NAME="FontEffects" VALUE="1073741827">
        <PARAM NAME="FontHeight" VALUE="320">
        <PARAM NAME="FontCharSet" VALUE="0">
        <PARAM NAME="FontPitchAndFamily" VALUE="2">
        <PARAM NAME="ParagraphAlign" VALUE="3">
        <PARAM NAME="FontWeight" VALUE="700">
    </OBJECT>
</CENTER>
</BODY>
</HTML>
```

Scripting from the HTML Layout Control

Let's get set up to work with the tool we used at the end of Skill 1—the HTML Layout Control. This tool, you'll recall, enables you to lay out controls on a two-dimensional display, adjust their sizes, and assign values to their properties. We can also write script from the HTML Layout Control, as we'll see in this section. First, we have to start things off in the Text Editor.

Editing the HTML

Begin by using the ActiveX Control Pad to open the file second.htm from your skill 1 folder. Save it as second script in your skill 2 folder. While you're at it, copy layout for second from your skill 1 folder into your skill 2 folder. Rename it `layout for second script`. Change the title of the Web page to **My Second Scripted ActiveX Web Page**.

In the Text Editor, we're going to jazz up the text line by turning it into a *marquee*—a line that continuously moves across the page:

1. Delete the <CENTER> and </CENTER> tags before and after the text line.

2. Before the text line type **<MARQUEE DIRECTION=RIGHT BEHAVIOR=SCROLL SCROLLAMOUNT=10 SCROLLDELAY=100>**.

3. After the text line type **</MARQUEE>**.

The <MARQUEE> tags tell IE how to render the text line and the attributes supply the specifics. Table 2.2 shows all the attributes of the <MARQUEE> tag.

T A B L E 2 . 2 : Attributes of the HTML *<MARQUEE>* Tag

Attribute	What It Does
ALIGN	Sets up the alignment of the surrounding text with the marquee (TOP, MIDDLE, or BOTTOM)
BEHAVIOR	Indicates how the text behaves. SCROLL starts it off one side, moves it across and off the page, then back again on the other side. SLIDE starts it off one side, moves it across the page and stops at the opposite margin. ALTERNATE bounces it back and forth
BGCOLOR	Defines the marquee's background color (a hexadecimal number or a predefined color name)
DIRECTION	Sets the direction for the text to scroll (LEFT or RIGHT; LEFT is the default value)
HEIGHT	Defines the marquee's height in pixels, or as a percentage of the screen's height. If it's a percentage, it must end with %
HSPACE	Sets left and right margins in pixels outside the marquee
LOOP	Indicates the number of times the marquee loops
SCROLLAMOUNT	Sets the number of pixels in each move of the marquee
SCROLLDELAY	Sets the time (in milliseconds) between each apparent movement of the marquee
VSPACE	Sets the top and bottom margins in pixels for the outside of the marquee
WIDTH	Defines the marquee's width either in pixels or as a percentage of the screen width. If it's a percentage, it must end with %

Since we renamed the ALX file when we moved it to the `skill 2` folder, we have to change its references in the Web page. In the <OBJECT> tag, change the ID attribute to `"layoutforsecondscript_alx"` and change the REF VALUE attribute to `"layout for second script.alx"`.

Working in the HTML Layout Control

In the Text Editor, click on the HTML Layout Control push button symbol to the left of the <OBJECT> tag. This takes us to the HTML Layout Control. In the HTML Layout Control, select the Command Button and right-click to display its Properties sheet. Double-click on the Font property. In the dialog box that opens change the font to something comprehensible, like MS SystemEx, and change the font size to 12 pt. Eliminate the Strikeout and Underline Effects by clicking on the checkboxes next to these Special Effect names. Select the Caption property and type **Change the Label**.

TIP   To quickly work with a property in the Properties sheet, double-click on the property's name. This automatically selects the property and positions the cursor in the Setting Box. When you finish entering information in the Setting Box, hit Return or click Apply.

You're left with a Command Button that's too large for its caption. To automatically resize the button around its caption, select the button, and then choose Format ➤ Size ➤ To Fit. Drag the Command Button so that it's centered above the Label. Your Layout Control should now look like Figure 2.6.

The HTML Layout Control lets us easily create another Command Button. With the Command Button selected type Ctrl+C to copy the button to the clipboard. Type Ctrl+V to paste the button into the HTML Layout Control.

TIP   Another keystroke combination for pasting text is Shift+Ins.

Use the mouse to drag the newly created Command Button somewhere between the first Command Button and the Label. Don't spend a lot of time minutely positioning the new button. Get it somewhere near the correct location and you can tweak it shortly.

Open the new button's Properties sheet. Double-click on Caption and type **Restore the Label**. From now on, we'll refer to the first Command Button as the *Change* button and the second Command Button as the *Restore* button. As we did

on to change the Label and the other to restore the Label

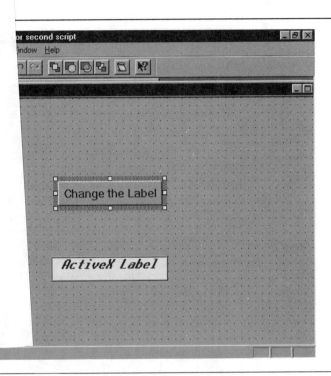

FIGURE 2.6: Your Layout Control after you update the Command Button

Select the Change button. Hold down the Shift key and select the Restore button. Now that you've selected both buttons, you can line them up. From the menu bar, select Format ➣ Align ➣ Centers. This snaps the Restore button into place. When you make a multiple selection (as we did with the two Command Buttons), which element takes precedence? The Layout Control uses the first selected element as the point of reference. Had you selected the Restore button and *then* the Change button, the Change button would have relocated when you selected Format ➣ Align ➣ Centers.

TIP   Properly aligning controls is an important part of User Interface design. When controls are aligned and meaningfully grouped, the eye and the brain have less work to do.

Open the Properties sheet for the Restore button. Change its ID property to cmdbtnRestore. Open the Properties sheet for the Change button. Change its ID property to cmdbtnChange.

Let's do one more thing with the two Command Buttons. When you use applications like a word processor or spreadsheet, you'll see that a button often has one underlined letter in its caption. This is called an *accelerator key*. Its purpose is to allow you to initiate the button's Click event without taking your hands off the keyboard. If you press Alt+the accelerator key, you activate the Click event.

The ActiveX Control Pad lets you add accelerator keys to your controls. Open the Properties sheet for the Change button. Double-click on the Accelerator property. In the Setting Box, type **C**. Follow the same steps for the Restore button, but type **R** in the Setting Box. The idea is to make one letter of the caption the accelerator (usually it's the first letter, unless a conflict would result). Figure 2.7 shows the appearance of your HTML Layout Control.

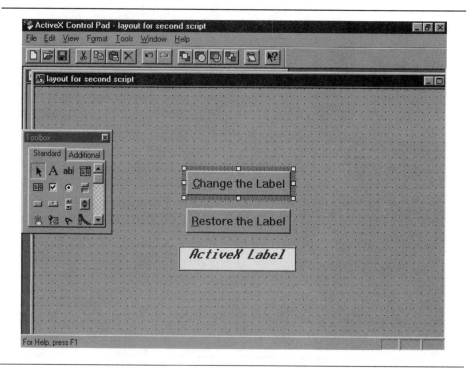

F I G U R E 2 . 7 : Your HTML Layout Control after you create a second Command Button (by copying the first), change the second button's caption, and assign accelerator keys

If you opened this Web page in IE, you'd see the first letter of each button's caption underlined (as they are in the HTML Layout Control). Alt+C would click the Change button and Alt+R would click the Restore button. Of course, we haven't scripted anything yet, so nothing would happen when you used these accelerators, or when you clicked the Command Buttons.

Rotating a Caption

At this point, we could open up the Script Wizard (by right-clicking in the Layout Control and selecting Script Wizard...), and go through all the steps we went through before to have the Command Buttons change aspects of the Label. Feel free to do this, and experiment until you feel comfortable with the Script Wizard.

I'd like to show you some new controls, however. Microsoft provides another Label control that allows for striking effects. We'll work with this control: We'll write a script that changes the angle of its caption text.

Examine the symbols on the Standard page of your Toolbox. The large, upper-case, black A is the symbol for the Label control we've been using. The symbol for the new Label control is a smaller uppercase A. Its tilted and blue. When you pass your cursor over this symbol, balloon help identifies it as IeLabel.

If you don't find this symbol on the Standard page, click on the Additional tab. If it's not on that page either, right-click on the lower part of the Standard page to bring up the Additional Controls list. Scroll through the list to find the Label control named Label Object. When you find it, click on the checkbox next to it. This adds the control to your Toolbox. If you can't find the Label Object in the Controls list, you have to go to the Microsoft ActiveX Component Gallery to download it.

DOWNLOADING ACTIVEX CONTROLS

This is a good time to learn how to download ActiveX controls. Fire up IE and navigate to `http://www.microsoft.com/activex/controls`. This is the ActiveX Component Gallery. A wealth of information, this site gives you the latest controls from Microsoft and other vendors.

continued ▶

Use the ActiveX Component Gallery's search engine to find the Microsoft Label control. Follow the instructions to see a demonstration and download the control. Note that watching a demonstration causes the control to download into (and register on) your computer. This exceptionally useful capability—automatic downloading and registration—is a cornerstone of ActiveX controls. We'll look into it further, I promise you.

After you watch the demo, go back to the ActiveX Control Pad, open the Controls list and select the Label Object to add it to your Toolbox.

To substitute the new Label control for the old one, and to work with the new Label's rotating caption property, here are the steps to follow:

1. Delete the original Label from the Layout. (Select it and hit Del.)

2. In its place, insert the Label Object.

3. Open its Properties list and select ID. Type **lblobjctScript**.

4. For the Caption property enter **ActiveX Label**.

5. Make the font bold by selecting True for the FontBold property.

6. For the FontSize property type **16**. For the Height property type **99**. For the Width type **150**.

7. While you're in the Properties list, take a moment to look at other properties of this control. The Angle property is the one we'll concentrate on for our scripts. Its default value is zero.

8. Close the Properties list.

9. Select the Restore button and then hold down the Shift key and select the Label control. (Both the Label and the button should be selected). Use Format ➢ Align ➢ Centers to center the Label under the buttons. Right-click to open the Script Wizard. In the Event pane open cmdbtnChange and select the Click event.

10. In the Actions pane open lblobjctScript and double-click on Angle. The dialog box (lblobjctScript Angle) prompts you for a value. Type **45** and click OK.

11. In the Event pane, close cmdbtnChange, open cmdbtnRestore, and select the Click event.

12. In the Actions pane, double-click once again on Angle.

13. In the dialog box, this time type **0** (zero) and click OK.

14. To save all these changes, click OK at the bottom of the Script Wizard.

15. Close the HTML Layout Control and save your work. Then save your work in the Text Editor.

Go to IE and take a look at the page. You should see the text ("I used the HTML Layout Control for this one") move across the top of the page. You should be able to tilt the Label's caption to 45 degrees by clicking the Change button. Figure 2.8 shows the Web page after clicking the Change button. You can bring the caption back to its original orientation by clicking the Restore button.

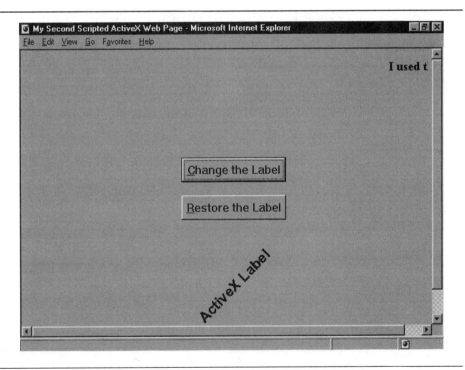

FIGURE 2.8: The Web page's appearance after you click the Change button. The text line "I used the HTML Layout Control for this one" is scrolling off the right side of the page.

Spinning and Rotating

Let's move on to another type of ActiveX control, the Spin Button. A Spin Button displays a pair of arrowheads. The arrowheads are closely linked to the Spin Button's Value property, which is numerical. Clicking on one arrowhead increases the Value, clicking on the other decreases the Value. The amount of increase or decrease is specified in the Spin Button's Small Change property (the default value for Small Change is 1). The Spin Button's value is never visible unless you design some way to show it (as the caption of a label, for instance).

We'll use this control's Value property to set the Label's Angle property and cause the caption to rotate to the number of degrees that the value specifies:

1. Delete the Change button.

2. In its place, insert a Spin Button control. Size the Spin Button so its dimensions are approximately the same as the Command Button.

3. Right-click on the Spin Button to open its Properties sheet.

4. Change the Spin Button's ID to **spnbtnRotate**.

5. For the Max property, type **360**. This gives us a range of 0 degrees to 360 degrees for rotating our Label's caption. (The default value for the Min property is 0, which is exactly what we want.)

6. Click on Apply, then click OK.

7. Select the Restore button, hold down the Shift key, and select the Spin Button.

8. In the menu bar, select Format ➢ Make the Same Size ➢ Both.

9. Then select Format ➢ Align ➢ Centers.

We're ready to insert another Label—an MS Forms 2.0 Label (the kind we worked with originally). Insert the Label and follow this sequence:

1. Set the Label's ID property to **frmslblScript**.

2. Set its Height property to **30** and its Width property to **30**.

3. Make its font 12 pt.

4. Delete its default caption and don't type anything in its place.

5. Set its BackColor property to white, and close the Properties sheet.

6. Move the new Label to the right of the Spin Button.

7. Select the Spin Button, hold down the Shift key, and select the new Label.

8. In the menu bar, select Format ➤ Make the Same Size ➤ Height.

9. Then select Format ➤ Align ➤ Tops.

After you make these changes, your HTML Layout Control should look like Figure 2.9.

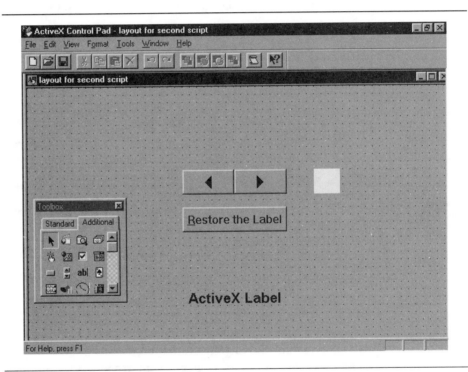

FIGURE 2.9: The HTML Layout Control after you insert and resize a Spin Button and a new Label

We're ready to do some scripting. Here are the behaviors we want to create:

- Clicking the Spin Button rotates the Label's caption.

- Clicking the Spin Button changes the caption in the Forms Label to the Spin Button's value (so we can keep track of how many degrees we rotate the caption).

- Clicking the Restore button returns the caption to its original orientation. (As you'll recall, we've already scripted this behavior in "Rotating a Caption.")

- Clicking the Restore button resets the Spin Button to zero and the Forms Label caption to zero.

Here are the steps to follow to make all this happen:

1. Open the Script Wizard.

2. In the Event pane click on the + next to spnbtnRotate.

3. Click on the Change event.

4. In the Actions pane click on lblobjctScript's +.

5. Double-click on Angle.

6. Click the Custom… button in the dialog box. Now the box prompts you to enter a single value or a variable name. We'll enter the variable name **spnbtnRotate.Value**. (Make sure you type the dot between **spnbtnRotate** and **Value**, but don't type the final period.)

Figure 2.10 shows what your screen looks like after you do this. Click on OK.

 NOTE   This "dot" notation—spnbtnRotate.Value, for example—is the way we'll represent a property (or other aspect) of a control.

In our last sequence of steps, Steps 3 through 6 deal with the Spin Button's Change event. This event is new in our discussion. It's a good one to learn, as many controls have a Change event. The Change event occurs as soon as a control's value changes—it doesn't wait for a Click, or a Double-Click, or anything else. (We examine the Change event more closely in Skill 5.)

Now that we've used the Change event to connect the Spin Button's Value with lblobjctScript's Angle property, let's connect the Spin Button's Value with the other Label's Caption property. With the Change event still selected, click on the + sign next to frmslblScript. Double-click on Caption. In the dialog box, click on Custom…. Type **spnbtnRotate.Value** and click OK.

We also have to update the Restore button's Click event. In the Event pane click on cmdbtnRestore's +. Select the Click event. In the Actions pane, click on the + for spnbtnRotate. Double-click on Value, type **0** (zero) in the dialog box,

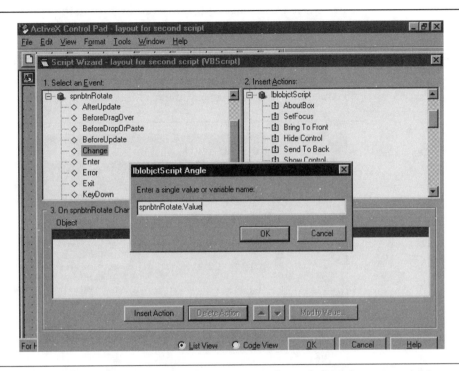

FIGURE 2.10: The dialog box prompts you for a single value or a variable name for IblobjctScript's Angle. Type the indicated expression, a variable that stands for the Spin Button's value.

and click OK. Also in the Actions pane, find fmslblScript's Caption property, double-click, type **0** in the dialog box, and click OK. Figure 2.11 shows what your Script Wizard looks like when you're done.

One more piece of business: In the Actions pane, click on the + next to Procedures. You'll see symbols that represent all the scripts we've created for this layout. One of those is cmdbtnChange_Click, a script for the Command Button we deleted. When you delete a control, the Script Wizard doesn't get rid of scripts you wrote for its events. You have to delete those scripts yourself. Here's how to do it: Select cmdbtnChange_Click, and right-click. From the little menu that opens, select Delete.

Click OK to close the Script Wizard and return to the HTML Layout Control. If we were in the Object Editor, we would close the Script Wizard and our VBS code would show up in the Text Editor. As we've seen, this doesn't happen with the HTML Layout Control. When we close it and return to the Text Editor, the only additional code is the pair of <OBJECT> tags for the layout. How do we see the VBS code if we're working with the HTML Layout Control?

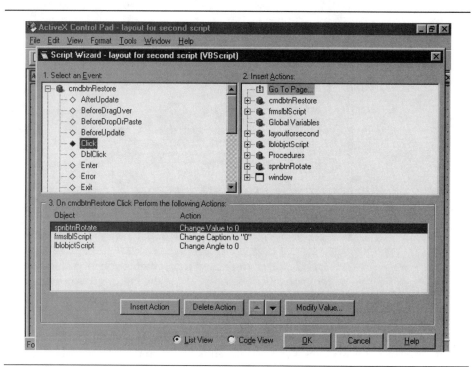

FIGURE 2.11: The Script Wizard shows your additions to the Restore button's Click event.

While you're still in the HTML Layout Control, right-click and select View Source Code. A dialog box warns you that if you proceed, you save changes and close the HTML Layout Control. Click Yes. Your VBS code is displayed in Notepad. It should look like the listing that follows (layout for second script.alx).

layout for second script.alx

```
<SCRIPT LANGUAGE="VBScript">
<!--
Sub cmdbtnRestore_Click()
spnbtnRotate.Value = 0
frmslblScript.Caption = "0"
lblobjctScript.Angle = 0
end sub
-->
</SCRIPT>

<SCRIPT LANGUAGE="VBScript">
<!--
Sub spnbtnRotate_Change()
lblobjctScript.Angle = spnbtnRotate.Value
frmslblScript.Caption = spnbtnRotate.Value
end sub
-->
</SCRIPT>
<DIV ID="layoutforsecond" STYLE="LAYOUT:FIXED;WIDTH:477pt;HEIGHT:293pt;">
    <OBJECT ID="cmdbtnRestore"
     CLASSID="CLSID:D7053240-CE69-11CD-A777-00DD01143C57"
    ➥STYLE="TOP:132pt;LEFT:173pt;WIDTH:118pt;HEIGHT:27pt;
    ➥TABINDEX:0;ZINDEX:0;">
        <PARAM NAME="Caption" VALUE="Restore the Label">
        <PARAM NAME="Size" VALUE="4163;953">
        <PARAM NAME="MousePointer" VALUE="12">
        <PARAM NAME="Accelerator" VALUE="82">
        <PARAM NAME="FontName" VALUE="MS SystemEx">
        <PARAM NAME="FontEffects" VALUE="1073741825">
        <PARAM NAME="FontHeight" VALUE="240">
        <PARAM NAME="FontCharSet" VALUE="0">
        <PARAM NAME="FontPitchAndFamily" VALUE="2">
        <PARAM NAME="ParagraphAlign" VALUE="3">
        <PARAM NAME="FontWeight" VALUE="700">
    </OBJECT>
    <OBJECT ID="lblobjctScript"
     CLASSID="CLSID:99B42120-6EC7-11CF-A6C7-00AA00A47DD2"
    ➥STYLE="TOP:182pt;LEFT:157pt;WIDTH:150pt;HEIGHT:99pt; ZINDEX:1;">
        <PARAM NAME="_ExtentX" VALUE="5292">
        <PARAM NAME="_ExtentY" VALUE="3493">
        <PARAM NAME="Caption" VALUE="ActiveX Label">
```

```
            <PARAM NAME="Angle" VALUE="0">
            <PARAM NAME="Alignment" VALUE="4">
            <PARAM NAME="Mode" VALUE="1">
            <PARAM NAME="FillStyle" VALUE="0">
            <PARAM NAME="FillStyle" VALUE="0">
            <PARAM NAME="ForeColor" VALUE="#000000">
            <PARAM NAME="BackColor" VALUE="#C0C0C0">
            <PARAM NAME="FontName" VALUE="Arial">
            <PARAM NAME="FontSize" VALUE="16">
            <PARAM NAME="FontItalic" VALUE="0">
            <PARAM NAME="FontBold" VALUE="1">
            <PARAM NAME="FontUnderline" VALUE="0">
            <PARAM NAME="FontStrikeout" VALUE="0">
            <PARAM NAME="TopPoints" VALUE="0">
            <PARAM NAME="BotPoints" VALUE="0">
        </OBJECT>
        <OBJECT ID="frmslblScript"
         CLASSID="CLSID:978C9E23-D4B0-11CE-BF2D-00AA003F40D0"
        ➥STYLE="TOP:91pt;LEFT:322pt;WIDTH:30pt;HEIGHT:27pt; ZINDEX:2;">
            <PARAM NAME="BackColor" VALUE="16777215">
            <PARAM NAME="Size" VALUE="1058;953">
            <PARAM NAME="FontHeight" VALUE="240">
            <PARAM NAME="FontCharSet" VALUE="0">
            <PARAM NAME="FontPitchAndFamily" VALUE="2">
            <PARAM NAME="FontWeight" VALUE="0">
        </OBJECT>
        <OBJECT ID="spnbtnRotate"
         CLASSID="CLSID:79176FB0-B7F2-11CE-97EF-00AA006D2776"
        ➥STYLE="TOP:91pt;LEFT:173pt;WIDTH:118pt;HEIGHT:27pt; TABINDEX:2; ZINDEX:3;">
            <PARAM NAME="Size" VALUE="4163;953">
            <PARAM NAME="Max" VALUE="360">
        </OBJECT>
</DIV>
```

Notice the <DIV> and </DIV> tags in your code. These tags set up a *division* within a document. They group related items—in this case, ActiveX controls.

Save your work in the Text Editor and examine your Web page in IE. Click the Spin Button's right arrowhead. The caption rotates by an amount corresponding to the number of times you click the Spin Button, and the Spin Button's value appears in the smaller Label control. If you hold down the mouse button while it's on the Spin Button, the caption rotates continuously. Click the Restore button to reset everything to zero. Figure 2.12 shows the Web page after you click the Spin Button.

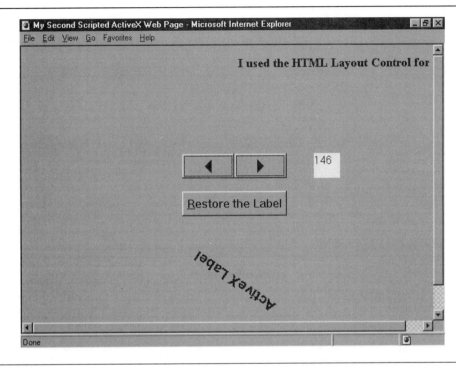

FIGURE 2.12: The appearance of your Web page after you click the Spin Button to rotate the Label's caption. The smaller Label shows how many degrees the caption has rotated from its starting position.

Understanding the Naming Convention

Why should we bother changing control ID properties when the Object Editor and the HTML Layout Control supply default IDs?

The idea is to make the IDs as meaningful as possible. Our demonstration scripts have few controls and it might seem easy to use the default ID property to keep track of the controls, but as your Web pages get more complex, however, the controls will add up.

Long after you've written a script, controls that follow a systematic naming convention will help you remember what they're supposed to do. If you have to work with a script that someone else has written, you'll appreciate the value of a systematic naming convention even more.

Our convention is simple. The first part of any ID property is a lowercase sequence of letters that indicates the type of control. We keep the first part short by omitting noninitial vowels and (optionally) some consonants. The second part begins with an uppercase letter (it can contain more than one) and conveys something specific about the control. Examples from what we've done so far include:

- cmdbtnRestore

- lblFirst

- spnbtnRotate

Summing Up

At this point, you've mastered some important skills: You can embed ActiveX controls into Web pages, and you can script behaviors into those controls. You've learned *how* to do these things, but you haven't learned *why*. We'll examine the whys and the wherefores in the next Skill.

Are You Experienced?

Now you can...

☑ **use the Script Wizard to create VBScript**

☑ **embed ActiveX controls that take input from users**

☑ **have ActiveX controls interact with each other**

☑ **use the Text Editor to edit ActiveX controls**

☑ **understand essential keyboard-based and mouse-based events**

☑ **script a Spin Button control**

☑ **work with HTML tags to create hypertext links**

☑ **work with HTML tags to generate a scrolling marquee**

Examining ActiveX Objects

❏ **Dissecting your controls**

❏ **Understanding the <*OBJECT*> tag**

❏ **Working with ActiveX and the Windows 95 Registry**

❏ **Examining VBS scripts**

In Skills 1 and 2, I've taken you step-by-step through the process of embedding ActiveX controls and assigning behaviors to those controls through scripts. The idea was to immerse you in the ActiveX development environment and familiarize you with the world of ActiveX.

In this Skill, we build your understanding of ActiveX ideas. ActiveX rests on a number of foundational concepts that are important to understand. Many of these concepts reveal themselves as you examine the HTML code you've written and the scripts you've created.

Dissecting Your Controls

Let's go back to the first script you wrote in Skill 2. The part of the script that defines the first Command Button is:

```
<OBJECT ID="cmdbtnScript1" WIDTH=171 HEIGHT=29
    CLASSID="CLSID:D7053240-CE69-11CD-A777-00DD01143C57">
        <PARAM NAME="Caption" VALUE="Scripted Command Button 1">
        <PARAM NAME="Size" VALUE="4234;767">
        <PARAM NAME="MousePointer" VALUE="3">
        <PARAM NAME="FontEffects" VALUE="1073741825">
        <PARAM NAME="FontCharSet" VALUE="0">
        <PARAM NAME="FontPitchAndFamily" VALUE="2">
        <PARAM NAME="ParagraphAlign" VALUE="3">
        <PARAM NAME="FontWeight" VALUE="700">
    </OBJECT>
```

The HTML <OBJECT> tags surround the relevant Command Button information, and the four attributes—ID, WIDTH, HEIGHT, and CLASSID—specify the particulars. The <PARAM> tags represent settable properties of the Command Button. Two of the properties are the most important:

- The ID identifies the instance of the control-type and is extremely important. It's the control's name and it enables other controls to refer to it. In the Script Wizard, as we've seen, we write scripts that enable one named control to influence another.

- The CLASSID identifies the type of control. Any time you embed an ActiveX control, you embed an instance of a control-type. In the jargon of software builders, a control-type is a *class*—hence the term "CLASSID." (For example, "Command Button" is a class; "Label" is a class, and so on.)

You can specify values for ID, WIDTH, and HEIGHT. The CLASSID property is read-only, however.

Working in the Windows 95 Registry

As you can see in the code fragment from the first script, the value for the CLASSID attribute is 32 (hexadecimal) digits long:

```
D7053240-CE69-11CD-A777-00DD01143C57
```

This identifier is a registration number for this control, telling you how the control is registered in the *Registry*. The Registry is the Windows 95 central repository of information on how you've configured software and hardware on your computer.

Let's find this Command Button control in the Registry. To do this we'll need a tool called the Registry Editor.

WARNING   When you're in the Registry, look but don't touch! Unless you have a black belt in Windows 95, *don't change anything.* You might change something that's crucial to your computer's operation, and your computer might not work properly (or it might not work at all).

To start the Registry Editor, go to the Windows 95 Start menu. Choose Start ➤ Run. Type **Regedit** and click OK. The Registry window opens (see Figure 3.1).

The Registry Editor window has two panes. The left pane shows a hierarchy with an icon representing your computer at the top. Folders, called *keys*, constitute the rest of the hierarchy. The keys in the level directly below the computer icon (shown in Figure 3.1) are *root keys*. These root keys can each hold a number of *subkeys*. All of these keys hold settings pertaining to your software and hardware. Whenever you install a program or add a new piece of hardware, you add information to these keys—probably without even knowing it.

The left pane in Figure 3.1 shows six root keys. Only two of them, however, are "real" root keys—HKEY_LOCAL_MACHINE and HKEY_USERS. The others are shortcuts to branches within these two. For example, HKEY_CLASSES_ROOT is actually a branch of HKEY_LOCAL_MACHINE.

You work with the left pane the same way you work with panes in the Script Wizard: click on a plus sign (+) next to a key and it becomes a minus sign (-) as it reveals the subkeys it contains. The pane on the right presents information about selections you make in the left pane.

Skill 3

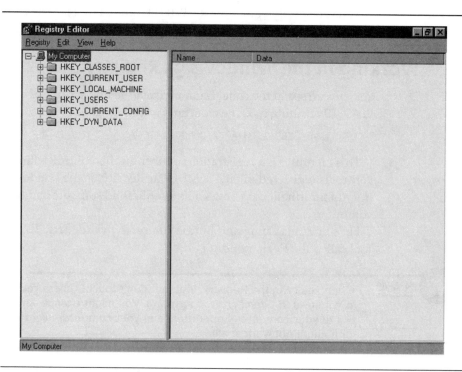

FIGURE 3.1: The Windows 95 Registry Editor window

Click on the + for HKEY_CLASSES_ROOT. The first items that appear are the file extensions you typically work with. Remember the .ALX extension for layouts that you build with the HTML Layout Control? Find the subkey for this extension and click on it (not the +). Information that appears in the right pane indicates this extension is for HTML layouts. Now scroll down to find the subkey for .DOC and click on it. If Microsoft Word is your word processor, information in the right pane tells you this extension is for Word documents.

Recall that the type of Command Button we used in Skill 2 was an MS Forms 2.0 CommandButton. Scroll down until you find Forms.CommandButton.1. Click on the subkey and you'll see that the data column in the right pane says "Microsoft Forms 2.0 CommandButton." This lets us know we've come to the right place. Now click on the subkey's +. A subkey entitled CLSID appears. Click on this subkey and the right pane's data column shows {D7053240-CE69-11CD-A777-00DD01143C57}, the 32-digit ID that is the value for CLASSID in the <OBJECT> tag of your first script (see Figure 3.2).

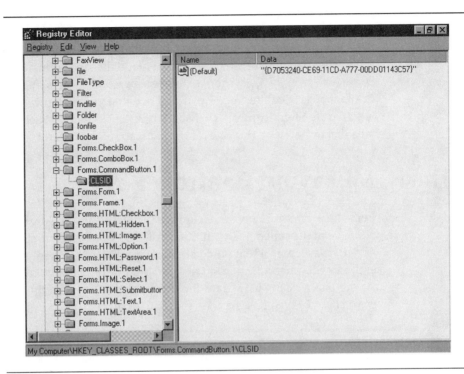

FIGURE 3.2: The Registry Editor window looks like this when you find the CLASSID for the Command Button control.

Other controls that we've used are nearby. If you scroll down, you'll find the subkey for Label. If you want, you can see that the value in its CLSID subkey is the same as the value in the CLASSID attribute of lblFirst's <OBJECT> tag.

Registered Controls

The Command Button and the Label are controls that came with the ActiveX Control Pad. Other controls that the ActiveX Control Pad provides are also in the Registry. When you install the ActiveX Control Pad, registration information for these controls is entered automatically in the Registry.

The controls in the Registry are said to be *registered*. When you work in the ActiveX Control Pad, the names of the registered controls are what appear in the Controls list.

At this point, it's a good idea to close the Registry Editor.

Now let's find the controls themselves. In the Windows 95 Start menu, select Start ➤ Find ➤ Files or Folders…. In the dialog box, type ***.ocx** and click Find Now. The search results will point you to the files for your ActiveX controls. Some will be in the C:\Windows\System directory; others might be in C:\Windows\Occache. When you find one that you recognize from the Controls list (like the Slider control or IeLabel), right-click on it and select Properties. The tabs that appear will provide information about the control.

The HTML Layout Control

Let's dissect another important ActiveX control—the HTML Layout Control. Notice that it's called a Layout "Control" and not a Layout "Editor" or a Layout "Tool." It's a control that you embed in an HTML document the same way you embed a Command Button, a Label, a Spin Button, or any other control.

Let's examine the HTML for the first page that we used the Layout Control to create in Skill 1. Here's the code (second.htm):

 second.htm

```
<HTML>
<HEAD>
<TITLE>My Second ActiveX Web Page</TITLE>
</HEAD>
<BODY> <!-- These tags adjust the text line --> <B> <BIG> <CENTER>
<!--- This is the text line -->
I Used the HTML Layout Control for this one
</CENTER> </BIG> </BIG>
<!-- This object is the layout -->
<OBJECT CLASSID="CLSID:812AE312-8B8E-11CF-93C8-00AA00C08FDF"
ID="layoutforsecond_alx" STYLE="LEFT:0;TOP:0">
<PARAM NAME="ALXPATH" REF VALUE="layout for second.alx">
</OBJECT>
</BODY>
</HTML>
```

Note that the <OBJECT> tag has a value for the CLASSID attribute and the ID. The STYLE attribute sets up the layout's position on the page. The <PARAM>

element's NAME directs the browser to follow a path to the file `layout for second.alx`, the REF VALUE.

The ID attribute names a control so other controls in the document can refer to it. This is important in VBScript when you assign one control's events to influence another control's actions. Thus, if we open the Script Wizard for this document, we should find an object whose name is the value, `layoutforsecond`, for the ID attribute (see Figure 3.3).

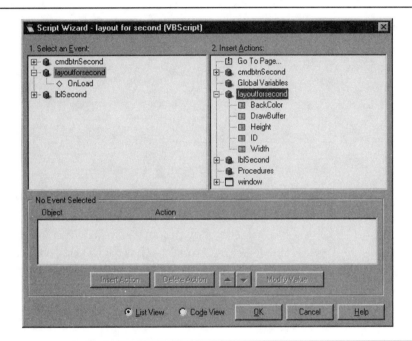

FIGURE 3.3: The Script Wizard for a document with an embedded Layout Control. The Layout Control appears as an object in the Event pane and in the Actions pane.

The HTML Layout Control has one event, OnLoad. As its name suggests, OnLoad occurs when the control opens. This control has five properties that events can modify: BackColor, DrawBuffer, Height, ID, and Width.

THE IMPORTANCE OF THE ACTIVEX CONTROL PAD

Perhaps you're starting to appreciate what a terrific invention the ActiveX Control Pad is. Suppose the Control Pad didn't exist. What would you have to do to embed ActiveX controls into HTML documents?

First, you'd have to use the Registry Editor to open the Registry. Then you'd have to search the Registry for the control you wanted to insert into HTML. Once you found it, you'd have to copy the CLASSID for the control—a possible source of error, since the CLASSID consists of 32 hexadecimal digits. Then you'd enter the CLASSID into the document. You'd have to remember the syntax for the <OBJECT> tag and you'd have to know and enter the parameters for the control's properties.

The ActiveX Control Pad handles all these steps for you:

- When you have to find a control, it gives you a list to select from.
- When you have to enter values for a control's properties, it gives you a Properties sheet.
- When you finish entering property values in the Object Editor and go back to the Text Editor, the control's 32-digit Class ID is automatically entered in the HTML document, in the proper syntax for the <OBJECT> tag.

Understanding the *<OBJECT>* Tag

The <OBJECT> tag is the HTML structure that enables you to embed ActiveX controls. It's also the structure for embedding Java applets and images. We generically refer to controls, applets, and images as *objects*.

What happens when your browser encounters an <OBJECT> tag in an HTML document? It first sets aside an area whose width and height equal the specified values for WIDTH and HEIGHT.

SOME FINE POINTS OF *WIDTH* AND *HEIGHT*... AND A CAVEAT

Because you're using the ActiveX Control Pad's Object Editor and the HTML Layout Control, you set values for WIDTH and HEIGHT by moving sizing handles. Even so, it might help you to know some of the fine points of these attributes:

- According to a working draft from the World Wide Web Consortium, the values for WIDTH and HEIGHT can be in centimeters, inches, percentage of the display area, or pixels.

- To designate a width or height in a particular unit, add a suffix to a floating-point number. Here are some examples: 0.5in, 3.51cm, 50%, 156pt.

- Some potentially useful conversion information: 72pt = 1in = 2.54cm

- For WIDTH, "percentage" refers to the space between the current left and right margins.

- For HEIGHT, "percentage" refers to the height of the current window (or other current display area, like a cell in a table).

Now that I've told you all this, I ought to fill you in on an important caveat. Except for %, the unit suffixes don't work in IE—at least not yet. The browser renders values with these suffixes as though they denote pixels. Thus, if you try WIDTH=2in HEIGHT=1in for an object, you'll see nothing. The % suffix can be useful, however, in laying out a page.

If the specified CLASSID is in your Registry, the browser renders the control on the Web page. If the CLASSID's value isn't in your Registry—in other words, if the control isn't installed and registered on your computer, the OBJECT's CODEBASE attribute comes into play.

The *CODEBASE* Attribute

When you went to the Microsoft ActiveX Component Gallery to get the Label control, you found yourself on a page that gave you the opportunity to click and see a demonstration of the Label. If you clicked and the Label wasn't registered on your computer, you downloaded it so IE could render it. The download happens automatically if your browser can't find the CLASSID. How does your browser know where to get the control? The CODEBASE attribute tells it.

We haven't worked with this attribute so far. We didn't have to, as all the controls we've embedded have been registered on your machine.

When you build a Web page, you can't be sure that the user who gets to look at it has registered all the necessary controls to render the page in all its glory. To ensure that a user can see your creations, you assign a value to CODEBASE. The value you assign is the WWW address to download the control from. If the user doesn't have the control, the user's browser goes and gets it. Sometimes this takes a few minutes (depending on the size of the file, the speed of the connection, and the speed of the computer). During the installation, you might see a message in the IE status bar that says "Installing Components...".

For example, if you were writing a Web page that uses the IeLabel Label control, you could assign the following value to the Label's CODEBASE:

```
"http://activex.microsoft.com/controls/iexplorer/ielabel.ocx#
Version=4,70,0,1161".
```

This ensures that the user gets the Label control if it isn't already installed. Note the version number (4,70,0,1161) in the CODEBASE value. This translates to version 4.70.0.1161 and directs the browser to see if that version or later is installed. If it's not, the newer version downloads.

To check the version of any registered control, find that control's file, right-click on its icon, select Properties and then select the Version tag. When I do this to check the Label control on my machine, the result of this process takes me to the display in Figure 3.4.

To assign a value to a control's Codebase, open that control's Properties sheet and select the Codebase property. Type in the URL and you're done.

NOTE   URL stands for *Uniform Resource Locator*, a way to specify where things reside and what you'll need to access them. The URL for the Label control's Codebase, http://activex.microsoft.com/controls/iexplorer/ielabel.ocx, is an example. The first part, http:, tells you that you'll need your Web browser. The second part, activex.microsoft.com, gives you the address of the computer that holds the Label control. The third part, /controls/iexplorer/ielabel.ocx , is the path that takes you to the Label's file. (If the file you want to refer to is on your own system, the URL is just the file's path.)

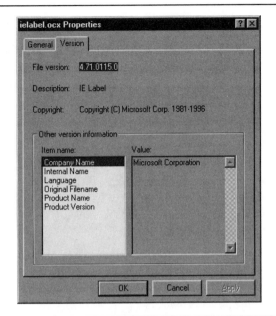

FIGURE 3.4: Checking the version of the Label control

The key question is: How do you get the value for the Codebase? If you build a Web site that resides on your own server, the Codebase is the path that leads to the control's filename on your server.

Another possibility is to give the URL for the site of the vendor (including, of course, the control's location at that site). The Codebase I gave you for the Label is an example of this.

How can you get that URL for the Label? Follow these steps:

1. Use IE to go to the Microsoft ActiveX Component Gallery, and get to the Label's page (see Figure 3.5).

2. In the frame (a dedicated area of the page) devoted to the Label, right-click your mouse.

3. In the menu that pops up, select View Source. The HTML code for the page appears in a Notepad file.

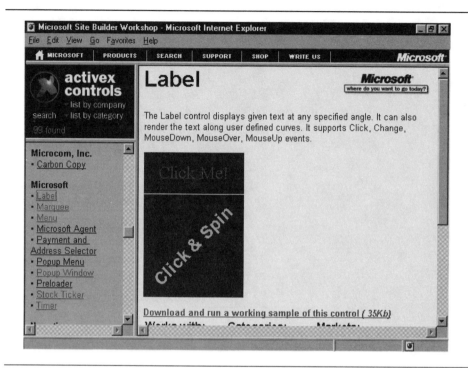

FIGURE 3.5: The Microsoft ActiveX Component Gallery page that presents the Label control

4.   Find the <OBJECT> tag. For the Label, the HTML code is:

```
<OBJECT
    ID="label1"
    CLASSID="clsid:99B42120-6EC7-11CF-A6C7-00AA00A47DD2"
        CODEBASE="http://activex.microsoft.com/controls/iexplorer/
        ➥ielabel.ocx#version=4,70,0,1161"TYPE="application/x-oleobject"
    WIDTH=150
    HEIGHT=150
    VSPACE=0
    ALIGN=left
>
    <PARAM NAME="Angle" VALUE="0">
    <PARAM NAME="Alignment" VALUE="4" >
    <PARAM NAME="BackStyle" VALUE="1" >
    <PARAM NAME="BackColor" VALUE="#0000ff" >
    <PARAM NAME="Caption" VALUE="Click & Spin">
```

```
        <PARAM NAME="FontName" VALUE="Arial">
        <PARAM NAME="FontSize" VALUE="20">
        <PARAM NAME="ForeColor" VALUE="#F0f000" >
        <PARAM NAME="FontBold" VALUE="1" >
    </OBJECT>
```

5. Note the value for the CODEBASE and use it in your work.

That's all there is to it.

Another way that you can sometimes get a clue about the URL for CODEBASE is to examine a particular file associated with the control. If you open the folder that contains the Label control file (ielabel.ocx), you'll find a file called ielabel.inf. The INF extension indicates an "information" file. It provides information about setting up the control. Double-click on ielabel.inf and you'll open it in Notepad. It looks like this:

```
[Add.Code]
ielabel.ocx=ielabel.ocx

[ielabel.ocx]
file-win32-x86=thiscab
file-win32-alpha=http://activex.microsoft.com/controls/iexplorer/alpha/ielabel.cab
file-win32-mips=http://activex.microsoft.com/controls/iexplorer/mips/ielabel.cab
file-win32-ppc=http://activex.microsoft.com/controls/iexplorer/ppc/ielabel.cab
clsid={99B42120-6EC7-11CF-A6C7-00AA00A47DD2}
FileVersion=4,71,115,0
```

If you've ever looked at an .INI file, this type of file may look somewhat familiar. Without going through a detailed explanation of all parts of this file, we see three URLs. Each one ends with a .CAB extension. We also see a reference to another .CAB file. In Windows 95 a .CAB file is a type of compressed file used in software installations (*cab* is short for "cabinet").

Each URL provides a download file for a different type of system—the first one, for instance, downloads the control to a DEC alpha computer. If you anticipate that users will access your Web page through several kinds of systems (like PCs, PowerPCs, and DEC alphas), this type of INF file is a useful way of getting your controls installed. We're interested in this file for a different reason right now. The reference to the other cab file (file-win32-x86=thiscab) gives us a value for CODEBASE for our Windows 95 system. That value is http://activex .microsoft.com/controls/iexplorer/ielabel.cab.

Yes, we made a little leap here. We assume that since we're using the most popular operating system, we don't have to have a qualifier like *alpha* or *ppc*.

Two *CODEBASE* Experiments

To give you a feel for the way CODEBASE works, let's try two experiments that show this attribute in action.

Here's the first experiment: In the ActiveX Control Pad, open the Object Editor and select the IeLabel control. Use the sizing handles to size the control. Enter a value for the caption and make it bold. Since we'll just concern ourselves with the Codebase property of the object we're inserting, we won't worry about details like text lines, titles, or anything about the HTML file other than the <OBJECT> tags. We're not particularly concerned with the exact values of the WIDTH and HEIGHT of the object as long as its caption is visible.

Your Text Editor should now have HTML code that looks like this:

```
HTML>
<HEAD>
<TITLE>New Page</TITLE>
</HEAD>
<BODY>

<OBJECT ID="IeLabel1" WIDTH=127 HEIGHT=93
 CLASSID="CLSID:99B42120-6EC7-11CF-A6C7-00AA00A47DD2">
    <PARAM NAME="_ExtentX" VALUE="3334">
    <PARAM NAME="_ExtentY" VALUE="2461">
    <PARAM NAME="Caption" VALUE="Just a test">
    <PARAM NAME="Angle" VALUE="0">
    <PARAM NAME="Alignment" VALUE="4">
    <PARAM NAME="Mode" VALUE="1">
    <PARAM NAME="FillStyle" VALUE="0">
    <PARAM NAME="FillStyle" VALUE="0">
    <PARAM NAME="ForeColor" VALUE="#000000">
    <PARAM NAME="BackColor" VALUE="#C0C0C0">
    <PARAM NAME="FontName" VALUE="Arial">
    <PARAM NAME="FontSize" VALUE="12">
    <PARAM NAME="FontItalic" VALUE="1">
    <PARAM NAME="FontBold" VALUE="1">
    <PARAM NAME="FontUnderline" VALUE="0">
    <PARAM NAME="FontStrikeout" VALUE="0">
    <PARAM NAME="TopPoints" VALUE="0">
    <PARAM NAME="BotPoints" VALUE="0">
</OBJECT>

</BODY>
</HTML>
```

Name this file `codebase exp1`, save it in a folder called `skill 3`, and open it in IE. You'll see a page open with a Label in the upper-left corner. Close IE and close the Active X Control Pad. Follow these steps to proceed with the experiment:

1. Open the directory that holds `ielabel.ocx`. Insert a floppy diskette into your A: drive.

2. Move (don't copy) `ielabel.ocx` to the diskette for safekeeping should anything go wrong.

3. Remove the diskette. The Label control is now off your system. (To be thorough, we'd change the Registry, but remember, we don't change anything in the Registry!)

4. Reopen `codebase exp1` in IE. The Label no longer shows up, but the page presents an area that equals your specifications in `WIDTH` and `HEIGHT`. IE knows how to set up the area you wanted, but without the Label control in the system, it can't do anything else.

5. Add a value for the `CODEBASE` attribute. In the Text Editor, between the end of the value for `CLASSID` and the closing angle-bracket for `<OBJECT>` type **CODEBASE="http://activex.microsoft.com/controls/iexplorer/ielabel.ocx# Version=4,70,0,1161"**.

6. Now let's add a value for the `TYPE` attribute. Enter **TYPE="application/ x-oleobject"**. (I'll explain this in the next section "Other Attributes of the *<OBJECT>* Tag.") Save the file.

7. Connect to the Internet, and open your file in IE. After a few minutes (depending on Net traffic volume, your connection, and your CPU) "Installing Components…" will appear on your status bar.

8. If an *Authenticode* certificate opens on your screen asking if you want to install and run the Label control, click Yes. Figure 3.6 shows an example of this certificate (for downloading Microsoft's Preloader control). It's a safeguard against downloading virus-laden software.

9. After you click Yes on the Authenticode certificate, the Label appears on your page. Close IE and disconnect from the Internet.

10. If you open the folder that you removed `ielabel.ocx` from, you'll see that this file has returned.

FIGURE 3.6: The Authenticode certificate that appears before you install an ActiveX control. This one is for the Microsoft Preloader control.

AUTHENTICODE

Authenticode™, a feature that Microsoft developed for IE, is a technology for verifying that no one has tampered with code that you download. Through a digital "certificate," Authenticode identifies the publisher of the software. When the certificate appears onscreen, you have the opportunity to either install and run the software or to refuse it. Displaying the name of the software's publisher on the certificate gives you a piece of information to help you decide.

continued ▶

Certificates serve another purpose. Software publishers use them to sign off on the software they produce. It's similar to the shrink-wrap on a software package that you buy in a computer store or the safety seal on a bottle of medicine.

Authenticode doesn't meet all the security challenges that the Internet presents, but it's a welcome line of defense.

For more on security-related issues, visit `http://www.microsoft.com/security`.

On to the second experiment. Go through the same steps, taking care to move `ielabel.ocx` to a floppy diskette. Remove the CODEBASE attribute and its value from the HTML file. Open the page in IE and you shouldn't see any Label. These steps complete the second experiment:

1. In the Text Editor type **CODEBASE="http://activex.microsoft.com/controls/iexplorer/ielabel.cab"**.

2. Save the file.

3. Connect to the Internet and you should see the same results as in the first experiment.

The download and installation process may take a bit longer as the CAB file takes some time to decompress. In either experiment, if anything goes wrong and the Label's OCX file doesn't download properly, copy it back over from the diskette.

Other Attributes of the <*OBJECT*> Tag

The designers of the <OBJECT> tag intended that the tag cover a multitude of possibilities. With so many development organizations formulating their own paradigms for Web objects (for example, Java applets, ActiveX controls) and with so many possible types of objects that one might embed, they had (and still have) their work cut out for them.

NOTE Who, exactly, are "they?" They, in fact, are the World Wide Web Consortium (W3C). W3C is a group devoted to making the Web a safer, kinder, gentler place for all of us. Get acquainted with them at http://www.w3.org. You'll be glad you did.

Their solution was an <OBJECT> tag with a large set of attributes. In this section, we examine some of those attributes. Although WIDTH, HEIGHT, CLASSID, and CODEBASE are the attributes you're likely to use the most, knowing some of the other attributes will solidify your understanding of this important structure.

In the last section, I asked you to enter a value for TYPE. This attribute name is short for *MIME type*. MIME is an acronym for Multipurpose Internet Mail Extension—an outmoded name since MIME types no longer just apply to electronic mail. They identify any file that travels over the Internet. A MIME type definition consists of a *type*, a slash, and a *subtype*. Types are either text, image, video, audio, message, multipart, or application. Subtypes are much more numerous and are either *official* or *unofficial*. You can spot an unofficial type by the "x-" that precedes it. This just means that the organization that maintains the MIME standard (the Internet Working Group) hasn't made it official yet. Thus, application/x-oleobject denotes a MIME-type definition that contains an unofficial subtype.

The TYPE can be an important attribute. It refers to the type of data that IE is trying to download (referenced by another attribute called DATA). If you haven't supplied a value for CLASSID, IE examines TYPE's value and if it's not supported, it can ignore the control without accessing the network.

Additional attributes determine the appearance of the object defined in the <OBJECT> tag. On Web pages that will present substantial amounts of text, you'll use the Object Editor to build the page, and these attributes are very useful. ALIGN, for example, tells IE where to place the object. Its possible values, which give specific directions for lining up the object in relation to surrounding text, are:

- BASELINE lines up the bottom of the object with the baseline of surrounding text

- CENTER centers the object between the left and right margins. Subsequent text starts on the next line after the object

- LEFT aligns the object with the left margin, and wraps subsequent text along the object's right side

- MIDDLE lines up the middle of the object with the baseline of surrounding text

- RIGHT lines up the object with the right margin, and wraps subsequent text along the object's left side

- TEXTBOTTOM aligns the bottom of the object with the bottom of surrounding text

- TEXTMIDDLE aligns the middle of the object between the text-baseline and the x-height of the font of the text that surrounds the object. The term "x-height" refers to the height of the lowercase x in Western alphabets. If the font is an all-uppercase style, use the height of the uppercase X. For non-Western alphabets, line up the middle of the object with the middle of the text

- TEXTTOP aligns the top of the object with the top of surrounding text

HSPACE, a numerical value, specifies the amount of space to the left and right of the object. VSPACE, also a numerical value, specifies the amount of space to the top of the object and to the bottom of the object. Imagine the object at the center of a picture frame. HSPACE gives the thickness of the left and right panels. VSPACE gives the thickness of the top and bottom panels.

One more attribute, STANDBY, might prove handy. When you send a Web page with images and other information that takes time to download, you can use STANDBY to display a message that stays onscreen during the process. The message is a text-string (enclosed by quotes) that you assign as STANDBY's value.

Dissecting VBS

To proceed with our dissection of ActiveX controls, let's analyze some of the scripts we've written. We'll look at how they represent ActiveX controls and how they represent what those controls do.

Understanding the *<SCRIPT>* Tag

When you use the Script Wizard to create VBS, the Wizard helps you by putting the VBS into a format that can reside in an HTML document. It puts a <SCRIPT> tag at the beginning of the code and a </SCRIPT> tag at the end.

Just as the <OBJECT> tag has WIDTH and HEIGHT attributes (and many others), the <SCRIPT> tag has a LANGUAGE attribute. For our scripts, the value of this attribute is

"VBScript." Another possibility is JScript, although we won't be working with that language. In principle, one could adapt many existing programming languages to the task of scripting ActiveX controls. Work is underway to do just that.

The VBS code appears between <!– and –>, characters that indicate a comment in HTML. Why should HTML enclose perfectly good code within comment indicators? The reason is that some browsers cannot work with VBS. If they encounter VBS, the comment indicators around the code enable them to ignore it.

Revisiting Your First Script

The first event we scripted in Skill 2 was the Click event for a Command Button. Working with the Script Wizard we created this VBS code:

```
Sub cmdbtnScript1_Click()
lblFirst.BackColor = &H00FFFFFF
lblFirst.Caption = "Hello World!"
end sub
```

The term *sub*—short for *subroutine*—refers to a sequence of steps (a *procedure*) that does a job and finishes up without *returning* a value. VBS has a term for a procedure that *does* return a value—*function*. We'll meet up with it in Skill 5.

Much like a pair of HTML tags, Sub and end sub form the boundaries of the subroutine. The term after Sub, cmdbtnScript1_Click, helps form the title of the procedure, indicates the control that the sub is for, and (following the underscore character) specifies the control event that the sub addresses. It's important for a sub (and for a function, too) to have a title so other procedures can refer to it when they have to call it into action.

This particular piece of VBS, like others we've written, assigns values to properties of another control in the HTML document. This shows the power of the <OBJECT> tag: one control can refer to another because of the <OBJECT> tag's ID attribute. The value assigned to the ID in a particular object can be referenced by other objects in the HTML document.

As you'll recall from working with first script's Web page, this code changes the Label's color from gray to white and the Label's caption from "ActiveX Label" to "Hello World!" The label is indicated by its ID, lblFirst. Its color is indicated by BackColor, separated from Label's ID by a dot. Similarly, its caption is indicated by Caption, separated from the ID by a dot.

 TIP   In most documentation that refers to ActiveX, or to ActiveX controls, or to objects in general, you'll find the name of an object on the left side of a dot and the name of one of its properties on the right side of the dot.

In the Object Editor and the HTML Layout Control, the Properties sheet makes it easy for us to work with this notation. When you use the Properties sheet to assign a value like "ActiveX Label" to the Caption property of lblFirst, in effect you tell IE that

```
lblFirst.Caption = "ActiveX Label"
```

In HTML, this translates to

```
<PARAM NAME="Caption" VALUE="ActiveX Label">
```

within the <OBJECT> tag for lblFirst.

You'll also find a dot separating the object name from an event that it's associated with as in cmdbtnScript1.Click. The Script Wizard's panes make it easy for us to work with this notation when we deal with events.

More from the First Script

For each Command Button in Skill 2, you'll recall, we wrote a sub that takes an action as a result of the KeyDown event and a sub that does the same for the KeyUp event. Here's the VBS for these events for the second Command Button:

```
Sub cmdbtnScript2_KeyDown(KeyCode, Shift)
lblFirst.TextAlign = 3
end sub
Sub cmdbtnScript2_KeyUp(KeyCode, Shift)
lblFirst.TextAlign = 2
end sub
```

When the focus is on cmdbtnScript2, pressing a key causes the text of the caption to shift to the right (in other words, lblFirst.TextAlign = 3) and releasing the key puts the text back in the center of the label (lblFirst.TextAlign = 2).

In the title of each sub, you see two terms enclosed by parentheses—KeyCode and Shift. These terms are called *arguments*. They're values that the sub works with.

Why are they there? In some applications, it's important to keep track of keys that users press and release because specific actions depend on specific keystrokes. (For example, in most Windows applications, when the user types Alt+F, the File menu opens.) Although we used the KeyDown and KeyUp events to show that we can make keyboard-contingent actions occur onscreen, the real reason for their existence is to track key-presses and key-releases.

The arguments do that for us. When you press a key, a numerical code for that key is assigned to the KeyCode argument. When you press the Shift key, or the Ctrl key, or the Alt key, you assign a non-zero value to the Shift argument (Shift = 1, Ctrl = 2, Alt = 4; these keys are called *modifiers*). For any other key, the value of the Shift argument is zero.

Skill 3

Let's work with these arguments. Specifically, we'll program a way to show ourselves the numerical codes for the keys we press. In the prehistoric days of computing (around 1970 or so), people often did this by saturating a program with *print* statements and generating paper printouts of the information they wanted. Today, we accomplish much the same thing by opening onscreen *Message Boxes* that display information. We'll use a VBS procedure called *MsgBox* to do this for us.

NOTE   Sometimes a line of VBS code is extremely long. It might not fit into the width of a book's page or it might not fit conveniently within the width of your Text Editor. Although you can scroll your Text Editor to the right to see the end of a line, for convenience we'll use the VBS *line continuation character* to continue a line of code into the next line. The VBS line continuation character is an underscore (_). Thus, if you see an underscore at the end of a line, that indicates that the code continues on the next line.

Save `first script` in the `skill 3` folder under the name `keycodes`. In the HTML file, change the title to **KeyCodes and Arguments**. In the code for cmdbtnScript2_ KeyDown, use the Text Editor to insert this line of VBS code just before `end sub`:

```
MsgBox  "The code of the pressed key is: " _
        & KeyCode & " " & _
        "The shift code is: " & Shift
```

Make sure you type the spaces, quotes, and ampersands (&) just as I've typed them. The quoted strings will appear in the Message Box. In VBS, an ampersand puts strings together. In computerese, we'd say that the ampersand *concatenates* strings. (In even more hardcore computerese, we'd say that the ampersand is a *concatenation operator*.) This line of code tells VBS to

- give us a Message Box
- put the string "The code of the pressed key is: " in the Message Box (note the space between the colon and the close quote)
- concatenate the numerical code for the pressed key
- concatenate a blank space
- concatenate the string "The shift code is: " (again, note the space between the colon and the close quote)

- concatenate the shift code for the pressed key.

Your code for sub `cmdbtnScript2_KeyDown` should now look like this:

```
Sub cmdbtnScript2_KeyDown(KeyCode, Shift)
lblFirst.TextAlign = 3
MsgBox  "The code of the pressed key is: " _
      & KeyCode & " " & _
        "The shift code is: " & Shift
end sub
```

Save your work, and open the document in IE. Perform the same operations as before, clicking and double-clicking and noting the effects on the label. After you've clicked on the second Command Button, press a key. You should see a Message Box that looks like the one in Figure 3.7.

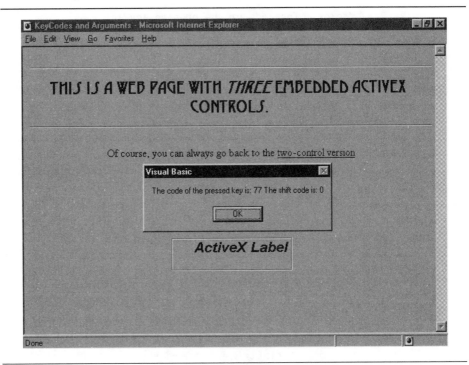

FIGURE 3.7: The Message Box that appears in response to the KeyDown event in *keycodes* with the focus on the second Command Button

We can put our new script to some use. The Message Box we created is a little cluttered because we've put everything on one line. It would look a little cleaner with one line for the key code and another for the shift code. In order to do this, we have to somehow insert a line-feed into our concatenated string. When we're typing, the Enter key is the key that gives us a new line. If we had the keycode for the Enter key, we could put it into the string on our Message Box. This would be like having our script press the Enter key for us.

How can we get the code for the Enter key? In IE, open the Web page, click on the second Command Button to give it the focus, and then press Enter. The Message Box tells you that the key code for Enter is 13.

Now that you know this, go back to the script for cmdbtnScript2's KeyDown event. In the MsgBox line, you'll see a blank space (" ") concatenated into the string. Replace this with **chr(13)**. That line should now look like this:

```
MsgBox  "The code of the pressed key is: " _
        & KeyCode & chr(13) _
        & "The shift code is: " & Shift
```

NOTE   chr(*code*) is a VBS function. Its argument is a code representing a character. It returns the character associated with that code.

Save the file, Alt+Tab back to IE, and click on Refresh. Click on the second Command Button to give it the focus. When you press a key, the Message Box that appears now has two lines. One identifies the KeyCode; the other identifies the Shift code.

You can also use the KeyPress event to monitor codes. This event has one argument—the code of the pressed key. This event differs from the other key-related events in an important way. Pressing the Shift key doesn't cause a KeyPress event, but it does modify the pressed key. Thus, as far as KeyPress is concerned, "A" has a different code value than "a."

To track similarities and differences between KeyPress and KeyDown, add a script for cmdbtnScript1's KeyPress event. Use the Text Editor to type this code into the area that holds the VBS for cmdbtnScript1:

```
Sub cmdbtnScript1_KeyPress(KeyCode
MsgBox "The code for the key you pressed is : " & KeyCode
end sub
```

Save your work and open the document in IE. Press keys with the focus on the first Command Button, and press keys with the focus on the second Command

Button. Note the differences in what the Message Boxes tell you and you'll understand how KeyPress differs from KeyDown and KeyUp.

Here's another little exercise to give you more of a feel for what arguments are all about. Take a look at the previous Note on chr, the VBS procedure we used to insert a line-feed. As the Note says, if you supply a keycode as the argument to chr, chr provides the key to which it corresponds. We can make that work for us if we add this code to the end of the MsgBox line in the sub for KeyPress:

```
& chr(13) & "The key you pressed: " & chr(KeyCode)
```

Your sub for cmdbtnScript1_KeyPress should now look like this:

```
Sub cmdbtnScript1_KeyPress(KeyCode)
MsgBox "The code for the key you pressed is : " & KeyCode _
       & chr(13) & "The key you pressed: " & chr(KeyCode)
end sub
```

Now when you press a key with the focus on cmdbtnScript1, the subsequent Message Box tells you the pressed key as well as the keycode.

If you want to experiment a bit more with arguments and Message Boxes, have a look at lblFirst's MouseUp event. This event has four arguments: Button, Shift, X, and Y. I could tell you what each of these arguments means and what their values indicate, but it's more challenging to discover the meanings and indications on your own.

To do that, type this line into the existing VBS for lblFirst_MouseUp:

```
MsgBox "Mouse Button: " & Button & chr(13) _
       & "Shift: " & Shift _
       & chr(13) & "X-co-ordinate: " & X _
       & chr(13) & "Y-co-ordinate: " & Y
```

Type it in just before end sub. Your code for lblFirst_MouseUp should look like this when you're done:

```
Sub lblFirst_MouseUp(Button, Shift, X, Y)
lblFirst.BackColor = &H00C0C0C0
MsgBox "Mouse Button: " & Button & chr(13) & "Shift: " & Shift _
       & chr(13) & "X-co-ordinate: " & X & chr(13) & _
       "Y-co-ordinate: " & Y
end sub
```

With these additions in place, go back to IE and experiment with mouse-placement and mouse-clicks on the Label. A four-line Message Box will appear with all the details whenever you click either the left or right mouse button and release it.

After all your updates, the HTML for this file (`keycodes.htm`) is:

 keycodes.htm

```
<HTML>
<HEAD>
<TITLE>KeyCodes and Arguments</TITLE>
</HEAD>
<BODY>
<!-- These tags adjust the text line -->
<CENTER>
<H2>
<!-- This is the text line -->
<HR> <FONT FACE = Desdemona>
This is a Web Page with <EM>three</EM> embedded ActiveX Controls
</FONT> <HR>
</H2>
</CENTER>
<CENTER>Of course, you can always go back to the <A Href =
➥"E:\ActiveX No Exp Req\skill 1\first.htm">two-control version</A></CENTER>
<!-- These commands add two line-breaks -->
<BR> <BR>
<CENTER>
<!-- This is an embedded Command Button -->
    <SCRIPT LANGUAGE="VBScript">
<!--
Sub cmdbtnScript1_KeyDown(KeyCode, Shift)
lblFirst.TextAlign = 1
end sub
Sub cmdbtnScript1_KeyUp(KeyCode, Shift)
lblFirst.TextAlign = 2
end sub
Sub cmdbtnScript1_KeyPress(KeyCode)
MsgBox "The code for the key you pressed is: " & " " & KeyCode _
        & chr(13) & "The key pressed: " & chr(Keycode)
end sub
Sub cmdbtnScript1_DblClick(Cancel)
lblFirst.Font.Italic = False
lblFirst.Font.Underline = True
end sub
Sub cmdbtnScript1_Click()
lblFirst.BackColor = &H00FFFFFF
lblFirst.Caption = "Hello World!"
end sub
-->
```

```
    </SCRIPT>
    <OBJECT ID="cmdbtnScript1" WIDTH=171 HEIGHT=29
     CLASSID="CLSID:D7053240-CE69-11CD-A777-00DD01143C57">
        <PARAM NAME="Caption" VALUE="Scripted Command Button 1">
        <PARAM NAME="Size" VALUE="4234;767">
        <PARAM NAME="MousePointer" VALUE="3">
        <PARAM NAME="FontEffects" VALUE="1073741825">
        <PARAM NAME="FontCharSet" VALUE="0">
        <PARAM NAME="FontPitchAndFamily" VALUE="2">
        <PARAM NAME="ParagraphAlign" VALUE="3">
        <PARAM NAME="FontWeight" VALUE="700">
    </OBJECT>
</CENTER>
<!-- This command adds a line-break -->
<BR>
<CENTER>
<!-- This is an embedded Command Button -->
    <SCRIPT LANGUAGE="VBScript">
<!--
Sub cmdbtnScript2_KeyDown(KeyCode, Shift)
lblFirst.TextAlign = 3
MsgBox  "The code of the pressed key is: " & KeyCode & _
        chr(13) & "The shift code is:" & Shift
end sub
Sub cmdbtnScript2_KeyUp(KeyCode, Shift)
lblFirst.TextAlign = 2
end sub
Sub cmdbtnScript2_DblClick(Cancel)
lblFirst.Font.Italic = True
lblFirst.Font.Underline = False
end sub
Sub cmdbtnScript2_Click()
lblFirst.BackColor = &H00C0C0C0
lblFirst.Caption = "ActiveX Label"
end sub
-->
    </SCRIPT>
    <OBJECT ID="cmdbtnScript2" WIDTH=171 HEIGHT=29
     CLASSID="CLSID:D7053240-CE69-11CD-A777-00DD01143C57">
        <PARAM NAME="Caption" VALUE="Scripted Command Button 2">
        <PARAM NAME="Size" VALUE="4234;767">
        <PARAM NAME="MousePointer" VALUE="3">
        <PARAM NAME="FontEffects" VALUE="1073741825">
        <PARAM NAME="FontCharSet" VALUE="0">
        <PARAM NAME="FontPitchAndFamily" VALUE="2">
        <PARAM NAME="ParagraphAlign" VALUE="3">
```

Skill 3

```
            <PARAM NAME="FontWeight" VALUE="700">
        </OBJECT>
</CENTER>
 <BR>
<!-- Center the object which follows -->
<CENTER>
<!-- This is an embedded label -->
    <SCRIPT LANGUAGE="VBScript">
<!--
Sub lblFirst_MouseDown(Button, Shift, X, Y)
lblFirst.BackColor = &H00FFFF80
end sub
Sub lblFirst_MouseUp(Button, Shift, X, Y)
lblFirst.BackColor = &H00C0C0C0
MsgBox "Mouse Button: " & Button & chr(13) & "Shift: " & Shift _
            & chr(13) & "X-co-ordinate: " & X _
            & chr(13) & "Y-co-ordinate: " & Y
end sub
-->
    </SCRIPT>
    <OBJECT ID="lblFirst" WIDTH=181 HEIGHT=48
     CLASSID="CLSID:978C9E23-D4B0-11CE-BF2D-00AA003F40D0">
        <PARAM NAME="Caption" VALUE="ActiveX Label">
        <PARAM NAME="Size" VALUE="4798;1270">
        <PARAM NAME="SpecialEffect" VALUE="3">
        <PARAM NAME="FontName" VALUE="Arial">
        <PARAM NAME="FontEffects" VALUE="1073741827">
        <PARAM NAME="FontHeight" VALUE="320">
        <PARAM NAME="FontCharSet" VALUE="0">
        <PARAM NAME="FontPitchAndFamily" VALUE="2">
        <PARAM NAME="ParagraphAlign" VALUE="3">
        <PARAM NAME="FontWeight" VALUE="700">
    </OBJECT>
</CENTER>
</BODY>
</HTML>
```

Adding Methods to the Madness

In addition to events and properties, controls also have associated *methods*. A method is a behavior that is built into a control. Another way to say this is that a method is a procedure that a control knows how to follow automatically. For example, a Label control knows how to open a dialog box that gives you some information about the Label control's implementation. Other controls, as you'll discover, have other methods. Some know how to add and delete items from lists.

Some know how to set the focus to a control (see Skill 2 for more information). Some multimedia controls know how to move to various locations within a media file. When you write scripts, you use these methods in much the same way that you set actions in motion.

Let's add some methods to a script we've already written so you can get a better idea of how methods work. Just as we used the Script Wizard to work with events and actions, we'll use the Script Wizard to add methods. We'll add a script that calls a method when we click on a Label control. We'll call the method to display an About Box.

Skill 3

To write the script, follow these steps:

1. Go to the skill 2 folder and open second script.

2. Save it in the skill 3 folder as method.

3. Copy layout for second script from skill 2 to skill 3, and rename it layout for method.

4. In the Text Editor, change the title to **Method**.

5. Also in the Text Editor, make the necessary changes to method regarding the layout file: in the <OBJECT> tag, change the ID and the REF VALUE to reflect the new layout file.

6. Click on the symbol to the left of the <OBJECT> tag to open the HTML Layout Control.

7. Open the Script Wizard.

8. In the Event pane, select lblobjctScript, open its events, and choose the Click event.

9. In the Actions pane, select lblobjctScript and click on its +. The items we haven't discussed yet open directly underneath lblobjctScript in the Actions pane. Represented by a little yellow box with an exclamation point through the middle, each of these items represents a method.

10. Double-click on AboutBox. The Script pane shows the results of our selection.

11. We've done something different this time, however, and we can only see it if we switch the Script pane to Code View. Do this by selecting the Code View radio button below the Script pane. Figure 3.8 shows the Script Wizard after you do this.

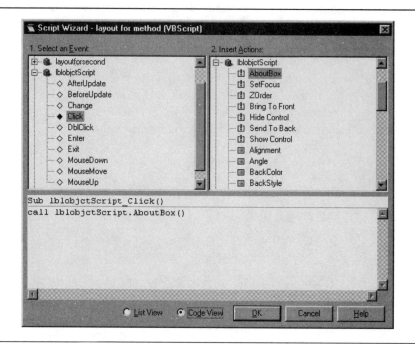

FIGURE 3.8: The Script Wizard after you link the Label's Click event with its About Box method and switch the Script pane to Code View. Note the methods displayed below lblobjctScript in the Actions pane.

The Script pane shows the VBS code created by your selections in the Event pane and the Actions pane. The second line of that code is different from anything we've done up to now:

```
call lblobjctScript.AboutBox()
```

This line tells us that we're invoking a particular object's procedure, as the word call indicates. We reference the procedure by stating the object that the procedure belongs to, followed by a dot, followed by the name of the procedure (this one takes no arguments). Incidentally, it's not always the case that scripts for methods involve call. Some will look like scripts that assign values.

WARNING   You don't have to insert end sub into the Code View in the Script Wizard. The Wizard takes care of this for you.

Save this script, save the Layout Control, and save the HTML. Open this document in IE. When you click on the Label at the bottom of the screen, a Message Box appears. The box provides some information about the Label control (see Figure 3.9).

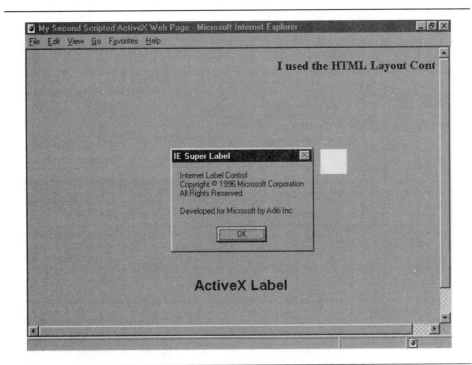

FIGURE 3.9: The box that appears as a result of the Label's About Box method

One more exercise will get you more acquainted with methods and how they work. In the ActiveX Control Pad, open a new HTML file, call it `label methods`, and save it in `skill 3`. In the Text Editor, give this file the title `Label Methods`. Insert the cursor in the blank line between <BODY> and </BODY>. From the Menu Bar, select Edit ➤ Insert HTML Layout.... Start a new layout and call it `layout for label methods` and save this new layout in `skill 3`. Back in the Text Editor, click on the layout push button symbol to open the HTML Layout Control.

We're going to build a Web page that has three Label controls on it. Clicking and double-clicking the labels will activate some of the labels' methods. Select the original Forms Label control that we worked with—the one that does *not* have the rotating-caption capability. On your Toolbox tab, it's the one symbolized by the black uppercase "A" that is not tilted. Use the sizing handles to make the label a reasonable size. Change its ID to frmslbl1. Change its caption to **First Label**, and make it bold. Leave the text alignment where it is. Change its background color to white.

Use copy and paste techniques that we discussed in Skill 2 to make two more labels just like the first. Change their IDs to frmslbl2 and frmslbl3, and change their captions to **Second Label** and **Third Label**. Make the color of the second label light blue (or some other light color that distinguishes it from the first). Make the color of the third label black, and change the ForeColor property to white.

Arrange the three labels so that they look like Figure 3.10.

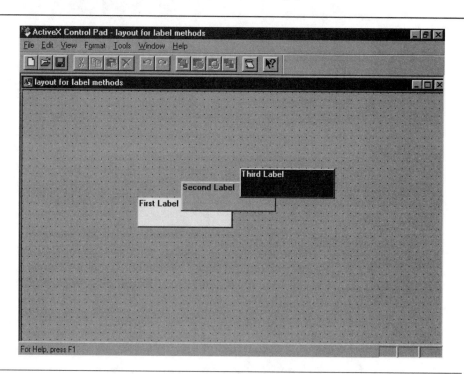

FIGURE 3.10: The arrangement of the labels in the layout for label methods

Now open the Script Wizard and select the Code View button at the bottom of the Wizard's window. In the Event pane, open frmslbl1's events. In the Actions pane, open frmslbl1's methods and properties. In the Event pane, select the Click event. In the Actions pane, double-click on the Bring to Front method. The Script Wizard should now look like Figure 3.11.

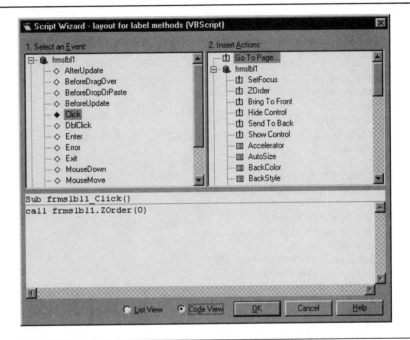

FIGURE 3.11: The Script Wizard, in Code View, after you select the first label's Click event and its Bring to Front method.

The second line of the Script pane shows the method that the Click event will call. This method, the ZOrder, specifies the back-to-front positioning of a control. Where does the name come from? The left-right location is the *x*-coordinate, the top-to-bottom location is the *y*-coordinate. Imagine a third dimension coming out of (and going back into) this x-y coordinate system—that's the ZOrder. When you bring a control to the front its ZOrder position is 0, as the value in the argument indicates.

In the Event pane select the DblClick event, and in the Actions pane double-click on the Send to Back method. (In the Script pane, note that the argument to ZOrder is now 1.) You've probably figured out what all this will do: in the finished Web page, clicking on a label will bring it to the front of our three-label arrangement, and double-clicking on a label will send it to the rear.

To make this happen, duplicate for frmslbl2 and frmslbl3 the selections and double-clicks you performed for frmslbl1. Save your work. When you examine the VBS for this layout, (layout for label methods.alx) it should look like this:

 layout for label methods.alx

```
<SCRIPT LANGUAGE="VBScript">
<!--
Sub frmlbl3_Click()
call frmlbl3.ZOrder(0)
end sub
Sub frmlbl3_DblClick(Cancel)
call frmlbl3.ZOrder(1)
end sub
-->
</SCRIPT>
<SCRIPT LANGUAGE="VBScript">
<!--
Sub frmlbl2_Click()
call frmlbl2.ZOrder(0)
end sub
Sub frmlbl2_DblClick(Cancel)
call frmlbl2.ZOrder(1)
end sub
-->
</SCRIPT>
<SCRIPT LANGUAGE="VBScript">
<!--
Sub frmlbl1_Click()
call frmlbl1.ZOrder(0)
end sub
Sub frmlbl1_DblClick(Cancel)
call frmlbl1.ZOrder(1)
end sub
-->
</SCRIPT>
<DIV ID="layoutforlabelmethods" STYLE="LAYOUT:FIXED;WIDTH:477pt;HEIGHT:293pt;">
    <OBJECT ID="frmlbl1"
     CLASSID="CLSID:978C9E23-D4B0-11CE-BF2D-00AA003F40D0"
    ➡STYLE="TOP:116pt;LEFT:132pt;WIDTH:107pt;HEIGHT:33pt;ZINDEX:0;">
        <PARAM NAME="BackColor" VALUE="16777215">
```

```
                <PARAM NAME="Caption" VALUE="First Label">
                <PARAM NAME="Size" VALUE="3775;1164">
                <PARAM NAME="SpecialEffect" VALUE="1">
                <PARAM NAME="FontEffects" VALUE="1073741825">
                <PARAM NAME="FontCharSet" VALUE="0">
                <PARAM NAME="FontPitchAndFamily" VALUE="2">
                <PARAM NAME="FontWeight" VALUE="700">
        </OBJECT>
        <OBJECT ID="frmlbl2"
         CLASSID="CLSID:978C9E23-D4B0-11CE-BF2D-00AA003F40D0"
        ➡STYLE="TOP:98pt;LEFT:181pt;WIDTH:107pt;HEIGHT:33pt;ZINDEX:1;">
                <PARAM NAME="BackColor" VALUE="16776960">
                <PARAM NAME="Caption" VALUE="Second Label">
                <PARAM NAME="Size" VALUE="3775;1164">
                <PARAM NAME="SpecialEffect" VALUE="1">
                <PARAM NAME="FontEffects" VALUE="1073741825">
                <PARAM NAME="FontCharSet" VALUE="0">
                <PARAM NAME="FontPitchAndFamily" VALUE="2">
                <PARAM NAME="FontWeight" VALUE="700">
        </OBJECT>
        <OBJECT ID="frmlbl3"
         CLASSID="CLSID:978C9E23-D4B0-11CE-BF2D-00AA003F40D0"
        ➡STYLE="TOP:83pt;LEFT:247pt;WIDTH:107pt;HEIGHT:33pt;ZINDEX:2;">
                <PARAM NAME="ForeColor" VALUE="16777215">
                <PARAM NAME="BackColor" VALUE="4194368">
                <PARAM NAME="Caption" VALUE="Third Label">
                <PARAM NAME="Size" VALUE="3775;1164">
                <PARAM NAME="SpecialEffect" VALUE="1">
                <PARAM NAME="FontEffects" VALUE="1073741825">
                <PARAM NAME="FontCharSet" VALUE="0">
                <PARAM NAME="FontPitchAndFamily" VALUE="2">
                <PARAM NAME="FontWeight" VALUE="700">
        </OBJECT>
</DIV>
```

Open the document in IE, click and double-click on the labels, and watch the Bring to Front and Send to Back methods in action.

Summarizing...

Skills 1 and 2 showed you how to embed ActiveX controls and got you accustomed to working with the ActiveX Control Pad, the HTML Layout Control, and the Script Wizard. Skill 3 examined Registered Controls, Codebase, the <SCRIPT> tag, and the <OBJECT> tag—important parts of ActiveX.

Now that you have some foundational concepts in hand, as well as experience with the tools, Skill 4 will get back to specific ActiveX controls and widen the scope of your knowledge.

Are You Experienced?

Now you can...

☑ track down ActiveX controls in the Windows 95 Registry

☑ understand the HTML *<OBJECT>* tag

☑ work with the *<OBJECT>* tag's *CODEBASE* attribute

☑ work with the dot notation for objects and their properties, methods, and events

☑ create VBS subroutines and work with their arguments

☑ open a Message Box to track important values in your scripts

☑ write scripts that involve methods as well as properties and actions

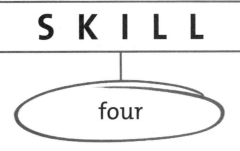

SKILL

four

4

Working with Graphics

- ❏ Using HTML tags to embed graphics into HTML documents
- ❏ Using ActiveX controls to embed graphics into HTML documents
- ❏ Heating things up with Hot Spots
- ❏ Making graphics interactive
- ❏ Hyperlinking from graphics to the World Wide Web
- ❏ Using images to create controls
- ❏ Introducing animation

In Skills 1 through 3, you developed Web pages that have a few controls and a little text. In this skill, you liven things up with graphics. You'll explore an ActiveX control that enables you to embed images into your HTML documents, and you'll examine another that makes those images respond to events that you initiate with your mouse. You'll finish up by showing you how to jump from your graphics to other sites on the Web.

Before you journey into the world of graphics, however, let's pick up some fundamentals.

The ABCs of Graphics Formats

Graphics formats that you may be accustomed to working with are typically too cumbersome for Web applications. Bitmap format (graphics files with the .BMP extension) takes up a lot of space, even for simple drawings. Try drawing something in Paint (the graphics-creation accessory that comes with Windows 95), and you'll see what I mean: A bitmap of just three simple overlapping shapes filled with color can occupy more than 900KB of disk space. For more meaningful images, the file size can really explode. Graphics of this size translate into long, frustrating waits as a Web page unfolds.

Instead, people who are concerned with graphic transmission over the Internet have come up with a few solutions. The solutions center around compressing images into small packages that traverse the Internet quickly.

One of the first groups to tackle the challenges of graphic transmission was CompuServe. Their solution is called *GIF* (Graphic Interchange Format). Each pixel in a GIF image can store up to eight bits. For our purposes, this means that a GIF image can have up to 256 colors.

Another organization that took on this challenge was the Joint Photographic Experts Group. Their initials, JPEG, form the name of the format they derived for transmitting complex images such as photographs. JPEG (pronounced "JAY-peg") stores 24 bits in each pixel. As a result, an image in this format can have more than 16 million colors.

Although 16 million colors sounds like a lot, a JPEG image, when decompressed, isn't exactly the same as the precompressed original image. Because JPEG compression yields a loss of information, JPEG is said to be *lossy*. The information that JPEG loses, however, is typically imperceptible to the human eye. Lossiness is adjustable: If you decrease the degree of compression, you increase the image quality and lower the lossiness.

Acquiring Images

In order to proceed you'll need some image files in the proper format. The Web is the best place to get them. As you cruise the Web, it's easy to copy any image from a Web page for your own personal use. Position your cursor anywhere on an image and right-click. In the pop-up menu that appears, select Save Picture As.... In the resulting dialog box, indicate the folder where you want to store a copy of the image file and click OK.

NOTE   Because this Skill shows you the fundamentals of working with graphics, we only cover the care and feeding of ready-made graphics files. We don't deal with graphics creation, a subject that typically takes up a whole book. If you have a need to create your own graphics, you can find some surprisingly inexpensive yet powerful tools on the Web. Many of them are shareware packages. Three good places to start looking are http://www.shareware.com, http://www.Windows95.com, and http://www.tucows.com.

A map of the United States is an image that will prove useful as a basis for our work. To get one, visit the Web site of the Foundation for Independent Higher Education (http://www.fihe.org/). The Foundation for Independent Higher Education is a national network of 38 state and regional funds representing 630 private colleges and universities, including many of the nation's finest liberal arts institutions. One of the applications at their site relies on a map of the 48 contiguous states in the United States. The map they use is a GIF image, and the Foundation has kindly consented to let us use this map in our exercises. The map is at http://www.fihe.org/fihe/college/map.htm. If you're in the market for a college, you might find their application useful: Click on a state and your screen will display information about independent colleges and universities in that state.

Figure 4.1 shows a copy of this application's Web page. Save the map's GIF file (it's called usmap.gif) in your skill 4 folder.

Other graphic images will also be useful. You'll want pictures, backgrounds, small-sized images, and multicolored straight lines. California-based Lassen Technologies maintains a library of GIF images you can use to decorate your personal Web pages. You will use some of these images in exercises in this Skill and in the next two. Lassen Technologies' image library is at http://www.lassentech.com/images.html. The images are in five categories: patterned backgrounds, photo backgrounds, bars, little guys (small images you can use as buttons and bullets) and pictures. Table 4.1 shows the categories and the names of the Lassen Technologies images that I use in the exercises. You can substitute others if you like. When you're on one of the Lassen Technologies pages that presents these images, you can find out the name of an image's file by hovering the mouse over the image: The filename appears in the status bar at the bottom of the IE window, along with some other information.

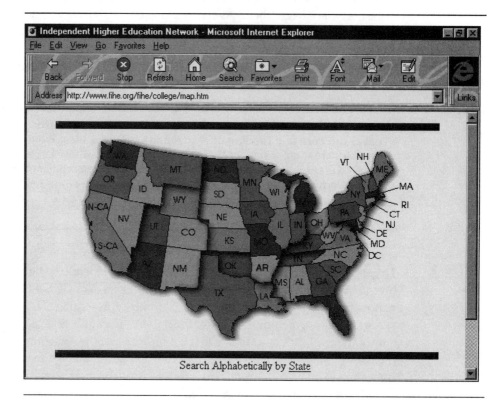

FIGURE 4.1: At the Web site of the Foundation for Independent Higher Education, this application provides information on independent colleges and universities throughout the United States. Store a copy of this map on your computer, as we'll use it in this Skill.

TABLE 4.1: Images from the Lassen Technologies Site Used in Our Exercises

Category	File
Solid/Patterned Backgrounds	`ltbke.gif, ltbk3.gif`
Pictures	`forest.gif, pine1.gif`
Bars	`ltbarrdy.gif, ltbarred.gif, ltbarbly.gif`
Little Guys	`ltb5.gif, ltb20.gif, ltb34.gif`

TIP   Make sure you've set Windows 95 to use IE to open JPEG files and GIF files. This enables you to preview a graphics file by double-clicking on it and having it appear in IE (which is a good thing to do, because you'll never remember what every file looks like, and the filenames often don't provide a clue).

Save the images in a folder called graphics. Within graphics, set up a folder for each category to make it easy to find an image when you need it. (I use the names backgrounds, bars, pictures, and small for my folders.) When you decide on an image to use, make a copy of it and store it in skill 4. (That way, we'll only have to specify the name of the file when we use it in conjunction with HTML tags.)

NOTE   Two more good sources of GIF files are http://www.3dcafe.com and http://www.mccannas.com.

Working with Graphics and HTML

You'll start our graphics adventures by adding a fancy background to a Web page. The background will be tiled, meaning that the browser copies a small image many times until all the viewing space is occupied. The result of your work will be a Web page that looks like Figure 4.2.

You'll eventually make some sharp-looking additions to this page, but let's just start with the heading and the tiling. In the ActiveX Control Pad, open a new file and call it graphics. Save it in skill 4.

NOTE   Just a reminder: You can use these filenames and folder names to reference and download the files from the Sybex Web site at http://www.sybex.com/. Click on the Catalog link and then click on the No Experienced Required link.

Now that you've set up a file, follow these steps:

1. In the Text Editor, change the title to **Graphics**.

2. Add the background by using the BACKGROUND attribute of the <BODY> tag. Set the BACKGROUND equal to the name of one of the background GIF files you copied from the Lassen Technologies site (I used 1tbk3.gif). Put double quotes around the filename, and don't forget the GIF extension.

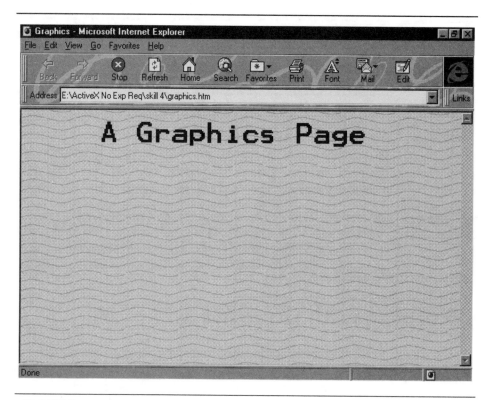

FIGURE 4.2: A Web page with a tiled background

3. Add the heading **A Graphics Page**, center it, and render it in Terminal font. (You would probably never use this font face for a heading, but this gives you the chance to try out some things.)

4. Set the SIZE attribute to 7.

The HTML in your Text Editor for graphics.htm should look something like this:

```
<HTML>
<HEAD>
<TITLE>Graphics</TITLE>
</HEAD>
<BODY BACKGROUND = "ltbk3.gif">
<FONT FACE=Terminal SIZE = 7>
<H1><CENTER>
A Graphics Page
```

```
</CENTER> </FONT>
</H1></BODY>
</HTML>
```

Open the page in IE. If you used `ltbk3.gif` as your background, it looks like Figure 4.2.

Add a horizontal line to set the heading off from the rest of the page. Before, you used the <HR> tag to draw a horizontal line. This time, you'll use a GIF file. After the </H1> tag—and before </BODY>—type **<IMG SRC="ltbarbly.gif"> </IMG>**.

Now let's add a main image to the document using the <IMG> tag. After the ending </IMG> tag that specifies the horizontal line, type four line-break tags (**
) and then type **<IMG SRC="pine1.gif" ALIGN=LEFT> </IMG>. Figure 4.3 shows how the page now looks in IE.

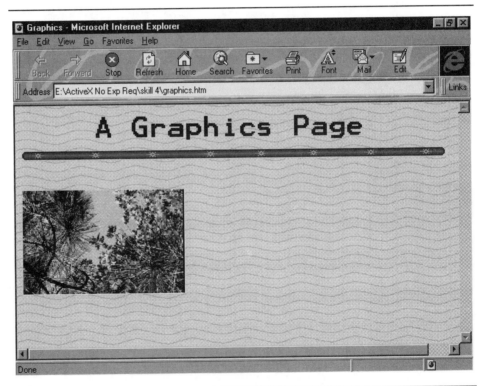

FIGURE 4.3: Your graphics Web page with two embedded images. One of them is the bar that separates the heading from the rest of the page. The other is a photograph of a pine.

Now line up the graphic with some text. In the Text Editor, update your file to look like this:

```
<HTML>
<HEAD>
<TITLE>Graphics</TITLE>
</HEAD>
<BODY BACKGROUND = "ltbk3.gif">
<FONT FACE=Terminal SIZE = 7>
<H1><CENTER>
A Graphics Page
</CENTER> </FONT>
</H1>
<IMG SRC = "ltbarbly.gif"> </IMG> <BR> <BR> <BR> <BR>
<IMG SRC="pine1.gif" ALIGN=LEFT>
</IMG>
ALIGN=LEFT. This text is with the image. It's called "mumble" text.
Mmmmmm mmmm mmmm mmm
mmm. Mmmmm mmm mmmmmmmm mmmmmm
mmmmm mm mmmmmmmmm mmmmmm mmm.
<P>This is a new paragraph:
Mmmm mmmmmmm mmmmmm mmm
mmmmm mmmmmmm mmm. Mmm mmmmmmm
mmmmmm mmmmm mm mmmmmmm mmmmm.
Mmm mmmm mmmmmmm mm.
</P>
</BODY>
</HTML>
```

TIP   For the text in this HTML document, we've borrowed a technique from Usability Engineering, a field concerned with making software intuitive and easy to work with. Usability engineers put text in the so-called "mumble" format (strings consisting of repetitions of the letter "m") to examine whether users can derive information from a layout without focusing on the information in text. It's a good idea to use mumble text in your initial layouts, too. While readable text is an extremely important consideration, it's not always a necessary one in the early stages of layout design.

Within the text, ALIGN=LEFT is not necessary to align the image. (It *is* necessary, of course, within the <IMG> tag.) You use the statement about ALIGN in the text so you can remember how you've set the ALIGN attribute when we open the document in IE. The <P> tags set off a paragraph.

Figure 4.4 shows the HTML document that IE renders. If you look closely at the way you typed the text in the Text Editor and the way IE renders it, you'll see that the two do not correspond. In the ActiveX Control Pad Text Editor, What You See *Ain't* What You Get (WYSAWYG?). If you want to break a line after a particular word, use the
 (line-break) tag you learned in Skill 1.

To learn how the other possible values of ALIGN (RIGHT, TOP, MIDDLE, BOTTOM) affect the display, change the value of ALIGN in the <IMG> tag (and change it in the text as well, just to keep track). After each change, save your work and view the page in IE.

NOTE   ALIGN=TOP **has an especially intriguing behavior. It lines up the top of the first line of the text with the top of the image, and causes the next line to appear after the bottom of the image.**

One of the major strengths of an HTML document is that it can contain links to other HTML documents. When we think of this capability, we usually associate it with text: Clicking on a word or a phrase anchored to a URL takes us to that URL.

Graphic images can also contain links to other HTML documents. An <IMG> attribute called ISMAP makes this work. This attribute identifies the graphic as an *image map*, a structure that links areas of images to URLs. The image map's file holds the linkages between image regions defined by pixel-coordinates and the URLs.

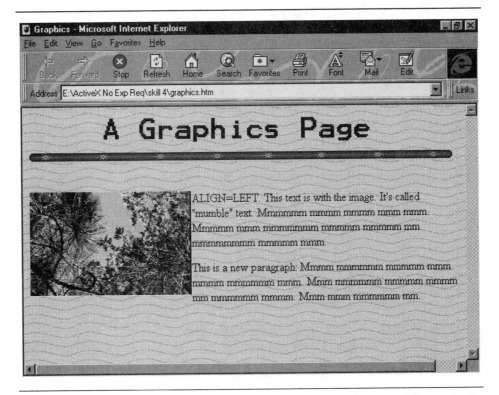

FIGURE 4.4: The HTML document with the embedded images and some text. The text is aligned by setting the main image's *ALIGN* attribute to *LEFT*.

To use the ISMAP attribute, you have to know the coordinates of the pixels within the image. You also have to specify the shapes of the regions. Although HTML developers have come up with applications that enable you to read an image map's pixel coordinates, image interactivity can be cumbersome to implement and difficult to manage in HTML.

ActiveX offers an easier way.

Graphics and ActiveX

Two ActiveX controls will concern us in this section. The first one, the Image control, is analogous to using the HTML <IMG> tag. You use it to add a picture to an HTML document. The second, the Hot Spot control, is analogous to an HTML image map. You use the Hot Spot control to divide the picture into areas that respond to user-initiated events like mouse-movements, mouse-clicks, or keystrokes.

Objects and Images

Let's first look at the ActiveX analogue for the <IMG> tag. Start with the graphics file you've been using (graphics.htm). Save it as ActiveX graphics in skill 4. Remove the line and the graphic. In the Text Editor, change the title to **Active X Graphics**, and change the <H1> header to **An ActiveX Graphics Page**. Just for variety, change the background to **ltbke.gif**. Add a bar you downloaded from Lassen Technology, like ltbarred.gif. To add the bar, type **<IMG SRC = "ltbarred.gif"></IMG>**, and then make sure you have four line-breaks (**
**) to put some separation between the line and the image that we'll embed.

Position the cursor where the pine1 image used to be. From the menu bar, select Edit ➤ Insert ActiveX Control…. Select Microsoft ActiveX Image Control 1.0. When the Object Editor opens, work with the Properties sheet to set these property values:

1. For ID type **imgForest**.

2. Change Autosize to -1-True.

3. Change PictureAlignment to 2-Center.

4. If you have copied forest.gif to your Skill 4 subdirectory, type **forest.gif** for PicturePath. You could also type the full file path, **E:\ActiveX No Exp Req\skill 4\forest.gif**.

Setting Autosize to True enables the Image control to automatically adjust its size to accommodate the size of the image.

When you finish typing the filename and click Apply, the image appears within the ActiveX Image control. In the Text Editor, position your cursor within the newly created <OBJECT> tag, just after the value for the HEIGHT attribute. Type **ALIGN = LEFT**.

In your Text Editor, the HTML code for ActiveX graphics.htm should look like this:

```
<HTML>
<HEAD>
<TITLE>ActiveX Graphics</TITLE>
</HEAD>
<BODY BACKGROUND = "ltbke.gif">
<FONT FACE=Terminal  SIZE = 7>
<H1><CENTER>
An ActiveX Graphics Page
</FONT>
</CENTER></H1>
<IMG SRC = "ltbarred.gif"></IMG> <BR> <BR> <BR> <BR>
<OBJECT ID="imgForest" WIDTH=200 HEIGHT=200 ALIGN=LEFT
 CLASSID="CLSID:D4A97620-8E8F-11CF-93CD-00AA00C08FDF">
    <PARAM NAME="PicturePath" VALUE=" forest.gif">
    <PARAM NAME="AutoSize" VALUE="-1">
    <PARAM NAME="BorderStyle" VALUE="0">
    <PARAM NAME="SizeMode" VALUE="3">
    <PARAM NAME="Size" VALUE="5292;5292">
    <PARAM NAME="VariousPropertyBits" VALUE="19">
</OBJECT>

ALIGN=LEFT. This  text is with the image. It's called "mumble" text.
Mmmmmm mmmm mmmm mmm
mmm. Mmmmm mmm mmmmmmmm mmmmm
mmmmm mm mmmmmmmmm mmmmm mmm.

<P>This is a new paragraph:
Mmmm mmmmmm mmmmm mmm
mmmm mmmmmmm mmm. Mmm mmmmmmm
mmmmm mmmm mm mmmmmmm mmmm.
Mmm mmmm mmmmmm mm.
</P>
</BODY>
</HTML>
```

When you open this document in IE, it will look like Figure 4.5. As you did with the <IMG> tag, experiment with different values for ALIGN (see Skill 3) and note the consequences.

FIGURE 4.5: The IE rendering of the HTML code in *ActiveX graphics.htm*

See the U.S.A.

Now we'll lay out a graphic that displays a map of the United States. We'll script it to display a variety of pieces of information that depend on what you do with the mouse.

First, open a new file. Call this file USA Map and store it in skill 4. Change the title of this document to **USA Applications**. The map we'll use has a white background, so we'll eventually change the layout's background to white. To make the rest of the page match up with the layout, change the <BODY> tag to **<BODY BGCOLOR = "WHITE">**. After the newly changed <BODY> tag, type **<H1>**

<CENTER> USA Applications </CENTER> </H1> <HR> to give the page a heading above a horizontal line. Press Enter to put a blank line before </BODY>. Now, follow these steps:

1. Position the cursor in the blank line before </BODY> and select Edit ➤ Insert HTML Layout....

2. Create a new layout called layout for USA and store it in skill 4.

3. In the Text Editor, click on the symbol to the left of the newly created <OBJECT> tag to open the HTML Layout Control.

4. From the Toolbox, select the Image control. Position it on the Layout Grid, and set its Height property to 281 and its Width property to 370.

5. In the Properties sheet, give the image an ID of imgMapUSA and set the PicturePath property to usamap.gif (the name of the U.S. map's GIF file—don't forget the gif extension). You should see the map appear within the boundaries of the Image control.

6. Set the PictureAlignment property to 2-Center and close the Properties sheet.

7. Since the background of the map is white, let's change the background of the layout to white as well. Outside the boundaries of the image, right-click anywhere in the layout and select Properties from the pop-up menu. Select the BackColor property and click on the ellipsis to open the color palette. From the palette, select white and click OK.

Your HTML Layout Control should resemble Figure 4.6.

Sections of the Country

We'll divide our map into sections and name each section. Commonly used section names for the United States are Midwest, South, Northeast, Southeast, Southwest, West, Northwest, Alaska, and Hawaii. Let's use these names as areas for our map.

The Hot Spot control is the mechanism for dividing the map into areas. A Hot Spot is an area (invisible on the page when it appears in IE) that responds to your mouse-movements and your button-clicks. When we finish our work here, we'll have a map that displays the name of a section of the United States when you pass your mouse over that section.

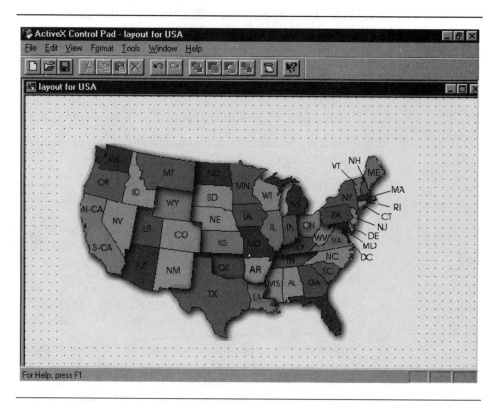

FIGURE 4.6: The HTML Layout Control with the U.S. map as the image for the Image control

From the Toolbox, select the Hot Spot control and draw it out over the map area that corresponds to the Midwest. (Don't worry if you don't get the Hot Spot's area exactly over all the Midwest.) Figure 4.7 shows the appearance of your Layout Control.

Now that we've set the foundation, here are the steps to follow:

1. In the Hot Spot's Properties sheet type **htsptMidwest** in the ID property.

2. Cover the U.S. map with Hot Spots for the other sections. Use these names for their IDs: htsptNortheast, htsptSouth, htsptSoutheast, htsptSouthwest, htsptWest, and htsptNorthwest.

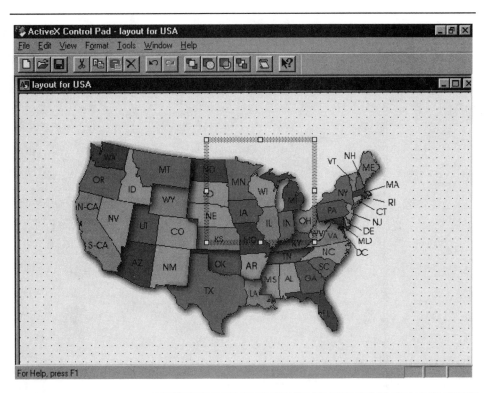

FIGURE 4.7: The Layout Control with a Hot Spot over the Midwestern United States

3. Select the Forms Label control and place it in the center of htsptMidwest.

- Make its ID **frmslblMidwest**, its BackColor yellow, and its font bold.

- Change its Caption to **Midwest**, and adjust the label so that it's just large enough to display its caption.

- Change one more property: For the Visible property, select 0-False. This makes the label invisible when the page opens in IE.

4. Make similar labels for all the other sections, and change their IDs, sizes, Captions, and Visibilities accordingly. They should all be invisible when the Web page opens (although they remain visible in the layout).

Your layout should now look like Figure 4.8.

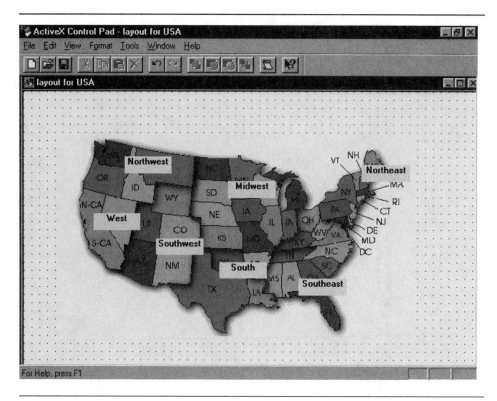

FIGURE 4.8: The Layout Control with a label over each section of the United States

Now script the Hot Spots and labels:

1. Open the Script Wizard.

2. In the Event pane, open the list of events for htsptMidwest. In the Actions pane, open the list of properties and methods for frmslblMidwest.

3. Back in the Event pane, select htsptMidwest's MouseEnter event.

4. In the Actions pane, double-click on the Visible property and select True in the dialog box that opens.

5. Again in the Event pane, select htsptMidwest's MouseExit event.

6. In the Actions pane, double-click on the Visible property and select False in the dialog box.

7. Repeat steps 2 through 6 for each Hot Spot and Label.

Save your work. When you open this page in IE, move the mouse across the map. Each time you move the cursor over a Hot Spot control, the associated label appears. It disappears when you move the cursor out of that section.

Adding Functionality

Let's add some features to the clickable map of the United States. One major use for a map is to present weather-related information. You can use your map to provide four-day forecasts for major U.S. cities. In addition to building a spiffy application, completing this exercise will broaden your horizons in both ActiveX and VBS.

First, you'll develop the capability to display the names of major cities on the map. Then, you'll develop a capability to jump to a destination that contains a weather forecast when you click on the name of a city.

Open the HTML Layout Control. Select the Forms Label control from the Toolbox. Drag the label to the area of the map that corresponds to New York City. In the Label's Properties sheet, make these adjustments:

1. Change the ID to **frmslblNY**.

2. Change the ForeColor to white.

3. Set the font to Bold.

4. Set the BackStyle to 0-Transparent.

5. Type **New York** in the Caption property.

6. Set the Visible property to 0-False.

7. Set the Enabled property to 0-False.

Setting Enabled to False ensures that a mouse-click on the Label control does not generate a Click event. Use the sizing handles to make the Label just large enough to display its caption.

With the Label selected, make a copy of the Label (Ctrl+C) and paste the copy (Ctrl+V). Change the new Label's caption to **Chicago** and change its ID to frmslblChicago. Drag frmslblChicago to the part of the map that corresponds to Chicago. Repeat this process to create and position Labels for Atlanta, Miami, Dallas, Denver, Los Angeles, San Francisco, and Seattle. Create IDs accordingly. Reposition the section labels if necessary.

When this HTML document opens in IE, the city names will not be visible. We'll use a Toggle Button control to make them appear. We'll script the Toggle Button so when it's down, the city names are visible, and when it's up they're not. When the city names are visible, clicking on one will take us to a weather forecast for that city.

In the Toolbox, select the Toggle Button control. Position it about an inch to the right of Florida. Give it an ID of **tglbtnCities**, a caption of **Cities Off**, and a size just large enough to accommodate the caption. Make the caption bold.

In the Script Wizard, we have to tie a number of things to the Toggle Button's Click event. When the Toggle Button is down, the following changes must occur:

- change each frmslbl's Visible property to True

- change each frmslbl's Enabled property to True

- change the Toggle Button's Caption to Cities On

When the Toggle Button is up, these changes occur:

- change each frmslbl's Visible property to False

- change each frmslbl's Enabled property to False

- change the Toggle Button's Caption to Cities Off

To accomplish all this, you'll use a bit of VBS magic that you haven't seen yet. You'll use the Script Wizard, but you have to go beyond simply clicking and double-clicking in the Wizard's dialog box. You'll have to write some VBS code, so in the Script Wizard click the option button (at the bottom of the window) for Code View.

The code that you'll write centers around a `Select Case` structure. This structure allows a program to go in one of several directions depending on the value of a condition or expression. For this script, the condition is "What is the Toggle Button's Caption?" Two *cases* are possible. The Caption can say either "Cities Off" or "Cities On." In either case, you want a click to change the Caption to the opposite of what it currently says. Here's the VBS that does this:

```
Select Case tglbtnCities.Caption
    Case "Cities On"
        tglbtnCities.Caption = "Cities Off"
    Case "Cities Off"
        tglbtnCities.Caption = "Cities On"
End Select
```

Note the `End Select` statement that ends this structure.

Remember that you also want the Click event to make city names visible and to make them Enabled. You have to add code to each case to make this happen. The following is an example for showing only two city names, New York and Chicago:

```
Select Case tglbtnCities.Caption
    Case "Cities On"
```

```
                tglbtnCities.Caption = "Cities Off"
                frmslblChicago.Visible = False
                frmslblChicago.Enabled = False
                frmslblNY.Visible = False
                frmslblNY.Enabled = False
        Case "Cities Off"
                tglbtnCities.Caption = "Cities On"
                frmslblChicago.Visible = True
                frmslblChicago.Enabled = True
                frmslblNY.Visible = True
                frmslblNY.Enabled = True
    End Select
```

In the Script Wizard, select tglbtnCities' Click event. In the Script pane type the VBS for the Select Case statement just as it appears in the preceding listing. To ease the typing load, when you get to the name of a property, like `tglbtnCities .Caption`, double-click on the property in the Actions pane and it will appear in the Script pane. When you're done typing, click OK.

Save your work and open the page in IE. Clicking the Toggle Button into the Down position should change its caption and display the two city names. Clicking it into the up position should return the caption to its original value and make the city names invisible. When you're convinced that the Toggle Button is behaving properly, add the appropriate VBS code for the remaining city names to the Select Case statement. Although this sounds like a daunting task, you can make it easier by using standard select, copy, and paste techniques. When you are finished, save your work and retest the Toggle Button in IE to ensure that it works correctly.

Now let's work on the weather forecasts. The Intellicast Web site (`http://www .intellicast.com/weather`) provides weather information for a number of U.S. cities. You'll write a script that makes clicking on a city name take you to the Intellicast page for that city. Table 4.2 contains the Intellicast URLs for the four-day forecasts for the cities on your map.

T A B L E 4 . 2 : Intellicast URLs for Four-Day Weather Forecasts for Selected U.S. Cities

City	Intellicast URL for Four-Day Weather Forecast
New York	`http://www.intellicast.com/weather/lga/#fourday`
Chicago	`http://www.intellicast.com/weather/ord/#fourday`
Atlanta	`http://www.intellicast.com/weather/atl/#fourday`
Miami	`http://www.intellicast.com/weather/mia/#fourday`

Skill 4

TABLE 4.2 CONTINUED: Intellicast URLs for Four-Day Weather Forecasts for Selected U.S. Cities

City	Intellicast URL for Four-Day Weather Forecast
Dallas	http://www.intellicast.com/weather/dfw/#fourday
Denver	http://www.intellicast.com/weather/den/#fourday
Los Angeles	http://www.intellicast.com/weather/lax/#fourday
San Francisco	http://www.intellicast.com/weather/sfo/#fourday
Seattle	http://www.intellicast.com/weather/sea/#fourday

Here's how to do it:

1. Open the Script Wizard.

2. Select the Click event for frmslblNY. At the top of the Actions pane, you'll see the Go to Window method.

3. Double-click on Go to Window. In the dialog box that appears, type the URL for New York from Table 4.1. (You don't have to type quotes. The Script Wizard adds them as necessary.)

4. Repeat these steps for the Click event for the other city labels.

After all your work, the VBS for the layout (layout for USA apps.alx) looks like this listing.

 layout for USA apps.alx

```
<SCRIPT LANGUAGE="VBScript">
<!--
Sub htsptWest_MouseEnter()
frmslblWest.Visible = True
end sub
Sub htsptWest_MouseExit()
frmslblWest.Visible = False
end sub
-->
</SCRIPT>
<SCRIPT LANGUAGE="VBScript">
<!--
Sub htsptSouthwest_MouseEnter()
frmslblSouthwest.Visible = True
end sub
Sub htsptSouthwest_MouseExit()
frmslblSouthwest.Visible = False
end sub
```

```
-->
</SCRIPT>
<SCRIPT LANGUAGE="VBScript">
<!--
Sub htsptSoutheast_MouseEnter()
frmslblSoutheast.Visible = True
end sub
Sub htsptSoutheast_MouseExit()
frmslblSoutheast.Visible = False
end sub
-->
</SCRIPT>
<SCRIPT LANGUAGE="VBScript">
<!--
Sub htsptSouth_MouseEnter()
frmslblSouth.Visible = True
end sub
Sub htsptSouth_MouseExit()
frmslblSouth.Visible = False
end sub
-->
</SCRIPT>
<SCRIPT LANGUAGE="VBScript">
<!--
Sub htsptNorthwest_MouseEnter()
frmslblNorthwest.Visible = True
end sub
Sub htsptNorthwest_MouseExit()
frmslblNorthwest.Visible = False
end sub
-->
</SCRIPT>
<SCRIPT LANGUAGE="VBScript">
<!--
Sub htsptNortheast_MouseEnter()
frmslblNortheast.Visible = True
end sub
Sub htsptNortheast_MouseExit()
frmslblNortheast.Visible = False
end sub
-->
</SCRIPT>
<SCRIPT LANGUAGE="VBScript">
<!--
Sub htsptMidwest_MouseEnter()
frmslblMidwest.Visible = True
end sub
Sub htsptMidwest_MouseExit()
frmslblMidwest.Visible = False
end sub
```

```
-->
</SCRIPT>
<SCRIPT LANGUAGE="VBScript">
<!--
Sub tglbtnCities_Click()
Select Case tglbtnCities.Caption
    Case "Cities On"
        tglbtnCities.Caption = "Cities Off"
        frmslblChicago.Visible = False
        frmslblChicago.Enabled = False
        frmslblNY.Visible = False
        frmslblNY.Enabled = False
        frmslblDallas.Visible = False
        frmslblDallas.Enabled = False
        frmslblDenver.Visible = False
        frmslblDenver.Enabled = False
        frmslblLosAngeles.Visible = False
        frmslblLosAngeles.Enabled = False
        frmslblMiami.Visible = False
        frmslblMiami.Enabled = False
        frmslblSanFrancisco.Visible = False
        frmslblSanFrancisco.Enabled = False
        frmslblSeattle.Visible = False
        frmslblSeattle.Enabled = False
        frmslblAtlanta.Visible = False
        frmslblAtlanta.Enabled = False
    Case "Cities Off"
        tglbtnCities.Caption = "Cities On"
        frmslblChicago.Visible = True
        frmslblChicago.Enabled = True
        frmslblNY.Visible = True
        frmslblNY.Enabled = True
        frmslblDallas.Visible = True
        frmslblDallas.Enabled = True
        frmslblDenver.Visible = True
        frmslblDenver.Enabled = True
        frmslblLosAngeles.Visible = True
        frmslblLosAngeles.Enabled = True
        frmslblMiami.Visible = True
        frmslblMiami.Enabled = True
        frmslblSanFrancisco.Visible = True
        frmslblSanFrancisco.Enabled = True
        frmslblSeattle.Visible = True
        frmslblSeattle.Enabled = True
        frmslblAtlanta.Visible = True
        frmslblAtlanta.Enabled = True
End Select
end sub
-->
```

```
</SCRIPT>
<SCRIPT LANGUAGE="VBScript">
<!--
Sub frmslblSeattle_Click()
Window.location.href = "http://www.intellicast.com/weather/sea/#fourday"
end sub
-->
</SCRIPT>
<SCRIPT LANGUAGE="VBScript">
<!--
Sub frmslblSanFrancisco_Click()
Window.location.href = "http://www.intellicast.com/weather/sfo/#fourday"
end sub
-->
</SCRIPT>
<SCRIPT LANGUAGE="VBScript">
<!--
Sub frmslblMiami_Click()
Window.location.href = "http://www.intellicast.com/weather/mia/#fourday"
end sub
-->
</SCRIPT>
<SCRIPT LANGUAGE="VBScript">
<!--
Sub frmslblLosAngeles_Click()
Window.location.href = "http://www.intellicast.com/weather/lax/#fourday"
end sub
-->
</SCRIPT>
<SCRIPT LANGUAGE="VBScript">
<!--
Sub frmslblDenver_Click()
Window.location.href = "http://www.intellicast.com/weather/den/#fourday"
end sub
-->
</SCRIPT>
<SCRIPT LANGUAGE="VBScript">
<!--
Sub frmslblDallas_Click()
Window.location.href = "http://www.intellicast.com/weather/dfw/#fourday"
end sub
-->
</SCRIPT>
<SCRIPT LANGUAGE="VBScript">
<!--
Sub frmslblChicago_Click()
Window.location.href = "http://www.intellicast.com/weather/ord/#fourday"
end sub
-->
```

Skill 4

```
</SCRIPT>
<SCRIPT LANGUAGE="VBScript">
<!--
Sub frmslblAtlanta_Click()
Window.location.href = "http://www.intellicast.com/weather/atl/#fourday"
end sub
-->
</SCRIPT>
<SCRIPT LANGUAGE="VBScript">
<!--
Sub frmslblNY_Click()
Window.location.href = "http://www.intellicast.com/weather/lga/#fourday"
end sub
-->
</SCRIPT>
<DIV BACKGROUND="#ffffff" ID="layoutforUSA"
STYLE="LAYOUT:FIXED;WIDTH:477pt;HEIGHT:293pt;">
    <OBJECT ID="imgMapUSA"
     CLASSID="CLSID:D4A97620-8E8F-11CF-93CD-00AA00C08FDF"
    ➥STYLE="TOP:8pt;LEFT:41pt;WIDTH:371pt;HEIGHT:281pt;ZINDEX:0;">
        <PARAM NAME="PicturePath" VALUE="usmap.gif">
        <PARAM NAME="BackColor" VALUE="16777215">
        <PARAM NAME="BorderStyle" VALUE="0">
        <PARAM NAME="SizeMode" VALUE="3">
        <PARAM NAME="Size" VALUE="13088;9913">
        <PARAM NAME="VariousPropertyBits" VALUE="19">
    </OBJECT>
    <OBJECT ID="htsptMidwest"
     CLASSID="CLSID:2B32FBC2-A8F1-11CF-93EE-00AA00C08FDF"
    ➥STYLE="TOP:50pt;LEFT:198pt;WIDTH:116pt;HEIGHT:98pt;ZINDEX:1;">
        <PARAM NAME="VariousPropertyBits" VALUE="8388627">
        <PARAM NAME="Size" VALUE="4092;3457">
    </OBJECT>
    <OBJECT ID="htsptNortheast"
     CLASSID="CLSID:2B32FBC2-A8F1-11CF-93EE-00AA00C08FDF"
    ➥STYLE="TOP:58pt;LEFT:322pt;WIDTH:74pt;HEIGHT:83pt;ZINDEX:2;">
        <PARAM NAME="VariousPropertyBits" VALUE="8388627">
        <PARAM NAME="Size" VALUE="2611;2928">
    </OBJECT>
    <OBJECT ID="htsptSoutheast"
     CLASSID="CLSID:2B32FBC2-A8F1-11CF-93EE-00AA00C08FDF"
    ➥STYLE="TOP:157pt;LEFT:281pt;WIDTH:74pt;HEIGHT:83pt;ZINDEX:3;">
        <PARAM NAME="VariousPropertyBits" VALUE="8388627">
        <PARAM NAME="Size" VALUE="2611;2928">
    </OBJECT>
    <OBJECT ID="htsptSouth"
     CLASSID="CLSID:2B32FBC2-A8F1-11CF-93EE-00AA00C08FDF"
    ➥STYLE="TOP:149pt;LEFT:206pt;WIDTH:66pt;HEIGHT:74pt;ZINDEX:4;">
        <PARAM NAME="VariousPropertyBits" VALUE="8388627">
```

```
        <PARAM NAME="Size" VALUE="2328;2611">
</OBJECT>
<OBJECT ID="htsptSouthwest"
 CLASSID="CLSID:2B32FBC2-A8F1-11CF-93EE-00AA00C08FDF"
➡STYLE="TOP:140pt;LEFT:116pt;WIDTH:83pt;HEIGHT:83pt;ZINDEX:5;">
        <PARAM NAME="VariousPropertyBits" VALUE="8388627">
        <PARAM NAME="Size" VALUE="2928;2928">
</OBJECT>
<OBJECT ID="htsptWest"
 CLASSID="CLSID:2B32FBC2-A8F1-11CF-93EE-00AA00C08FDF"
➡STYLE="TOP:107pt;LEFT:66pt;WIDTH:50pt;HEIGHT:83pt;ZINDEX:6;">
        <PARAM NAME="VariousPropertyBits" VALUE="8388627">
        <PARAM NAME="Size" VALUE="1764;2928">
</OBJECT>
<OBJECT ID="htsptNorthwest"
 CLASSID="CLSID:2B32FBC2-A8F1-11CF-93EE-00AA00C08FDF"
➡STYLE="TOP:50pt;LEFT:74pt;WIDTH:74pt;HEIGHT:57pt;ZINDEX:7;">
        <PARAM NAME="VariousPropertyBits" VALUE="8388627">
        <PARAM NAME="Size" VALUE="2611;2011">
</OBJECT>
<OBJECT ID="frmslblMidwest"
 CLASSID="CLSID:978C9E23-D4B0-11CE-BF2D-00AA003F40D0"STYLE=
➡"TOP:91pt;LEFT:215pt;WIDTH:50pt;HEIGHT:17pt;DISPLAY:NONE;ZINDEX:8;">
        <PARAM NAME="BackColor" VALUE="8454143">
        <PARAM NAME="Caption" VALUE="Midwest">
        <PARAM NAME="Size" VALUE="1764;600">
        <PARAM NAME="FontEffects" VALUE="1073741825">
        <PARAM NAME="FontCharSet" VALUE="0">
        <PARAM NAME="FontPitchAndFamily" VALUE="2">
        <PARAM NAME="ParagraphAlign" VALUE="3">
        <PARAM NAME="FontWeight" VALUE="700">
</OBJECT>
<OBJECT ID="frmslblSouth"
 CLASSID="CLSID:978C9E23-D4B0-11CE-BF2D-00AA003F40D0" STYLE=
➡"TOP:173pt;LEFT:206pt;WIDTH:50pt;HEIGHT:17pt;DISPLAY:NONE;ZINDEX:9;">
        <PARAM NAME="BackColor" VALUE="8454143">
        <PARAM NAME="Caption" VALUE="South">
        <PARAM NAME="Size" VALUE="1764;600">
        <PARAM NAME="FontEffects" VALUE="1073741825">
        <PARAM NAME="FontCharSet" VALUE="0">
        <PARAM NAME="FontPitchAndFamily" VALUE="2">
        <PARAM NAME="ParagraphAlign" VALUE="3">
        <PARAM NAME="FontWeight" VALUE="700">
</OBJECT>
<OBJECT ID="frmslblSoutheast"
 CLASSID="CLSID:978C9E23-D4B0-11CE-BF2D-00AA003F40D0" STYLE=
➡"TOP:190pt;LEFT:289pt;WIDTH:50pt;HEIGHT:17pt;DISPLAY:NONE;ZINDEX:10;">
        <PARAM NAME="BackColor" VALUE="8454143">
        <PARAM NAME="Caption" VALUE="Southeast">
```

```
            <PARAM NAME="Size" VALUE="1764;600">
            <PARAM NAME="FontEffects" VALUE="1073741825">
            <PARAM NAME="FontCharSet" VALUE="0">
            <PARAM NAME="FontPitchAndFamily" VALUE="2">
            <PARAM NAME="ParagraphAlign" VALUE="3">
            <PARAM NAME="FontWeight" VALUE="700">
        </OBJECT>
        <OBJECT ID="frmslblNortheast"
         CLASSID="CLSID:978C9E23-D4B0-11CE-BF2D-00AA003F40D0" STYLE=
        ➥ "TOP:74pt;LEFT:371pt;WIDTH:50pt;HEIGHT:17pt;DISPLAY:NONE;ZINDEX:11;">
            <PARAM NAME="BackColor" VALUE="8454143">
            <PARAM NAME="Caption" VALUE="Northeast">
            <PARAM NAME="Size" VALUE="1764;600">
            <PARAM NAME="FontEffects" VALUE="1073741825">
            <PARAM NAME="FontCharSet" VALUE="0">
            <PARAM NAME="FontPitchAndFamily" VALUE="2">
            <PARAM NAME="ParagraphAlign" VALUE="3">
            <PARAM NAME="FontWeight" VALUE="700">
        </OBJECT>
        <OBJECT ID="frmslblSouthwest"
         CLASSID="CLSID:978C9E23-D4B0-11CE-BF2D-00AA003F40D0" STYLE=
        ➥ "TOP:149pt;LEFT:140pt;WIDTH:50pt;HEIGHT:17pt;DISPLAY:NONE;ZINDEX:12;">
            <PARAM NAME="BackColor" VALUE="8454143">
            <PARAM NAME="Caption" VALUE="Southwest">
            <PARAM NAME="Size" VALUE="1764;600">
            <PARAM NAME="FontEffects" VALUE="1073741825">
            <PARAM NAME="FontCharSet" VALUE="0">
            <PARAM NAME="FontPitchAndFamily" VALUE="2">
            <PARAM NAME="ParagraphAlign" VALUE="3">
            <PARAM NAME="FontWeight" VALUE="700">
        </OBJECT>
        <OBJECT ID="frmslblWest"
         CLASSID="CLSID:978C9E23-D4B0-11CE-BF2D-00AA003F40D0" STYLE=
        ➥ "TOP:124pt;LEFT:74pt;WIDTH:50pt;HEIGHT:17pt;DISPLAY:NONE;ZINDEX:13;">
            <PARAM NAME="BackColor" VALUE="8454143">
            <PARAM NAME="Caption" VALUE="West">
            <PARAM NAME="Size" VALUE="1764;600">
            <PARAM NAME="FontEffects" VALUE="1073741825">
            <PARAM NAME="FontCharSet" VALUE="0">
            <PARAM NAME="FontPitchAndFamily" VALUE="2">
            <PARAM NAME="ParagraphAlign" VALUE="3">
            <PARAM NAME="FontWeight" VALUE="700">
        </OBJECT>
        <OBJECT ID="frmslblNorthwest"
         CLASSID="CLSID:978C9E23-D4B0-11CE-BF2D-00AA003F40D0" STYLE=
        ➥ "TOP:66pt;LEFT:107pt;WIDTH:50pt;HEIGHT:17pt;DISPLAY:NONE;ZINDEX:14;">
            <PARAM NAME="BackColor" VALUE="8454143">
            <PARAM NAME="Caption" VALUE="Northwest">
```

```
        <PARAM NAME="Size" VALUE="1764;600">
        <PARAM NAME="FontEffects" VALUE="1073741825">
        <PARAM NAME="FontCharSet" VALUE="0">
        <PARAM NAME="FontPitchAndFamily" VALUE="2">
        <PARAM NAME="ParagraphAlign" VALUE="3">
        <PARAM NAME="FontWeight" VALUE="700">
    </OBJECT>
    <OBJECT ID="frmslblNY"
     CLASSID="CLSID:978C9E23-D4B0-11CE-BF2D-00AA003F40D0" STYLE=
    ➥"TOP:107pt;LEFT:322pt;WIDTH:50pt;HEIGHT:17pt;DISPLAY:NONE;ZINDEX:15;">
        <PARAM NAME="ForeColor" VALUE="16777215">
        <PARAM NAME="BackColor" VALUE="16777215">
        <PARAM NAME="VariousPropertyBits" VALUE="8388625">
        <PARAM NAME="Caption" VALUE="New York">
        <PARAM NAME="Size" VALUE="1764;600">
        <PARAM NAME="FontEffects" VALUE="1073750017">
        <PARAM NAME="FontCharSet" VALUE="0">
        <PARAM NAME="FontPitchAndFamily" VALUE="2">
        <PARAM NAME="ParagraphAlign" VALUE="3">
        <PARAM NAME="FontWeight" VALUE="700">
    </OBJECT>
    <OBJECT ID="frmslblChicago"
     CLASSID="CLSID:978C9E23-D4B0-11CE-BF2D-00AA003F40D0" STYLE=
    ➥"TOP:116pt;LEFT:248pt;WIDTH:50pt;HEIGHT:17pt;DISPLAY:NONE;ZINDEX:16;">
        <PARAM NAME="ForeColor" VALUE="16777215">
        <PARAM NAME="BackColor" VALUE="16777215">
        <PARAM NAME="VariousPropertyBits" VALUE="8388625">
        <PARAM NAME="Caption" VALUE="Chicago ">
        <PARAM NAME="Size" VALUE="1764;600">
        <PARAM NAME="FontEffects" VALUE="1073750017">
        <PARAM NAME="FontCharSet" VALUE="0">
        <PARAM NAME="FontPitchAndFamily" VALUE="2">
        <PARAM NAME="ParagraphAlign" VALUE="3">
        <PARAM NAME="FontWeight" VALUE="700">
    </OBJECT>
    <OBJECT ID="frmslblDallas"
     CLASSID="CLSID:978C9E23-D4B0-11CE-BF2D-00AA003F40D0" STYLE=
    ➥"TOP:190pt;LEFT:182pt;WIDTH:50pt;HEIGHT:17pt;DISPLAY:NONE;ZINDEX:17;">
        <PARAM NAME="ForeColor" VALUE="16777215">
        <PARAM NAME="BackColor" VALUE="16777215">
        <PARAM NAME="VariousPropertyBits" VALUE="8388625">
        <PARAM NAME="Caption" VALUE="Dallas ">
        <PARAM NAME="Size" VALUE="1764;600">
        <PARAM NAME="FontEffects" VALUE="1073750017">
        <PARAM NAME="FontCharSet" VALUE="0">
        <PARAM NAME="FontPitchAndFamily" VALUE="2">
        <PARAM NAME="ParagraphAlign" VALUE="3">
        <PARAM NAME="FontWeight" VALUE="700">
```

Skill 4

```
    </OBJECT>
    <OBJECT ID="frmslblDenver"
     CLASSID="CLSID:978C9E23-D4B0-11CE-BF2D-00AA003F40D0" STYLE=
    ➡"TOP:132pt;LEFT:149pt;WIDTH:50pt;HEIGHT:17pt;DISPLAY:NONE;ZINDEX:18;">
        <PARAM NAME="ForeColor" VALUE="16777215">
        <PARAM NAME="BackColor" VALUE="16777215">
        <PARAM NAME="VariousPropertyBits" VALUE="8388625">
        <PARAM NAME="Caption" VALUE="Denver">
        <PARAM NAME="Size" VALUE="1764;600">
        <PARAM NAME="FontEffects" VALUE="1073750017">
        <PARAM NAME="FontCharSet" VALUE="0">
        <PARAM NAME="FontPitchAndFamily" VALUE="2">
        <PARAM NAME="ParagraphAlign" VALUE="3">
        <PARAM NAME="FontWeight" VALUE="700">
    </OBJECT>
    <OBJECT ID="frmslblMiami"
     CLASSID="CLSID:978C9E23-D4B0-11CE-BF2D-00AA003F40D0" STYLE=
    ➡"TOP:223pt;LEFT:305pt;WIDTH:50pt;HEIGHT:17pt;DISPLAY:NONE;ZINDEX:19;">
        <PARAM NAME="ForeColor" VALUE="16777215">
        <PARAM NAME="BackColor" VALUE="16777215">
        <PARAM NAME="VariousPropertyBits" VALUE="8388625">
        <PARAM NAME="Caption" VALUE="Miami">
        <PARAM NAME="Size" VALUE="1764;600">
        <PARAM NAME="FontEffects" VALUE="1073750017">
        <PARAM NAME="FontCharSet" VALUE="0">
        <PARAM NAME="FontPitchAndFamily" VALUE="2">
        <PARAM NAME="ParagraphAlign" VALUE="3">
        <PARAM NAME="FontWeight" VALUE="700">
    </OBJECT>
    <OBJECT ID="frmslblLosAngeles"
     CLASSID="CLSID:978C9E23-D4B0-11CE-BF2D-00AA003F40D0" STYLE=
    ➡"TOP:149pt;LEFT:66pt;WIDTH:58pt;HEIGHT:17pt;DISPLAY:NONE;ZINDEX:20;">
        <PARAM NAME="ForeColor" VALUE="16777215">
        <PARAM NAME="BackColor" VALUE="16777215">
        <PARAM NAME="VariousPropertyBits" VALUE="8388625">
        <PARAM NAME="Caption" VALUE="Los Angeles">
        <PARAM NAME="Size" VALUE="2046;600">
        <PARAM NAME="FontEffects" VALUE="1073750017">
        <PARAM NAME="FontCharSet" VALUE="0">
        <PARAM NAME="FontPitchAndFamily" VALUE="2">
        <PARAM NAME="ParagraphAlign" VALUE="3">
        <PARAM NAME="FontWeight" VALUE="700">
    </OBJECT>
    <OBJECT ID="frmslblSanFrancisco"
     CLASSID="CLSID:978C9E23-D4B0-11CE-BF2D-00AA003F40D0" STYLE=
    ➡"TOP:107pt;LEFT:50pt;WIDTH:74pt;HEIGHT:17pt;DISPLAY:NONE;ZINDEX:21;">
        <PARAM NAME="ForeColor" VALUE="16777215">
        <PARAM NAME="BackColor" VALUE="16777215">
```

```
        <PARAM NAME="VariousPropertyBits" VALUE="8388625">
        <PARAM NAME="Caption" VALUE="San Francisco">
        <PARAM NAME="Size" VALUE="2611;600">
        <PARAM NAME="FontEffects" VALUE="1073750017">
        <PARAM NAME="FontCharSet" VALUE="0">
        <PARAM NAME="FontPitchAndFamily" VALUE="2">
        <PARAM NAME="ParagraphAlign" VALUE="3">
        <PARAM NAME="FontWeight" VALUE="700">
</OBJECT>
<OBJECT ID="frmslblSeattle"
 CLASSID="CLSID:978C9E23-D4B0-11CE-BF2D-00AA003F40D0" STYLE=
➡"TOP:58pt;LEFT:58pt;WIDTH:74pt;HEIGHT:17pt;DISPLAY:NONE;ZINDEX:22;">
        <PARAM NAME="ForeColor" VALUE="16777215">
        <PARAM NAME="BackColor" VALUE="16777215">
        <PARAM NAME="VariousPropertyBits" VALUE="8388625">
        <PARAM NAME="Caption" VALUE="Seattle">
        <PARAM NAME="Size" VALUE="2611;600">
        <PARAM NAME="FontEffects" VALUE="1073750017">
        <PARAM NAME="FontCharSet" VALUE="0">
        <PARAM NAME="FontPitchAndFamily" VALUE="2">
        <PARAM NAME="ParagraphAlign" VALUE="3">
        <PARAM NAME="FontWeight" VALUE="700">
</OBJECT>
<OBJECT ID="tglbtnCities"
 CLASSID="CLSID:8BD21D60-EC42-11CE-9E0D-00AA006002F3" STYLE=
➡"TOP:198pt;LEFT:363pt;WIDTH:52pt;HEIGHT:22pt;TABINDEX:22;ZINDEX:23;">
        <PARAM NAME="BackColor" VALUE="2147483663">
        <PARAM NAME="ForeColor" VALUE="2147483666">
        <PARAM NAME="DisplayStyle" VALUE="6">
        <PARAM NAME="Size" VALUE="1834;776">
        <PARAM NAME="Value" VALUE="0">
        <PARAM NAME="Caption" VALUE="Cities Off">
        <PARAM NAME="FontEffects" VALUE="1073741825">
        <PARAM NAME="FontCharSet" VALUE="0">
        <PARAM NAME="FontPitchAndFamily" VALUE="2">
        <PARAM NAME="ParagraphAlign" VALUE="3">
        <PARAM NAME="FontWeight" VALUE="700">
</OBJECT>
<OBJECT ID="frmslblAtlanta"
 CLASSID="CLSID:978C9E23-D4B0-11CE-BF2D-00AA003F40D0" STYLE=
➡"TOP:173pt;LEFT:281pt;WIDTH:50pt;HEIGHT:17pt;DISPLAY:NONE;ZINDEX:24;">
        <PARAM NAME="ForeColor" VALUE="16777215">
        <PARAM NAME="BackColor" VALUE="16777215">
        <PARAM NAME="VariousPropertyBits" VALUE="8388625">
        <PARAM NAME="Caption" VALUE="Atlanta">
        <PARAM NAME="Size" VALUE="1764;600">
        <PARAM NAME="FontEffects" VALUE="1073750017">
        <PARAM NAME="FontCharSet" VALUE="0">
```

```
        <PARAM NAME="FontPitchAndFamily" VALUE="2">
        <PARAM NAME="ParagraphAlign" VALUE="3">
        <PARAM NAME="FontWeight" VALUE="700">
    </OBJECT>
</DIV>
```

It's amazing how much VBS the Script Wizard creates with just a few mouse-clicks.

Connect to the Internet. Open the page in IE to verify that it works properly. Clicking the Toggle Button should change its caption and make the city names visible. Figure 4.9 shows the page with the Toggle Button clicked and the city names showing.

Click a city name to open Intellicast's page of the four-day forecast for that city's weather. To return to the map from the forecast, press the Back button on the button-bar at the top of IE or use the keystroke combination Alt+Left Arrow.

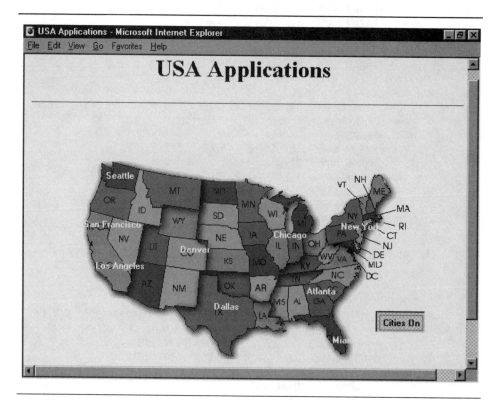

FIGURE 4.9: The U.S. map with the Toggle Button clicked into the Down position and the city names visible

TIP   If you want to add more cities to this application, check `http://www.intellicast .com/weather/usa/#cities` to find out the appropriate city codes.

A Little Trick with Click

Images and Hot Spots are a powerful combination. In addition to letting you build clickable maps, they also let you expand your arsenal of controls.

In your U.S. map application, a Toggle Button switches the display of city names on and off. Using small images from the Lassen Technologies Web site, you can develop your own Toggle Button and use it in the application. It won't be a button in the same sense as the Command Buttons and Toggle Button you've used, because the components are just images. To turn a pair of these images into something like a Toggle Button, you:

- stack one image on top of the other
- make the top one visible and the bottom one invisible
- set some SpecialEffect properties (in other words, make the top one look "raised" and the bottom one look "sunken")
- put a clickable Hot Spot control over them
- write a script that reacts to the Hot Spot control's Click event by toggling the Visible property of the images
- write actions into the script which depend on the Hot Spot's Click event

The result is a structure that behaves like a Toggle Button.

The Images

The two small images you'll use are shown here.

Together with a Hot Spot control, these two images can take the place of a Toggle Button control in our Web page. The open box image will represent the Toggle Button's Up position. The box with an X in it will represent the Toggle Button's Down position. In the discussion that follows, I assume that you've made a copy of each image in `skill 4`.

The Layout

Open a new HTML document. Save it as Click Trick in skill 4. Do the necessary typing in the Text Editor so that Click Trick looks like this:

```
<HTML>
<HEAD>
<TITLE>A Little Trick with Click</TITLE>
</HEAD>
<BODY>
<H1>
<FONT FACE = SCRIPT>
<CENTER> A Little Trick With Click </CENTER>
</FONT>
</H1>
<IMG SRC = ."ltbarrdy.gif">
<IMG>

</BODY>
</HTML>
```

The Script style would never appear in a heading, but this gives you a chance to see what it looks like. The file ltbarrdy.gif is another image from Lassen Technologies. It's from their library of bars, and we use it here to separate the heading from the rest of the page (in the same way that we've used the <HR> tag before).

In the menu bar, select Edit ➤ Insert HTML Layout... and select layout for USA apps.alx. When the layout opens, select File ➤ Save As... and save it as layout for USA Click Trick. Go back to the Text Editor (without closing the Layout). In the <OBJECT> tag, change the ID to **"layoutforUSAClickTrick_alx"** and change the REF VALUE to **"layout for USA Click Trick.alx"**. The HTML for the <OBJECT> tag should now be:'

```
<OBJECT CLASSID="CLSID:812AE312-8B8E-11CF-93C8-00AA00C08FDF"
ID="layoutforUSAClickTrick_alx" STYLE="LEFT:0;TOP:0">
<PARAM NAME="ALXPATH" REF VALUE="layout for USA Click Trick.alx">
</OBJECT>
```

The Properties

In the HTML Layout Control, delete the Toggle Button. From the ToolBox, select the Image control. Open the Properties sheet and follow these steps:

1. Set the ID property to **imgBoxButton**

2. Set the PicturePath property to **ltb34.gif**.

3. Set Autosize to 1-True

4. Set PictureAlignment to 2-Center

5. Make sure that Visible is 1-True.

Make a copy of this Image control. In the copy's Properties sheet:

1. Set the ID property to **imgXBoxButton**.

2. Set the PicturePath property to **ltb20.gif**.

3. Set Visible to 0-False.

Now we'll move things around a bit. Move imgXBoxButton to the location formerly occupied by the Toggle Button control, and place imgBoxButton on top of imgXBoxButton. From the ToolBox, select the Hot Spot control and lay it over the two buttons. Finish by setting the Hot Spot's ID to htsptImageButtons.

The Script

Open the Script Wizard and select Code View. In the Event pane, open the htsptImageButtons events and choose the Click event. In the Script pane, enter this VBS code:

```
Select Case imgBoxButton.Visible
    Case True
        imgBoxButton.Visible = False
        imgXBoxButton.Visible = True
        frmslblChicago.Visible = True
        frmslblChicago.Enabled = True
        frmslblNY.Visible = True
        frmslblNY.Enabled = True
    Case False
        imgBoxButton.Visible = True
        imgXBoxButton.Visible = False
        frmslblChicago.Visible = False
        frmslblChicago.Enabled = False
        frmslblNY.Visible = False
        frmslblNY.Enabled = False
End Select
```

As you can see, this is similar to the code for the Toggle Button. The test for the Select Case is the visibility of the imgBoxButton control. This VBS code works with the stacked button images and with the Labels for Chicago and New York.

Open the document in IE. Test the new button control you built. When you're satisfied that it works, go back to the Script Wizard and add the statements for the other city names to the Select Case statement. As before, Copy and Paste techniques *greatly* ease the typing load.

When you're finished, you'll have a button that behaves very much like a Toggle Button and changes its face when you click it. When you open the finished product in IE, you'll notice that the display response to the Click event isn't particularly smooth. The reason is that we've attached many actions to the Click event and they take time to execute. The idea, however, is an important one: you can develop your own controls by combining existing controls with a little scripting and a bit of ingenuity.

Animation: A Stitch in Time

Let's wrap things up with a look at a simple technique for animating your graphics.

Background Info

Animation is, of course, on optical illusion. An onscreen object that appears to move is really disappearing in one place and reappearing in another. An object that appears to rotate in place is really a series of objects that look just different enough from each other to give the appearance of rotation.

To create animation effects in HTML documents, we can take a GIF image, reposition it slightly, and keep repositioning it at regular intervals. If we're smart about how we set the time interval and the amount of repositioning, we'll have an animated image—an image that appears to move from position to position.

Specifics

Let's animate a sphere. The Lassen Technologies library has a stylized sphere labeled `ltb5.gif`. (This image is in their Little Guys category.) It's about .25KB. If you haven't copied this image, use another GIF image of that approximate size that you might have lying around. (To find one on your machine, select Windows 95 Start ➢ Find ➢ Files or Folders… and type *.gif in the dialog box.)

In order to set a time interval and associate it with an action (like repositioning an image), we'll use the Microsoft IE30 Timer control. If you haven't downloaded it yet from the Microsoft ActiveX Component Gallery (`http://www.microsoft.com/activex/controls`), now would be a good time to do that.

Laying Out the Objects

Open a new document in the ActiveX Control Pad. Save it as Simple Animation in skill 4. Between the <TITLE> tags, type **Animation Demo**. Use <H1> tags to place the heading **Moving an Image** in the document. Center the heading and follow it with a horizontal line <HR> (unless you've downloaded some line images that you want to use). Position the cursor before the </BODY> tag and select Edit ➤ Insert HTML Layout…. Create a layout called layout for simple animation and save it in skill 4. Open the HTML Layout Control.

If the Timer control isn't already in the Toolbox, add it. You might have to scroll almost all the way down the scrollable list to find it, as its name is *Timer Object*. Its icon on the Toolbar is a little clock with a light blue face. If you pass your mouse over this icon, the balloon help says *IeTimer*.

NOTE   The Timer control appears as Timer Object in the Additional Controls dialog box (for the Layout Control's Toolbox) and as both Microsoft IE 30 Timer Control and Timer Object in the Object Editor's list of controls.

Insert the Timer control into the layout. The Timer control's exact position and size don't matter because this control is invisible at runtime. In the Properties sheet, give the timer an ID of **tmrSphere** and set the Enabled property to 0-False. Set the Interval property to **100**. This tells the timer to fire an event every 100 milliseconds. It's as though we programmed a Command Button to click every tenth of a second. Just as we can write VBS that attaches a Click event to a set of actions, we can write VBS that attaches a Timer event to a set of actions. Those actions will then occur every 100 milliseconds (or whatever value we choose for the Timer's Interval property).

Insert an Image control. Give it an ID of **imgSphere** and a PicturePath that points to ltb5.gif (or to the image you are using).

Now let's go back to our old friend the Command Button. Create three Microsoft Forms 2.0 Command Buttons. Make their captions **Start**, **Stop**, and **Reset,** and make the captions bold. Give them IDs of cmdbtnStart, cmdbtnStop, and cmdbtnReset, respectively. Position everything so that your layout looks like Figure 4.10, and write down the value of imgSphere's Left property (in my Layout, that value is 66).

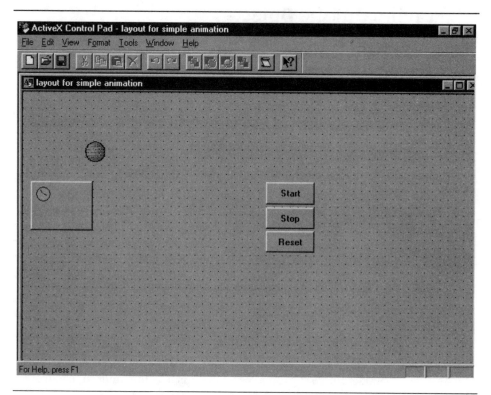

FIGURE 4.10: The Layout control for demonstrating animation

The Script

One Command Button will start the sphere moving (in a left-to-right direction), another will stop it in its tracks, and the third will reset the sphere's position back to its starting point. In order to make this happen, we have to write a script.

The script connects the Timer Interval with the sphere's Left property (in other words, its left-to-right position within the layout), and increases the value of this property. In other words, every 100 milliseconds the sphere will move a bit to the right.

We'll script the Start button to initiate the process (by enabling the Timer), the Stop button to stop the process (by disabling the Timer), and the Reset button to reposition the sphere back to where it started (by having it reset the sphere's Left property to its original value).

Open the Script Wizard. Start by clicking the + next to tmrSphere in the Event pane. Click on Timer. In the Actions pane, click on the + next to imgSphere. At the bottom of the Script Wizard, click on Code View. Using the method is most convenient for you (for example, double-clicking, typing), make the Script pane look like this:

```
Sub tmrSphere_Timer()
imgSphere.Left = imgSphere.Left + 20
```

This code means "whenever a Timer event occurs, make imgSphere appear 20 pixels to the right." The value we set for the Timer's Interval assures us that this script will run every 100 milliseconds.

Now let's turn our attention to the Command Buttons. First, go back to the Script Wizard's List View. In the Event pane, choose cmdbtnStart's Click event. In the Actions pane, double-click on tmrSphere's Enabled property and select True in the dialog box. Now go back to the Action pane and choose cmdbtnStop's Click event. Once again in the Actions pane, double-click on tmrSphere's Enabled property and select False in the dialog box. Finally, in the Event pane, choose cmdbtnReset's Click event. In the Actions pane double-click on imgSphere's Left property and type the value you wrote down for imgSphere's starting position.

Examine the script for the (layout for simple animation.alx) file. It looks like this listing.

layout for simple animation.alx

```
<SCRIPT LANGUAGE="VBScript">
<!--
Sub tglbtnSphere_Click()
tmrImages.Enabled = -1
end sub
-->
</SCRIPT>
<SCRIPT LANGUAGE="VBScript">
<!--
Sub cmdbtnStop_Click()
tmrSphere.Enabled = 0
end sub
-->
</SCRIPT>
<SCRIPT LANGUAGE="VBScript">
<!--
Sub cmdbtnStart_Click()
tmrSphere.Enabled = -1
end sub
```

```
-->
</SCRIPT>
<SCRIPT LANGUAGE="VBScript">
<!--
Sub cmdbtnReset_Click()
imgSphere.Left = 66
end sub
-->
</SCRIPT>
<SCRIPT LANGUAGE="VBScript">
<!--
Sub tmrSphere_Timer()
imgSphere.Left = imgSphere.Left + 20
end sub
-->
</SCRIPT>
<DIV ID="layout for simple animation"
➥STYLE="LAYOUT:FIXED;WIDTH:477pt;HEIGHT:293pt;">
    <OBJECT ID="tmrSphere"
     CLASSID="CLSID:59CCB4A0-727D-11CF-AC36-00AA00A47DD2"
     ➥STYLE="TOP:91pt;LEFT:8pt;WIDTH:66pt;HEIGHT:50pt;ZINDEX:0;">
        <PARAM NAME="_ExtentX" VALUE="2328">
        <PARAM NAME="_ExtentY" VALUE="1773">
        <PARAM NAME="Interval" VALUE="100">
        <PARAM NAME="Enabled" VALUE="False">
    </OBJECT>
    <OBJECT ID="imgSphere"
     CLASSID="CLSID:D4A97620-8E8F-11CF-93CD-00AA00C08FDF"
     ➥STYLE="TOP:50pt;LEFT:66pt;WIDTH:20pt;HEIGHT:20pt;ZINDEX:1;">
        <PARAM NAME="PicturePath"
        ➥VALUE="E:\ActiveX No Exp Req\ Graphics\Small\ltb5.gif">
        <PARAM NAME="AutoSize" VALUE="-1">
        <PARAM NAME="BorderStyle" VALUE="0">
        <PARAM NAME="SizeMode" VALUE="3">
        <PARAM NAME="Size" VALUE="688;688">
        <PARAM NAME="VariousPropertyBits" VALUE="17">
    </OBJECT>
    <OBJECT ID="cmdbtnStart"
     CLASSID="CLSID:D7053240-CE69-11CD-A777-00DD01143C57"
     ➥STYLE="TOP:91pt;LEFT:256pt;WIDTH:50pt;HEIGHT:22pt;TABINDEX:0;ZINDEX:2;">
        <PARAM NAME="Caption" VALUE="Start">
        <PARAM NAME="Size" VALUE="1764;776">
        <PARAM NAME="FontEffects" VALUE="1073741825">
        <PARAM NAME="FontCharSet" VALUE="0">
        <PARAM NAME="FontPitchAndFamily" VALUE="2">
        <PARAM NAME="ParagraphAlign" VALUE="3">
        <PARAM NAME="FontWeight" VALUE="700">
    </OBJECT>
```

```
<OBJECT ID="cmdbtnStop"
 CLASSID="CLSID:D7053240-CE69-11CD-A777-00DD01143C57"
➡STYLE="TOP:116pt;LEFT:256pt;WIDTH:50pt;HEIGHT:22pt;TABINDEX:1;ZINDEX:3;">
    <PARAM NAME="Caption" VALUE="Stop">
    <PARAM NAME="Size" VALUE="1764;776">
    <PARAM NAME="FontEffects" VALUE="1073741825">
    <PARAM NAME="FontCharSet" VALUE="0">
    <PARAM NAME="FontPitchAndFamily" VALUE="2">
    <PARAM NAME="ParagraphAlign" VALUE="3">
    <PARAM NAME="FontWeight" VALUE="700">
</OBJECT>
<OBJECT ID="cmdbtnReset"
 CLASSID="CLSID:D7053240-CE69-11CD-A777-00DD01143C57"
➡STYLE="TOP:140pt;LEFT:256pt;WIDTH:50pt;HEIGHT:22pt;TABINDEX:2;ZINDEX:4;">
    <PARAM NAME="Caption" VALUE="Reset">
    <PARAM NAME="Size" VALUE="1764;776">
    <PARAM NAME="FontEffects" VALUE="1073741825">
    <PARAM NAME="FontCharSet" VALUE="0">
    <PARAM NAME="FontPitchAndFamily" VALUE="2">
    <PARAM NAME="ParagraphAlign" VALUE="3">
    <PARAM NAME="FontWeight" VALUE="700">
</OBJECT>
</DIV>
```

It's time to save your work and test it in IE. Click the Start button to (literally) get the ball rolling. You should see it move progressively to the right. Click Stop to stop it, and Reset to reset it.

Summary

In this Skill, you've added graphics and some animation to your bag of tricks. You've seen how to use graphics that you encounter on the Web and how to make them work for you. Most importantly, you can make your graphics interactive.

In the next Skill, we amplify the interactivity theme. We explore controls that enable users to make choices and to enter text of their own.

Are You Experienced?

Now you can...

- ☑ embed images into your Web pages by using the HTML <IMG> tag
- ☑ copy and use graphics from sites you encounter on the Web
- ☑ use the ActiveX Object Editor and the HTML Layout Control to embed graphics into your HTML documents
- ☑ use the ActiveX Hot Spot control to make your graphics interactive
- ☑ develop Web pages with map-based front-ends
- ☑ use a graphic as a backdrop for jumping out into the Web
- ☑ combine images with a Hot Spot to develop new controls
- ☑ use the ActiveX Timer control to implement simple animation

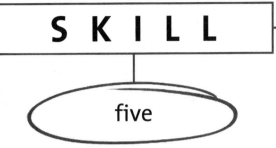

SKILL

five

Introducing Interactivity: The TextBox Control

- ❏ Setting up TextBox controls
- ❏ The Change event
- ❏ Handling errors
- ❏ Working with *If…Then*
- ❏ Crafting Message Box controls

With so much information on the Web vying for people's attention—and with attention spans as short as they are—the potential for interaction between a user and a Web page is great. And, with this high level of interaction, the likelihood that your message will get through to users is even greater. A cornerstone of ActiveX controls is their ability to draw users into meaningful interactions with the controls on your Web page. As a designer of ActiveX Web pages, it falls to you to create this interaction.

Users want to feel that they're are influencing the course of the information flow in observable ways. In other words, if you give users something to do (such as enter some text, click a button, or make a choice), they want to see results (such as new information, a change in the display, or a new graphic) as quickly as possible. The Command Buttons, Toggle buttons, and Click events we've worked with are steps in this direction.

ActiveX controls put a number of additional tools at your disposal to help you build interactivity into your Web pages. These tools form the subject of the next two Skills.

The Textbox: Entering a Value

One tried-and-true way to get users to interact with your Web page is to have them type values into controls. The Web page then uses these values to do its business. In this case, these controls are called *textboxes*. With a textbox, a user can copy, cut, and paste existing text, as well as type new text.

Microsoft provides an ActiveX TextBox control that makes it easy to design a textbox. To explore the properties of this control, we'll work with the Web page that we developed at the end of the preceding Skill. We'll use input from textboxes to set the parameters for our animation display.

Animation Revisited

At the end of Skill 4, I encouraged you to experiment with the two important parameters of our animated Web page:

- the time interval between movements of the GIF image
- the number of pixels that the image appears to move

This is a bit easier said than done. Whenever you want to change these parameters you have to go through this sequence:

1. Leave the Web page.

2. Open the Script Wizard.

3. Find the appropriate code (for the Timer control interval and the Timer event).

4. Change the code.

5. Close the Script Wizard.

6. Save the HTML Layout Control.

7. Alt+Tab back to the Web page.

8. Refresh the Web page.

Skill 5

This is extremely cumbersome and doesn't encourage experimentation. (It's entirely understandable if you tried a few settings and then decided it was just too much trouble.)

Textboxes offer us an easier way to provide input to other controls on our animated Web page. If we put some textboxes on the display and attach their values to the appropriate parts of the VBS, we can just open the Web page, enter values in the textboxes, and start the animation. We can then watch the consequences, change the values, and restart the animation—all without leaving the Web page.

To begin this simple process, follow these steps:

1. Copy `Simple Animation.htm` and `layout for simple animation.alx` from the `skill 4` folder to the `skill 5` folder.

2. Rename them `Animation With TextBoxes.htm` and `layout for animation with textboxes.alx`.

3. Open the ActiveX Control Pad and open `Animation With TextBoxes` in the Text Editor.

4. Delete what's between <TITLE> and </TITLE> and replace it with **Animation With TextBoxes**.

Now, let's add a heading and an image of a fancy horizontal line to separate the heading from the layout. From your file of graphics downloads from Lassen Technologies, copy `ltbarrdy.gif` (a red bar with yellow stars on it) into your `skill 5` folder, or you can use another graphic if you prefer. In the ActiveX

Control Pad Text Editor, edit the `Animation With TextBoxes` file so it looks like this up until the `<BODY>` tag:

```
<HTML>
<HEAD>
<TITLE>Animation With TextBoxes</TITLE>
</HEAD>
<H1> <FONT FACE = SCRIPT>
<CENTER> <B> Animation With TextBoxes </B> </CENTER>
</FONT>
<IMG SRC = "ltbarrdy.gif"></IMG>
<BODY>
      .
      .
      .
```

NOTE   The SCRIPT font is another one of those fonts that we'd probably never use for a heading, but we'll take the opportunity to see what it looks like here.

The Layout

At this point, you could use the Text Editor to update the `<OBJECT>` tag and make it point to the newly renamed ALX file in `skill 5`, but there's an easier way to do this. Just delete everything between (and including) `<OBJECT>` and `</OBJECT>` and then use Edit ➤ Insert HTML Layout… to insert `layout for animation with textboxes.alx`.

After you've done this, click on the symbol to the left of `<OBJECT>` to open the HTML Layout Control and then follow these steps:

1. Select a TextBox control from the Toolbox and position it approximately midway between the Timer control (which is invisible at runtime, but visible in the Layout Control) and the Command Buttons.

2. Open the TextBox's Properties sheet and set the ID to **txtbxMilliseconds**.

3. Select the TextBox. Use Ctrl+C to make a copy of the TextBox control and Ctrl+V to paste the copy.

4. In the new TextBox's Properties sheet, change the ID to **txtbxPixels**. Position the new TextBox control below the first one.

5. Select a Label control from the Toolbox and position it above txtbxMilliseconds.

6. Change the Label's ID to **lblMilliseconds**. Change the caption to **Milliseconds Between Moves:** and make the font bold.

7. Make a copy of the label, paste the copy, and change the copy's ID to **lblPixels**. Change the caption to **Pixels Per Move:**.

8. Position lblPixels just above txtbxPixels.

Adjust the controls so your layout looks like Figure 5.1.

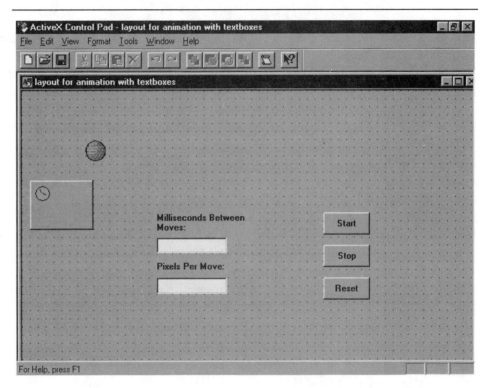

FIGURE 5.1: Laying out the controls for Animation With TextBoxes

Writing the Script

Time to do some scripting. Here are our goals:

- The value typed into txtbxMilliseconds becomes the value of the Timer's Interval property.

- The value typed into txtbxPixels becomes the amount by which the Left property of imgSphere (the red sphere) increases after each Timer event.

Open the Script Wizard and we'll attach TextBox events in appropriate places.

NAMING THE LAYOUT

Examine the objects in the Script Wizard. You'll see something that's called `layoutforsimpleanimation` in both the Event pane and the Actions pane. Wait a minute! Wasn't that the *old* name for this layout? Didn't we rename the file?

As you saw in Skill 2, some things hang around unless you explicitly change them or delete them. These fossils usually have no effect on the working of the code. If you want to change the name of a layout object for the Script Wizard, however, go back to the Layout Control *before* you start scripting. Right-click and select View Source Code.... In the Notepad, make the changes. To change the name of the object that represents the Layout Control in the Script Wizard panes, scroll down to the <DIV> tag and change the value of the ID attribute.

A very important point: If you change the ID attribute, make sure the new value has no spaces. (The temptation is to use spaces because Windows 95 allows spaces in filenames. Don't do it.) For very long names, separate the words with an underscore. If you use spaces, you'll have a huge problem when you try to script the Layout's one event, which we'll do in the next section.

Go through these steps:

1. In the Event pane, open the events for txtbxMilliseconds and choose the Change event.

2. In the Actions pane, click on the + next to tmrSphere (the Timer control). Double-click on Interval.

3. In the dialog box that opens, Click on Custom.... In the dialog box, type **txtbxMilliseconds.Value**.

This sets up the script that changes the Timer's Interval to the value typed into txtbxMilliseconds whenever you type in a new value. Exactly when does that value change? As soon as you type something. Just for instructional purposes, change the Script Wizard from List View to Code View. The code should look like this:

```
Sub txtbxMilliseconds_Change()
tmrSphere.Interval = txtbxMilliseconds.Value
```

Keep the Wizard in Code View. In the Event pane, click on the + next to tmrSphere and choose the Timer event. In the Script pane, the code left over from prior work with in Skill 4 will have a line that looks something like this:

```
imgSphere.Left = imgSphere.Left + 30
```

Your numerical value on the right side may be different, depending on any changes you may have made while experimenting with the animation in the previous Skill. We want the line to look like this

```
imgSphere.Left = imgSphere.Left + txtbxPixels.Value
```

to indicate that the value in txtbxPixels determines the number of pixels that the sphere "advances" from left to right when the Timer event occurs. Make the necessary changes in the Script pane and click OK to close the Script Wizard.

Save your work and open `Animation With Textboxes` in IE. You'll be able to type numerical values into the TextBoxes and note the effects on the animation (see Figure 5.2).

If you type anything other than a number, you'll see an error message. We'll show you how to deal with this in "Handling Errors," but first I want to familiarize you with the Change event.

The Change Event: A Closer Look

We've worked with a Change event before, but for a different control—the Spin Button. The Change event is like a watchdog: It watches its control for a change in a value and swings into action whenever a change occurs. In the Spin Button, the Change event occurred when we clicked the Spin Button. In a TextBox, the Change event fires up any time you change the contents of the TextBox control.

Here's a little exercise to help you gain an intuitive understanding of the Change event:

1. In the ActiveX Control Pad, open a new file.

2. Save it in `skill 5` as `Change Event Demo`, and use **Change Event Demo** as the title that also acts as a centered heading.

3. Select Edit ➤ Insert ActiveX Control... and choose a Microsoft Forms 2.0 TextBox control from the list.

4. In the Object Editor, use the sizing handles to make the TextBox big enough to hold about four or five characters.

5. Set the ID to **txtbxDemo** and then close the Object Editor.

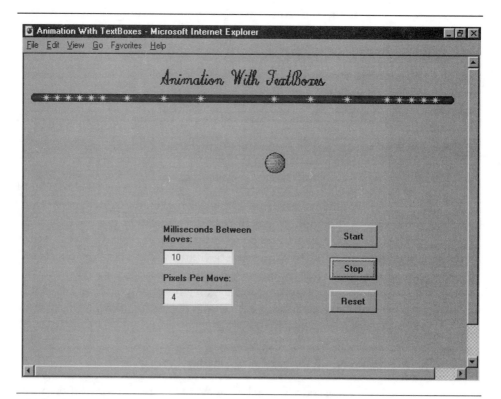

FIGURE 5.2: The Animation With TextBoxes Web page. The contents of the TextBoxes have set the sphere to move 4 pixels every 10 milliseconds. The Stop button has been clicked, stopping the sphere partway across the screen.

6.   In the Text Editor, use <BR> tags and <CENTER> tags to position the TextBox control. The exact location on the page doesn't matter.

7.   Once again, select Edit ➤ Insert ActiveX Control…. This time, select a Microsoft Forms 2.0 Label.

8.   Set its ID to **lblDemo**. Make it about the same width as the TextBox control and set its BackColor to white.

9.   Close the Object Editor and use <BR> tags and <CENTER> tags to position the Label (again, the exact location on the page doesn't matter).

  Now we have to write a script that, as a result of the TextBox Change event, puts the contents of the TextBox into the Caption of the Label. In other words, as soon as the value of the TextBox changes, the Label's appearance reflects that change. We could go into the Script Wizard, but it's just as easy to type these lines of code directly into the Text Editor, just before the <OBJECT> tag that defines the TextBox control:

```
<SCRIPT LANGUAGE="VBScript">
<!--
Sub txtbxDemo_Change()
lblDemo.Caption = txtbxDemo.Value
end sub
-->
    </SCRIPT>
```

When you have finished, the file (Change Event Demo.htm) should look like this:

Change Event Demo.htm

```
<HTML>

<HEAD>
<TITLE>Change Event Demo</TITLE>
</HEAD>
<BODY> <CENTER> <H1> Change Event Demo </H1> <CENTER><HR>
<CENTER> <BR> <BR> <BR>
    <SCRIPT LANGUAGE="VBScript">
<!--
Sub txtbxDemo_Change()
lblDemo.Caption = txtbxDemo.Value
end sub
-->
    </SCRIPT>
    <OBJECT ID="txtbxDemo" WIDTH=127 HEIGHT=35
 CLASSID="CLSID:8BD21D10-EC42-11CE-9E0D-00AA006002F3">
    <PARAM NAME="VariousPropertyBits" VALUE="746604571">
    <PARAM NAME="Size" VALUE="3351;917">
    <PARAM NAME="FontCharSet" VALUE="0">
    <PARAM NAME="FontPitchAndFamily" VALUE="2">
    <PARAM NAME="FontWeight" VALUE="0">
</OBJECT>
</CENTER> <BR><BR><BR>
<CENTER>
    <OBJECT ID="lblDemo" WIDTH=127 HEIGHT=35
 CLASSID="CLSID:978C9E23-D4B0-11CE-BF2D-00AA003F40D0">
    <PARAM NAME="BackColor" VALUE="16777215">
    <PARAM NAME="Size" VALUE="3351;917">
    <PARAM NAME="FontCharSet" VALUE="0">
    <PARAM NAME="FontPitchAndFamily" VALUE="2">
    <PARAM NAME="FontWeight" VALUE="0">
</OBJECT>
</CENTER>
</BODY>
</HTML>
```

Skill 5

Now open up this page in IE, and start typing (anything you like) into the TextBox. You'll find that whatever you type into the TextBox appears immediately in the Label. You don't have to click anything, press the Enter key, or do anything else. The Change event takes care of everything. Figure 5.3 shows this page in action.

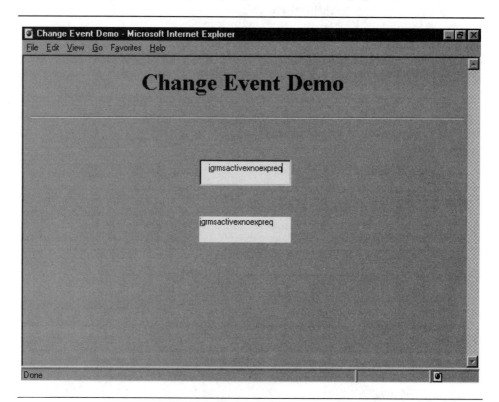

FIGURE 5.3: The Change Event Demo page in action. Anything you type into the TextBox (upper rectangle) immediately appears in the Label (lower rectangle).

When you finish with this exercise, close the Change Event Demo page and go back to Animation with Textboxes.htm. Reopen layout for Animation with Textboxes.alx and we'll move on.

Handling Errors

When you build a Web page and put it out on the Web, you open it up to a potential audience in the tens of millions. With the huge diversity of users, it's highly probable someone will make a mistake when entering information into a textbox.

In `Animation With TextBoxes.htm`, an error occurs when a user types text instead of numbers. When that happens, a messy-looking error message results (see Figure 5.4). Another kind of error results when users push the Start button without entering any values in the textboxes. Errors like these can bring the application to a crashing halt—or alter its operations in ways that you can't predict.

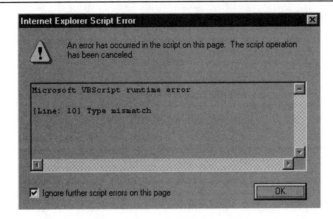

FIGURE 5.4: An error message that appears when the user types the wrong kind of information into a textbox

Setting Up Safeguards

To avoid the unsightly messes that errors produce, we'll put safeguards in our VBS code—safeguards that let the user know what went wrong and present a chance to try again without messing up the program.

Our safeguards will depend on testing the values in the TextBox controls. Specifically, we'll test to see whether the values are numeric. If the user types a non-numeric value in a TextBox control, its Change event will open a Message Box that tells the user to enter a numeric value. If the user clicks the Start button without entering a value in either TextBox, the Start button's Click event will open a Message Box that tells the user to enter a value in the appropriate TextBox.

We might also want to keep the users' entries within a particular range—say 1 to 300 milliseconds and 1 to 80 pixels. We can script these safeguards into the Start Button's Click event.

Some Helpful VBS Concepts

To accomplish these objectives, we'll work with two new VBS concepts. One is the If...Then structure. The other is a VBS *function* called IsNumeric.

First things first. If...Then sets up a *condition*. If the condition is true, the code that follows the word "Then" executes. This structure ends with the two words "End If." If the condition is not true, the code after the word "Then" (and before "End If") doesn't execute, and the code after "End If" executes.

It looks like this:

```
If condition is True Then
... code executes...
End If
```

We'll add an extra wrinkle: In our script, we want the "If" condition to be true if the value in our TextBox is *not* a number. If it's not a number, we'll show a Message Box and stop the whole process. If it is a number, we won't show the Message Box and we'll let the process continue.

This leads us to the next concept, IsNumeric, as I said, is a VBS *function*. A function is like the subroutines we've been using, but with one important difference: A function returns a value; a subroutine does not. The IsNumeric function returns a value representing whether the value passed in its argument is a numeric value. The argument that we'll give IsNumeric is the value in a TextBox. The value it returns is *True* if the value is a numerical one, *False* if it's not.

Before we start scripting, here's a non-computerese version of what the subroutine should look like:

```
If the value in the TextBox is not a number Then
Show a Message Box that tells the user that the
➥entered value is not a number
End the subroutine without doing anything more
End the "If Then"
You've come this far, so you must have a number;
➥set the value in the timer to the value in the TextBox
End the subroutine
```

Writing the Scripts

Here we go. In the Script Wizard, open the events for txtbxMilliseconds and choose the Change event. Put the Script Wizard in Code View.

In the Script pane, type these lines before the line that sets the value of `tmrSphere.Interval` to the value of `txtbxMilliseconds.Value`:

```
If Not IsNumeric(txtbxMilliseconds.Value) Then
    MsgBox "You must enter a numeric value", 64, _
        "Wrong Type for Milliseconds"
    Exit Sub
End If
```

Some explanation:

- The underscore at the end of the second line is the line continuation character.

- The `MsgBox` statement takes three arguments, the second of which specifies a symbol that appears on the message box or specifies which buttons appear on the message box. Each possible symbol or button-combination is associated with a number. The number we used, 64, causes a stylized "i" to appear (indicating that the message box supplies information). Table 5.1 shows all the numbers and what they stand for.

- The first argument (the string "You must enter a numeric value") is the contents of the message box.

- The third argument ("Wrong Type for Milliseconds") is the message box's title.

T A B L E 5 . 1 : Numerical Arguments for the MsgBox Display

Number	What Appears on the Message Box
0	OK button
1	OK button and Cancel button
2	Abort, Retry, and Ignore buttons
3	Yes, No, and Cancel buttons
4	Yes button and No button
5	Retry button and Cancel button
16	X (often used to indicate a Critical Error)
32	Question-Mark
48	Exclamation Point (indicates a warning)
64	I (indicates an informational message)

Skill 5

NOTE   You can use the numbers in Table 5.1 in combinations. For example, if the second argument to MsgBox is 2+ 48, the Abort, Retry, and Cancel buttons appear along with an exclamation point. Another tidbit: If you forget the MsgBox numbers and what they mean, 0 (zero) is always safe as the second argument for MsgBox. If you forget what zero means, two commas separated by blank space (,) also work (as the equivalent of zero).

When you finish typing, the Script pane should say:

```
Sub txtbxMilliseconds_Change()
If Not IsNumeric(txtbxMilliseconds.Value) Then
    MsgBox "You must enter a numeric value", 64, _
        "Wrong Type for Milliseconds"
    Exit Sub
End If
tmrSphere.Interval = txtbxMilliseconds.Value
```

The line Exit Sub tells us that this subroutine terminates after you click the OK button on the message box. The line after End If tells us that the program sets the interval to the value in txtbxMilliseconds if that value is a number.

WARNING   When you use the VBS line continuation character (the underscore) be sure you leave a space after the character that precedes it. If you don't, you'll get an error message.

In similar fashion, open the Script pane for the Change event for txtbxPixels. Type this code into the Script pane:

```
Sub txtbxPixels_Change()
If Not IsNumeric(txtbxPixels.Value) Then
    MsgBox "You must enter a numeric value", 64, _
        "Wrong Type for Pixels"
    Exit Sub

End If
```

The Start button's Click event should display a message box if either textbox is empty when the user clicks on Start (having no value in a textbox is like having a non-numeric value). The Start button's Click event should also generate a message box if a TextBox value is out of range. Otherwise, the Click event activates the timer and the animation starts. To make all this happen, enter the following code in the Script pane for the Start button's Click event:

```
Sub cmdbtnStart_Click()
If Not IsNumeric(txtbxMilliseconds.Value) Then
    MsgBox "You must enter a value for Milliseconds", 64, _
        "No Value Entered For Milliseconds"
    tmrSphere.Enabled = False
    Exit sub
End If

If Not IsNumeric(txtbxPixels.Value) Then
    MsgBox "You must enter a value for Pixels", 64, _
        "No Value Entered For Pixels"
    tmrSphere.Enabled = False
    Exit sub
End If

If txtbxMilliseconds.Value > 300 or _
        txtbxMilliseconds.Value < 1 Then
    MsgBox "Keep Milliseconds between 1 and 300", 64, _
        "Milliseconds Value Out of Range"
    Exit sub
End If

If txtbxPixels.Value > 80 or txtbxPixels.Value < 1 Then
    MsgBox "Keep Pixels between 1 and 80", 64, _
        "Pixels Value Out of Range"
    Exit sub
End If
tmrSphere.Enabled = True
```

The first two If...Then structures trap errors caused by clicking the Start button with either textbox missing a value. The last two trap out-of-range values.

We're all set. Save your work and open the page in IE. Enter values as before and note the effects on the animation. Enter some erroneous values and watch the message boxes appear. In particular, try entering out-of-range values and try clicking on the Start button without a value in either textbox. By the way, when you backspace to clear a textbox, you'll see the Message Box. Why? Because the backspace is not a numeric character. (Given what we know about key-press events from Skill 3, it wouldn't be difficult to eliminate this behavior.)

The beauty of the message box approach to trapping errors is that you can use them to tell users where they went wrong, point out the right thing to do, and allow them to click on the message box to continue using the program. Figure 5.5 shows the Web page in IE displaying one of the message boxes that we created.

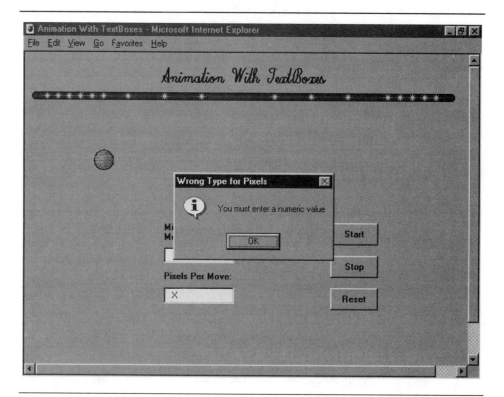

FIGURE 5.5: The Animation With TextBoxes Web page shows a Message Box that traps an error.

Examine the VBS for this file (layout for animation with textboxes.alx). You'll see code that looks like this listing.

 layout for animation with textboxes.alx

```
<SCRIPT LANGUAGE="VBScript">
<!--
Sub cmdbtnStop_Click()
tmrSphere.Enabled = 0
end sub
```

```
-->
</SCRIPT>
<SCRIPT LANGUAGE="VBScript">
<!--
Sub cmdbtnStart_Click()
If Not IsNumeric(txtbxMilliseconds.Value) Then
    MsgBox "You must enter a value for Milliseconds", 64, _
        "No Value Entered For Milliseconds"
    tmrSphere.Enabled = False
    Exit sub
End If

If Not IsNumeric(txtbxPixels.Value) Then
    MsgBox "You must enter a value for Pixels", 64, _
        "No Value Entered For Pixels"
    tmrSphere.Enabled = False
    Exit sub
End If

If txtbxMilliseconds.Value > 300 or txtbxMilliseconds.Value < 1 Then
    MsgBox "Keep Milliseconds between 1 and 300", 64, _
    "Milliseconds Value Out of Range"
    Exit sub
End If

If txtbxPixels.Value > 80 or txtbxPixels.Value < 1 Then
    MsgBox "Keep Pixels between 1 and 80", 64, _
    "Pixels Value Out of Range"
    Exit sub
End If
tmrSphere.Enabled = True
end sub
-->
</SCRIPT>
<SCRIPT LANGUAGE="VBScript">
<!--
Sub cmdbtnReset_Click()
imgSphere.Left = 66
end sub
-->
</SCRIPT>
<SCRIPT LANGUAGE="VBScript">
<!--
Sub tmrSphere_Timer()
imgSphere.Left = imgSphere.Left + txtbxPixels.Value
end sub
-->
</SCRIPT>
```

Skill 5

```
<SCRIPT LANGUAGE="VBScript">
<!--

Sub txtbxMilliseconds_Change()
If Not IsNumeric(txtbxMilliseconds.Value) Then
    MsgBox "You must enter a numeric value", 64, _
        "Wrong Type for Milliseconds"
    Exit Sub
End If
tmrSphere.Interval = txtbxMilliseconds.Value
end sub
-->
</SCRIPT>
<SCRIPT LANGUAGE="VBScript">
<!--

Sub txtbxPixels_Change()
If Not IsNumeric(txtbxPixels.Value) Then
    MsgBox "You must enter a numeric value", 64, _
        "Wrong Type for Pixels"
    Exit Sub
End If

end sub
-->
</SCRIPT>
<DIV ID="layout_for_animation_with_textboxes"
➥STYLE="LAYOUT:FIXED;WIDTH:477pt;HEIGHT:293pt;">
    <OBJECT ID="tmrSphere"
     CLASSID="CLSID:59CCB4A0-727D-11CF-AC36-00AA00A47DD2"
     ➥STYLE="TOP:91pt;LEFT:8pt;WIDTH:66pt;HEIGHT:50pt;ZINDEX:0;">
        <PARAM NAME="_ExtentX" VALUE="2328">
        <PARAM NAME="_ExtentY" VALUE="1773">
        <PARAM NAME="Interval" VALUE="100">
        <PARAM NAME="Enabled" VALUE="False">
    </OBJECT>
    <OBJECT ID="imgSphere"
     CLASSID="CLSID:D4A97620-8E8F-11CF-93CD-00AA00C08FDF"
     ➥STYLE="TOP:50pt;LEFT:66pt;WIDTH:20pt;HEIGHT:20pt;ZINDEX:1;">
        <PARAM NAME="PicturePath"
        ➥VALUE="E:\ActiveX No Exp Req\graphics\small\ltb5.gif">
        <PARAM NAME="AutoSize" VALUE="-1">
        <PARAM NAME="BorderStyle" VALUE="0">
        <PARAM NAME="SizeMode" VALUE="3">
        <PARAM NAME="Size" VALUE="688;688">
        <PARAM NAME="VariousPropertyBits" VALUE="17">
    </OBJECT>
    <OBJECT ID="cmdbtnStart"
```

```
          CLASSID="CLSID:D7053240-CE69-11CD-A777-00DD01143C57"
        ➥STYLE="TOP:124pt;LEFT:314pt;WIDTH:50pt;HEIGHT:22pt;TABINDEX:0;ZINDEX:2;">
            <PARAM NAME="Caption" VALUE="Start">
            <PARAM NAME="Size" VALUE="1764;776">
            <PARAM NAME="FontEffects" VALUE="1073741825">
            <PARAM NAME="FontCharSet" VALUE="0">
            <PARAM NAME="FontPitchAndFamily" VALUE="2">
            <PARAM NAME="ParagraphAlign" VALUE="3">
            <PARAM NAME="FontWeight" VALUE="700">
        </OBJECT>
        <OBJECT ID="cmdbtnStop"
          CLASSID="CLSID:D7053240-CE69-11CD-A777-00DD01143C57"
        ➥STYLE="TOP:157pt;LEFT:314pt;WIDTH:50pt;HEIGHT:22pt;TABINDEX:1;ZINDEX:3;">
            <PARAM NAME="Caption" VALUE="Stop">
            <PARAM NAME="Size" VALUE="1764;776">
            <PARAM NAME="FontEffects" VALUE="1073741825">
            <PARAM NAME="FontCharSet" VALUE="0">
            <PARAM NAME="FontPitchAndFamily" VALUE="2">
            <PARAM NAME="ParagraphAlign" VALUE="3">
            <PARAM NAME="FontWeight" VALUE="700">
        </OBJECT>
        <OBJECT ID="cmdbtnReset"
          CLASSID="CLSID:D7053240-CE69-11CD-A777-00DD01143C57"
        ➥STYLE="TOP:190pt;LEFT:314pt;WIDTH:50pt;HEIGHT:22pt;TABINDEX:2;ZINDEX:4;">
            <PARAM NAME="Caption" VALUE="Reset">
            <PARAM NAME="Size" VALUE="1764;776">
            <PARAM NAME="FontEffects" VALUE="1073741825">
            <PARAM NAME="FontCharSet" VALUE="0">
            <PARAM NAME="FontPitchAndFamily" VALUE="2">
            <PARAM NAME="ParagraphAlign" VALUE="3">
            <PARAM NAME="FontWeight" VALUE="700">
        </OBJECT>
        <OBJECT ID="txtbxMilliseconds"
          CLASSID="CLSID:8BD21D10-EC42-11CE-9E0D-00AA006002F3"
        ➥STYLE="TOP:149pt;LEFT:140pt;WIDTH:74pt;HEIGHT:16pt;TABINDEX:3;ZINDEX:5;">
            <PARAM NAME="VariousPropertyBits" VALUE="746604571">
            <PARAM NAME="Size" VALUE="2611;564">
            <PARAM NAME="FontCharSet" VALUE="0">
            <PARAM NAME="FontPitchAndFamily" VALUE="2">
            <PARAM NAME="FontWeight" VALUE="0">
        </OBJECT>
        <OBJECT ID="txtbxPixels"
          CLASSID="CLSID:8BD21D10-EC42-11CE-9E0D-00AA006002F3"
        ➥STYLE="TOP:190pt;LEFT:140pt;WIDTH:74pt;HEIGHT:16pt;TABINDEX:4;ZINDEX:6;">
            <PARAM NAME="VariousPropertyBits" VALUE="746604571">
            <PARAM NAME="Size" VALUE="2611;564">
            <PARAM NAME="FontCharSet" VALUE="0">
            <PARAM NAME="FontPitchAndFamily" VALUE="2">
```

Skill 5

```
        <PARAM NAME="FontWeight" VALUE="0">
   </OBJECT>
   <OBJECT ID="lblMilliseconds"
    CLASSID="CLSID:978C9E23-D4B0-11CE-BF2D-00AA003F40D0"
➡️STYLE="TOP:124pt;LEFT:140pt;WIDTH:107pt;HEIGHT:25pt;ZINDEX:7;">
        <PARAM NAME="Caption" VALUE="Milliseconds Between Moves:">
        <PARAM NAME="Size" VALUE="3775;882">
        <PARAM NAME="FontEffects" VALUE="1073741825">
        <PARAM NAME="FontCharSet" VALUE="0">
        <PARAM NAME="FontPitchAndFamily" VALUE="2">
        <PARAM NAME="FontWeight" VALUE="700">
   </OBJECT>
   <OBJECT ID="lblPixels"
    CLASSID="CLSID:978C9E23-D4B0-11CE-BF2D-00AA003F40D0"
➡️STYLE="TOP:173pt;LEFT:140pt;WIDTH:83pt;HEIGHT:17pt;ZINDEX:8;">
        <PARAM NAME="Caption" VALUE="Pixels Per Move:">
        <PARAM NAME="Size" VALUE="2928;600">
        <PARAM NAME="FontEffects" VALUE="1073741825">
        <PARAM NAME="FontCharSet" VALUE="0">
        <PARAM NAME="FontPitchAndFamily" VALUE="2">
        <PARAM NAME="FontWeight" VALUE="700">
    </OBJECT>
</DIV>
```

Other Properties of the TextBox Control

We've only examined a few of the properties of the TextBox control. This control has a number of other properties that often come in handy. I've outlined some of them for you in Table 5.2.

TABLE 5.2: Some Useful Properties of the TextBox Control

Property	Explanation
Multiline	If this is set to True, the TextBox can display multiple lines. If it's False, all the text appears on one line
WordWrap	If Multiline is True, the words wrap inside the TextBox. If Multiline is False, this property is ignored
LineCount	Indicates the number of lines in the TextBox
PasswordChar	Emulates what happens when you type a password. In the Properties sheet, you specify a character for this property: that character becomes the only character that appears no matter what the user types

Summing Up

What we've seen thus far introduces some important concepts of Web page interactivity. We've set up TextBoxes that allow a lot of flexibility, but that flexibility comes with a price: the more flexibility you allow, the more you have to worry about input errors and how to handle them in your code.

Sometimes it's helpful and appropriate to provide choices rather than the capability for free-form input. The next skill covers ActiveX controls that do just that.

Are You Experienced?

Now you can...

☑ **work with the TextBox control to build interactivity into your Web pages**

☑ **understand all the aspects of the Change event**

☑ **use the VBS *If...Then* statement to control the flow of your scripts**

☑ **work with some built-in VBS functions**

☑ **set up informative Message Boxes**

☑ **trap user errors and display instructive error messages that don't disrupt program flow**

Skill 5

Building Interactivity: ListBoxes, ComboBoxes, Option Buttons, and PopUp Menus

❑ **Setting up ListBox controls**

❑ **Combining the ListBox control with the TextBox control**

❑ **Using Option Buttons in radio button groups**

❑ **Working with global variables**

❑ **Popping up menus on your Web pages**

❑ **Putting options into choice-based controls**

While the TextBox we learned about in Skill 5 is a useful control, sometimes it allows the user too much freedom. We saw this when we examined ways to handle errors in the previous Skill.

If your Web page requires only a few possible values as input, it's not always best to use a TextBox—although you almost always have to worry about handling errors. When you present only a limited number of choices, some controls may be more appropriate than the TextBox control. This Skill covers ActiveX controls that present choices to the user. Once again, we'll work in the context of the simple animation we've created.

The ListBox

The ListBox control provides interaction capabilities, but it limits the values that a user can choose. A listbox is a sequence of rows, and each row presents a value. When we refer to the *value* of a listbox, we mean the value that the user has selected (typically the row the user has clicked on). This row is highlighted and this selection will be the value of the control.

Suppose, for example, we find that users of our textbox-based animated Web page typically enter millisecond values of 10, 20, 50, 100, 200, and 300, and pixel values of 2, 4, 8, 12, 16, and 20. If this occurs frequently enough, we might set up listboxes with these values built-in—rather than textboxes that permit all kinds of entries. We'll still have to worry about trapping errors; for example, when the page first opens, a user might mistakenly click on the Start button without first selecting a value from either listbox.

Getting Started

To see how the ListBox control works, let's examine it in the context of our animation page. We'll set up a new page that substitutes listbox controls for the textbox controls—based on `Animation With TextBoxes` from Skill 5. We'll save ourselves some layout time by building on the layout we just used for the Text-Box controls in Skill 5 (isn't reusability wonderful?):

1. Start by copying `layout for Animation with TextBoxes.alx` from your `skill 5` folder to your `skill 6` folder.

2. In the ActiveX Control Pad, open the `Animation With TextBoxes` file and save it as `Animation With ListBoxes` in `skill 6`.

3. Enter **Animation With ListBoxes** as the title and create a heading of the same name.

4. Click on the symbol next to the <OBJECT> tag to open the HTML Layout Control that resides in skill 6.

5. In the Layout Control select Edit ➤ Save As... and save the layout as layout for animation with listboxes in skill 6.

6. Still in the Layout Control, open the Script Wizard. Take a look at the object in the Event pane and the object in the Actions pane that represent the layout. They carry the name over from the previous incarnation of this file.

7. Let's update the name. Click on OK to return to the HTML Layout Control.

8. Right-click and select View Source Code.... Click Yes in the resulting dialog box.

9. In the Notepad window that opens, find the <DIV> tag and change the value of the ID attribute to **layout_for_animation_with_listboxes**. (Make sure you include the underscores here.)

10. Save what you've done, close the Notepad, and return to the Text Editor.

11. Make sure you change the ID attribute in the <OBJECT> tag to **layoutforanimationwithlistboxes_alx** and the REF VALUE to **layout for animation with listboxes.alx**.

We're ready to roll if your Animation With ListBoxes.htm file in the Text Editor looks like this:

```
<HTML>
<HEAD>
<TITLE>Animation With ListBoxes</TITLE>
</HEAD>
<H1> <FONT FACE = SCRIPT>
<CENTER> <B> Animation With ListBoxes </B> </CENTER>
</FONT> </CENTER>
<IMG SRC = "ltbarrdy.gif"></IMG>
<BODY>
<OBJECT CLASSID="CLSID:812AE312-8B8E-11CF-93C8-00AA00C08FDF"
ID="layoutforanimationwithlistboxes_alx" STYLE="LEFT:0;TOP:0">
<PARAM NAME="ALXPATH" REF VALUE=
➥"layout for animation with listboxes.alx">
 </OBJECT>
</BODY>
</HTML>
```

Skill 6

Working with the Layout

Reopen the HTML Layout Control and remove the two TextBox controls. In their place put two ListBox controls (which you select from the Toolbox). Give the first one an ID of **lstbxMilliseconds**. Give the second one an ID of **lstbxPixels**. Your layout should resemble Figure 6.1.

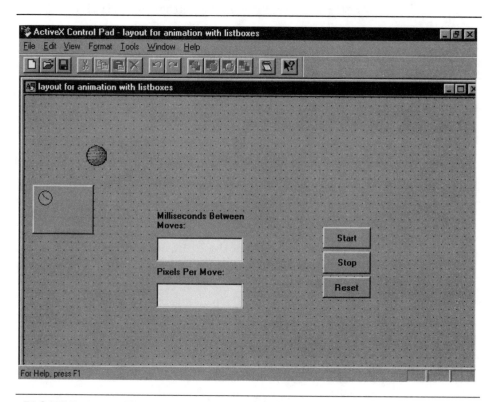

FIGURE 6.1: The layout for Animation With ListBoxes

Finally, open the Properties sheet for the Timer and make sure its Enabled property is set to 0-False.

Writing the ListBoxes Script

Open the Script Wizard and check the events for the cmdbtnStart Command Button. It still has some error-trapping code related to the TextBox controls that have been deleted. Some of this code is still useful. In Code View, delete the code that pertains to the out-of-range errors, and change the remaining code to reflect working with ListBoxes now. The subroutine for cmdbtnStart's Click event should be:

```
Sub cmdbtnStart_Click()
If Not IsNumeric(lstbxMilliseconds.Value) Then
    MsgBox "You must select a value for Milliseconds", 64, _
        "No Value Selected For Milliseconds"
    tmrSphere.Enabled = False
    Exit sub
End If

If Not IsNumeric(lstbxPixels.Value) Then
    MsgBox "You must select a value for Pixels", 64, _
        "No Value Selected For Pixels"
    tmrSphere.Enabled = False
    Exit sub
End If
tmrSphere.Enabled = True
```

Now let's address the listboxes. Specifically, we want to assign the functionality that we previously scripted for the textboxes to the listboxes instead—but without the error-trapping code. Error-trapping code is not necessary here because users will select from predefined values rather than enter values themselves.

In the Event pane, open the events for lstbxMilliseconds. Choose the Change event. Our goal is to attach the Change event to tmrSphere's Interval property. That is, whenever the value in lstbxMilliseconds changes (because the user has selected a new value), we want the new value to become the Timer's interval. Type this line in the Change event's subroutine:

tmrSphere.Interval = lstbxMilliseconds.Value

> **TIP**
>
> Here's a different way to enter that line into the Script pane (and save you a bit of typing). Double-click on `tmrSphere`'s Interval property in the Actions pane, type the equal sign (=), and then double-click on `lstbxMilliseconds`' Value property in the Actions pane.

Now take a look at tmrSphere's Timer event. In the Script pane, you'll see this line left over from the TextBox version:

```
imgSphere.Left = imgSphere.Left + txtbxPixels.Value
```

Of course, we want this line to work with lstbxPixels, so change it to:

```
imgSphere.Left = imgSphere.Left + lstbxPixels.Value
```

Here's where things get interesting. We have to *populate* the listboxes. In English, rather than computerese, that means we have to put values into the rows of the listboxes (10, 20, 50, 100, 200, and 300 into lstbxMilliseconds, and 2, 4,8, 12, 16, and 20 into lstbxPixels). Users will select one of these values in each control to run the animation. How do you put the values into the listboxes? Read on.

The trick is to invoke a particular method that is part and parcel of a ListBox control. This method, called *AddItem*, does just what its name suggests—it adds an item to a ListBox control. Each time you invoke the AddItem method, it adds another row to the control. AddItem can work with either one or two arguments. The first argument is the item to add to the ListBox. The (optional) second argument is the row in the ListBox to add it to. We'll work with just the first argument.

In order to use the AddItem method we have to attach it to an event. In the Event pane, click on the + next to layout_for_animation_with_listboxes. The layout's one event, OnLoad, becomes visible. This event occurs when you open up its Web page that used the Layout Control). We'll use the OnLoad event to add items to the listbox controls—or more accurately, we'll make OnLoad cause each listbox to add items to itself.

Select OnLoad and switch the Script Wizard into Code View. In the Actions pane, click on the + to the left of lstbxMilliseconds, and then double-click on the AddItem method. This line appears in the Script pane:

```
call lstbxMilliseconds.AddItem(pvargItem, pvargIndex)
```

Replace everything in the parentheses with the number **10**, representing the first millisecond value that we want in lstbxMilliseconds. Copy this line, paste it into the next line, and replace the 10 in the new line with **20**. In similar fashion, create subsequent lines for 50, 100, 200, and 300.

When you finish, go back to the Actions pane. Make sure that the cursor in the Script pane is on a new, blank line. Click on the + next to lstbxPixels and double-click on AddItem. This line appears in the Script pane:

```
call lstbxPixels.AddItem(pvargItem, pvargIndex)
```

Replace everything in the parentheses with **2**, the first pixel value for lstbxPixels. Use copy and paste techniques to create lines for 4, 8, 12, 16, and 20.

In the Script pane, the completed subroutine for the layout's OnLoad event should be:

```
Sub layout_for_animation_with_listboxes_OnLoad()
call lstbxMilliseconds.AddItem(10)
call lstbxMilliseconds.AddItem(20)
call lstbxMilliseconds.AddItem(50)
```

```
call lstbxMilliseconds.AddItem(100)
call lstbxMilliseconds.AddItem(200)
call lstbxMilliseconds.AddItem(300)
call lstbxPixels.AddItem(2)
call lstbxPixels.AddItem(4)
call lstbxPixels.AddItem(8)
call lstbxPixels.AddItem(12)
call lstbxPixels.AddItem(16)
call lstbxPixels.AddItem(20)
```

The result of all this code will be two ListBox controls filled with the values you specified. Click on OK to close the Script Wizard and return to the Layout Control.

The Animation Web Page

Save your work and open the `Animation With ListBoxes` Web page in IE. Select values from the ListBoxes, click the Start button and see the effects of the different values on the animation.

One of the convenient aspects of working with a listbox is the ability to type a character and have the highlight shift to the next row whose entry begins with that character. If no subsequent row has an entry that begins with that character, the highlight moves back to the previous one that does. This behavior results from the ListBox control's MatchEntry property. We've left it at the default value, 0-First Letter. Other possible values are 1-Complete (the ListBox looks for an entry that matches all the characters entered) and 2-None (no matching).

Figure 6.2 shows the Web page in action.

The Web page looks as it does because IE is rendering this code for the layout (`layout for animation with listboxes.alx`).

 layout for animation with listboxes.alx

```
<SCRIPT LANGUAGE="VBScript">
<!--
Sub cmdbtnStop_Click()
tmrSphere.Enabled = 0
end sub
-->
</SCRIPT>
<SCRIPT LANGUAGE="VBScript">
<!--
Sub cmdbtnStart_Click()
```

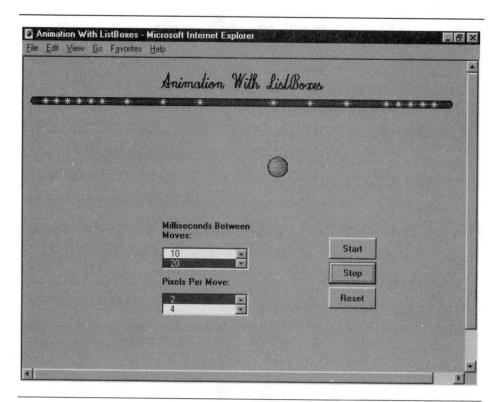

FIGURE 6.2: The Animation With ListBoxes Web page. Scrollbars help you navigate through the ListBox controls.

```
If Not IsNumeric(lstbxMilliseconds.Value) Then
    MsgBox "You must select a value for Milliseconds", 64, _
        "No Value Selected For Milliseconds"
    tmrSphere.Enabled = False
    Exit sub
End If

If Not IsNumeric(lstbxPixels.Value) Then
    MsgBox "You must select a value for Pixels", 64, _
        "No Value Selected For Pixels"
    tmrSphere.Enabled = False
    Exit sub
End If

tmrSphere.Enabled = True
end sub
```

```
-->
</SCRIPT>
<SCRIPT LANGUAGE="VBScript">
<!--
Sub cmdbtnReset_Click()
imgSphere.Left = 66
end sub
-->
</SCRIPT>
<SCRIPT LANGUAGE="VBScript">
<!--
Sub tmrSphere_Timer()
imgSphere.Left = imgSphere.Left + lstbxPixels.Value
end sub
-->
</SCRIPT>
<SCRIPT LANGUAGE="VBScript">
<!--
Sub layout_for_animation_with_listboxes_OnLoad()
call lstbxMilliseconds.AddItem(10)
call lstbxMilliseconds.AddItem(20)
call lstbxMilliseconds.AddItem(50)
call lstbxMilliseconds.AddItem(100)
call lstbxMilliseconds.AddItem(200)
call lstbxMilliseconds.AddItem(300)
call lstbxPixels.AddItem(2)
call lstbxPixels.AddItem(4)
call lstbxPixels.AddItem(8)
call lstbxPixels.AddItem(12)
call lstbxPixels.AddItem(16)
call lstbxPixels.AddItem(20)

end sub
-->
</SCRIPT>
<SCRIPT LANGUAGE="VBScript">
<!--
Sub lstbxMilliseconds_Change()
tmrSphere.Interval = lstbxMilliseconds.Value
end sub
-->
</SCRIPT>
<DIV ID="layout_for_animation_with_listboxes"
➥STYLE="LAYOUT:FIXED;WIDTH:477pt;HEIGHT:293pt;">
    <OBJECT ID="tmrSphere"
     CLASSID="CLSID:59CCB4A0-727D-11CF-AC36-00AA00A47DD2"
     ➥STYLE="TOP:91pt;LEFT:8pt;WIDTH:66pt;HEIGHT:50pt;ZINDEX:0;">
        <PARAM NAME="_ExtentX" VALUE="2328">
```

Skill 6

```
        <PARAM NAME="_ExtentY" VALUE="1773">
        <PARAM NAME="Interval" VALUE="100">
        <PARAM NAME="Enabled" VALUE="False">
</OBJECT>
<OBJECT ID="imgSphere"
 CLASSID="CLSID:D4A97620-8E8F-11CF-93CD-00AA00C08FDF"
➡STYLE="TOP:50pt;LEFT:66pt;WIDTH:20pt;HEIGHT:20pt;ZINDEX:1;">
        <PARAM NAME="PicturePath" VALUE=
        ➡"E:\ActiveX No Exp Req\graphics\small\ltb5.gif">
        <PARAM NAME="AutoSize" VALUE="-1">
        <PARAM NAME="BorderStyle" VALUE="0">
        <PARAM NAME="SizeMode" VALUE="3">
        <PARAM NAME="Size" VALUE="688;688">
        <PARAM NAME="VariousPropertyBits" VALUE="17">
</OBJECT>
<OBJECT ID="cmdbtnStart"
 CLASSID="CLSID:D7053240-CE69-11CD-A777-00DD01143C57"
➡STYLE="TOP:132pt;LEFT:314pt;WIDTH:50pt;HEIGHT:22pt;TABINDEX:0;ZINDEX:2;">
        <PARAM NAME="Caption" VALUE="Start">
        <PARAM NAME="Size" VALUE="1764;776">
        <PARAM NAME="FontEffects" VALUE="1073741825">
        <PARAM NAME="FontCharSet" VALUE="0">
        <PARAM NAME="FontPitchAndFamily" VALUE="2">
        <PARAM NAME="ParagraphAlign" VALUE="3">
        <PARAM NAME="FontWeight" VALUE="700">
</OBJECT>
<OBJECT ID="cmdbtnStop"
 CLASSID="CLSID:D7053240-CE69-11CD-A777-00DD01143C57"
➡STYLE="TOP:157pt;LEFT:314pt;WIDTH:50pt;HEIGHT:22pt;TABINDEX:1;ZINDEX:3;">
        <PARAM NAME="Caption" VALUE="Stop">
        <PARAM NAME="Size" VALUE="1764;776">
        <PARAM NAME="FontEffects" VALUE="1073741825">
        <PARAM NAME="FontCharSet" VALUE="0">
        <PARAM NAME="FontPitchAndFamily" VALUE="2">
        <PARAM NAME="ParagraphAlign" VALUE="3">
        <PARAM NAME="FontWeight" VALUE="700">
</OBJECT>
<OBJECT ID="cmdbtnReset"
 CLASSID="CLSID:D7053240-CE69-11CD-A777-00DD01143C57"
➡STYLE="TOP:182pt;LEFT:314pt;WIDTH:50pt;HEIGHT:22pt;TABINDEX:2;ZINDEX:4;">
        <PARAM NAME="Caption" VALUE="Reset">
        <PARAM NAME="Size" VALUE="1764;776">
        <PARAM NAME="FontEffects" VALUE="1073741825">
        <PARAM NAME="FontCharSet" VALUE="0">
        <PARAM NAME="FontPitchAndFamily" VALUE="2">
        <PARAM NAME="ParagraphAlign" VALUE="3">
        <PARAM NAME="FontWeight" VALUE="700">
</OBJECT>
```

```
<OBJECT ID="lblMilliseconds"
 CLASSID="CLSID:978C9E23-D4B0-11CE-BF2D-00AA003F40D0"
➡STYLE="TOP:116pt;LEFT:140pt;WIDTH:107pt;HEIGHT:25pt;ZINDEX:5;">
    <PARAM NAME="Caption" VALUE="Milliseconds Between Moves:">
    <PARAM NAME="Size" VALUE="3775;882">
    <PARAM NAME="FontEffects" VALUE="1073741825">
    <PARAM NAME="FontCharSet" VALUE="0">
    <PARAM NAME="FontPitchAndFamily" VALUE="2">
    <PARAM NAME="FontWeight" VALUE="700">
</OBJECT>
<OBJECT ID="lblPixels"
 CLASSID="CLSID:978C9E23-D4B0-11CE-BF2D-00AA003F40D0"
➡STYLE="TOP:173pt;LEFT:140pt;WIDTH:83pt;HEIGHT:17pt;ZINDEX:6;">
    <PARAM NAME="Caption" VALUE="Pixels Per Move:">
    <PARAM NAME="Size" VALUE="2928;600">
    <PARAM NAME="FontEffects" VALUE="1073741825">
    <PARAM NAME="FontCharSet" VALUE="0">
    <PARAM NAME="FontPitchAndFamily" VALUE="2">
    <PARAM NAME="FontWeight" VALUE="700">
</OBJECT>
<OBJECT ID="lstbxMilliseconds"
 CLASSID="CLSID:8BD21D20-EC42-11CE-9E0D-00AA006002F3"
➡STYLE="TOP:143pt;LEFT:140pt;WIDTH:91pt;HEIGHT:25pt;TABINDEX:5;ZINDEX:7;">
    <PARAM NAME="ScrollBars" VALUE="3">
    <PARAM NAME="DisplayStyle" VALUE="2">
    <PARAM NAME="Size" VALUE="3210;882">
    <PARAM NAME="MatchEntry" VALUE="0">
    <PARAM NAME="FontCharSet" VALUE="0">
    <PARAM NAME="FontPitchAndFamily" VALUE="2">
    <PARAM NAME="FontWeight" VALUE="0">
</OBJECT>
<OBJECT ID="lstbxPixels"
 CLASSID="CLSID:8BD21D20-EC42-11CE-9E0D-00AA006002F3"
➡STYLE="TOP:190pt;LEFT:140pt;WIDTH:91pt;HEIGHT:25pt;TABINDEX:6;ZINDEX:8;">
    <PARAM NAME="ScrollBars" VALUE="3">
    <PARAM NAME="DisplayStyle" VALUE="2">
    <PARAM NAME="Size" VALUE="3210;882">
    <PARAM NAME="MatchEntry" VALUE="0">
    <PARAM NAME="FontCharSet" VALUE="0">
    <PARAM NAME="FontPitchAndFamily" VALUE="2">
    <PARAM NAME="FontWeight" VALUE="0">
</OBJECT>
</DIV>
```

Skill 6

When you examine your code for this ALX file, you'll probably see some sub-routines for TextBox controls left over from the previous version. Just delete them (along with their tags) and save the file.

ComboBoxes

Suppose we find that people who use our animation Web page enjoy selecting values from the listboxes and seeing the resulting animation effects. Suppose, however, that they also tell us they would occasionally like to enter a millisecond value or a pixel value that we didn't put into the listboxes.

To accommodate them, we'd need a control that combines the flexibility of a textbox with the selection capabilities of a listbox. The ComboBox control does just that. Let's now explore this control.

Setting Up

By now, you probably know how to do the Reusability Shuffle. To create a Web page that uses ComboBox controls, follow these steps:

1. Start with the HTML file we just created, `Animation With ListBoxes`.

2. Save the file in `skill 6` as `Animation With ComboBoxes`.

3. Update the title and the heading to reflect the change.

4. Open the Layout Control and save it as `layout for animation with comboboxes` in `skill 6`.

5. View the Source Code in Notepad and change the ID attribute of the <DIV> tag to **layout_for_animation_with_comboboxes**.

6. Save the Source Code, close Notepad, return to the Text Editor, and open the HTML Layout Control.

7. In the Layout Control, delete the ListBox controls and replace them with ComboBox controls.

8. Position the ComboBoxes where the ListBoxes used to be. Give one an ID of **cmbbxMilliseconds** and give the other an ID of **cmbbxPixels**.

9. Open the Script Wizard.

In the Script Wizard, we have to replace the error-trapping functionality that we removed from the ListBox version. We do this because users are free to enter any value they like in the ComboBox controls.

Start with the Click event for cmdbtnStart. With all the error-trapping functionality, the subroutine for this event should be:

```
Sub cmdbtnStart_Click()
If Not IsNumeric(cmbbxMilliseconds.Value) Then
MsgBox "You must supply a value for Milliseconds", 64, _
```

```
                      "No Value Selected Or Entered For Milliseconds"
          tmrSphere.Enabled = False
          Exit sub
    End If

    If Not IsNumeric(cmbbxPixels.Value) Then
        MsgBox "You must supply a value for Pixels", 64, _
              "No Value Selected Or Entered For Pixels"
        tmrSphere.Enabled = False
        Exit sub
    End If

    tmrSphere.Enabled = True
```

Make the necessary changes in the Script pane.

On to the ComboBoxes. In the Event pane, open the events for cmbbxMilliseconds. Select the Change event. Edit the Script pane so that it winds up looking like this:

```
Sub cmbbxMilliseconds_Change()
If Not IsNumeric(cmbbxMilliseconds.Value) Then
MsgBox "You must enter a numeric value or select a value", _
    64, "Wrong Type for Milliseconds"
Exit Sub
End If
tmrSphere.Interval = cmbbxMilliseconds.Value
In the Event pane, select the Change event for cmbbxPixels. Edit the
Script pane to produce:
Sub cmbbxPixels_Change()
If Not IsNumeric(cmbbxPixels.Value) Then
MsgBox "You must enter a numeric value or select a value", _
    64, "Wrong Type for Pixels"
Exit Sub
End If
```

Change the subroutine for tmrSphere's Timer event to read:

```
Sub tmrSphere_Timer()
imgSphere.Left = imgSphere.Left + cmbbxPixels.Value
```

Finally, script the subroutine for populating the ComboBoxes the same way we populated the ListBoxes. In the Event pane, click on the + next to layout_for_animation_with_comboboxes. Click on the OnLoad event. In Code View, change the code in the Script pane to create:

```
Sub layout_for_animation_with_comboboxes_OnLoad()
call cmbbxMilliseconds.AddItem(10)
call cmbbxMilliseconds.AddItem(20)
call cmbbxMilliseconds.AddItem(50)
call cmbbxMilliseconds.AddItem(100)
call cmbbxMilliseconds.AddItem(200)
call cmbbxMilliseconds.AddItem(300)
```

Skill 6

```
call cmbbxPixels.AddItem(2)
call cmbbxPixels.AddItem(4)
call cmbbxPixels.AddItem(8)
call cmbbxPixels.AddItem(12)
call cmbbxPixels.AddItem(16)
call cmbbxPixels.AddItem(20)
```

Again, you can use copy and paste techniques to help you along.

Click on OK to close the Script Wizard. Save your work in the HTML Layout Control.

The ComboBox Web Page

Open the Web page in IE. You'll see a page that looks like Figure 6.3. Note the down-arrow on the right side of each combobox. Clicking this arrow produces a drop-down list of the values in the combobox. You can also enter a value that's not in the list. To test your error-trapping code, enter alphabetic characters and perform other actions that bring on error messages.

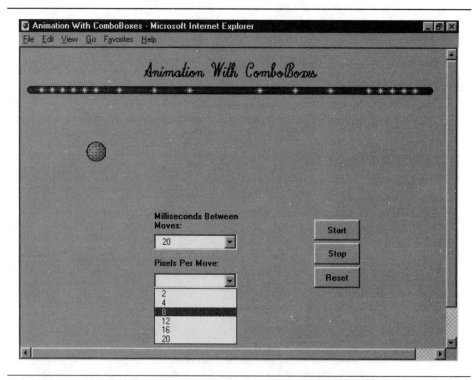

FIGURE 6.3: The Web page for Animation With ComboBoxes

Option Buttons

We now turn our attention to another vehicle for interacting with users. The *option button* is popular because a group of them displays all the possible choices at the same time. Because this type of onscreen device is intuitive, it's reminiscent of the type of button you'd find on a prehistoric car radio. In fact, the term "radio buttons" refers to a group of option buttons set up so the user can select only one—just like using a button on a radio to select a station.

Grouping radio buttons is a natural way to present the possible values for our animation application—that is, if (as in the ListBox version) we can narrow the set of choices down to a manageable number. We can use one group of radio buttons to represent the values for milliseconds, and another to represent the values for pixels. A user can select from each group, hit the Start button, and watch the animation. For this exercise, we'll use the same millisecond values and pixel values we used for the previous exercises.

Reusing Reusability

Again, we'll start with the Reusability Shuffle. To create a Web page using radio buttons, follow these steps:

1. In the ActiveX Control Panel's Text Editor, open `Animation With ComboBoxes.htm`.

2. Save the file in `skill 6` as `Animation With Option Buttons`.

3. Update the title and the heading to reflect the change.

4. Open the Layout Control and save it as `layout for animation with option buttons` in `skill 6`.

5. View the Source Code in Notepad and change the ID attribute of the <DIV> tag to **layout_for_animation_with_option_buttons**.

6. Save the Source Code and return to the Text Editor.

Laying It All Out

Our objective is to build a layout that looks like Figure 6.4.

Begin by opening the HTML Layout Control. Delete the two ComboBox controls and reposition the Labels controls so lblMilliseconds is to the left of lblPixels. Use the sizing handles on lblPixels to make it narrower and force the word "Move" onto another line. That way, the labels look more like each other (an important User Interface detail for two labels side-by-side). Position both labels at about the level of the Start button.

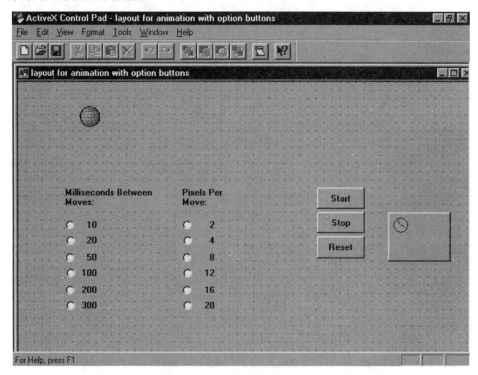

FIGURE 6.4: The layout for Animation With Option Buttons

Now select an Option Button control from the Toolbox and position it below lblMilliseconds. In its Properties Sheet, give it an ID of **optbtn10Milliseconds**. Set the GroupName to **Milliseconds**. If a group of Option Buttons has the same GroupName, selecting one makes it impossible to select another at the same time.

Use copy and paste techniques to create and position five more Option Buttons and line them up under the first one. Give each one an ID that indicates its associated millisecond value:

- optbtn20Milliseconds

- optbtn50Milliseconds

- optbtn100 Milliseconds

- optbtn200Milliseconds
- optbtn300Milliseconds

Create a label (a Microsoft Forms 2.0 Label) for each button (again, after the first one, use the copy and paste methods), and give each one an ID that lets you know what it stands for: lbl10Milliseconds, lbl20Milliseconds, … , lbl300Milliseconds. Put each Label to the immediate right of its option button. Give each one the appropriate caption (in other words, the number of milliseconds for the radio button right next to it) and make the caption bold. It's also a good idea to use the Properties sheets to align the text to the right within each label.

When you finish setting up the buttons and labels under lblMilliseconds, repeat the process and create option buttons and labels to form columns below lblPixels. The easiest way to do this is select as a group all the buttons and labels you just created, Ctrl+C (to copy the group), and Ctrl+V or Shift+Ins (to paste the group).

Move the new group of labels and buttons so they sit below lblPixels. Our pixel values, as before, are 2, 4, 8, 12, 16, and 20. Analogous to the IDs we set up for the Milliseconds buttons and labels, make sure the IDs for the buttons and labels reflect the pixel values, and make sure these new buttons all have **Pixels** as the value for their GroupName. Your layout should now resemble Figure 6.4.

Writing the Script

We now build the VBS that assigns functionality to the Option Buttons—functionality we formerly assigned to TextBoxes, ListBoxes, and ComboBoxes.

Open the Script Wizard and open the events for optbtn100Milliseconds. When the user clicks on this button, we want the value of tmrSphere's Interval to change to 100 milliseconds. To script this, select the Click event. In the Actions pane, open the methods and properties for tmrSphere and double-click on Interval. In the dialog box that opens and asks you for a value for Interval, type **100** and click OK. Follow the same steps for the other Milliseconds Option Buttons, and type the appropriate values.

Skill 6

For the Pixels Options Buttons, we've come to a little impasse. In the previous versions, we've always had a variable—either txtbxPixels.Value, lstbxPixels.Value, or cbbxPixels.Value—that stored the number of pixels that the image advances. We had this luxury because the Value property of a single object acted as the variable. When the value changed, the variable changed, and the image advanced the correct amount because of the statement:

```
imgSphere.Left = imgSphere.Left + Object.Value
```

Now we don't have just one object to deal with—either for the Pixels or the Milliseconds—we have six for each. The problem is that we still require a single value for the right side of the statement that modifies imgSphere.Left. Put another way, when we click on one of the Milliseconds Option Buttons we change a value, tmrSphere.Interval. When we click on a Pixels Option Button, we don't have an analogous value to change. So we'll just have to create one.

We'll use a VBS concept that we haven't looked at yet: the *global variable*. A global variable is a variable that all the subroutines and functions in a script can work with. (By contrast, a *local* variable can only live and work in one subroutine or function.) We'll create a global variable that stores the value when someone clicks a Pixels Option Button. Then we'll use that value to modify imgSphere.Left.

The Script Wizard gives us an easy way to create global variables. In the Actions pane, you'll see an object called Global Variables. Right-click on this object and a pop-up menu appears. In this menu, click on New Global Variable…. A dialog box opens, asking you to supply a name for the new variable. Type **glblvarPixels** and click OK. From now on, when you click on the + next to the Global Variables object, glblvarPixels will appear. Figure 6.5 shows the new global variable in the Actions pane.

The variable's prefix, glblvar, indicates that we've created a global variable, and the rest of the name tells us what the variable is for. We'll write a script that changes the value of that variable in response to the Click event for each Pixels Option button.

We'll use our new global variable in the statement that modifies the value of imgSphere.Left:

```
imgSphere.Left = imgSphere.Left + glblvarPixels
```

Put the Script Wizard in List View. In the Actions pane, click on the + next to Global Variables to make our variable appear. In the Event pane, find each Option Button that sets a value for pixels. Find each one's Click event and in the Actions pane, double-click on glblvarPixels. In the dialog box that opens, type the appropriate number (for optnbtn2Pixels type **2**, for optnbtn4Pixels type **4**, and so on).

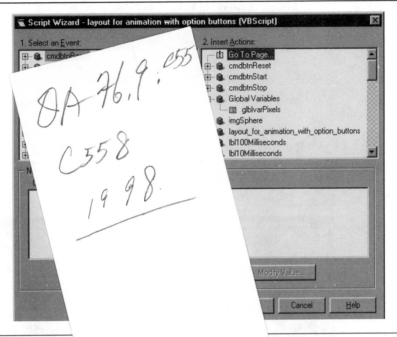

FIGURE 6.5: ░░░░░░░░░░░░░░░░░░░░░░░░░░░ ike glblvarPixels, you can see it in the Actions pa░

Now let's turn our ░░░░░░░░░░░░░░░░░░░░. The Stop button and the Reset button are the sa░░░░░░░░░░░░░░░░ addition to kicking off the animation, has to t░░░░░░░░░░░░░░ on Start with no value selected for either para░░░░

This could happen wh░░░░░░░░░░░░░ the page opens, the value of tmrSphere.Inter░░░░░░░░░░░░░s is empty, because nothing has been assigned to i░░░░░░░░░░tart's Click event, we test for both conditions. The test for glblva░░ixels depends on *IsEmpty*, a VBS function that returns "True" if its argument is empty (if it has never had a value assigned to it), "False" otherwise.

In Code View, update the Click event of cmdbtnStart to read:

```
Sub cmdbtnStart_Click()
If tmrSphere.Interval = 0 Then
    MsgBox "You must select a value for Milliseconds", 64, _
        "No Value Selected For Milliseconds"
    tmrSphere.Enabled = False
    Exit sub
End If
```

```
If IsEmpty(glblvarPixels) Then
    MsgBox "You must select a value for Pixels", 64, _
        "No Value Selected  For Pixels"
    tmrSphere.Enabled = False
    Exit sub
End If

tmrSphere.Enabled = True
```

Close the Script Wizard and save your work in the HTML Layout Control. Open the Web page in IE, and when it first opens click on Start to check our error-traps. Work with the Options Buttons to set the parameters of the animation and note the effects of different combinations. Figure 6.6 shows the Web page in IE.

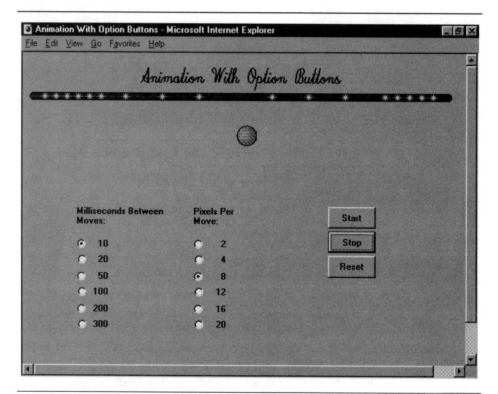

FIGURE 6.6: The Option Buttons Web page in IE

Here's most of the code for layout for option buttons.alx. (I've cut out the long, long HTML for the labels and buttons.) It's instructive to look through this because it will show you how the Script Wizard inserts a global variable into VBS. I've inserted a comment to highlight it for you.

```
<SCRIPT LANGUAGE="VBScript">
<!--
Sub cmdbtnStop_Click()
tmrSphere.Enabled = 0
end sub
-->
</SCRIPT>
<SCRIPT LANGUAGE="VBScript">
<!--
Sub cmdbtnStart_Click()
If tmrSphere.Interval = 0 Then
    MsgBox "You must select a value for Milliseconds", 64, _
        "No Value Selected For Milliseconds"
    tmrSphere.Enabled = False
    Exit sub
End If

If IsEmpty(glblvarPixels) Then
    MsgBox "You must select a value for Pixels", 64, _
        "No Value Selected  For Pixels"
    tmrSphere.Enabled = False
    Exit sub
End If

tmrSphere.Enabled = True
end sub
-->
</SCRIPT>
<SCRIPT LANGUAGE="VBScript">
<!--
Sub cmdbtnReset_Click()
imgSphere.Left = 66
end sub
-->
</SCRIPT>
<SCRIPT LANGUAGE="VBScript">
<!--
Sub tmrSphere_Timer()
imgSphere.Left = imgSphere.Left + glblvarPixels
end sub
-->
</SCRIPT>
<SCRIPT LANGUAGE="VBScript">
<!--
```

```
'========================================
'      The global variable follows
'========================================

dim glblvarPixels

Sub cmbbxMilliseconds_Change()
If Not IsNumeric(cmbbxMilliseconds.Value) Then
    MsgBox "You must enter a numeric value or select a value", 64, _
        "Wrong Type for Milliseconds"
    Exit Sub
End If

tmrSphere.Interval = cmbbxMilliseconds.Value
end sub
-->
</SCRIPT>
<SCRIPT LANGUAGE="VBScript">
<!--
Sub optbtn8Pixels_Click()
glblvarPixels = 8
end sub
-->
</SCRIPT>
<SCRIPT LANGUAGE="VBScript">
<!--
Sub optbtn4Pixels_Click()
glblvarPixels = 4
end sub
-->
</SCRIPT>
<SCRIPT LANGUAGE="VBScript">
<!--
Sub optbtn2Pixels_Click()
glblvarPixels = 2
end sub
-->
</SCRIPT>
<SCRIPT LANGUAGE="VBScript">
<!--
Sub optbtn20Pixels_Click()
glblvarPixels = 20
end sub
-->
</SCRIPT>
<SCRIPT LANGUAGE="VBScript">
<!--
Sub optbtn16Pixels_Click()
glblvarPixels = 16
end sub
```

```
-->
</SCRIPT>
<SCRIPT LANGUAGE="VBScript">
<!--
Sub optbtn12Pixels_Click()
glblvarPixels = 12
end sub
-->
</SCRIPT>
<SCRIPT LANGUAGE="VBScript">
<!--
Sub optbtn100Milliseconds_Click()
tmrSphere.Interval = 100
end sub
-->
</SCRIPT>
<SCRIPT LANGUAGE="VBScript">
<!--
Sub optbtn50Milliseconds_Click()
tmrSphere.Interval = 50
end sub
-->
</SCRIPT>
<SCRIPT LANGUAGE="VBScript">
<!--
Sub optbtn300Milliseconds_Click()
tmrSphere.Interval = 300
end sub
-->
</SCRIPT>
<SCRIPT LANGUAGE="VBScript">
<!--
Sub optbtn20Milliseconds_Click()
tmrSphere.Interval = 20
end sub
-->
</SCRIPT>
<SCRIPT LANGUAGE="VBScript">
<!--
Sub optbtn200Milliseconds_Click()
tmrSphere.Interval = 200
end sub
-->
</SCRIPT>
<SCRIPT LANGUAGE="VBScript">
<!--
Sub optbtn10Milliseconds_Click()
tmrSphere.Interval = 10
end sub
```

Skill 6

```
-->
</SCRIPT>
<DIV ID="layout_for_animation_with_option_buttons"
            .
            .
            .
      [HTML for objects]
            .
            .
            .
</DIV>
```

Tying It All Together: A PopUp Menu

Textboxes, listboxes, comboboxes, option buttons… all of these enable users to make choices. One of the most familiar mechanisms, however, is one we haven't dealt with yet—the menu. One type of menu is the *pop-up menu*, a menu that appears when you click inside a window or a Web page. In the preceding section, we used a pop-up menu in the Script Wizard to create a global variable when we right-clicked on Global Variables in the Actions pane.

Let's put together a Web page that uses a pop-up menu to take us to the Web pages we built in this Skill. (If the PopUp Menu Object isn't in your list of available ActiveX controls, visit the Microsoft ActiveX Component Gallery Web site to download it.) In the Text Editor, create a new document and save it as Animation Home Page. Make this the title of the page as well. Create a centered <H1> heading that says **The Fabulous Animation Home Page!**, and follow the heading with an <HR> tag. Create a new HTML Layout and save it as **layout for animation home page**.

In this layout, select a Label control from the Toolbox and center it. The Label is going to display the text for this page, so make it wide (about 150) and tall (around 200). Give the Label an ID of lblAnimation. Make its BackColor white, and its Font 14 pt Comic Sans MS. To set the Label's Caption, click on the Label, and when diagonal stripes appear on its borders, type (directly into the Label): **Welcome to the Fabulous Animation Home Page! Click anywhere in this white space to get a PopUp Menu. The Menu presents a variety of ways to enter parameters for an animation!** Set the TextAlign property to 2-Center, and set the SpecialEffect to Bump (or some other effect, if you prefer).

From the Toolbox, select the PopUp Menu control. Position it anywhere. Don't use sizing handles to make it larger than its original appearance. In its Properties sheet, in fact, make sure that its Height and Width are both zero and give it an ID of ppmnuAnimation. Your layout should now look like Figure 6.7.

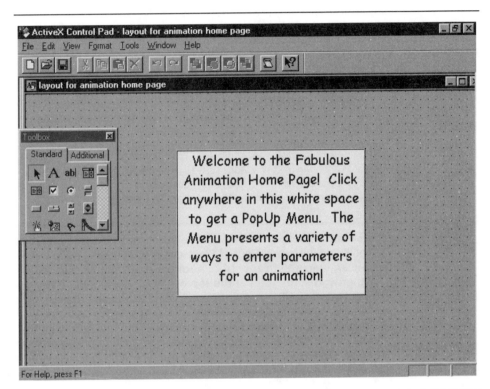

FIGURE 6.7: The layout for the animation home page

Open the Script Wizard, and put it in Code View. We want users to be able to click anywhere in the Label and pop up the menu. Make the Label's Click event appear in the Event pane and select it. In the Actions pane, open ppmnuAnimation's methods and properties. With the Label's Click event selected, double-click on the PopUp method to make the menu pop-up contingent on clicking in the Label. If you don't specify where you want the menu to pop up, it opens with its upper-left corner at the coordinates of the cursor.

Now let's populate the menu. Each menu choice will correspond to one of the pages we designed. Just as we did when we populated ListBoxes and ComboBoxes, we use the menu's AddItem method in the Layout's OnLoad event. Follow these steps:

1. Make sure that the Script Wizard is in Code View.

2. In the Event pane, make the Layout's OnLoad event visible, and select it.

3. In the Actions pane, make the PopUp Menu's AddItem method visible and double-click on it.

This line appears in the Script pane:

```
call ppmnuAnimation.AddItem(item, index)
```

The first argument is a string that represents the menu choice, the optional second argument indicates the choice's position in the menu. If you don't give a value for the second argument, the item just gets appended as the last item in the menu. Type this code into the Script pane for the OnLoad subroutine:

```
Sub layoutforanimationhomepage_OnLoad()
call ppmnuAnimation.AddItem("TextBoxes")
call ppmnuAnimation.AddItem("ListBoxes")
call ppmnuAnimation.AddItem("ComboBoxes")
call ppmnuAnimation.AddItem("Option Buttons")
```

TIP   Documentation about the AddItem event for ListBoxes and ComboBoxes (which you'll find in Help ≻ Control Pad Help Topics) leads you to believe that the second argument to this control's AddItem event should start at 0, rather than 1. In other words, the item at the top of the menu should be the zeroth item. This turns out to not be the case. If you give the second argument a value of zero— for example, *call ppmnuAnimation.AddItem("TextBoxes",0)*—the menu puts "TextBoxes" at the bottom rather than the top, and has no idea what you mean if you click on this choice. So if you want to include a value for the second argument, start at 1 instead of 0. Go figure.

Now that we've populated the menu, we've got one more piece of business to take care of to make the pop-up menu functional. When someone clicks on the menu, we have to know what he or she clicked so we can make something happen as a result.

The menu's Click event is set up to provide the necessary information. It works with one argument, the row number of the selected item. That is, when a user makes a menu selection, the Click event tells us the selection's row. If we find that the user selects "TextBoxes," (in row 1 of the menu) we'll open the TextBox page, if the selection is "Option Buttons" (row 4) we'll open the Options Button page, and so on.

The appropriate VBS structure for this task is Select Case, which we worked with in the previous Skill. We'll use Select Case test the selected row and open one of the four Web pages depending on which row the user selected. Select the ppmnuAnimation Click event and add code to the Script pane (in Code View) to produce:

```
Sub ppmnuAnimation_Click(item)
Select Case item
Case 1
```

```
Window.location.href =
➡"E:\ActiveX No Exp Req\skill 5\Animation With TextBoxes.htm"
Case 2
Window.location.href =
➡"E:\ActiveX No Exp Req\skill 6\Animation With ListBoxes.htm"
Case 3
Window.location.href =
➡"E:\ActiveX No Exp Req\skill 6\Animation WithComboBoxes.htm"
Case 4
Window.location.href =
➡"E:\ActiveX No Exp Req\skill 6\Animation With Option Buttons.htm"
End Select
```

Note that in the first case we open a file in skill 5, and in the others we open files in skill 6.

Save your work and open the Web page in IE. Click anywhere in the Label, and then click on any choice in the menu. Figure 6.8 shows what the display looks like.

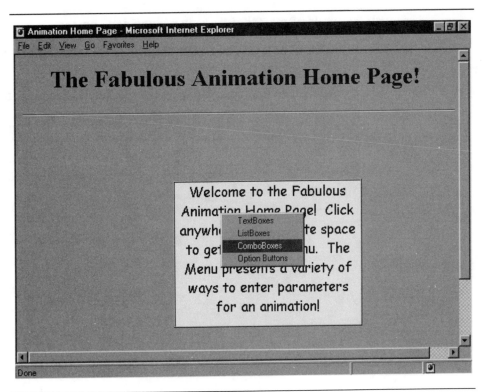

FIGURE 6.8: The Animation home page

Taking Stock

In addition to a variety of ActiveX controls, you've also seen a substantial number of VBS concepts (`Select Case`, `If...Then`, global variables). What we've done thus far will enable you to build some pretty sharp-looking Web pages with a lot of interactivity.

In the next Skill, we'll explore ways to display some concepts that go beyond straightforward graphics. Stay tuned.

Are You Experienced?

Now you can...

- ☑ set up ListBoxes that display predefined choices

- ☑ build ComboBoxes that combine the power of ListBoxes with the flexibility of TextBoxes

- ☑ create Option Buttons and group them into sets of radio buttons

- ☑ use the Script Wizard to create and work with global variables

- ☑ program PopUp Menus

- ☑ use the AddItem method to populate ListBoxes, ComboBoxes, and Menus

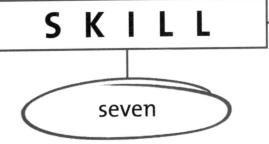

S K I L L

seven

Displaying Data, Documents, and Ideas

7

If you've followed along with the exercises in the previous Skills, you can display images, text, and controls that result in some great-looking Web pages. Sometimes, however, it's necessary to go even further by embedding visual displays of data into a Web page.

Some Web sites, like those for government agencies and regulatory bodies, must show documents in formats that resemble the originals. Figure 7.1 shows you what I mean. This document is from the Consumer Product Safety Commission, a federal agency that regulates consumer products with the goal of maximizing safety.

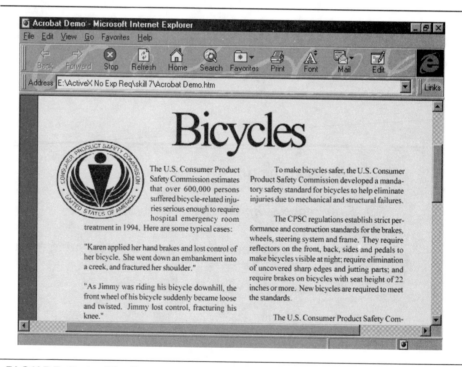

FIGURE 7.1: The Consumer Product Safety Commission's Web site displays documents that resemble the originals.

With a new generation of ActiveX tools emerging, still other Web sites can display interactive diagrams that depict models and processes and allow users to diagram their own ideas. This Skill gives you a chance to work with tools that build on your knowledge and go beyond buttons, graphics, and text.

Charting a Course

People have used charts from time immemorial to present easily understandable summaries of complex sets of data. It's been my experience that people typically prefer a picture to a table, a chart to a dataset, a graph to a report.

One of the great aspects of the Web (and ActiveX in particular) is its tendency to adapt to people's preferences. Designers of Web sites use images that are familiar and comfortable to help draw attention to the pages they build. ActiveX controls are often based on everyday objects transformed into onscreen objects whose functionality mirrors the objects they mimic.

This is the case with ActiveX controls that present visual representations of data. The controls offer familiar chart formats that most of us have seen before and can intuitively understand. Some of them go above and beyond, offering newer formats that exploit today's technology, but the basis for these styles is still the simple chart that we all learned long ago.

The Microsoft Chart Control

The first control we'll explore is Microsoft's Chart control. Originally a part of the Internet Explorer 3 package, Microsoft is phasing this control out. It is still available via automatic download, however, so sites that use it will function properly.

We include this control in our discussion to introduce you to a data visualization control that you can download. The idea is to give you an understanding of these types of controls if you have to use a commercially available Chart control (or this Chart) in your own work.

Setting Up the Chart

Imagine a fictional institution of higher learning called the University of Cyberspace. A fully accredited university, UC conducts its lectures, classes, seminars, and exams on the Web. Within the virtually hallowed halls of its Net-based campus are Divisions of Arts & Sciences (A&S), Engineering (Eng), Education (Ed), Medicine (Med), and Law. UC has been a thriving institution since 1994, and its administration has tracked enrollment in each of its divisions since the day the virtual doors opened. Table 7.1 shows the figures year-by-year.

TABLE 7.1: Yearly Enrollment by Division at the University of Cyberspace

	A&S	Eng	Ed	Med	Law
1994	1200	1650	1550	820	1010
1995	1350	1700	1480	850	1150
1996	1420	1760	1495	840	1180
1997	1465	1800	1490	845	1185

UC wants to build a Web page that displays these enrollment numbers. Let's set up a Web page that illustrates these figures in a Chart control along with ListBox controls. This will allow us to examine different types of charts and vary the way it looks.

Open the ActiveX Control Pad. In the Text Editor, open a new file and save it as UC in skill 7. Change the title to **The University of Cyberspace**, give it a centered <H1> heading of **Enrollment at the University of Cyberspace**, and follow it with an <HR> tag.

The next step is to open the HTML Layout Control. Since we're starting from scratch, set up a new layout, call it layout for UC, and save it in skill 7. Open this layout (click the symbol to the left of <OBJECT> in UC.htm) and select the Chart control from the Toolbox. If this control isn't in your Toolbox, right-click on the Toolbox page and select Additional Controls…. Scroll down the list until you find Chart Object (or Microsoft IE 3.0 Chart) and click on the checkbox next to it to add it to the Toolbox.

TIP   If you have neither Microsoft IE 3.0 Chart nor Chart Object, open UC.htm at the No Experience Required area on the Sybex Web site. The Codebase property that I've written into the Chart Object will download it for you.

Select the Chart control and position it slightly to the left of center and drag it out to a height of about 225 and a width of about 320. Let's now open the Properties sheet and specify some of the characteristics of the chart. First, let's give the chart an ID of **chrtUC**. Next, we'll set the ChartType property. The Chart control offers 21 types; the most straightforward one for our purposes is 11-Simple Column Chart.

It's important to specify the number of rows and the number of columns to put in the chrtUC control. In the Properties sheet, set the Columns property to **5** (the five divisions at UC). Set the Rows property to **4**.

If you expand the Properties sheet vertically, it will look something like Figure 7.2. Two properties above Rows, you'll see the RowIndex property (which I've highlighted in Figure 7.2). Notice that it's 0 (zero), and that the RowName property just below it is R0. At the top of the Properties sheet, you'll see that the ColumnIndex property is also 0 and that ColumnName is C0. This indexing (keeping track of row number and column number) begins at zero, and it lets you know the default names of the rows and columns.

Properties	
Apply	0
ColumnIndex	0
ColumnName	C 0
Columns	5
DataItem	9
DisplayLegend	1 - On
ForeColor	32768
GridPlacement	0 - Bottom
Height	222.75
hgridStyle	0 - No Grid
HorizontalAxis	0
ID	chrtUC
Left	17
RowIndex	0
RowName	R 0
Rows	4
Scale	100
Top	33
URL	
VerticalAxis	200
vgridStyle	0 - No Grid
Visible	-1 - True

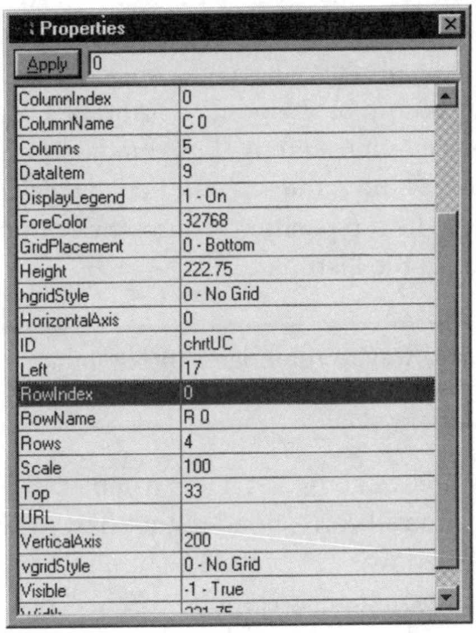

FIGURE 7.2: The Properties sheet for chrtUC, the Chart control in *layout for UC.alx*

If you click on RowName and try to rename the row "1994" and click on ColumnName to try rename the column "A&S," the new names will show up on the layout. You can do that with all the rows and columns and see the new names show up on the layout, but you'd be wasting your time. These new values don't show up on the Web page when you open it in IE. When you reopen the Properties sheet to figure out what happened, you'd find the original values (R0, C0, ..., R3, C4) in place. You'll have to change the names of the rows and columns programmatically (in other words, by having a script do it).

Skill 7

The BoundColumn Property

Close the Properties sheet, select a ListBox control from the Toolbox, and position it to the upper-right corner of the chart. Open the ListBox control's Properties sheet and set its ID to **lstbxChartStyle**. Set the value of the BoundColumn property to **0** (zero).

The BoundColumn property usually comes into play when your ListBox has more than one column. In that case, VBS has to know which column supplies the ListBox's value when a user selects a ListBox row. The BoundColumn provides the answer.

But wait, don't we have just one column? Why do we bother to set the BoundColumn property at all? And why do we set it to zero? When a ListBox has only one column, setting the BoundColumn property to 0 specifies that the ListBox's value is the selected item's *index*. An item's index is its position in the ListBox. The top position is zero, the bottom position is one less than the number of items in the ListBox.

 TIP   As easy way to remember the definition of the word "index" is to think of it as the "row number."

Why are we going to all this trouble? The properties that our ListBox selections will change all correspond to the chart's numbers. For example, the ChartType we selected was "11-Simple Column Chart." The system sees that value as "11." The numbers that correspond to Chart properties will be indexes in our listboxes. These numbers will enable us to use the ListBox's Change event to set the value of the ChartType property.

If all we have to do is make the ChartType property depend on a ListBox Change event, we don't have to have a VBS statement for each possible ListBox value. We won't need statements such as:

```
If lstbxChartStyle.Value = 'Simple Chart' Then chrtUC.ChartStyle = 11
```

Since a Chart control can have one of 21 Chart Styles, 5 Color Schemes, 5 Horizontal Grid Styles, and 5 Vertical Grid Styles, we would have to write many lines of code. With the Change event, eight statements can handle all the work.

Back to the Layout

We'll need a label to let users know what the ListBox is for, so select a Label control from the Toolbox and position it just above the ListBox. Set its ID to **lblChartStyle**, set its Caption to **Chart Style:**, and set its Font to 10 pt Bold.

Follow these steps to complete the layout:

1. Select both the Label and the ListBox.

2. Ctrl+C to copy the two, and Ctrl+V to paste the two copies.

3. Position the copies just below the originals.

4. Repeat this procedure two more times. You'll have four ListBoxes, each with a corresponding Label.

5. Change the Label captions to **Color Scheme:**, **Horizontal Grid:**, and **Vertical Grid:**.

6. Change the Label IDs to **lblColorScheme**, **lblHorizontalGrid**, and **lblVerticalGrid**, respectively.

7. Change the ListBox IDs to **lstbxColorScheme**, **lstbxHorizontalGrid**, and **lstbxVerticalGrid**, respectively.

Your HTML Layout Control should now look like Figure 7.3.

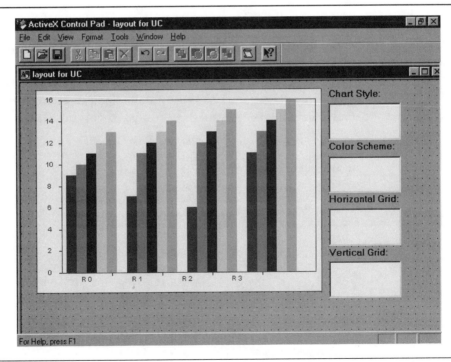

FIGURE 7.3: The layout for UC, with the Chart Control, ListBoxes, and Labels

Putting the Data into the Chart

We've done just about everything to the chart except put in the data, and several possibilities are available. You can work with the HTML file in either of two ways, you can work with a URL, you can use the Properties sheet, or you can write a script that enters the data. Let's examine each one.

Working with the HTML File

Right-click in the layout to open the pop-up menu and select View Source Code…. In the ALX file that opens in NotePad, find the <DIV> tag and move down until you find this line:

```
<PARAM NAME="Data[0][0]" VALUE="9">
```

This line and the ones like it that follow set up the default data that you see in your chart before you put your own data in. The [0][0] indicates that the VALUE, 9, is in the first row, first column. The data for the first row, first column is 1200. Change the 9 to 1200. The next line

```
<PARAM NAME="Data[0][1]" VALUE="10">
```

tells you the VALUE, 10, is in the first row, second column. The data for the first row, second column is 1650. Change the 10 to 1650.

By now you're probably getting the hang of it. The first bracketed number indicates the row, the second bracketed number indicates the column. Change the default data until the relevant lines in layout for uc.alx look like this:

```
<PARAM NAME="Data[0][0]" VALUE="1200">
<PARAM NAME="Data[0][1]" VALUE="1650">
<PARAM NAME="Data[0][2]" VALUE="1550">
<PARAM NAME="Data[0][3]" VALUE="820">
<PARAM NAME="Data[0][4]" VALUE="1010">
<PARAM NAME="Data[1][0]" VALUE="1350">
<PARAM NAME="Data[1][1]" VALUE="1700">
<PARAM NAME="Data[1][2]" VALUE="1480">
<PARAM NAME="Data[1][3]" VALUE="850">
<PARAM NAME="Data[1][4]" VALUE="1150">
<PARAM NAME="Data[2][0]" VALUE="1420">
<PARAM NAME="Data[2][1]" VALUE="1760">
<PARAM NAME="Data[2][2]" VALUE="1495">
<PARAM NAME="Data[2][3]" VALUE="840">
<PARAM NAME="Data[2][4]" VALUE="1180">
<PARAM NAME="Data[3][0]" VALUE="1465">
<PARAM NAME="Data[3][1]" VALUE="1800">
<PARAM NAME="Data[3][2]" VALUE="1490">
```

```
<PARAM NAME="Data[3][3]" VALUE="845">
<PARAM NAME="Data[3][4]" VALUE="1185">
```

If you save your file and open up the page in IE, you'll see the data in the chart.

HTML: Another Way

You can also work with the HTML file in a way that makes the <PARAM> tags look more like a table. Instead of using two indexes (the row and the column) on each line within the <PARAM> tag, use just one—the row. This turns everything associated with the VALUE attribute into data for the entire row. For this data, you can edit the relevant lines to look like this:

```
<PARAM NAME="Data[0]" VALUE="1200 1650 1550 820 1010">
<PARAM NAME="Data[1]" VALUE="1350 1700 1480 850 1150">
<PARAM NAME="Data[2]" VALUE="1420 1760 1495 840 1180">
<PARAM NAME="Data[3]" VALUE="1465 1800 1490 845 1185">
```

The advantage to the two HTML-oriented approaches is that they circumvent the ActiveX Control Pad and depend only on simple text-editing.

Working with a URL

Another approach that depends only on text-editing works with the URL property. The value for this property is the address of a file that contains the data you want to display. The idea is to put this file together in a text editor, reference it in the URL property, and you've taken care of data-entry. The file must follow a specific format. For this data, here's what the file (UCTable.txt) looks like this listing.

C UCTable.txt

```
11
4
5        "A&S"    "Eng"    "Ed"     "Med"    "Law"
"1994"   1200     1650     1550     820      1010
"1995"   1350     1700     1480     850      1150
"1996"   1420     1760     1495     840      1180
"1997"   1465     1800     1490     845      1185
```

The 11 in the first row specifies the ChartType (11-Simple Column Type). The 4 in the next row indicates the number of rows, and the 5 in the following row indicates the number of columns. The quoted column names appear to the right of the 5. Successive items on any line are separated by tabs.

In theory, this is a fine idea: change the file and you change the chart—all without opening the ActiveX Control Pad or writing any script. In my version of the ActiveX Control Pad, this procedure is a little finicky. The file as I've outlined it changes the data values in the <PARAM> tags of the ALX file and is thus a quick way to get them into the chart. The row names, column names, and the Legend all appear immediately in the Chart in the HTML Layout Control, but they don't appear when you open the Chart in IE.

Using the Properties Sheet

If you scroll through the Chart control's Property sheet, you'll see a property called DataItem. A DataItem is a particular piece of data. For example, 1200 in the first row and first column of our table is one possible value of DataItem.

DataItem is connected to the ColumnIndex and RowIndex properties. In the Properties sheet, you can set RowIndex and ColumnIndex, and then set the value of DataItem. When you do this, you have input the data value for the appropriate row and column.

The Properties sheet opens with RowIndex and ColumnIndex both set to 0. Change DataItem to **1200**. Now change ColumnIndex to **1**, and note that ColumnName changes automatically from C0 to C1. Change DataItem to **1650**. Keep changing ColumnIndex and changing DataItem until you get to the end of the first row of our table.

Now it's time to change the RowIndex. Change it to **1**, and you'll see that RowName changes automatically from R0 to R1. Change ColumnIndex back to **0** and change DataItem to **1350**. Again, keep changing ColumnIndex and DataItem until you get to the end of the second row.

Go through the third row and the fourth row the same way. The advantage to this approach is that you can see your data appear in the chart as you make the changes. When you're done, examine the source code for `layout for UC.alx` and you'll find that the <PARAM> tags contain the data you have specified.

Scripting Data-Entry

The last alternative is the one I like best. It requires some typing, but it gets the job done and it introduces a couple of ActiveX and VBS concepts that you should know. What we'll do is write a script that does automatically what we did manually in the previous sections.

From the HTML Layout Control, open the Script Wizard. In the Event pane, click on the + to the left of layoutforUC to open up this object's OnLoad event. We will use the OnLoad event to:

- name the rows and columns

- enter data into the chart

- populate the listboxes

Click on OnLoad to open up a Code View Script pane. In the Actions pane, find chrtUC and open its methods and properties. Double-click on RowIndex to put it in the Script pane. In the Script pane, specify that the RowIndex = 0. Now that we've set the index, we'll name the row. In the Actions pane, find chrtUC's RowName and double-click on it. On a new line in the Script pane, set the RowName to "1994." The first three lines of this subroutine should be:

```
Sub layoutforUC_OnLoad()
chrtUC.RowIndex = 0
chrtUC.RowName = "1994"
```

Next, set the ColumnIndex to 0, name the column, and assign a value to the data in the first row, first column. To do this, add these three lines to the Script pane:

```
chrtUC.ColumnIndex = 0
chrtUC.ColumnName = "A&S"
chrtUC.DataItem = 1200
```

Our next step is to specify the name and enter the data for the next column of the first row:

```
chrtUC.ColumnIndex = 1
chrtUC.ColumnName = "Eng"
chrtUC.DataItem = 1650
```

Keep going this way, until you've entered all the values for the first row. Your code for the entire first row should look like this:

```
chrtUC.RowIndex = 0
chrtUC.RowName = "1994"
chrtUC.ColumnIndex = 0
chrtUC.ColumnName = "A&S"
chrtUC.DataItem = 1200
chrtUC.ColumnIndex = 1
chrtUC.ColumnName = "Eng"
chrtUC.DataItem = 1650
chrtUC.ColumnIndex = 2
```

```
chrtUC.ColumnName = "Ed"
chrtUC.DataItem = 1550
chrtUC.ColumnIndex = 3
chrtUC.ColumnName = "Med"
chrtUC.DataItem = 820
chrtUC.ColumnIndex = 4
chrtUC.ColumnName = "Law"
chrtUC.DataItem = 1010
```

Now, move on to the second row:

```
chrtUC.RowIndex = 1
chrtUC.RowName = "1995"
chrtUC.ColumnIndex = 0
chrtUC.DataItem = 1350
```

Notice that because you've already named all the columns, you don't have to name them a second time when you encounter them in another row.

When you finish with the second row, move on to the third, and start the process again. When you're done with the rows and columns, type this line to ensure that the chart displays the legend when we open this page in IE:

```
chrtUC.DisplayLegend = 1
```

Next, we turn our attention to the lstbxChartStyle ListBox control. In the Script pane for the Layout's OnLoad event, double-click on lstbxChartStyle's AddItem method. Between the parentheses type **"Simple Pie", 0**. The first argument is the string that AddItem adds to the listbox, and the second is the string's position in the listbox (positioning starts at 0, not 1). Because the Chart control has 20 additional CharType settings, we have 20 more lines like this to type. Table 7.2 shows all the values to enter using the lstbxChartStyle.AddItem method.

T A B L E 7 . 2 : The List of Items and Indexes to Type into lstbxChartStyle.AddItem

ListBox Item	Index
"Simple Pie"	0
"Special Pie"	1
"Simple Point"	2
"Stacked Point"	3
"Full Point"	4
"Simple Line"	5
"Stacked Line"	6

TABLE 7.2 CONTINUED: The List of Items and Indexes to Type into lstbxChartStyle.AddItem

ListBox Item	Index
"Full Line"	7
"Simple Area"	8
"Stacked Area"	9
"Full Area"	10
"Simple Column"	11
"Stacked Column"	12
"Full Column"	13
"Simple Bar"	14
"Stacked Bar"	15
"Full Bar"	16
"HLC Simple Stock"	17
"HLC WSJ Stock"	18
"OHLC Simple Stock"	19
"OHLC" WSJ Stock"	20

Similarly, we have to type five pairs of arguments for lstbxColorScheme.AddItem. In the Script pane for the Layout's OnLoad event, double-click on lstbxColorScheme.AddItem method. Between the parentheses, type the arguments listed in Table 7.3.

TABLE 7.3: The List of Items and Indexes to Type into lstbxColorScheme

ListBox Item	Index
"Scheme 1"	0
"Scheme 2"	1
"Scheme 3"	2
"Scheme 4"	3
"Scheme 5"	4

We also have to type five pairs of arguments into lstbxHorizontalGrid and five pairs of arguments into lstbxVerticalGrid. Fortunately, the values are the same. Table 7.4 shows the values to use for the AddItem method for both the lstbxHorizontalGrid and the lstbxVerticalGrid ListBox controls.

T A B L E 7 . 4 : The List of Items and Indexes to Type into lstbxHorizontalGrid and lstbxVerticalGrid

ListItem	Index
"None"	0
"Solid"	1
"Bold"	2
"Dotted"	3
"Bold Dotted"	4

In all long, repetitious subroutines like this one, it helps if you use copy and paste techniques. They'll reduce the typing load considerably.

Four more short subroutines and we're done. In each subroutine, we use a Listbox Change event to set the value of a property of the Chart. For example, we use lstbxChartStyle's Change event to set the value of chrtUC.ChartType. Click on that ListBox's Change event and in the Actions pane, double-click on chrtUC.ChartType. In the Script pane, do the typing and clicking that produces

```
chrtUC.ChartType = lstbxChartStyle.Value
```

If we opened the Web page in IE at this point, an error message would appear. The error message would let us know that this line tried to match up two different types of quantities. If we clicked OK on the error message, we could proceed as though nothing happened and everything would work smoothly.

Why do we get that error message? When the page opens in IE, no value has been assigned to any of the ListBox controls. Therefore their value is said to be *null*. Trying to use null values in an expression that assigns a value will generate an error message and stop things temporarily.

The quickest way to get around this is to type **On Error Resume Next** as the first line of code in the lstbxChartStyle control's Change event. This statement tells the VBS interpreter to ignore errors it encounters, and continue processing the script. This type of error is different from the errors described in the last two Skills (and for which we built error-traps). This error is a system inconsistency that we're telling VBS to ignore because it irons itself out very quickly. The kinds of errors we examined before were errors users made inputting data. In that case, it was useful to tell the user why the error occurred, and what to do to correct it.

The code for the subroutine that links the ListBox's Change event to the Chart's ChartType is:

```
Sub lstbxChartStyle_Change()
On Error Resume Next
chrtUC.ChartType = lstbxChartStyle.Value
```

In a similar way, we have to script the Change event for each of the other three listboxes. Here are the scripts:

```
Sub lstbxVerticalGrid_Change()
On Error Resume Next
chrtUC.vgridStyle = lstbxVerticalGrid.Value

Sub lstbxHorizontalGrid_Change()
On Error Resume Next
chrtUC.hgridStyle = lstbxHorizontalGrid.Value

Sub lstbxColorScheme_Change()
On Error Resume Next
chrtUC.ColorScheme = lstbxColorScheme.Value
```

When we're done, the entire HTML code for your Layout Control (layout for UC.alx) looks like this.

C **Layout for UC.alx**

```
<SCRIPT LANGUAGE="VBScript">
<!--
Sub layoutforUC_OnLoad()

chrtUC.RowIndex = 0
chrtUC.RowName = "1994"
chrtUC.ColumnIndex = 0
chrtUC.ColumnName = "A&S"
chrtUC.DataItem = 1200
chrtUC.ColumnIndex = 1
chrtUC.ColumnName = "Eng"
chrtUC.DataItem = 1650
chrtUC.ColumnIndex = 2
chrtUC.ColumnName = "Ed"
chrtUC.DataItem = 1550
chrtUC.ColumnIndex = 3
chrtUC.ColumnName = "Med"
chrtUC.DataItem = 820
chrtUC.ColumnIndex = 4
```

```
chrtUC.ColumnName = "Law"
chrtUC.DataItem = 1010
chrtUC.RowIndex = 1
chrtUC.RowName = "1995"
chrtUC.ColumnIndex = 0
chrtUC.DataItem = 1350
chrtUC.ColumnIndex =1
chrtUC.DataItem = 1700
chrtUC.ColumnIndex =2
chrtUC.DataItem = 1480
chrtUC.ColumnIndex =3
chrtUC.DataItem = 850
chrtUC.ColumnIndex =4
chrtUC.DataItem = 1150
chrtUC.RowIndex = 2
chrtUC.RowName = "1996"
chrtUC.ColumnIndex =0
chrtUC.DataItem = 1420
chrtUC.ColumnIndex =1
chrtUC.DataItem = 1760
chrtUC.ColumnIndex =2
chrtUC.DataItem = 1495
chrtUC.ColumnIndex =3
chrtUC.DataItem = 840
chrtUC.ColumnIndex =4
chrtUC.DataItem = 1180
chrtUC.RowIndex = 3
chrtUC.RowName = "1997"
chrtUC.ColumnIndex =0
chrtUC.DataItem = 1465
chrtUC.ColumnIndex =1
chrtUC.DataItem = 1800
chrtUC.ColumnIndex =2
chrtUC.DataItem = 1490
chrtUC.ColumnIndex =3
chrtUC.DataItem = 845
chrtUC.ColumnIndex =4
chrtUC.DataItem = 1185
chrtUC.DisplayLegend = 1
call lstbxChartStyle.AddItem("Simple Pie", 0)
call lstbxChartStyle.AddItem("Special Pie", 1)
call lstbxChartStyle.AddItem("Simple Point", 2)
call lstbxChartStyle.AddItem("Stacked Point", 3)
call lstbxChartStyle.AddItem("Full Point", 4)
call lstbxChartStyle.AddItem("Simple Line", 5)
call lstbxChartStyle.AddItem("Stacked Line", 6)
call lstbxChartStyle.AddItem("Full Line", 7)
call lstbxChartStyle.AddItem("Simple Area", 8)
```

```
call lstbxChartStyle.AddItem("Stacked Area", 9)
call lstbxChartStyle.AddItem("Full Area", 10)
call lstbxChartStyle.AddItem("Simple Column", 11)
call lstbxChartStyle.AddItem("Stacked Column", 12)
call lstbxChartStyle.AddItem("Full Column", 13)
call lstbxChartStyle.AddItem("Simple Bar", 14)
call lstbxChartStyle.AddItem("Stacked Bar", 15)
call lstbxChartStyle.AddItem("Full Bar", 16)
call lstbxChartStyle.AddItem("HLC Simple Stock", 17)
call lstbxChartStyle.AddItem("HLC WSJ Stock", 18)
call lstbxChartStyle.AddItem("OHLC Simple Stock", 19)
call lstbxChartStyle.AddItem("OHLC WSJ Stock", 20)
call lstbxColorScheme.AddItem("Scheme 1", 0)
call lstbxColorScheme.AddItem("Scheme 2", 1)
call lstbxColorScheme.AddItem("Scheme 3", 2)
call lstbxColorScheme.AddItem("Scheme 4", 3)
call lstbxColorScheme.AddItem("Scheme 5", 4)
call lstbxHorizontalGrid.AddItem("None", 0)
call lstbxHorizontalGrid.AddItem("Solid", 1)
call lstbxHorizontalGrid.AddItem("Bold", 2)
call lstbxHorizontalGrid.AddItem("Dotted", 3)
call lstbxHorizontalGrid.AddItem("Bold Dotted", 4)
call lstbxVerticalGrid.AddItem("None", 0)
call lstbxVerticalGrid.AddItem("Solid", 1)
call lstbxVerticalGrid.AddItem("Bold", 2)
call lstbxVerticalGrid.AddItem("Dotted", 3)
call lstbxVerticalGrid.AddItem("Bold Dotted", 4)

end sub
-->
</SCRIPT>
<SCRIPT LANGUAGE="VBScript">
<!--
Sub lstbxChartStyle_Change()
On Error Resume Next
chrtUC.ChartType = lstbxChartStyle.Value

end sub
-->
</SCRIPT>
<SCRIPT LANGUAGE="VBScript">
<!--
Sub lstbxVerticalGrid_Change()
On Error Resume Next
chrtUC.vgridStyle = lstbxVerticalGrid.Value
end sub
-->
</SCRIPT>
<SCRIPT LANGUAGE="VBScript">
```

Skill 7

```
<!--
Sub lstbxHorizontalGrid_Change()
On Error Resume Next
chrtUC.hgridStyle = lstbxHorizontalGrid.Value
end sub
-->
</SCRIPT>
<SCRIPT LANGUAGE="VBScript">
<!--
Sub lstbxColorScheme_Change()
On Error Resume Next
chrtUC.ColorScheme = lstbxColorScheme.Value
end sub
-->
</SCRIPT>
<DIV ID="layoutforUC" STYLE="LAYOUT:FIXED;WIDTH:477pt;HEIGHT:293pt;">
    <OBJECT ID="chrtUC"
      CLASSID="CLSID:FC25B780-75BE-11CF-8B01-444553540000"
CODEBASE="http://activex.microsoft.com/controls/iexplorer/iechart.ocx#Version=
➥4,70,0,1161" STYLE="TOP:17pt;LEFT:17pt;WIDTH:322pt;HEIGHT:223pt;ZINDEX:0;">
        <PARAM NAME="_ExtentX" VALUE="11351">
        <PARAM NAME="_ExtentY" VALUE="7858">
        <PARAM NAME="Rows" VALUE="4">
        <PARAM NAME="Columns" VALUE="5">
        <PARAM NAME="ChartType" VALUE="11">
        <PARAM NAME="Data[0][0]" VALUE="9">
        <PARAM NAME="Data[0][1]" VALUE="10">
        <PARAM NAME="Data[0][2]" VALUE="11">
        <PARAM NAME="Data[0][3]" VALUE="12">
        <PARAM NAME="Data[0][4]" VALUE="13">
        <PARAM NAME="Data[1][0]" VALUE="7">
        <PARAM NAME="Data[1][1]" VALUE="11">
        <PARAM NAME="Data[1][2]" VALUE="12">
        <PARAM NAME="Data[1][3]" VALUE="13">
        <PARAM NAME="Data[1][4]" VALUE="14">
        <PARAM NAME="Data[2][0]" VALUE="6">
        <PARAM NAME="Data[2][1]" VALUE="12">
        <PARAM NAME="Data[2][2]" VALUE="13">
        <PARAM NAME="Data[2][3]" VALUE="14">
        <PARAM NAME="Data[2][4]" VALUE="15">
        <PARAM NAME="Data[3][0]" VALUE="11">
        <PARAM NAME="Data[3][1]" VALUE="13">
        <PARAM NAME="Data[3][2]" VALUE="14">
        <PARAM NAME="Data[3][3]" VALUE="15">
        <PARAM NAME="Data[3][4]" VALUE="16">
        <PARAM NAME="HorizontalAxis" VALUE="0">
        <PARAM NAME="VerticalAxis" VALUE="200">
        <PARAM NAME="hgridStyle" VALUE="0">
```

```
            <PARAM NAME="vgridStyle" VALUE="0">
            <PARAM NAME="ColorScheme" VALUE="0">
            <PARAM NAME="BackStyle" VALUE="1">
            <PARAM NAME="Scale" VALUE="100">
            <PARAM NAME="DisplayLegend" VALUE="0">
            <PARAM NAME="BackColor" VALUE="16777215">
            <PARAM NAME="ForeColor" VALUE="32768">
</OBJECT>
<OBJECT ID="lblChartStyle"
 CLASSID="CLSID:978C9E23-D4B0-11CE-BF2D-00AA003F40D0"
➡STYLE="TOP:8pt;LEFT:347pt;WIDTH:91pt;HEIGHT:17pt;ZINDEX:1;">
            <PARAM NAME="Caption" VALUE="Chart Style:">
            <PARAM NAME="Size" VALUE="3210;600">
            <PARAM NAME="FontEffects" VALUE="1073741825">
            <PARAM NAME="FontHeight" VALUE="200">
            <PARAM NAME="FontCharSet" VALUE="0">
            <PARAM NAME="FontPitchAndFamily" VALUE="2">
            <PARAM NAME="FontWeight" VALUE="700">
</OBJECT>
<OBJECT ID="lblColorScheme"
 CLASSID="CLSID:978C9E23-D4B0-11CE-BF2D-00AA003F40D0"
➡STYLE="TOP:66pt;LEFT:347pt;WIDTH:91pt;HEIGHT:17pt;ZINDEX:2;">
            <PARAM NAME="Caption" VALUE="Color Scheme:">
            <PARAM NAME="Size" VALUE="3210;600">
            <PARAM NAME="FontEffects" VALUE="1073741825">
            <PARAM NAME="FontHeight" VALUE="200">
            <PARAM NAME="FontCharSet" VALUE="0">
            <PARAM NAME="FontPitchAndFamily" VALUE="2">
            <PARAM NAME="FontWeight" VALUE="700">
</OBJECT>
<OBJECT ID="lblHorizontalGrid"
 CLASSID="CLSID:978C9E23-D4B0-11CE-BF2D-00AA003F40D0"
➡STYLE="TOP:125pt;LEFT:347pt;WIDTH:91pt;HEIGHT:17pt;ZINDEX:3;">
            <PARAM NAME="Caption" VALUE="Horizontal Grid:">
            <PARAM NAME="Size" VALUE="3210;600">
            <PARAM NAME="FontEffects" VALUE="1073741825">
            <PARAM NAME="FontHeight" VALUE="200">
            <PARAM NAME="FontCharSet" VALUE="0">
            <PARAM NAME="FontPitchAndFamily" VALUE="2">
            <PARAM NAME="FontWeight" VALUE="700">
</OBJECT>
<OBJECT ID="lblVerticalGrid"
 CLASSID="CLSID:978C9E23-D4B0-11CE-BF2D-00AA003F40D0"
➡STYLE="TOP:182pt;LEFT:347pt;WIDTH:91pt;HEIGHT:17pt;ZINDEX:4;">
            <PARAM NAME="Caption" VALUE="Vertical Grid:">
            <PARAM NAME="Size" VALUE="3210;600">
            <PARAM NAME="FontEffects" VALUE="1073741825">
            <PARAM NAME="FontHeight" VALUE="200">
```

Skill 7

```
            <PARAM NAME="FontCharSet" VALUE="0">
            <PARAM NAME="FontPitchAndFamily" VALUE="2">
            <PARAM NAME="FontWeight" VALUE="700">
        </OBJECT>
        <OBJECT ID="lstbxColorScheme"
         CLASSID="CLSID:8BD21D20-EC42-11CE-9E0D-00AA006002F3"
        ➥STYLE="TOP:83pt;LEFT:347pt;WIDTH:83pt;HEIGHT:41pt;TABINDEX:3;ZINDEX:5;">
            <PARAM NAME="ScrollBars" VALUE="3">
            <PARAM NAME="DisplayStyle" VALUE="2">
            <PARAM NAME="Size" VALUE="2928;1446">
            <PARAM NAME="BoundColumn" VALUE="0">
            <PARAM NAME="MatchEntry" VALUE="0">
            <PARAM NAME="FontCharSet" VALUE="0">
            <PARAM NAME="FontPitchAndFamily" VALUE="2">
            <PARAM NAME="FontWeight" VALUE="0">
        </OBJECT>
        <OBJECT ID="lstbxVerticalGrid"
         CLASSID="CLSID:8BD21D20-EC42-11CE-9E0D-00AA006002F3"
        ➥STYLE="TOP:198pt;LEFT:347pt;WIDTH:83pt;HEIGHT:40pt;TABINDEX:7;ZINDEX:6;">
            <PARAM NAME="ScrollBars" VALUE="3">
            <PARAM NAME="DisplayStyle" VALUE="2">
            <PARAM NAME="Size" VALUE="2928;1411">
            <PARAM NAME="BoundColumn" VALUE="0">
            <PARAM NAME="MatchEntry" VALUE="0">
            <PARAM NAME="FontCharSet" VALUE="0">
            <PARAM NAME="FontPitchAndFamily" VALUE="2">
            <PARAM NAME="FontWeight" VALUE="0">
        </OBJECT>
        <OBJECT ID="lstbxChartStyle"
         CLASSID="CLSID:8BD21D20-EC42-11CE-9E0D-00AA006002F3"
        ➥STYLE="TOP:26pt;LEFT:347pt;WIDTH:83pt;HEIGHT:41pt;TABINDEX:0;ZINDEX:7;">
            <PARAM NAME="ScrollBars" VALUE="3">
            <PARAM NAME="DisplayStyle" VALUE="2">
            <PARAM NAME="Size" VALUE="2928;1446">
            <PARAM NAME="BoundColumn" VALUE="0">
            <PARAM NAME="MatchEntry" VALUE="0">
            <PARAM NAME="FontCharSet" VALUE="0">
            <PARAM NAME="FontPitchAndFamily" VALUE="2">
            <PARAM NAME="FontWeight" VALUE="0">
        </OBJECT>
        <OBJECT ID="lstbxHorizontalGrid"
         CLASSID="CLSID:8BD21D20-EC42-11CE-9E0D-00AA006002F3"
        ➥STYLE="TOP:140pt;LEFT:347pt;WIDTH:83pt;HEIGHT:41pt;TABINDEX:5;ZINDEX:8;">
            <PARAM NAME="ScrollBars" VALUE="3">
            <PARAM NAME="DisplayStyle" VALUE="2">
            <PARAM NAME="Size" VALUE="2928;1446">
            <PARAM NAME="BoundColumn" VALUE="0">
            <PARAM NAME="MatchEntry" VALUE="0">
```

```
        <PARAM NAME="FontCharSet" VALUE="0">
        <PARAM NAME="FontPitchAndFamily" VALUE="2">
        <PARAM NAME="FontWeight" VALUE="0">
    </OBJECT>
</DIV>
```

Pick the method of data-entry you like best. Whichever one you choose, you still have to programmatically name the rows and columns and populate the listbox controls. The Web page you open in IE will resemble Figure 7.4.

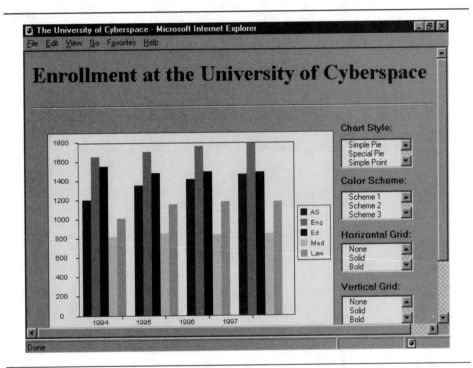

FIGURE 7.4: The Web page with the Chart of Enrollment at the University of Cyberspace

Figure 7.4 shows the "Simple Columns" Chart type with the default color scheme. The "Special Pie Chart" in Figure 7.5 is another useful Chart type. Figure 7.5 displays this Chart type with a different color scheme.

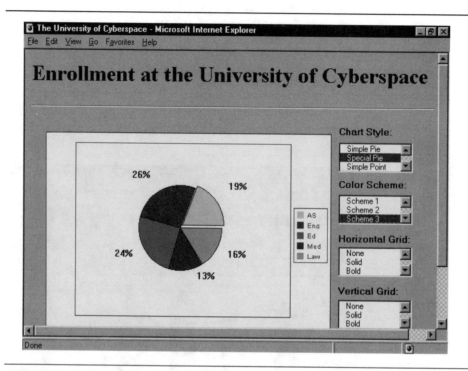

F I G U R E 7 . 5 : The University of Cyberspace Enrollment Data presented in a "Special Pie Chart"

Try changing values in the ListBox controls to examine the variety of possible permutations of the Chart control's features. It might be helpful for you to save this code and reuse it as necessary when you need to create a chart on a Web page.

A More Advanced Chart Control: First Impression

If you took a moment to think of all the capabilities you'd like to add to the Chart control, I'm sure you'd come up with quite a few. In a new, improved version you'd probably like the ability to:

- add a title to the chart
- name the x-axis and the y-axis

- add and change data in a fast, intuitive way

- show your data in three dimensions

Kansas-based Visual Components Inc. created an ActiveX control called First Impression that addresses these issues and many, many more. Visit their Web site at `http://www.visualcomp.com` to find out about this control and others that they've created. You can purchase a 30-day evaluation copy of First Impression from Visual Components (1-800-884-8665). To give you a feel for how this control works, I created a chart that uses the same data as the MS Chart control. I used a sample of the control which doesn't have all the features of the full version (you get all the features in the evaluation copy).

Figure 7.6 shows a Web page that holds the First Impression control.

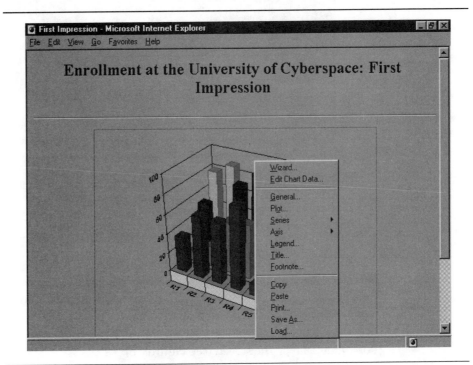

FIGURE 7.6: The Web page with the First Impression control and the pop-up menu that appears when you right-click on the chart.

To enter the data into the chart. First Impression gives you a Data Grid Editor to work with, which you open by clicking on Edit Chart Data…, the second item on the pop-up menu (see Figure 7.7). (Ordinarily, you would enter the data in the layout at designtime, but I was working with a sample copy that didn't transmit the data from the layout to the Web page.)

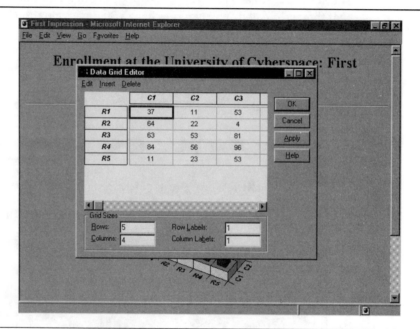

FIGURE 7.7: The Data Grid Editor in First Impression

First, in the appropriate places near the bottom of the Editor, I input the number of rows in our data (**4**) and the number of columns (**5**). Then, onto the grid to type in the names of the rows and columns. After any entry, clicking on Apply makes that entry appear immediately in the chart. After the data are in the appropriate parts of the grid, closing the Editor puts a three-dimensional representation of the data on the screen (see Figure 7.8).

Some more mouse-clicking gets a legend into the picture.

The real star of the show is the Wizard, which offers numerous options for the style of the chart. It's only a right-click away (see Figure 7.9).

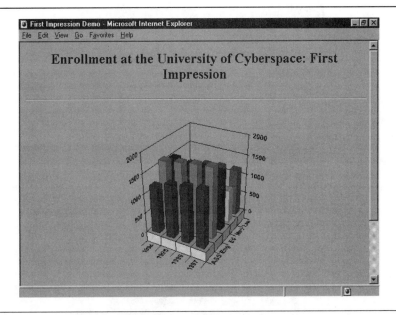

FIGURE 7.8: A three-dimensional chart of the University of Cyberspace's enrollment data

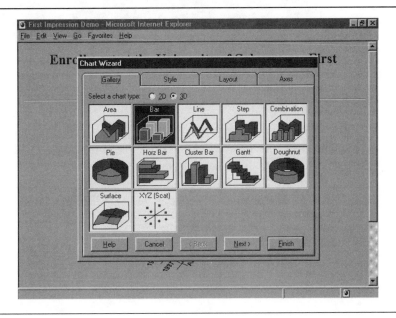

FIGURE 7.9: The First Impression Wizard opens with a set of options for the style of the chart.

The Wizard is also the tool that puts labels on the chart's axes and inserts footnote information. Figure 7.10 shows the chart after all the additions and some resizing.

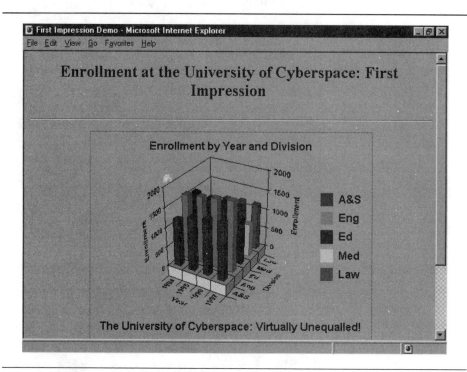

FIGURE 7.10: The First Impression chart with labeled axes, a title, a footnote, and a legend

In the previous section, you'll recall, we worked with a two-dimensional "Simple Column" chart. How does First Impression render a chart like that? Working with the Wizard, I generated Figure 7.11.

It would take an entire book to cover all the features of First Impression. Now that I've taken you this far, however, you'll be in a good position to explore them on your own if you purchase a copy.

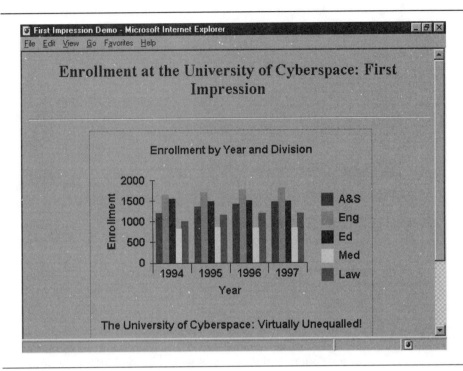

FIGURE 7.11: A two-dimensional First Impression chart of our data

Document Acrobatics

The text around us comes in a variety of formats. Its appearance varies from books, to magazines, to academic journals, to tech manuals, and so on. We've become accustomed to these different formats, and therefore it's often helpful to bring these formats to the Web. If you have some documents you want users to read, it might be easier for them to read the documents in the format in which they originally appeared, rather than in an HTML form.

Adobe Systems Inc. provides a vehicle that makes this happen. Their portable document format (PDF) preserves the original format of a document and makes it accessible across a wide variety of hardware that people use to access the Internet. An extremely popular format, PDF is graphically oriented and designed specifically for electronic communication. Adobe derived PDF from PostScript, their page-description language, and they designed it to use with their Acrobat software.

The Acrobat software is required to create a PDF document. Once a document is in PDF, a developer can use Adobe's software to add links to other parts of the document, to other files, to other applications, and to other URLs on the Web. To read a PDF document, you have to have Adobe's Acrobat reader. Fortunately, Adobe provides this reader for free. Adobe also provides a free ActiveX Acrobat control that works with the reader. You can get the control from the Microsoft ActiveX Component Gallery. The installation file you download will put the control, the reader, and useful documentation in PDF on your computer.

PDF is a popular format with government agencies. The Internal Revenue Service, for example, puts tax forms in PDF that you can download and print. Some states also put their forms in PDF. To demonstrate the ActiveX Acrobat control, we'll display documents from two federal agencies, the Bureau of Economic Analysis (BEA) and the Consumer Product Safety Commission (CPSC).

 NOTE   The BEA is the "accountant" of the United States. It integrates and interprets huge volumes of data. Its objective is to build a complete picture of the U.S. economy. The CPSC, as I mentioned earlier, regulates consumer products to ensure their safety. Enjoy the documents—your tax dollars paid for them.

Setting Up the Controls

Let's take a look at the ActiveX Acrobat control in action and make it work with some Command Buttons. When we're finished, we'll have a Web page that:

- opens a PDF document
- has a Command Button that prints the document
- has a Command Button that shows an About... box for the Acrobat control
- has Command Buttons that display PDF documents

Begin by opening up a new HTML file in the ActiveX Control Pad. Save it as Acrobat Demo in skill 7 and use **Acrobat Demo** as the title. From the Menu Bar, select Edit ➢ Insert ActiveX Control... and select Acrobat control for ActiveX from the list.

In the Object Editor, type **acrbtReader** in the ID property of the Properties sheet. In the src property, type **http://www.bea.doc.gov/bea/scb/0696od.pdf**. This is the BEA document that the Reader control will display when we open this Web page in IE. It's BEA's Mid-Decade Strategic Plan. The "scb" in the URL stands for *Survey of Current Business*, BEA's monthly publication.

Close the Object Editor. In the Text Editor, set 811 for the Width and 1056 for the Height. These are larger numbers than we've ever used for these attributes, but it's a good idea to use them as documents tend to look better the more room they're allowed onscreen.

Now, let's create the Command Buttons. With the cursor below the </OBJECT> tag that closes the identifying information for the Acrobat control, select Edit ➤ Insert ActiveX Control… and choose the Microsoft Forms 2.0 Command Button control. Set its ID to **cmdbtnAcrobatPrint**, make its Caption **Print**, and make its Font 10 pt Bold. Close the Object Editor to return to the Text Editor.

Using copy and paste, create three more Command Buttons. Caption the first one **About…**, the second one **Bicycle Safety**, and the third one **BEA**. Make the ID **cmdbtnAcrobatAbout** for the first one, **cmdbtnAcrobatBike** for the second, and **cmdbtnAcrobatBEA** for the third.

Scripting the Controls

To write the script, open the Script Wizard and follow these steps:

1. In the Event pane, open the events for cmdbtnAcrobatPrint and select Click.

2. In the Actions pane open the methods and properties for acrbtReader. Double-click on the Print method.

3. Back in the Event pane, open the events for cmdbtnAcrobatAbout and select Click.

4. In the Actions pane, double-click on acrbtReader's AboutBox method.

5. In the Event pane, open the events for cmdbtnAcrobatBike and select Click.

6. In the Actions pane, double-click on acrbtReader's src property. In the dialog box that appears, type **http://www.cpsc.gov/cpscpub/pubs/bicycle.pdf**. (This is the CPSC document in Figure 7.1.)

7. Almost done! In the Event pane, open the events for cmdbtnAcrobatBEA and select (you guessed it!) Click.

8. In the Actions pane, double-click on the src property, and this time in the dialog box type **http://www.bea.doc.gov/bea/scb/0696od.pdf**. (Clicking the last Command Button will take you back to the document that displays when the Web page opens.)

Close the Script Wizard. Here's how your HTML file (`Acrobat Demo.htm`) should look.

 Acrobat Demo.htm

```
<HTML>
<HEAD>
<TITLE>Acrobat Demo</TITLE>
</HEAD>
<BODY>
    <OBJECT ID="acrbtReader" WIDTH=811 HEIGHT=1056
     CLASSID="CLSID:CA8A9780-280D-11CF-A24D-444553540000">
        <PARAM NAME="_Version" VALUE="65539">
        <PARAM NAME="_ExtentX" VALUE="21449">
        <PARAM NAME="_ExtentY" VALUE="27940">
        <PARAM NAME="_StockProps" VALUE="0">
        <PARAM NAME="SRC" VALUE="http://www.bea.doc.gov/bea/scb/0696od.pdf">
    </OBJECT>
    <SCRIPT LANGUAGE="VBScript">
<!--
Sub cmdbtnAcrobatPrint_Click()
call acrbtReader.Print()
end sub
-->
    </SCRIPT>
    <OBJECT ID="cmdbtnAcrobatPrint" WIDTH=115 HEIGHT=39
     CLASSID="CLSID:D7053240-CE69-11CD-A777-00DD01143C57">
        <PARAM NAME="Caption" VALUE="Print">
        <PARAM NAME="Size" VALUE="3034;1023">
        <PARAM NAME="FontEffects" VALUE="1073741825">
        <PARAM NAME="FontHeight" VALUE="200">
        <PARAM NAME="FontCharSet" VALUE="0">
        <PARAM NAME="FontPitchAndFamily" VALUE="2">
        <PARAM NAME="ParagraphAlign" VALUE="3">
        <PARAM NAME="FontWeight" VALUE="700">
    </OBJECT>
    <SCRIPT LANGUAGE="VBScript">
<!--
Sub cmdbtnAcrobatAbout_Click()
call acrbtReader.AboutBox()
end sub
-->
```

```
    </SCRIPT>
    <OBJECT ID="cmdbtnAcrobatAbout" WIDTH=115 HEIGHT=39
     CLASSID="CLSID:D7053240-CE69-11CD-A777-00DD01143C57">
        <PARAM NAME="Caption" VALUE="About...">
        <PARAM NAME="Size" VALUE="3034;1023">
        <PARAM NAME="FontEffects" VALUE="1073741825">
        <PARAM NAME="FontHeight" VALUE="200">
        <PARAM NAME="FontCharSet" VALUE="0">
        <PARAM NAME="FontPitchAndFamily" VALUE="2">
        <PARAM NAME="ParagraphAlign" VALUE="3">
        <PARAM NAME="FontWeight" VALUE="700">
    </OBJECT>
    <SCRIPT LANGUAGE="VBScript">
<!--
Sub cmdbtnAcrobatBike_Click()
acrbtReader.src = "http://www.cpsc.gov/cpscpub/pubs/bicycle.pdf"
end sub
-->
    </SCRIPT>
    <OBJECT ID="cmdbtnAcrobatBike" WIDTH=115 HEIGHT=39
     CLASSID="CLSID:D7053240-CE69-11CD-A777-00DD01143C57">
        <PARAM NAME="Caption" VALUE="Bicycle Safety">
        <PARAM NAME="Size" VALUE="3034;1023">
        <PARAM NAME="FontEffects" VALUE="1073741825">
        <PARAM NAME="FontHeight" VALUE="200">
        <PARAM NAME="FontCharSet" VALUE="0">
        <PARAM NAME="FontPitchAndFamily" VALUE="2">
        <PARAM NAME="ParagraphAlign" VALUE="3">
        <PARAM NAME="FontWeight" VALUE="700">
    </OBJECT>
    <SCRIPT LANGUAGE="VBScript">
<!--
Sub cmdbtnAcrobatBEA_Click()
acrbtReader.src = "http://www.bea.doc.gov/bea/scb/0696od.pdf"
end sub
-->
    </SCRIPT>
    <OBJECT ID="cmdbtnAcrobatBEA" WIDTH=115 HEIGHT=39
     CLASSID="CLSID:D7053240-CE69-11CD-A777-00DD01143C57">
        <PARAM NAME="Caption" VALUE="BEA">
        <PARAM NAME="Size" VALUE="3034;1023">
        <PARAM NAME="FontEffects" VALUE="1073741825">
        <PARAM NAME="FontHeight" VALUE="200">
        <PARAM NAME="FontCharSet" VALUE="0">
        <PARAM NAME="FontPitchAndFamily" VALUE="2">
        <PARAM NAME="ParagraphAlign" VALUE="3">
        <PARAM NAME="FontWeight" VALUE="700">
    </OBJECT>
</BODY>
</HTML>
```

Skill 7

Save your work, and open the Web page in IE. It will resemble Figure 7.12.

FIGURE 7.12: The Acrobat Demo Web page. The PDF document is from the Bureau of Economic Analysis.

The Acrobat Reader tools appear in a toolbar just below the IE toolbar, and the area on the left of the document enables you to navigate to bookmarked areas within the document. Scroll down to the bottom of the page and you'll see your Command Buttons just below some more Acrobat tools.

Click on our Print button and the Acrobat Print dialog box opens, as in Figure 7.13. This box allows you to select a print range. (The Print button duplicates the function of the Printer icon in the Acrobat toolbar.) Selecting IE's File ➤ Print only prints the document's first page.

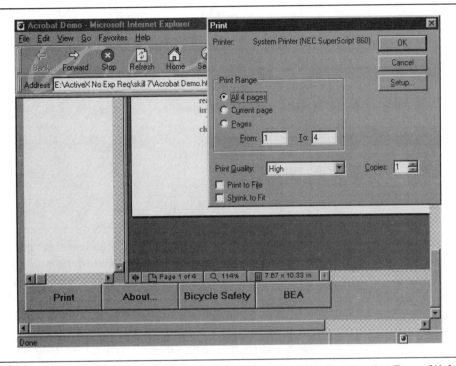

FIGURE 7.13: The Command Buttons we created for the Acrobat Demo Web page. Clicking on our Print button opens the Acrobat Print dialog box.

Clicking on our About… Button opens a box that provides information about the Acrobat control. The Bicycle Safety button will display the aforementioned document from the CPSC, and the BEA button takes you back to the BEA Mid-Decade Strategic Plan.

Two questions might be forming in your mind:

> Why didn't we use the Acrobat control with the HTML Layout Control?
>
> and
>
> Why didn't we use Acrobat documentation in PDF files on our hard drive for this exercise instead of going out on the Web?

The answers are:

> That won't work.
>
> and
>
> That won't work.

Setting up the Acrobat control inside the HTML Layout Control doesn't get the necessary information transmitted to the HTML file. When you try to open the Web page in IE, you'll just get a blank space. The inability to read local files (or local files referenced with a local pathname rather than with an http-type URL) is a known limitation of this control.

These limitations aside, the Acrobat control is a slick little tool that you should place in your arsenal of Web development gadgets. It enables you to use PDF, a wonderful vehicle that expands the functionality of the World Wide Web.

Big Ideas: InterAct

We complete our look at controls that go beyond simple graphics and text with a look at a control that allows users to visualize ideas and express them as diagrams.

These modeling tools are coming into increasing prominence in the world of computing. Evolving beyond the paper-based flowchart, computer-based visual tools allow a flexibility in diagramming that was unheard of until recently. You can picture the steps in all kinds of real-world processes including business processes, scientific processes, and project plans. This is a great help when you want to communicate your ideas to others.

With its InterAct modeling tool, New Jersey–based ProtoView brings diagramming capabilities to the world of ActiveX controls. You can put this control on your Web page, and users can use it to build models of processes when they view your page in a browser. Download a sample of InterAct from the Microsoft ActiveX Component Gallery and we'll get started.

In the ActiveX Control Pad, open a new HTML file and save it as `InterAct` in `skill 7`. Then open a new HTML Layout Control and save it as `layout for InterAct`. Put the ProtoView InterAct control on the Toolbox, select it, and place it on the layout. Size it so it takes up at least half of the layout space. Save your work and open the page in IE.

The page opens with a grid in a work area. Right-click on the work area to pop up a menu, and make the selection that brings a Tools Palette onscreen. You can select shapes and lines from this palette to draw diagrams of processes. In Figure 7.14, you see the results of my handiwork in modeling the process for making an omelet. Try diagramming a few processes to get the feel for using the Tools Palette.

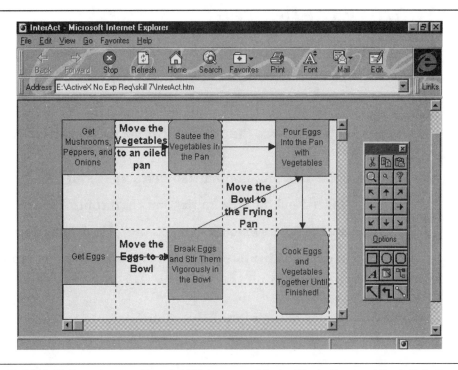

FIGURE 7.14: Our InterAct Web page with the Work Area and Tools Palette. The Work Area shows a diagram for a process that results in an omelet.

The Options choice in the Tools Palette enables users to save diagrams locally and load them in future sessions. This capability could make InterAct very useful in corporate intranets or in other environments where people visualize ideas and share them with one another.

Summarizing

We've progressed from graphics to data visualization to diagramming, and from simple text to text that looks like it came out of a printed publication. We've also learned some more ActiveX and VBS along the way.

In the next Skill, we'll enter the world of multimedia and explore its implementation in ActiveX.

Are You Experienced?

Now you can...

- ☑ visualize data in the Chart control
- ☑ enter data into the Chart control via the Properties sheet and via HTML
- ☑ enter data programmatically via a VBS script
- ☑ understand the First Impression Chart control and its features
- ☑ use the Adobe Acrobat ActiveX control to display documents in PDF
- ☑ understand the InterAct control for diagramming processes

S K I L L

8

eight

Multiplying the Media:
Music, Sound, and Video

❑ **Adding synthesized music to your Web pages**

❑ **Working with arrays**

❑ **Streaming audio into your Web pages**

❑ **Watching movies**

❑ **Tracking movie events**

Images, charts, and diagrams augment a user's experience with a Web page and add to the excitement of surfing the Net. Music, sounds, and videos turn up the volume on the fun and excitement even more. You can harness this collection of multimedia to make your Web pages come alive. In this Skill, we explore three controls that bring multimedia to the world of ActiveX.

In order to do the exercises in this Skill, you'll need a sound card and speakers installed in your computer. When we get to the third control, make sure you have your Windows 95 CD in your CD-ROM drive.

The Interactive Music Control

The ActiveX Interactive Music control is the latest addition to Microsoft's stable of ActiveX controls. It's is one of those why-didn't-I-think-of-it ideas. The Interactive Music control adds music to your Web pages while getting around the very thorny problem of copyrights. You see, if you play a music clip on your Web page, you may have to pay someone a royalty. One way to get around this is to play something original.

The Interactive Music control does just that: It plays a melody that no one has composed. How is that possible? Does it make the music up as it goes along? Well…yes. All you do is set some parameters, such as Style, Personality, and type of Band, and a software synthesizer plays the tune. So many permutations are possible that you can easily match a tune to the content of your Web page. The control handles transitions from page to page as well.

To obtain this control, head over to `http://www.microsoft.com/Home.htm` and follow the download instructions.

 TIP   In addition to installing and registering the control, the download and installation process puts Music control–related reference material on your hard drive. The material, in HTML files, includes a Tutorial, a Language Reference (which provides all of this control's associated procedures and possible values for their arguments), and information that gets you off to a quick start.

Facing the Music

To help you become aware of all the different types and combinations of available music—and more importantly, what they sound like—Microsoft provides an

Express tool as part of the reference package that installs with the Interactive Music control. You can make all kinds of selections in this tool and immediately hear the results.

Let's have a look—and a listen. Go to the folder called `Microsoft Interactive Music Web Reference` that holds the reference material. You'll see many subfolders that hold a wealth of information.

Open the `Express` folder, and you'll see a couple of familiar icons. One is the icon for an HTML file; the other is an icon for an ALX file. Double-click on the HTML file, `default`, to open the Express tool in Internet Explorer (see Figure 8.1).

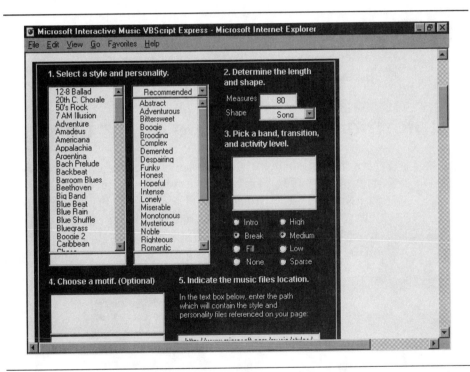

FIGURE 8.1: The Web page for the Interactive Music control's Express tool

Two large listboxes ask you to select a Style and a Personality for the music. Every type of music from Rock to Beethoven has its own characteristic pattern of notes, and the Style property lets you select this pattern. More than a hundred styles are available (including Bluegrass, Caribbean, and Country). The Personality property sets up the progression of chords for the selected style. (Funky, Intense, and Mysterious are a few Personalities.)

In the second group of controls, you select a Length (the number of measures) for the music and a Shape (the way the intensity changes over time).

The third group offers selections for Band (the set of instruments that plays the style), type of transition (the way the music sounds when you move from one Web page to another), and Activity Level (how frequently the chords change).

In the fourth group, a listbox, you can select an optional motif (a musical flourish, such as a Guitar Lick). You don't have to be concerned about the fifth group, which is for setting a file path in a URL.

Start clicking and start listening!

NOTE   If you don't know anything about chords, chord changes, flourishes, or measures, don't worry. It won't diminish your enjoyment of this control. You may even learn a thing or two about music composition.

Exploring the Interactive Music Control

Now let's take a look at the Interactive Music control up close and personal. Open a new HTML file and save it as `music` in `skill 8`. Give it **Interactive Music** as a title and **The Great Music Demo!** as a centered heading. Just for appearances, follow the heading with a horizontal line. Select Edit ➤ Insert ActiveX Control..., and select Microsoft Music Control from the list. In the Object Editor, right-click on the control, and you'll see a pop-up menu with two entries (see Figure 8.2).

FIGURE 8.2: The menu that pops up when you right-click on the Interactive Music control

The two choices are related to the properties of the Interactive Music control. The first, Properties, opens the same Properties sheet we've worked with before. The second is Music Properties. If you click on this, the Control Properties dialog box opens with two tabbed pages (see Figure 8.3). This type of Properties page, with buttons to open Help files, is the probable wave of the future for viewing and setting the properties of ActiveX controls.

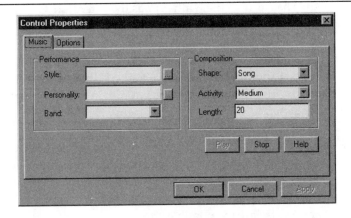

FIGURE 8.3: When you click on Music Properties, the Control Properties dialog box appears.

The first tab in the Control Properties dialog box, Music, has two groups. One group offers choices for Performance; the other for Composition. The second tab, Options, also has two groups, one for Optimization and one for Section (see Figure 8.4).

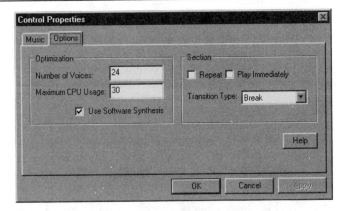

FIGURE 8.4: In the Control Properties dialog box, the Options tab has one group of choices for Optimization and another group for Section.

Let's examine each of these tabs in the Control Properties dialog box.

The Music Tab

In the Performance group you select the music's Style, Personality, and Band. Each style has its own file, with .STY as the extension. Clicking on the ellipsis to the right of the Style box opens a File Open dialog box from which you can select the STY file you want to use. Like Style, each Personality has its own file. These files have .PER as their extension.

The Band property contains a set of "instruments" to play the selected Style. The drop-down list examines your Style and Personality choices and figures out a set of Bands for you to choose from. The Bands have names like OtherWorld, Good Vibes, and Honky Tonk.

In the Compositions group, the Shape property determines how the intensity of the selected Style changes over time. Possible values include Rising, Falling, and Level.

Activity specifies the frequency of chord changes. Dense, Frequent, Medium, and Sparse are the possible values.

Length specifies the duration of the music (in measures). In the Options tab, you can select Repeat, which causes the composition to repeat after the designated number of measures.

The Options Tab

The Options tab of the Control Properties dialog box contains two groups: Optimization and Section. In the Optimization group, Number of Voices sets the minimum number of voices (or instruments) to use. This one works only if the checkbox (Use Software Synthesis) below the group is checked. Checking this checkbox plays music through the Microsoft Synthesizer (which you can download along with the Interactive Music control). If you have a MIDI device that you want the music played through, make sure you clear this checkbox.

Maximum CPU Usage is the percentage of the CPU you want devoted to playing the music. To meet this percentage, your computer might have to make some adjustments (like compressing data or omitting a few instruments).

In the Section group, the Repeat checkbox specifies whether you want the music replayed after the number of measures you entered in the Music tab's Length property. If you check the box, the music repeats. If you don't, it plays only once.

The Play Immediately checkbox determines whether the music plays as soon as the page opens (if the box is checked), or if it waits for some other event, like a Click event (if the box is cleared).

It's possible that you'll want one type of music on one page within your site and another type on another. During the time that the user goes from page to page, what do you want the music to do? You use the Transition Type property to specify the transition effects between pages. Possible values are Break, End and Intro, Fill, and None.

In addition to setting these parameters in the pages of the Control Properties dialog box, you can set them programmatically.

While you're still in the Object Editor, you can experiment with all these parameters and hear what the music sounds like by clicking the Play button on the Music tab. It's extremely helpful to be able to hear the results of your tinkering at designtime, rather than having to wait for a page to open in IE. It's not quite as smooth as working with the Express tool, but it's a welcome capability.

When you've finished experimenting with the parameters, close the Music Properties pages and open the Properties sheet. Set the control's ID property to **imControl**. Close the Object Editor, and you'll find that your HTML file looks something like this:

```
<HTML>
<HEAD>
<TITLE>Interactive Music</TITLE>
</HEAD>
<BODY>
<CENTER> <H1> The Great Music Demo! </H1> </CENTER> <HR>
    <OBJECT ID="imControl" WIDTH=40 HEIGHT=40
 CLASSID="CLSID:D2377D41-E6FD-11CF-8DCF-00AA00C01802">
       <PARAM NAME="NumVoices" VALUE="24">
       <PARAM NAME="MaxCPU" VALUE="30">
       <PARAM NAME="UseSoftwareSynthesis" VALUE="1">
       <PARAM NAME="Style" VALUE="">
       <PARAM NAME="Personality" VALUE="">
       <PARAM NAME="Template" VALUE="">
       <PARAM NAME="Section" VALUE="">
       <PARAM NAME="Band" VALUE="Default">
       <PARAM NAME="Shape" VALUE="8">
       <PARAM NAME="Activity" VALUE="1">
       <PARAM NAME="Repeat" VALUE="0">
       <PARAM NAME="Length" VALUE="20">
       <PARAM NAME="Transition" VALUE="32">
       <PARAM NAME="PlayImmediate" VALUE="0">
    </OBJECT>

    </BODY>
    </HTML>
```

Skill 8

Note that we eliminate the Values for Style and Personality, because we'll write a script that sets them. For NumVoices, retain the default value (24).

Leave this page open as we move on.

Mixing, Matching, and Music

Adding music to a Web page is as simple as selecting the parameters that create the music you want and inserting the Interactive Music control into your HTML document.

Even so, let's tinker a bit with some of the Interactive Music control's events, properties, and methods. We'll add a few controls to this HTML document to emulate a few capabilities of the Express tool. In so doing, we'll build a page that allows a user to mix and match some of the control's features, and in the process we'll pick up some more VBS concepts (and a little HTML, too).

Laying Out the Document

In your `music.htm` file, just below the </OBJECT> tag, type:

**<P> <B>Here's a little something for your listening enjoyment.
**

**In the box on the left, select a Style.
**

**In the box in the center, pick a Personality.
**

**In the box on the right, strike up the Band!
**

To stop the music at any time, click on the Stop Button.

</B></P>

This gives you an idea of the controls we'll embed in the document. We'll have three ListBoxes side-by-side. One ListBox will present choices for music Styles, one for Personalities, and one for Bands. Each ListBox's Change event will immediately trigger a new value. Below the ListBox controls, we'll put a Command Button.

 NOTE   Why do we embed our controls directly in the HTML document rather than in the HTML Layout Control? As it happens, the Layout Control doesn't work with some of the Interactive Music control's methods.

First, use Edit ➤ Insert ActiveX Control… to insert a Microsoft Forms 2.0 ListBox control just below the paragraph we've written. Set the Listbox's ID property to **lstbxStyle**. Use copy and paste techniques to create two more ListBox controls and insert them just below the first one. Set the first one's ID property to **lstbxPersonality** and the second one's to **lstbxBand**.

This next part is important: For lstbxStyle and lstbxPersonality, open the control property sheet and set the BoundColumn property to **0**. For lstbxBand, set the BoundColumn property to **1**. These values tell you that for the first two ListBoxes we'll work with the index of a selection, and for the third, we'll work with the selection itself.

Next, insert a Microsoft Forms 2.0 Command Button. Set its ID property to **cmdbtnStop** and its Caption property to **Stop** with the text bold. Here's how the file looks at this point:

```
<HTML>
<HEAD>
<TITLE>Interactive Music</TITLE>
</HEAD>
<BODY>
<CENTER> <H1> The Great Music Demo! </H1> </CENTER> <HR>
    <OBJECT ID="imControl" WIDTH=40 HEIGHT=40
 CLASSID="CLSID:D2377D41-E6FD-11CF-8DCF-00AA00C01802">
    <PARAM NAME="NumVoices" VALUE="24">
    <PARAM NAME="MaxCPU" VALUE="30">
    <PARAM NAME="UseSoftwareSynthesis" VALUE="1">
    <PARAM NAME="Style" VALUE="">
    <PARAM NAME="Personality" VALUE="">
    <PARAM NAME="Template" VALUE="">
    <PARAM NAME="Section" VALUE="">
    <PARAM NAME="Band" VALUE="Default">
    <PARAM NAME="Shape" VALUE="8">
    <PARAM NAME="Activity" VALUE="1">
    <PARAM NAME="Repeat" VALUE="0">
    <PARAM NAME="Length" VALUE="20">
    <PARAM NAME="Transition" VALUE="32">
    <PARAM NAME="PlayImmediate" VALUE="0">
</OBJECT>

<P> <B>Here's a little something for your listening enjoyment. <BR>
In the box on the left, select a Style. <BR>
In the box in the center, pick a Personality. <BR>
In the box on the right, strike up the Band!
</B></P>

    <OBJECT ID="lstbxPersonality" WIDTH=131 HEIGHT=95
     CLASSID="CLSID:8BD21D20-EC42-11CE-9E0D-00AA006002F3">
        <PARAM NAME="ScrollBars" VALUE="3">
        <PARAM NAME="DisplayStyle" VALUE="2">
        <PARAM NAME="Size" VALUE="3466;2512">
```

```
            <PARAM NAME="BoundColumn" VALUE="0">
            <PARAM NAME="MatchEntry" VALUE="0">
            <PARAM NAME="FontCharSet" VALUE="0">
            <PARAM NAME="FontPitchAndFamily" VALUE="2">
            <PARAM NAME="FontWeight" VALUE="0">
        </OBJECT>

        <OBJECT ID="lstbxBand" WIDTH=131 HEIGHT=95
          CLASSID="CLSID:8BD21D20-EC42-11CE-9E0D-00AA006002F3">
            <PARAM NAME="ScrollBars" VALUE="3">
            <PARAM NAME="DisplayStyle" VALUE="2">
            <PARAM NAME="Size" VALUE="3466;2512">
            <PARAM NAME="BoundColumn" VALUE="1">
            <PARAM NAME="MatchEntry" VALUE="0">
            <PARAM NAME="FontCharSet" VALUE="0">
            <PARAM NAME="FontPitchAndFamily" VALUE="2">
            <PARAM NAME="FontWeight" VALUE="0">
        </OBJECT>

        <OBJECT ID="cmdbtnStop" WIDTH=96 HEIGHT=32
          CLASSID="CLSID:D7053240-CE69-11CD-A777-00DD01143C57">
            <PARAM NAME="Caption" VALUE="Stop">
            <PARAM NAME="Size" VALUE="2540;846">
            <PARAM NAME="FontCharSet" VALUE="0">
            <PARAM NAME="FontPitchAndFamily" VALUE="2">
            <PARAM NAME="ParagraphAlign" VALUE="3">
            <PARAM NAME="FontWeight" VALUE="0">
        </OBJECT>
    </BODY>
</HTML>
```

If we opened the page in IE as it is right now, it would be a sorry sight indeed. (And, come to think of it, a sorry site, too.) The controls would be on top of each other. Fortunately, we can use a little HTML magic to straighten things out. The magic comes in the form of the <TABLE> tag.

Most of the time, when you think of a table, you probably think of a structure that holds data arranged in rows and columns, with the rows and columns intersecting to form cells. In HTML, a table isn't confined to data. It can also hold text, images, and (most importantly, for our purposes) ActiveX controls. Let's put the three ListBoxes in one row of a table and the Command Button in another:

1. We start the table by inserting a **<TABLE>** tag just before the lstbxStyle <OBJECT> tag and end the table by inserting **</TABLE>** after cmdbtnStop. This, of course, is just the beginning.

2. In the opening <TABLE> tag, insert two attributes **COLS = 3** and **CELLPADDING = 30**. The opening <TABLE> tag should then look like this: <TABLE COLS = 3 CELLPADDING = 30>. The first attribute sets up the number of columns in the table. The second sets up, in pixels, the amount of space between the sides of a cell and its contents. (This gives us some space between successive controls in the same row.)

3. Now we'll set up our rows. To build the first row, type **<TR>** just before the lstbxStyle <OBJECT> tag and **</TR>** right after the lstbxBand <OBJECT> tag.

4. To build the second row, type **<TR>** just before cmdbtnStop and **</TR>** right after cmdbtnStop.

5. We finish by setting up the cells. The <TD> tag does this. We'll want each control in its own cell, so before each control type **<TD>**, and after each control type **</TD>**.

Here's how it all comes out:

```
<HTML>
<HEAD>
<TITLE>Interactive Music</TITLE>
</HEAD>
<BODY>
<CENTER> <H1> The Great Music Demo! </H1> </CENTER> <HR>
    <OBJECT ID="imControl" WIDTH=40 HEIGHT=40
 CLASSID="CLSID:D2377D41-E6FD-11CF-8DCF-00AA00C01802">
    <PARAM NAME="NumVoices" VALUE="24">
    <PARAM NAME="MaxCPU" VALUE="30">
    <PARAM NAME="UseSoftwareSynthesis" VALUE="1">
    <PARAM NAME="Style" VALUE="">
    <PARAM NAME="Personality" VALUE="">
    <PARAM NAME="Template" VALUE="">
    <PARAM NAME="Section" VALUE="">
    <PARAM NAME="Band" VALUE="Default">
    <PARAM NAME="Shape" VALUE="8">
    <PARAM NAME="Activity" VALUE="1">
    <PARAM NAME="Repeat" VALUE="0">
    <PARAM NAME="Length" VALUE="20">
    <PARAM NAME="Transition" VALUE="32">
    <PARAM NAME="PlayImmediate" VALUE="0">
</OBJECT>

<P> <B>Here's a little something for your listening enjoyment. <BR>
In the box on the left, select a Style. <BR>
```

Skill 8

```
In the box in the center, pick a Personality. <BR>
In the box on the right, strike up the Band!
</B></P>

<TABLE COLS = 3 CELLPADDING = 30>
<TR> <TD>
    <OBJECT ID="lstbxStyle" WIDTH=131 HEIGHT=95
    CLASSID="CLSID:8BD21D20-EC42-11CE-9E0D-00AA006002F3">
        <PARAM NAME="ScrollBars" VALUE="3">
        <PARAM NAME="DisplayStyle" VALUE="2">
        <PARAM NAME="Size" VALUE="3457;2505">
        <PARAM NAME="BoundColumn" VALUE="0">
        <PARAM NAME="MatchEntry" VALUE="0">
        <PARAM NAME="FontCharSet" VALUE="0">
        <PARAM NAME="FontPitchAndFamily" VALUE="2">
        <PARAM NAME="FontWeight" VALUE="0">
    </OBJECT>
</TD>
<TD>
    <OBJECT ID="lstbxPersonality" WIDTH=131 HEIGHT=95
    CLASSID="CLSID:8BD21D20-EC42-11CE-9E0D-00AA006002F3">
        <PARAM NAME="ScrollBars" VALUE="3">
        <PARAM NAME="DisplayStyle" VALUE="2">
        <PARAM NAME="Size" VALUE="3466;2512">
        <PARAM NAME="BoundColumn" VALUE="0">
        <PARAM NAME="MatchEntry" VALUE="0">
        <PARAM NAME="FontCharSet" VALUE="0">
        <PARAM NAME="FontPitchAndFamily" VALUE="2">
        <PARAM NAME="FontWeight" VALUE="0">
    </OBJECT>
</TD>
<TD>
    <OBJECT ID="lstbxBand" WIDTH=131 HEIGHT=95
    CLASSID="CLSID:8BD21D20-EC42-11CE-9E0D-00AA006002F3">
        <PARAM NAME="ScrollBars" VALUE="3">
        <PARAM NAME="DisplayStyle" VALUE="2">
        <PARAM NAME="Size" VALUE="3466;2512">
        <PARAM NAME="BoundColumn" VALUE="1">
        <PARAM NAME="MatchEntry" VALUE="0">
        <PARAM NAME="FontCharSet" VALUE="0">
        <PARAM NAME="FontPitchAndFamily" VALUE="2">
        <PARAM NAME="FontWeight" VALUE="0">
    </OBJECT>
</TD>
```

```
<TR> <TD>
    <OBJECT ID="cmdbtnStop" WIDTH=96 HEIGHT=32
     CLASSID="CLSID:D7053240-CE69-11CD-A777-00DD01143C57">
        <PARAM NAME="Caption" VALUE="Stop">
        <PARAM NAME="Size" VALUE="2540;846">
        <PARAM NAME="FontCharSet" VALUE="0">
        <PARAM NAME="FontPitchAndFamily" VALUE="2">
        <PARAM NAME="ParagraphAlign" VALUE="3">
        <PARAM NAME="FontWeight" VALUE="0">
    </OBJECT>
</TD>
</TR> </TABLE>
</BODY>
</HTML>
```

That's the layout. When you open the page in IE, it should look like Figure 8.5.

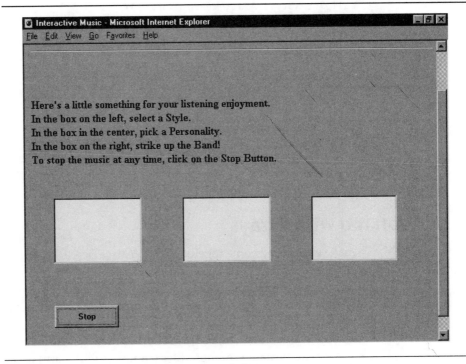

FIGURE 8.5: IE's rendering of *music.htm*

Populating the ListBoxes

Now we have to put values into the ListBoxes. The first one will display Styles, the second will show Personalities, and the third will have Bands. I decided on four Styles: 50s Rock, Beethoven, Hip 60s Rock, and Rock Ballads. If you prefer different styles, by all means use them. The same with Personalities: I selected Righteous, Honest, Sophisticated, and Adventurous. The Bands I chose were Classical, Clockwork, Twangs, and Default. With so many possible combinations, you're sure to find a set you like.

To put these values (or the ones you like) into the ListBoxes, use the Script Wizard to embed this code in the HTML document (right after <HEAD>):

```
<SCRIPT LANGUAGE="VBScript">
<!--
Sub window_onLoad()
call lstbxStyle.AddItem("50s Rock",0)
call lstbxStyle.AddItem("Beethoven", 1)
call lstbxStyle.AddItem("Hip 60s Rock", 2)
call lstbxStyle.AddItem("Rock Ballad", 3)
call lstbxPersonality.AddItem("Righteous", 0)
call lstbxPersonality.AddItem("Honest", 1)
call lstbxPersonality.AddItem("Sophisticated", 2)
call lstbxPersonality.AddItem("Adventurous", 3)
call lstbxBand.AddItem("Classical", 0)
call lstbxBand.AddItem("Clockwork", 1)
call lstbxBand.AddItem("Twangs", 2)
call lstbxBand.AddItem("Default", 3)
-->
    </SCRIPT>
```

Working with Arrays

To make everything come together, we'll learn a new VBS concept: arrays. Before we do that, however, I'll tell you why.

We're going to put the Style, Personality, and Band selections together (along with some default values) and have the control compose a piece of music called a *Section*. Every Style and Personality has its own individual file. The built-in procedure we'll use (it's called EZPlaySection) uses the names of those files. If we could present the names of those files (complete with path) in our Style and Personality ListBoxes, we could just pass the values of the ListBoxes directly to EZPlaySection.

Doing that would present a problem: It's not user-friendly to populate a ListBox with choices like E:\Multimedia Files\MINAEO.per instead of choices like Adventurous. What we need is a mechanism that translates the ListBox choice into its filename, and then turns the filename over to EZPlaySection.

Recall from the preceding Skill that when you set the BoundColumn property of a ListBox to 0, the value of the ListBox isn't the selection, it's the index of the selection. In lstbxPersonality, for example, the first item is Righteous. If you select that item—and if the BoundColumn is 0—the value of the ListBox is 0 (because the index of the first item is 0), not Righteous. The second item is Honest, and if you select it, the value of the ListBox is 1 (because the second item's index is 1).

What we'll do is match up the items in the ListBox with the items in a structure called an *array*. An array is a collection of items that we tie together. We tie them together because they're similar in some way and so we can refer to them by the name of the array and the index number. If this makes you think of a table and its rows (where the table is the array, and the row numbers are indexes) you've pretty much got it.

The idea is to take the ListBox value—let's say it's 1—and then go to an array of filenames. We'll have to build this array, but for the moment, let's pretend we already have. If we've set the array up correctly, the item whose index is 1 corresponds to the filename for the item in lstbxPersonality whose index is 1. (That value—on my computer—will be E:\Multimedia Files\JAZZ.PER.) We take the item from the array, and give it to EZPlaySection. Think of the filename array as a dictionary in which you look up the filename of the ListBox choice.

How do we build an array? In the Script Wizard, go to the Actions pane and find Global Variables. Right-click on Global Variables and select New Global Variable… from the pop-up menu. In the dialog box, type the name you want to give the array, followed by an open parenthesis, followed by the number of items that will go in the array minus one (because indexing starts from 0, not 1), followed by a close parenthesis.

We'll need two arrays, so you'll go through this process twice. The first time, type **style_path_array(3)** in the dialog box and click OK. The second time, type **personality_path_array(3)** and click OK.

If you then click OK to close the Script Wizard, you'll see these lines somewhere in your HTML document:

```
dim style_path_array(3)
dim personality_path_array(3)
```

We'll assign the array items in the Window OnLoad event. First, of course, you have to know what those items are. Table 8.1 shows the specifics for style_path_array, and Table 8.2 does the same for personality_path_array. You can get these values, or the ones for the Styles and Personalities you like, by working with the

Express tool. When you make a selection from either of the first two boxes in Express, the filename (not the whole path) appears at the bottom of the box.

 WARNING   Bear in mind that the file paths I use are probably *not* the same as the ones on your machine. I stored the files in a folder on my E: drive. The default installation puts them on the C: drive. You may have done something completely different.

T A B L E   8 . 1 : The Items in the style_path_array

Index	Path
0	"E:\Multimedia Files\50SROCK.STY"
1	"E:\Multimedia Files\BETHOVEN.STY"
2	"E:\Multimedia Files\HIP60S.STY"
3	"E:\Multimedia Files\ROCKBLD.STY"

T A B L E   8 . 2 : The Items in the personality_path_array

Index	Path
0	"E:\Multimedia Files\CLASSICL.PER"
1	"E:\Multimedia Files\JAZZ.PER"
2	"E:\Multimedia Files\CNTRY.PER"
3	"E:\Multimedia Files\MINAEO.PER"

Now that you know the items, you can put them into the arrays by typing this code in the Window_OnLoad subroutine (just after the lines that populate the ListBoxes):

```
style_path_array(0) = "E:\Multimedia Files\50SROCK.STY"
style_path_array(1) = "E:\Multimedia Files\BETHOVEN.STY"
style_path_array(2) = "E:\Multimedia Files\HIP60S.STY"
style_path_array(3) = "E:\Multimedia Files\ROCKBLD.STY"
personality_path_array(0) = "E:\Multimedia Files\CLASSICL.PER"
personality_path_array(1) = "E:\Multimedia Files\JAZZ.PER"
personality_path_array(2) = "E:\Multimedia Files\CNTRY.PER"
personality_path_array(3) = "E:\Multimedia Files\MINAEO.PER"
```

The *EZPlaySection* Function

EZPlaySection is a method built into the Interactive Music control that you use to play a section of music. If you open the Script Wizard and put it into Code View, you'll see this method in the Actions pane when you click on the + next to imControl.

This method is more complex than any we've worked with thus far. It takes nine arguments, and we have to be careful about the way we specify each argument. Table 8.3 presents the arguments to EZPlaySection.

TABLE 8.3: The Arguments of *EZPlaySection*

Argument	Description	Possible Values
style file	Specifies the style	File path in string form
personality file	Specifies the personality	File path in string form
number of measures	Provides the length of the section in measures	An integer (the default is 80)
transition	Specifies the type of transition from section to section	C_NONE, C_FILL, C_INTRO, C_BREAK
band name	Gives the name of the band	Band name in string form
shape	Defines the section's musical "shape"	S-FALLING, S_LEVEL, S_LOOPABLE, S_LOUD, S_QUIET, S_PEAKING, S_RANDOM, S_RISING, S_SONG
activity	Gives the rate of chord changes	An integer from 0 (most activity) to 3 (least activity)
playImmediate	Defines whether to play the section as soon as it's ready	TRUE (play it as soon as it's ready), FALSE (wait for an event)
repeat	Makes a looping section or uses the number of repeats built into the section file	TRUE (make a looping section), FALSE (use built-in repeats)

Since we're only working with three listboxes, we're just allowing the user to change three of the nine arguments. We'll enter the values for the other arguments as part of the VBS code.

The objective is to get this function to work each time a ListBox value changes. Thus, we'll associate each ListBox Change event with this function. The Change event for lstbxStyle and for lstbxPersonality will make use of the array functionality we just discussed. The Change event for lstbxBand will pass lstbxBand's value directly to EZPlaySection.

Skill 8

Let's start with the Change event for lstbxStyle. When the user makes a selection in this ListBox (and activates the Change event), we want these things to happen:

1. Stop playing a section.

2. Note the index of the selection.

3. Use that index as the index of the style_path_array.

4. Take the element in style_path_array which has that index and send it to EZPlaySection.

To accomplish the first step, we invoke the Interactive Music control's Stop method. You can use the Script Wizard to do this in the usual way. (Select lstbxStyle's Change event, and double-click on imControl's Stop method.)

I'll break the remaining steps down:

1. Set the index of lstbxStyle's selection to lstbxStyle.Value (because we've set lstbxStyle's BoundColumn to 0).

2. Since the expression lstbxStyle.Value is a number, we can use it as the index for style_path_array. Thus, the corresponding element in style_path_array is style_path_array(lstbxStyle.Value).

3. This expression becomes the first argument to EZPlaySection.

In a similar way, the second argument for EZPlaySection is personality_path_array(lstbxPersonality.Value).

Here, then, is the code for lstbxStyle's Change event:

```
Sub lstbxStyle_Change()
call imControl.Stop(flags)
On Error Resume Next
call imControl.EZPlaySection(style_path_array(lstbxStyle.Value),
➥personality_path_array(lstbxPersonality.Value), 20,
➥imControl.C_INTRO, lstbxBand.Value, imControl.S_RISING,
➥1, TRUE, FALSE)
end sub
```

Similarly, the code for lstbxPersonality's Change event is:

```
Sub lstbxPersonality_Change()
call imControl.Stop(flags)
On Error Resume Next
call imControl.EZPlaySection(style_path_array(lstbxStyle.Value),
➥personality_path_array(lstbxPersonality.Value), 20,
```

```
➥imControl.C_BREAK, lstbxBand.Value, imControl.S_RISING,
➥1, TRUE, FALSE)
end sub
```

And, finally, the code for lstbxBand's Change event:

```
Sub lstbxBand_Change()
call imControl.Stop(flags)
On Error Resume Next
call imControl.EZPlaySection(style_path_array(lstbxStyle.Value),
➥personality_path_array(lstbxPersonality.Value), 20,
➥imControl.C_FILL, lstbxBand.Value, imControl.S_RISING,
➥1, TRUE, FALSE)
end sub
```

You can use the Script Wizard to input much of this code. As we pointed out in the last Skill, the statement On Error Resume Next takes care of some minor inconsistencies at startup (like matching up one variable with another before one of them has been assigned a value).

If you look closely at the code for the three Change events, you'll see that I've made them different from one another in the fourth argument. This is the one that deals with transitions from one section to another. I did it that way just to hear what the different transitions sound like and to make the transitions sound different for the three events. Use those, or others from the third column of the fourth row of Table 8.3.

For completeness, here's the code for our music file (music.htm).

music.htm

```
<HTML>
<HEAD>
 <SCRIPT LANGUAGE="VBScript">
<!--
Sub window_onLoad()
call lstbxStyle.AddItem("50s Rock",0)
call lstbxStyle.AddItem("Beethoven", 1)
call lstbxStyle.AddItem("Hip 60s Rock", 2)
call lstbxStyle.AddItem("Rock Ballad", 3)
call lstbxPersonality.AddItem("Righteous", 0)
call lstbxPersonality.AddItem("Honest", 1)
call lstbxPersonality.AddItem("Sophisticated", 2)
call lstbxPersonality.AddItem("Adventurous", 3)
call lstbxBand.AddItem("Classical", 0)
call lstbxBand.AddItem("Clockwork", 1)
call lstbxBand.AddItem("Twangs", 2)
call lstbxBand.AddItem("Default", 3)
```

Skill 8

```
style_path_array(0) = "E:\Multimedia Files\50SROCK.STY"
style_path_array(1) = "E:\Multimedia Files\BETHOVEN.STY"
style_path_array(2) = "E:\Multimedia Files\HIP60S.STY"
style_path_array(3) = "E:\Multimedia Files\ROCKBLD.STY"
personality_path_array(0) = "E:\Multimedia Files\CLASSICL.PER"
personality_path_array(1) = "E:\Multimedia Files\JAZZ.PER"
personality_path_array(2) = "E:\Multimedia Files\CNTRY.PER"
personality_path_array(3) = "E:\Multimedia Files\MINAEO.PER"
end sub
-->
    </SCRIPT>


<TITLE>Interactive Music</TITLE>
</HEAD>
<BODY>
<CENTER> <H1> The Great Music Demo! </H1> </CENTER> <HR>
    <OBJECT ID="imControl" WIDTH=40 HEIGHT=40
 CLASSID="CLSID:D2377D41-E6FD-11CF-8DCF-00AA00C01802">
    <PARAM NAME="NumVoices" VALUE="24">
    <PARAM NAME="MaxCPU" VALUE="30">
    <PARAM NAME="UseSoftwareSynthesis" VALUE="1">
    <PARAM NAME="Style" VALUE="">
    <PARAM NAME="Personality" VALUE=" ">
    <PARAM NAME="Template" VALUE="">
    <PARAM NAME="Section" VALUE="">
    <PARAM NAME="Band" VALUE="Default">
    <PARAM NAME="Shape" VALUE="8">
    <PARAM NAME="Activity" VALUE="1">
    <PARAM NAME="Repeat" VALUE="0">
    <PARAM NAME="Length" VALUE="20">
    <PARAM NAME="Transition" VALUE="32">
    <PARAM NAME="PlayImmediate" VALUE="0">
</OBJECT>

<P> <B>Here's a little something for your listening enjoyment. <BR>
In the box on the left, select a Style. <BR>
In the box in the center, pick a Personality. <BR>
In the box on the right, strike up the Band! <BR>
To stop the music at any time, click on the Stop Button.
</B></P>

    <SCRIPT LANGUAGE="VBScript">
<!--
Sub cmdbtnStop_Click()
call imControl.Stop(flags)
end sub
-->
    </SCRIPT>
```

```
<TABLE COLS = 3 CELLPADDING = 30>
<TR> <TD>
    <SCRIPT LANGUAGE="VBScript">
<!--
Sub lstbxStyle_Change()
call imControl.Stop(flags)
On Error Resume Next
call imControl.EZPlaySection(style_path_array(lstbxStyle.Value),
➡personality_path_array(lstbxPersonality.Value), 20,
➡imControl.C_INTRO, lstbxBand.Value, imControl.S_RISING, 1, TRUE, FALSE)
end sub
-->
    </SCRIPT>
    <OBJECT ID="lstbxStyle" WIDTH=131 HEIGHT=95
     CLASSID="CLSID:8BD21D20-EC42-11CE-9E0D-00AA006002F3">
        <PARAM NAME="ScrollBars" VALUE="3">
        <PARAM NAME="DisplayStyle" VALUE="2">
        <PARAM NAME="Size" VALUE="3457;2505">
        <PARAM NAME="BoundColumn" VALUE="0">
        <PARAM NAME="MatchEntry" VALUE="0">
        <PARAM NAME="FontCharSet" VALUE="0">
        <PARAM NAME="FontPitchAndFamily" VALUE="2">
        <PARAM NAME="FontWeight" VALUE="0">
    </OBJECT>
</TD>
<TD>
    <SCRIPT LANGUAGE="VBScript">
<!--
Sub lstbxPersonality_Change()
call imControl.Stop(flags)
On Error Resume Next
call imControl.EZPlaySection(style_path_array(lstbxStyle.Value),
➡personality_path_array(lstbxPersonality.Value), 20,
➡imControl.C_BREAK, lstbxBand.Value, imControl.S_RISING, 1,TRUE, FALSE)
end sub
-->
    </SCRIPT>
    <OBJECT ID="lstbxPersonality" WIDTH=131 HEIGHT=95
     CLASSID="CLSID:8BD21D20-EC42-11CE-9E0D-00AA006002F3">
        <PARAM NAME="ScrollBars" VALUE="3">
        <PARAM NAME="DisplayStyle" VALUE="2">
        <PARAM NAME="Size" VALUE="3466;2512">
        <PARAM NAME="BoundColumn" VALUE="0">
        <PARAM NAME="MatchEntry" VALUE="0">
        <PARAM NAME="FontCharSet" VALUE="0">
        <PARAM NAME="FontPitchAndFamily" VALUE="2">
        <PARAM NAME="FontWeight" VALUE="0">
    </OBJECT>
</TD>
```

Skill 8

```
<TD>
    <SCRIPT LANGUAGE="VBScript">
<!--
Sub lstbxBand_Change()
call imControl.Stop(flags)
On Error Resume Next
call imControl.EZPlaySection(style_path_array(lstbxStyle.Value),
➥personality_path_array(lstbxPersonality.Value), 10,
➥imControl.C_FILL, lstbxBand.Value, imControl.S_RISING, 1, TRUE, FALSE)
end sub
-->
    </SCRIPT>
    <OBJECT ID="lstbxBand" WIDTH=131 HEIGHT=95
     CLASSID="CLSID:8BD21D20-EC42-11CE-9E0D-00AA006002F3">
        <PARAM NAME="ScrollBars" VALUE="3">
        <PARAM NAME="DisplayStyle" VALUE="2">
        <PARAM NAME="Size" VALUE="3466;2512">
        <PARAM NAME="BoundColumn" VALUE="1">
        <PARAM NAME="MatchEntry" VALUE="0">
        <PARAM NAME="FontCharSet" VALUE="0">
        <PARAM NAME="FontPitchAndFamily" VALUE="2">
        <PARAM NAME="FontWeight" VALUE="0">
    </OBJECT>
</TD>

<TR> <TD>
    <OBJECT ID="cmdbtnStop" WIDTH=96 HEIGHT=32
 CLASSID="CLSID:D7053240-CE69-11CD-A777-00DD01143C57">
    <PARAM NAME="Caption" VALUE="Stop">
    <PARAM NAME="Size" VALUE="2540;847">
    <PARAM NAME="FontEffects" VALUE="1073741825">
    <PARAM NAME="FontCharSet" VALUE="0">
    <PARAM NAME="FontPitchAndFamily" VALUE="2">
    <PARAM NAME="ParagraphAlign" VALUE="3">
    <PARAM NAME="FontWeight" VALUE="700">
</OBJECT>
</TD>
    <SCRIPT LANGUAGE="VBScript">
<!--
dim style_path_array(3)

dim personality_path_array(3)

-->
    </SCRIPT>
</TR> </TABLE>
</BODY>
</HTML>
```

Opened in IE, this document looks like Figure 8.6.

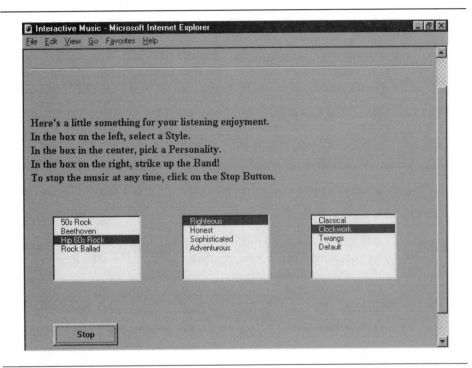

FIGURE 8.6: Our *music.htm* file in IE

Microsoft's Interactive Music control is as rich in possibilities as it is in sounds. Take some time to explore as many of the possibilities as you can, and happy listening!

The RealAudio Control

One of the problems with Web-based multimedia has been the size of the files. Until recently, you had to wait while a sizable file downloaded before you got to experience it.

In the world of audio, Progressive Networks met that challenge with the Real-Audio Player. The RealAudio Player, which Progressive Networks distributes for free, enables you to play RealAudio files in their proprietary .RA or .RAM format as they stream into your computer. In other words, you don't have to wait until the file is in your computer before you can start listening. This process enables you to listen to events like radio broadcasts live over the Web.

By now, many who lurk on the Web have downloaded and installed the RealAudio Player and enjoyed streamed audio. You can even use the Player to get on the Web and listen to audio files without going through your browser.

Progressive Networks now provides an ActiveX Control version of the RealAudio Player. Embed this control into your Web page, provide a source file, and audio streams in. You can get this control at Microsoft's ActiveX Component Gallery. In this section, we'll show you how this control works.

The Layout

Start by opening a new page in the ActiveX Control Pad's Text Editor. Save it as RAudio in skill 8 and type **The RealAudio Player** between <Title> and </Title>. Open a new HTML Layout Control, save it as layout for RAudio in skill 8, and open it up. If you haven't put the RealAudio Player control on a page in the Toolbox yet, do that now and select it. Draw the control out to a reasonable set of dimensions (about 200 pixels wide by 100 pixels high).

In the Properties sheet, give the RealAudio Player an ID of **raRMN** (the reason for this ID will be clear in a moment). When you right-clicked to get to the Properties sheet, you undoubtedly noticed RealAudio Properties on the pop-up menu. Select that choice now and you'll see the tabbed page with a textbox for typing the Source URL that provides the file you'll listen to. In the Source URL textbox enter: **http://www.real.com/products/ramfiles/ra3.0/nixon288v.ram**. Figure 8.7 shows the tabbed page with this URL entered.

 NOTE   In case you're wondering, this URL points to a RealAudio file of Richard Nixon's resignation speech. It's a mono version for a 28.8 modem and it resides at the RealAudio Web site. If your system and modem require a different version—or if you prefer, say, a Mozart composition to a Nixon speech—head on up to their Web site at http://www.real.com and look around for a different file.

Put three more controls into the HTML Layout Control, as we'll play with a few of the RealAudio Control's events and methods:

1. Just below the RealAudio control, insert two Command Buttons side-by-side.

2. Center a Microsoft Forms 2.0 Label control below the two buttons, and make its dimensions 60 (Height) by 400 (Width).

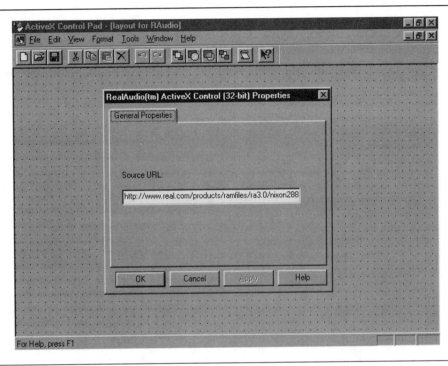

FIGURE 8.7: This tabbed page opens when you choose RealAudio Properties from the RealAudio control's pop-up menu.

3. Set the caption the left Command Button **Preferences...** and set the caption the right Command Button to **Statistics**. We're going to use one button to display the RealAudio Preferences dialog box, and the other to display statistics that pertain to the transmission of the audio file.

4. Give the left Command Button an ID of **cmdbtnPreferences**, and give the right Command Button an ID of **cmdbtnStatistics**.

5. We'll use the Label to track the beginning and end of the sound clip, so type **lblClip** as its ID.

6. Make the Label's BackColor white and its Font 10 pt Bold, center-aligned. Remove its caption, as we'll set the caption programmatically.

Your Layout Control should resemble Figure 8.8.

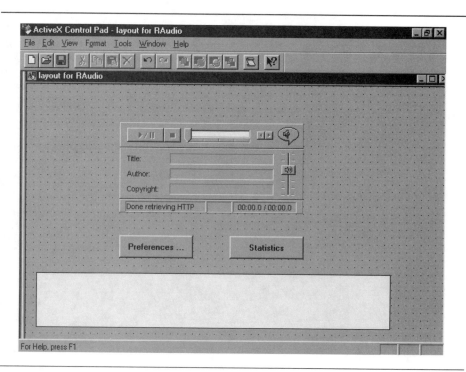

FIGURE 8.8: The layout for RAudio

The Script

In the Script Wizard, attach cmdbtnPreferences' Click event to raRMN's EditPreferences method, and attach cmdbtnStatistics' Click event to raRMN's HideShowStatistics method. With the Script Wizard in Code View, go to the Event pane and click the + next to cmdbtnPreferences to display its events. Select the Click event of cmdbtnPreferences and in the Actions pane, open raRMN's properties and methods and then double-click on EditPreferences. Back in the Event pane, display the events for cmdbtnStatistics, select its Click event, and double-click raRMN's HideShowStatistics method in the Actions pane.

Now we'll hook up two of raRMN's events to the lblClip Label control. The OnClipOpened event fires when the clip starts playing. The OnClipClosed event fires when the clip has finished (or when the user stops it by clicking on raRMN's Stop button). When the clip opens, we'd like the caption in the Label to reflect that, and when it closes, we'd like the caption to reflect that, too.

First, let's address the OnClipOpened event. If you click on this event with the Script Wizard in Code View, you'll see that it takes two arguments. We'll focus on the second argument, url. In the Script pane, do the typing and clicking to produce these lines of VBS:

```
Sub raRMN_OnClipOpened(shortClipName, url)
lblClip.Caption = "The clip has started!" & chr(13) _
    & "The URL is: " & chr(13) & url
```

Looks just like the kind of code we've done for Message Boxes, doesn't it? You can use similar statements for label captions, and this capability turns out to be helpful here. Why am I asking you to display a URL that you already know? When we open the page in IE, you're in for a little surprise.

Set the OnClipClosed event to change lblClip's caption to **The clip has finished!**

Here's all the code for our layout (layout for Raudio.alx).

(C) layout for Raudio.alx

```
<SCRIPT LANGUAGE="VBScript">
<!--
Sub cmdbtnPreferences_Click()
call raRMN.EditPreferences()
end sub
-->
</SCRIPT>

<SCRIPT LANGUAGE="VBScript">
<!--
Sub cmdbtnStatistics_Click()
call raRMN.HideShowStatistics()
end sub
-->
</SCRIPT>

<SCRIPT LANGUAGE="VBScript">
<!--
Sub raRMN_OnClipOpened(shortClipName, url)
lblClip.Caption = "The clip has started!" & chr(13) _
    & "The URL is: " & chr(13) & url
end sub
Sub raRMN_OnClipClosed()
lblClip.Caption = "The clip has finished!"
end sub
-->
```

Skill 8

```
</SCRIPT>
<DIV ID="layoutforRAudio" STYLE="LAYOUT:FIXED;WIDTH:477pt;HEIGHT:293pt;">
    <OBJECT ID="raRMN"
     CLASSID="CLSID:CFCDAA03-8BE4-11CF-B84B-0020AFBBCCFA"
    ➥STYLE="TOP:41pt;LEFT:107pt;WIDTH:206pt;HEIGHT:99pt;TABINDEX:0;ZINDEX:0;">
        <PARAM NAME="_ExtentX" VALUE="7276">
        <PARAM NAME="_ExtentY" VALUE="3493">
        <PARAM NAME="SRC"
        ➥VALUE="http://www.real.com/products/ramfiles/ra3.0/nixon288v.ram">
        <PARAM NAME="AUTOSTART" VALUE="0">
        <PARAM NAME="NOLABELS" VALUE="0">
    </OBJECT>
    <OBJECT ID="cmdbtnPreferences"
     CLASSID="CLSID:D7053240-CE69-11CD-A777-00DD01143C57"
    ➥STYLE="TOP:165pt;LEFT:107pt;WIDTH:83pt;HEIGHT:25pt;TABINDEX:1;ZINDEX:1;">
        <PARAM NAME="Caption" VALUE="Preferences ...">
        <PARAM NAME="Size" VALUE="2928;882">
        <PARAM NAME="FontEffects" VALUE="1073741825">
        <PARAM NAME="FontCharSet" VALUE="0">
        <PARAM NAME="FontPitchAndFamily" VALUE="2">
        <PARAM NAME="ParagraphAlign" VALUE="3">
        <PARAM NAME="FontWeight" VALUE="700">
    </OBJECT>
    <OBJECT ID="cmdbtnStatistics"
     CLASSID="CLSID:D7053240-CE69-11CD-A777-00DD01143C57"
    ➥STYLE="TOP:165pt;LEFT:231pt;WIDTH:83pt;HEIGHT:25pt;TABINDEX:3;ZINDEX:3;">
        <PARAM NAME="Caption" VALUE="Statistics">
        <PARAM NAME="Size" VALUE="2928;882">
        <PARAM NAME="FontEffects" VALUE="1073741825">
        <PARAM NAME="FontCharSet" VALUE="0">
        <PARAM NAME="FontPitchAndFamily" VALUE="2">
        <PARAM NAME="ParagraphAlign" VALUE="3">
        <PARAM NAME="FontWeight" VALUE="700">
    </OBJECT>
    <OBJECT ID="lblClip"
     CLASSID="CLSID:978C9E23-D4B0-11CE-BF2D-00AA003F40D0"
    ➥STYLE="TOP:206pt;LEFT:12pt;WIDTH:400pt;HEIGHT:60pt;ZINDEX:2;">
        <PARAM NAME="BackColor" VALUE="16777215">
        <PARAM NAME="Size" VALUE="14111;2117">
        <PARAM NAME="BorderStyle" VALUE="1">
        <PARAM NAME="FontEffects" VALUE="1073741825">
        <PARAM NAME="FontHeight" VALUE="200">
        <PARAM NAME="FontCharSet" VALUE="0">
        <PARAM NAME="FontPitchAndFamily" VALUE="2">
        <PARAM NAME="ParagraphAlign" VALUE="3">
        <PARAM NAME="FontWeight" VALUE="700">
    </OBJECT>
</DIV>
```

The Page

When you open the page in IE, you'll probably find that it starts working for you immediately. The RealAudio control starts looking around for the URL and prompts you to establish a connection to the Net if you're not already online. When you get connected and when the control's Play button activates, click on the Play Button to begin listening to the dulcet tones of our 37th President.

As the clip starts, the display looks like Figure 8.9.

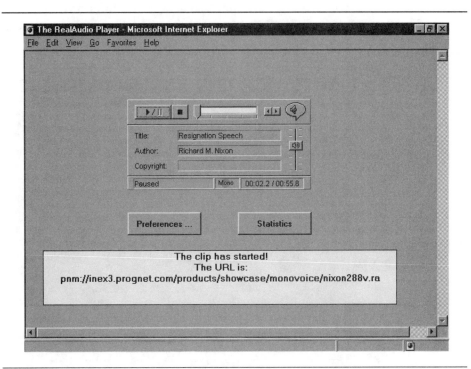

FIGURE 8.9: The appearance of the RAudio Web page when the Nixon clip begins

Whoa! What's that URL in the Label? That's not the one you typed into the URL property of raRMN's Properties sheet.

The URL you typed in was:

```
http://www.real.com/products/ramfiles/ra3.0/nixon288v.ram
```

The one in lblClip when Nixon starts speaking is:

`pnm://inex3.prognet.com/products/showcase/monovoice/nixon288v.ra`

Is this a meaningful change or just another Dirty Trick from Tricky Dick? As it happens, it's a trick from Progressive Networks and there's nothing at all dirty about it. You gave the RealAudio control an `http` URL that it used to find the RealAudio site. What you got back is in `pnm`, a protocol from Progressive Networks that you use to access computers that send RealAudio.

In the Web page, click on the Statistics button, and you'll see the display that appears in Figure 8.10. It's instructive to keep this open as the clip plays so you can see exactly what's going on during the transmission.

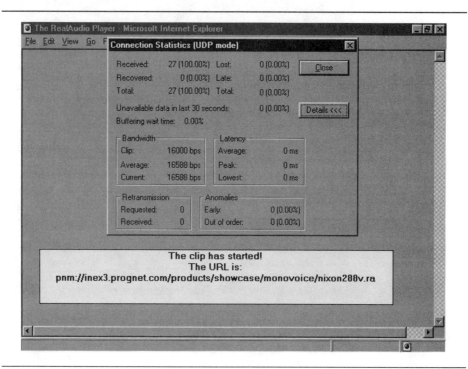

FIGURE 8.10: The RealAudio Statistics box

Click the Preferences... button and the tabbed pages shown in Figure 8.11 open. Tab through to see what's available. You probably won't want to reset anything, however.

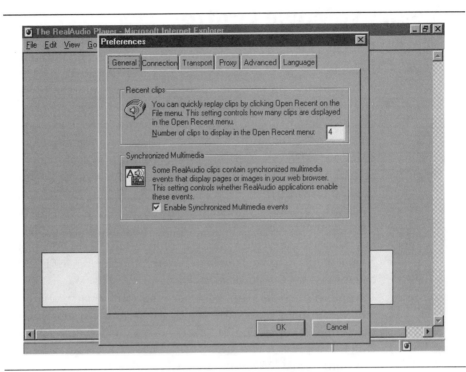

FIGURE 8.11: The RealAudio Preferences tabs

The RealAudio control presents a lot of possibilities for Web page enhancement. To embed streamed audio into your Web page, embed the RealAudio control into your Layout Control or your HTML document. You don't even have to make the control visible. A Web page devoted to the life of R. M. Nixon, for example, could have an image of Mr. Nixon with an overlayed Hot Spot. The Hot Spot's Click event could be scripted to run the RealAudio control's DoPlayPause method and play the file we played in our application.

As long as you can access a source file in the RealAudio format, you're all set. You might not want to leave it to chance as to whether a file pertaining to your subject matter resides on a server somewhere on the Web. Instead, you might want to build your own RealAudio files and put them on your own Web site. This is much more involved than installing the RealAudio Player or the RealAudio control. To find out how to do it, go to the RealAudio Web site at `http://www.real.com`.

The ActiveMovie Control

As we've seen, sprucing up your Web site with music and sound isn't all that difficult. Adding video is surprisingly straightforward, too, thanks to the ActiveMovie control. We wrap up this Skill by exploring this control; but first, a few words about video formats.

Video files are huge. The trick is to compress them for transport across the Web without losing image quality in the process. One organization that develops standards for video and audio compression is the Moving Pictures Expert Group, better known as MPEG. They gave their organization's initials to a format they devised for video. Like the JPEG format for images, the MPEG format uses a so-called *lossy* algorithm that loses information (undetectable to the human eye) when it compresses video files. It compresses video more than other formats do, but the downside is the amount of information it loses. The upside is that this format works on more than one type of computer. An MPEG file has one of these extensions: .MPEG, .MPG, or .MPE.

Apple's QuickTime, another cross-platform format, works on PCs, PowerPCs, and Macintoshes. QuickTime compression results in substantially larger files than MPEG compression, but the image quality is better. File extensions for QuickTime are .MOV and .QT.

A third format, AVI, is the one we'll work with. AVI is short for Audio/Video Interleaved. *Interleaving* combines video and audio into one signal. The format of choice for the Windows 95 multimedia architecture, AVI files run on Windows computers. They can run on other types of platforms equipped with special tools. AVI's image quality is better than MPEG's, but its resolution (because of the interleaving) is lower than QuickTime's. The AVI file extension, not surprisingly, is .AVI.

Setting the Scene

Our objective is to embed the ActiveMovie control into a Web page and use it to watch movies in AVI format. We'll do more than just watch movies, however. We'll choose from a list of movies and track some of the ActiveMovie control's events. In so doing, we'll solidify our knowledge of arrays.

We begin our trip to the movies with a new HTML document (call it Movies and save it in skill 8) and a new HTML Layout Control (call it layout for Movies and save it in skill 8). In the Text Editor, type **Movies** between <TITLE> and </TITLE> and put a centered <H1> heading **Let's Go To The Movies!** after <BODY> and before <OBJECT>.

Open the HTML Layout Control. Select and position the controls to match Figure 8.12.

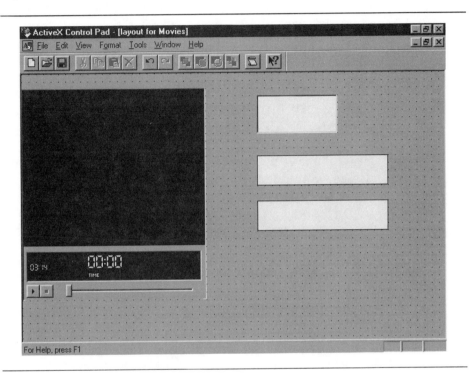

FIGURE 8.12: The layout for Movies

The control on the left of the layout is, of course, the ActiveMovie control. The uppermost control on the right is a ListBox, and the other two are Labels. Give the ActiveMovie control an ID of **acmControl**, and the ListBox an ID of **lstbxMovies**. We'll set up the ListBox to provide a list of movie titles for the user to choose from. While you're in the ListBox Properties sheet, set the value of its BoundColumn property to **0**.

In order to better understand the ActiveMovie control, we'll use the two Labels to track some of its events: We'll set the Label captions to reflect specific values that change as those events take place. You wouldn't do this on a finished Web page, but it's a good technique when you're trying to learn about a control (see Skill 15). We did this in the preceding section on the RealAudio control.

One event fires when the movie we're watching changes its *state*, which can be either Inactive, Paused, or Running. The other fires when we do something that changes the movie's *position* (how far along it is, in seconds, from the beginning). We'll track a third event—one that activates when a movie we've selected is ready for us to click the ActiveMovie control's Play button—but we'll track it with a Message Box rather than a Label. The first event is called *StateChange*, the second is called *PositionChange*. To stay consistent with these event names, let's assign **lblStateChange** as the ID of the upper Label and **lblPositionChange** as the ID of the lower Label. (The third event, by the way, is called *OpenComplete*.)

An ActiveMovie control would be worthless without movies to watch. Where will we get AVI files for the control? Make sure your Windows 95 CD is in your CD-ROM drive. Check the folder funstuff for a folder called videos. In that folder, you should find at least these three AVI files: goodtime, robroy, and weezer. I'll work with these three files; if you'd rather work with different AVI files, go right ahead.

We have to provide an initial value for the ActiveMovie control's FileName property. Since my CD-ROM drive is F:, here's what I entered for FileName: **F:\funstuff\videos\goodtime.avi**.

A Script for the Movies

In the Script Wizard, we have to populate the ListBox with the titles of our three movies. Then, we'll script the ListBox's Change event to send the selected title to the ActiveMovie control.

We face, however, the same challenge that we met previously with the Interactive Music control (see "Working with Arrays" for more information). We can't pass a title as the FileName. Instead, we must pass a file path. Once again, we'll do that by setting up an array that contains file paths. The file paths in this array will occupy the same positions that the titles occupy in the ListBox, and we'll match them up by position. We're able to do that because we've set the ListBox's BoundColumn to 0, which means that the ListBox's Value is the index of the selection, rather than the selection itself.

In the Script Wizard, create the array by right-clicking on Global Variables in the Actions pane and typing **movie_files_array(2)** in the dialog box.

As always, we populate our ListBox and array in the Layout's OnLoad event. Here's the VBS:

```
Sub layoutforMovies_OnLoad()
call lstbxMovies.AddItem("Good Times", 0)
call lstbxMovies.AddItem("Rob Roy", 1)
call lstbxMovies.AddItem("Weezer", 2)
lstbxMovies.Value = 0
movie_files_array(0) = "F:\funstuff\videos\goodtime.avi"
```

```
movie_files_array(1) = "F:\funstuff\videos\robroy.avi"
movie_files_array(2) = "F:\funstuff\videos\weezer.avi"
```

The line that sets lstbxMovies.Value to 0 causes the page to open up with "Good Times" selected in the ListBox, which corresponds to the FileName we provided in acmControl's Properties sheet.

> **TIP**   Are you starting to get the idea that a ListBox is just an array? It's an array that a user can see and select from—an array that has properties, methods, and events—but otherwise it's just an array.

We want the wheels to start turning as soon as we make a selection, so this is a job for lstbxMovies' Change event. Here's how to script that event in the Script Wizard:

```
Sub lstbxMovies_Change()
On Error Resume Next
call acmControl.Stop()
acmControl.FileName = movie_files_array(lstbxMovies.Value)
```

The `On Error Resume Next` statement tells IE to overlook any minor inconsistencies that might occur when the page opens.

Now let's address the ActiveMovie control's StateChange event. This event fires when a movie stops, starts, or pauses. It tells us the state the movie started in and the new state. The possible values are 0 (Inactive), 1 (Paused), and 2 (Running). We'll want these values to display in the caption for the lblStateChange control, but we want something more informative than 0, 1, or 2. How can we do the translation from numbers to words? To keep you thinking about arrays, we'll use an array to handle the translation. The idea is to have the StateChange event return its 0, 1, or 2, and then use that number as an index to an array which holds the word "Inactive" in the 0th position, "Paused" in the 1st position, and "Running" in the 2nd position.

To build this array, create a new Global Variable. When you open the New Global Variable dialog box, type **state_array(2)**. Then add these three lines to layoutforMovies' OnLoad event:

```
state_array(0) = "Inactive"
state_array(1) = "Paused"
state_array(2) = "Running"
```

The subroutine for StateChange works with two arguments, *oldstate* and *newstate*. They give us the state the movie was in before the change and the state it changed into.

In the Event pane, open the events for acmControl, and select StateChange. With the Script Wizard in Code View, create these lines of VBS in the Script pane:

```
Sub acmControl_StateChange(oldState, newState)
lblStateChange.Caption = "Old State: " & _
    state_array(oldState) & chr(13) & _
    "New State: " & state_array(newState)
```

Our use of the arrays causes the Label's caption to show words rather than numbers for the states.

Now for acmControl's PositionChange event. This event also works with two arguments, oldPosition and newPosition. In the Event pane, select PositionChange and in the Script pane create:

```
Sub acmControl_PositionChange(oldPosition, newPosition)
lblPositionChange.Caption = "Old Position: " & _
    oldPosition & chr(13) & "New Position: " & newPosition
```

Finally, let's select acmControl's OpenComplete event. This one fires when a movie is queued up and ready to roll. Let's have it display a Message Box when the movie is ready. The Message Box will tell us to click the ActiveMovie control's Play button so we can start watching. We'll also want it to tell us which movie we'll see (a little unnecessary, as we just selected the title from the ListBox).

This presents a little problem. We want the Message Box to echo the title of the movie we just selected, but we can't use lstbxMovies' Value for this. Why? Remember that we set the BoundColumn to 0. This means that the value is a number (an index), not a title.

But wait. A few paragraphs ago, I told you that a ListBox is just an array. You can refer to an item in an array by using the item's index. ListBox has a property that enables us to treat a ListBox like any other array. This property is called *List*. Thus,

> lstbxMovies.List(0) = "Good Times"
>
> lstbxMovies.List(1) = "Rob Roy"
>
> lstbxMovies.List(2) = "Weezer"

Now, if lstbxMovies.Value = 1, then lstbxMovies.List(lstbxMovies.Value) = "Rob Roy."

We'll use this concept in the code for the OpenComplete event:

```
Sub acmControl_OpenComplete()
MsgBox "Ready!" & chr(13) & "Click the Play Button to watch "
➥& chr(13) & CAlstbxMovies.List(lstbxMovies.Value),64,
➥"Let's See A Movie!"
```

You'll recall that the second argument, 64, indicates that the Message Box will display an Information symbol. The third argument is the Message Box's title. The first argument gives the particulars of the message.

Here's the listing for our layout (layout for Movies.alx):

 layout for Movies.alx

```vbscript
<SCRIPT LANGUAGE="VBScript">
<!--
dim movie_files_array(2)
-->
</SCRIPT>
<SCRIPT LANGUAGE="VBScript">
<!--
Sub layoutforMovies_OnLoad()
call lstbxMovies.AddItem("Good Times", 0)
call lstbxMovies.AddItem("Rob Roy", 1)
call lstbxMovies.AddItem("Weezer", 2)
lstbxMovies.Value = 0
movie_files_array(0) = "F:\funstuff\videos\goodtime.avi"
movie_files_array(1) = "F:\funstuff\videos\robroy.avi"
movie_files_array(2) = "F:\funstuff\videos\weezer.avi"
state_array(0) = "Inactive"
state_array(1) = "Paused"
state_array(2) = "Running"
end sub
-->
</SCRIPT>
<SCRIPT LANGUAGE="VBScript">
<!--
Sub lstbxMovies_Change()
On Error Resume Next
call acmControl.Stop()
acmControl.FileName = movie_files_array(lstbxMovies.Value)
end sub
-->
</SCRIPT>
<SCRIPT LANGUAGE="VBScript">
<!--
Sub acmControl_OpenComplete()
MsgBox "Ready!" & chr(13) & "Click the Play Button to watch "
➥& chr(13) &
➥lstbxMovies.List(lstbxMovies.Value),64,
➥"Let's See A Movie!"
end sub

dim state_array(3)

Sub acmControl_StateChange(oldState, newState)
```

```
lblStateChange.Caption = "Old State: " & _
    state_array(oldState) & chr(13) & _
    "New State: " & state_array(newState)
end sub

Sub acmControl_PositionChange(oldPosition, newPosition)
lblPositionChange.Caption = "Old Position: " & _
    oldPosition & chr(13) & _
    "New Position: " & newPosition
end sub
-->
</SCRIPT>

<DIV ID="layoutforMovies" STYLE="LAYOUT:FIXED;WIDTH:477pt;HEIGHT:293pt;">
    <OBJECT ID="acmControl"
      CLASSID="CLSID:05589FA1-C356-11CE-BF01-00AA0055595A"
      ➥STYLE="TOP:17pt;LEFT:0pt;WIDTH:206pt;HEIGHT:231pt;TABINDEX:0;ZINDEX:0;">
        <PARAM NAME="_ExtentX" VALUE="7276">
        <PARAM NAME="_ExtentY" VALUE="8149">
        <PARAM NAME="MovieWindowWidth" VALUE="271">
        <PARAM NAME="MovieWindowHeight" VALUE="227">
        <PARAM NAME="FileName" VALUE="F:\funstuff\videos\goodtime.avi">
    </OBJECT>
    <OBJECT ID="lblPositionChange"
      CLASSID="CLSID:978C9E23-D4B0-11CE-BF2D-00AA003F40D0"
      ➥STYLE="TOP:140pt;LEFT:264pt;WIDTH:149pt;HEIGHT:33pt;ZINDEX:1;">
        <PARAM NAME="BackColor" VALUE="16777215">
        <PARAM NAME="Size" VALUE="5239;1164">
        <PARAM NAME="BorderStyle" VALUE="1">
        <PARAM NAME="FontEffects" VALUE="1073741825">
        <PARAM NAME="FontHeight" VALUE="200">
        <PARAM NAME="FontCharSet" VALUE="0">
        <PARAM NAME="FontPitchAndFamily" VALUE="2">
        <PARAM NAME="FontWeight" VALUE="700">
    </OBJECT>
    <OBJECT ID="lblStateChange"
      CLASSID="CLSID:978C9E23-D4B0-11CE-BF2D-00AA003F40D0"
      ➥STYLE="TOP:91pt;LEFT:264pt;WIDTH:149pt;HEIGHT:33pt;ZINDEX:2;">
        <PARAM NAME="BackColor" VALUE="16777215">
        <PARAM NAME="Size" VALUE="5239;1164">
        <PARAM NAME="BorderStyle" VALUE="1">
        <PARAM NAME="FontEffects" VALUE="1073741825">
        <PARAM NAME="FontHeight" VALUE="200">
        <PARAM NAME="FontCharSet" VALUE="0">
        <PARAM NAME="FontPitchAndFamily" VALUE="2">
        <PARAM NAME="FontWeight" VALUE="700">
    </OBJECT>
    <OBJECT ID="lstbxMovies"
```

```
CLASSID="CLSID:8BD21D20-EC42-11CE-9E0D-00AA006002F3"
➡STYLE="TOP:25pt;LEFT:264pt;WIDTH:91pt;HEIGHT:42pt;TABINDEX:3;ZINDEX:3;">
    <PARAM NAME="ScrollBars" VALUE="3">
    <PARAM NAME="DisplayStyle" VALUE="2">
    <PARAM NAME="Size" VALUE="3202;1480">
    <PARAM NAME="BoundColumn" VALUE="0">
    <PARAM NAME="MatchEntry" VALUE="0">
    <PARAM NAME="FontCharSet" VALUE="0">
    <PARAM NAME="FontPitchAndFamily" VALUE="2">
    <PARAM NAME="FontWeight" VALUE="0">
  </OBJECT>
</DIV>
```

The Movies Web Page

When you open Movies.htm in IE, you see "Good Times" selected in the ListBox, and a Message Box that tells you to click the Play button to watch Good Times (see Figure 8.13).

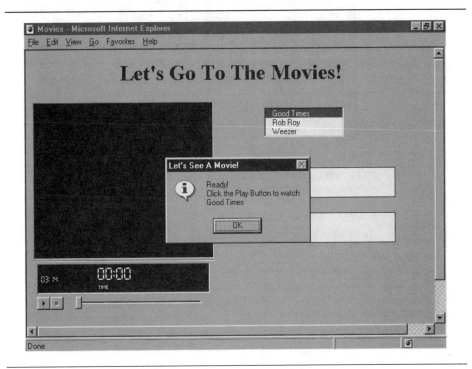

FIGURE 8.13: The Movies Web page opens with a selection in the ListBox and an open Message Box.

The Message Box appears because the page opens with a movie ready for viewing. The ListBox selection is in place because you set it up that way.

Clicking OK in the Message Box and clicking the Play button starts the movie. When the movie is rolling (and then paused), the Web page looks like Figure 8.14.

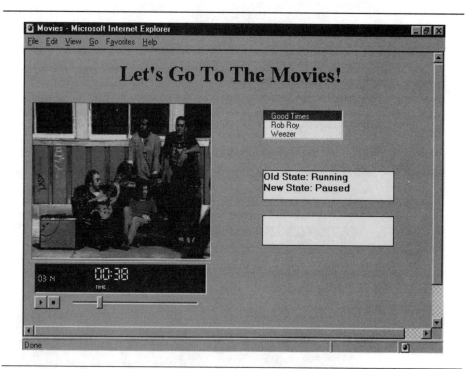

FIGURE 8.14: The Good Times movie in our Movies Web page

Note the state information in the (upper) StateChange label. As Figure 8.14 shows, no information is in the PositionChange label yet, because you haven't physically changed the position of the movie. When you do so, information appears in the PositionChange label, as in Figure 8.15.

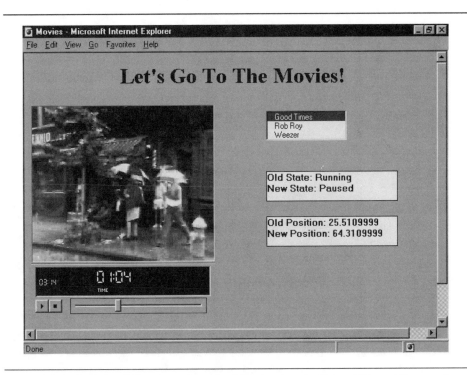

FIGURE 8.15: When you do something to change the position of the movie (like move the slider around), information appears in the (lower) PositionChange label.

The ActiveMovie control has another useful capability. People who interact with it on a Web page can make adjustments to the control. They can modify the volume, the stereo balance, the size of the viewing area, and more. The trick is to right-click on the control and select Properties from the pop-up menu. A dialog box appears with a set of tabbed pages, as Figure 8.16 shows. Users make the adjustments by making selections in these pages.

Skill 8

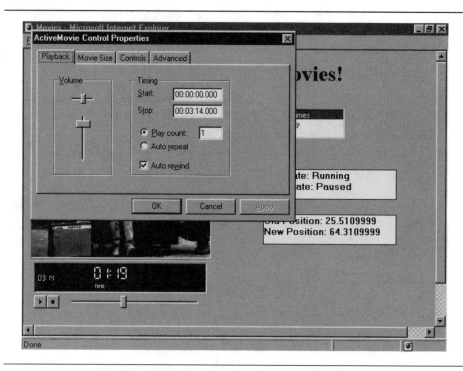

FIGURE 8.16: The dialog box for adjusting the ActiveMovie control at runtime

A number of shortcut keystroke combinations are available to end users. Table 8.4 shows these shortcuts. The one to try is Alt+Enter, which toggles between full-screen mode and Windows mode.

TABLE 8.4: Keystroke Combinations for the ActiveMovie Control

Keystroke Combination	Effect
Ctrl+D	Toggle Display
Ctrl+Left Arrow	Rewind
Ctrl+Right Arrow	Forward
Ctrl+R	Run
Ctrl+P	Pause
Ctrl+S	Stop

TABLE 8.4 CONTINUED: Keystroke Combinations for the ActiveMovie control

Keystroke Combination	Effect
Ctrl+T	Toggle Control Panel
Alt+Enter	Toggle Full Screen/Windows Modes
Ctrl+Shift+Left Arrow	Previous
Ctrl+Shift+Right Arrow	Next

In our application, the last two combinations just take you out of the movie you're watching.

Summing Up

Multimedia stimulates several senses at once. For that reason, it's a real attention-grabber, and it can enhance the power of a Web page many times over. In this Skill, we've presented a number of controls you can use for Web-based multimedia, but we've only scratched the surface. Every day new formats, tools, and possibilities emerge.

Keep your eyes (and ears) open.

Are You Experienced?

Skill 8

Now you can...

☑ **work with the Microsoft Interactive Music control to add synthesized royalty-free music to your Web pages**

☑ **understand the RealAudio ActiveX control for bringing streamed audio to your Web pages**

☑ **work with arrays in VBS**

☑ **apply useful VBS concepts to Label controls in order to track events**

☑ **work with the ActiveMovie control to enhance your Web pages with video**

536-555-3398.

PROGRAMMERS
C, C, VB, Cobol, exp. Call 534-555-6543 or fax 534-555-6544.

PROGRAMMING
MRFS Inc. is looking for a Sr. Windows NT developer. Reqs. 3-5 yrs. Exp. in C under Windows, Win95 & NT, using Visual C, Excl. OO design & implementations skills, a must. OLE2 & ODBC are a plus. Excl. Salary & bnfts. Resume & salary history to HR, 8779 HighTech Way, Computer City, AR

PROGRAMMERS
Contractors Wanted for short & long term assignments; Visual C, MFC Unix C/C, SQL Oracle Dev elop ers PC Help Desk Support Windows NT & NetWareTelecommunications Visual Basic, Access, HTML, CGI, Perl MMI & Co.. 885-555-9933

PROGRAMMER World Wide Web Links wants your HTML & Photoshop skills. Develop great WWW sites. Local & global customers. Send samples & resume to WWWL, 2000 Apple Road, Santa Rosa, CA.

TECHNICAL WRITER Software firm seeks writer/editor for manuals, research notes, project mgmt. Min 2 years tech. writing, DTP & programming experience. Send resume & writing samples to: Software Systems, Dallas, TX.

TECHNICAL Software development firm looking for Tech Trainers. Ideal candidates have programming experience in Visual C, HTML & JAVA. Need quick self starter. Call (443) 555-6868 for interview.

TECHNICAL WRITER/ Premier Computer Corp is seeking a combination of technical skills, knowledge and experience in the following areas: UNIX, Windows 95/NT, Visual Basic, on-line help & documentation, and the internet. Candidates must possess excellent writing skills, be comfortable working in a quality vs. deadline driven environment. Competitive salary. Fax resume & samples to Karen Fields, Premier Computer Corp, 444 Industrial Blvd. Concord, CA. Or send to our website at www.premier.com.

WEB DESIGNER
BA/BS or equivalent programming/multimedia production. 3 years of experience in use and design of WWW services streaming audio and video HTML, PERL, CGI, GIF, JPEG. Demonstrated interpersonal, organization, communications, multi-tasking skills. Send resume to The Learning People at www.learning.com.

WEBMASTER-TECHNICAL
BSCS or equivalent, 2 years of experience in CGI, Windows 95/NT, UNIX, C, Java, Perl. Demonstrated ability to design, code, debug and test on-line services. Send resume to The Learning People at www.learning.com.

PROGRAMMER World Wide Web Links wants your HTML & Photoshop skills. Develop great WWW sites. Local & global customers. Send sam-

ing tools. Experienced in documentation preparation & programming languages (Access, C, FoxPro) are a plus. Financial or banking customer service support is required along with excellent verbal & written communication skills with multi levels of end-users. Send resume to KKUP Enterprises, 45 Orange Blvd., Orange, CA.

COMPUTERS Small Web Design firm seeks indiv. w/NT, Webserver & Database management exp. Fax resume to 556-555-4221.

COMPUTER/ Visual C/C, Visual Basic Exp'd Systems Analysts/Programmers for growing software dev. team in Roseburg. Computer Science or related degree preferred. Develop adv. Engineering applications for engineering firm. fax resume to 707-555-8744.

COMPUTER Web Master for dynamic SF Internet co. Site Dev. test, coord. train. 2 yrs prog. Exp. C C Web C FTP. Fax resume to Best Staffing 845-555-7722.

COMPUTER PROGRAMMER
Ad agency seeks programmer w/exp. in UNIX/NT Platforms, Web Server, CGI/Perl. Programmer Position avail. on a project basis with the possibility to move into F/T. Fax resume & salary req. to R. Jones 334-555-8332.

COMPUTERS Programmer/Analyst Design and maintain C based SQL database applications, Required skills: Visual Basic, C, SQL, ODBC, Document existing and new applications. Novell or NT exp. a plus. Fax resume or salary history to 235-555-9935.

GRAPHIC DESIGNER
Webmaster's Weekly is seeking a creative Graphic Designer to design high impact marketing collateral, including direct mail promo's, CD-ROM packages, ads and WWW pages. Must be able to juggle multiple projects and learn new skills on the job very rapidly. Web design experience a big plus, technical troubleshooting also a plus. Call 435-555-1235.

GRAPHICS - ART DIRECTOR - WEB-MULTIMEDIA
Leading internet development company has an outstanding opportunity for a talented, high-end Web Experienced Art Director. In addition to a great portfolio and fresh ideas, the ideal candidate has excellent communication and presentation skills. Working as a team with innovative producers and programmers, you will create dynamic, interactive web sites and application interfaces. Some programming experience required. Send samples and resume to: SuperSites, 333 Main, Seattle, WA.

MARKETING
Fast paced software and services provider looking for MARKETING COMMUNICATIONS SPECIALIST to be responsible for its webpage, seminar coordination, and ad place-

PROGRAMMERS Multiple short term assignments available: Visual C, 3 positions SQL ServerNT Server, 2 positions JAVA & HTML, long term NetWare Various locations. Call for more info. 356-555-3398.

PROGRAMMERS
C, C, VB, Cobol, exp.
Call 534-555-6543
or fax 534-555-6544.

PROGRAMMING
MRFS Inc. is looking for a Sr. Windows NT developer. Reqs. 3-5 yrs. Exp. in C under Windows, Win95 & NT using Visual C, Excl. OO design & implementation skills a must. OLE2 & ODBC are a plus. Resume & salary history to HR, 8779 HighTech Way, Computer City, AR

PROGRAMMERS/ Contractors Wanted for short & long term assignments: Visual C, MFC Unix C/C, SQL Oracle Developers PC Help Desk Support Windows NT & NetWareTelecommunications Visual Basic, Access, HTML, CGI, Perl MMI & Co.. 885-555-9933

PROGRAMMER World Wide Web Links wants your HTML & Photoshop skills. Develop great WWW sites. Local & global customers. Send samples & resume to WWWL, 2000 Apple Road, Santa Rosa, CA.

TECHNICAL WRITER Software firm seeks writer/editor for manuals, research notes, project mgmt. Min 2 years tech. writing, DTP & programming experience. Send resume & writing samples to: Software Systems, Dallas, TX.

COMPUTER PROGRAMMER
Ad agency seeks programmer w/exp. in UNIX/NT Platforms, Web Server, CGI/Perl. Programmer Position avail. on a project basis with the possibility to move into F/T. Fax resume & salary req. to R. Jones 334-555-8332.

COMPUTERS Small Web Design firm seeks indiv. w/NT Webserver & Database management exp. fax resume to 556-555-4221.

COMPUTER Visual C/C, Visual Basic Exp'd Systems Analysts/Programmers for growing software dev. team in Roseburg. Computer Science or related degree preferred. Develop adv. Engineering applications for engineering firm. fax resume to 707-555-8744.

COMPUTER Web Master for dynamic SF Internet co. Site Dev. test coord. train. 2 yrs prog. Exp. C C Web C FTP. Fax resume to Best Staffing 845-555-7722.

COMPUTERS/ QA SOFTWARE TESTERS Qualified candidates should have 2 yrs exp. performing integration & system testing using automated testing tools. Experienced in documentation preparation & programming languages (Access, C, FoxPro) are a plus. Financial or banking customer service support is required along with excellent verbal & written communication skills with multi levels of end-users. Send resume to KKUP Enterprises, 45 Orange Blvd. Orange, CA.

COMPUTERS Programmer/Analyst Design and maintain C based SQL database applications, Required skills: Visual Basic, C, SQL, ODBC, Document existing and new applications. Novell or NT exp. a plus. Fax resume & salary history to 235-555-9935.

GRAPHIC DESIGNER
Webmaster's Weekly is seeking a creative Graphix Designer to design high impact marketing collateral, including direct mail promo's. CD-ROM packages, ads and WWW pages. Must be able to juggle multiple projects and learn new skills on the job very rapidly. Web design experience a big plus, technical troubleshooting also a plus. Call 435-555-1235.

GRAPHICS - ART DIRECTOR - WEB-MULTIMEDIA
Leading internet development company has an outstanding opportunity for a talented, high-end Web Experienced Art Director. In addition to a great portfolio and fresh ideas, the ideal candidate has excellent communication and presentation skills. Working as a team with innovative producers and programmers, you will create dynamic, interactive web sites and application interfaces. Some programming experience required. Send samples and resume to: SuperSites, 333 Main, Seattle, WA.

COMPUTER PROGRAMMER
Ad agency seeks programmer w/exp. in UNIX/NT Platforms, Web Server, CGI/Perl. Programmer Position avail. on a project basis with the possibility to move into F/T. Fax resume & salary req. to R. Jones 334-555-8332.

PROGRAMMERS / Established software company seeks programmers with extensive Windows NT

ment. Must be a self-starter, energetic, organized. Must have 2 yrs web experience. Programming a plus. Call 985-555-9854

PROGRAMMERS Multiple short term assignments available: Visual C, 3 positions SQL ServerNT Server, 2 positions JAVA & HTML, long term NetWare Various locations. Call more info. 356-555-3398.

PROGRAMMERS
C, C, VB, Cobol, exp. Call 534-555-6543 or fax 534-555-6544.

PROGRAMMING
MRFS Inc. is looking for a Windows NT developer. Reqs. 3 yrs. Exp. in C under Window Win95 & NT, using Visual C, Ex OO design & implementation sk a must. OLE2 & ODBC are a pl Excl. Salary & bnfts. Resume salary history to HR, 8779 HighTe Way, Computer City, AR

PROGRAMMERS/ Contractor Wanted for short & long term assig ments Visual C, MFCUnix C/C, S Oracle Developers PC Help De Support Windows NT & NetWa Telecommunications Visual Bas Access, HTML, CGI, Perl MMI & C 885-555-9933

PROGRAMMER World Wide W Links wants your HTML & Photosh skills. Develop great WWW sit Local & global customers. Send sa ples & resume to WWWL, 20 Apple Road, Santa Rosa, CA.

TECHNICAL WRITER Software fi seeks writer/editor for manua research notes, project mgmt. Mi years tech. writing, DTP & progra ming experience. Send resume writing samples to: Softwa Systems, Dallas, TX.

TECHNICAL Software developme firm looking for Tech Trainers. Id candidates have programming exp rience in Visual C, HTML & JAV Need quick self starter. Call (44 555-6868 for interview.

TECHNICAL WRITER Prem Computer Corp is seeking a com nation of technical skills, knowled and experience in the followi areas: UNIX, Windows 95/NT, Vis Basic, on-line help & documentatio and the internet. Candidates m possess excellent writing skills, a be comfortable working in a qual vs. deadline driven environmen Competitive salary. Fax resume samples to Karen Fields, Premi Computer Corp, 444 Industrial Bl Concord, CA. Or send to our websi at www.premier.com.

WEB DESIGNER
BA/BS or equivalent progra ming/multimedia production. years of experience in use a design of WWW services stream audio and video HTML, PERL, C GIF, JPEG. Demonstrated interp sonal, organization, communicat multi-tasking skills. Send resum The Learning People at www.lea ing.com.

WEBMASTER-TECHNICAL

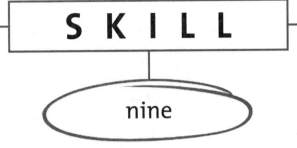

S K I L L

nine

Working with Agents

❑ **Understanding agents**

❑ **The Microsoft ActiveX Agent control**

❑ **Scripting speech output and animation**

❑ **Harnessing speech recognition**

So there I was, sitting at my computer, happily editing a document with my new Word 97. Nothing about the document was out of the ordinary: a couple of lines, some white space, and some more lines. Suddenly, out of nowhere, an animated paper clip with beady eyes and bushy eyebrows flew into view. It careened onto the screen from right to left, told me (via a text box) that I appeared to be working on a letter, and asked me if I needed its help. Although I had to admit that the little clip guy had a point (the document structure did fit the general configuration of a letter), it wasn't a letter that I was working on. I declined the offer, but I was grateful nonetheless. After all, how often do you have someone looking over your shoulder who's helpful, knowledgeable, and knows how to take "No" (or, for that matter, "Yes") gracefully? Pretty soon the answer just might be "very often." In fact, one day this type of interaction may be a common method of working on computers.

If you've used Office 97, you've probably had the same experience I had (or one very much like it). If so, then you too have had a close encounter with an *agent*. Researchers and developers in the new field of agent technology are starting to develop a consensus about what constitutes an agent. Agents, most agree, should have some form of intelligence that they apply toward carrying out a well-defined task. They should be helpful, and they should learn to anticipate the needs of the people they work for.

Agents are coming into increasing use on the Internet. The reason? With the expanding glut of Net-based information, agents are a valuable tool for intelligently finding the information you need.

We'll end Part I with a look at agent technology. It's the likely wave of the future, and you can experiment with it now in the context of ActiveX. As you do, you'll learn a couple more VBS concepts.

The Microsoft ActiveX Agent Control

Microsoft recently unveiled a beta version of its Microsoft Agent control for ActiveX. I couldn't resist the opportunity to tell you about it and help you explore some of its features.

To get this little treasure, point IE to the Microsoft ActiveX Component Gallery and scroll down the left frame (the area that arranges controls according to vendors) until you get to the Microsoft section. Click Microsoft Agent and the Agent's download and demo pages will appear. If you have the requisite memory and storage—16MB RAM and 8.5MB free hard drive space—follow the instructions to download the Agent control. The download page indicates that a Pentium100Mhz processor is necessary, but I let the Agent loose on a souped-up 486 (performing at about the level of a Pentium 75). Although things get a little sluggish at times on the 486, working with the Agent still offers a great computing experience.

TIP   You can find more information about the agent at `http://www.microsoft`
`.com/workshop/prog/agent`. **This Web site offers agent-related samples and documentation.**

The installation file that you download is almost 5MB, so be prepared to wait (how long, as always, depends on Web traffic and on your connection speed). Once the download is complete, installation proceeds smoothly.

You'll find that the Agent can perform more than two dozen animated gestures that seem surprisingly lifelike. In this Skill, you'll insert an Agent into an HTML document and you'll also insert a ListBox that will display the gestures. You'll select a gesture from the ListBox, and the Agent will perform it (as a result of VBS code in the ListBox Change event).

Then, you'll add controls to this page to learn about more of the Agent's capabilities (like movement across the screen and speech production). You'll develop some procedures that use these capabilities, and, if you have a microphone connected to your computer, you'll finish up by having a conversation with the Agent! (It can recognize and respond to spoken input!)

WARNING   The Microsoft Agent that we'll work with is a beta version, with all the attendant imperfections, inconsistencies, and insects. Don't plan on using this version in a real-life Web page. Keep checking the Microsoft ActiveX Component Gallery to see when a final version will be available.

Getting Started with the Agent

In the ActiveX Control Pad, open a new HTML document, save it as Agent in your skill 9 folder, and title this page Agent. We're going to work directly with this document, rather than with the HTML Layout Control. When you use the Agent with the HTML Layout Control, a warning appears each time you open your page in IE. The warning advises you that the combination of controls (the Layout and the Agent) is not known to be safe. The warning gives you the option to either proceed or cancel. Although nothing bad is likely to happen—I've used the Agent control and the HTML Layout Control together numerous times with no ill effects—why take a chance?

Select Edit ➢ Insert ActiveX Control... and select Microsoft Agent control from the list of controls. In the Object Editor, you'll see the fedora-wearing, sunglassed gentleman that appears in Figure 9.1.

FIGURE 9.1: The Agent's representation in the Object Editor

Apparently, the hat and the shades are intended to convey the impression of a "secret agent." This is a somewhat misleading way to get the ball rolling, because the little Agent icon bears absolutely no resemblance to the character who will emerge on your screen momentarily. In the future, of course, the resemblance might be closer. The genie is just one example of an agent's appearance. As the agent evolves from a beta into a product, the icon character might be another possible look for the agent.

Change the Agent's ID to **agntControl** and close the Object Editor.

Making the Agent Active

We now have to make sure the Agent is active when the Web page opens. To do this:

1. Open the Script Wizard, put it in Code View, and in the Event pane choose the Window OnLoad event.

2. In the Script pane, type **agntControl.Active = True**. While you're here, open agntControl both in the Event pane and in the Actions pane. This is a good place to start exploring the properties and methods of this control, as the Properties sheet doesn't provide much information. Close the Script Wizard when you finish exploring.

NOTE   **Once you make the agent active, it exhibits an unexpected behavior: Until you close it, it hangs around no matter what you do. Even if you Alt+Tab to another application, it stays visible, waiting to do your bidding.**

3. In the Text Editor select Edit ➤ ActiveX Control... once again and this time choose a Microsoft Forms 2.0 ListBox control.

4. Change its ID to **lstbxAnimation** and give the ListBox a Width of 121 and a Height of 264. Close the Object Editor. In the HTML document, lstbxAnimation should appear below agntControl.

5. Since we're not using the HTML Layout Control, we'll use HTML tags to position the ListBox. In the Text Editor, before the ListBox's <OBJECT> tag type **<TABLE ALIGN = RIGHT>** and after its </OBJECT> tag type **</TABLE>**.

6. Let's put the ListBox in its own row, and in its own cell within that row. Between <TABLE ALIGN = RIGHT> and the <OBJECT> tag, type **<TR> <TD>**. Between the </OBJECT> tag and the </TABLE> tag, type **</TD> </TR>**.

The HTML in your Text Editor should look like this:

```
<HTML>
<HEAD>
<TITLE>Agent</TITLE>
</HEAD>
<BODY>
<OBJECT ID="agntControl" WIDTH=32 HEIGHT=32
 CLASSID="CLSID:855B244C-FC5B-11CF-91FE-00C04FD701A5">
    <PARAM NAME="_Version" VALUE="65536">
    <PARAM NAME="_ExtentX" VALUE="847">
    <PARAM NAME="_ExtentY" VALUE="847">
    <PARAM NAME="_StockProps" VALUE="0">
</OBJECT>

<TABLE  ALIGN = RIGHT>
<TR> <TD>
<OBJECT ID="lstbxAnimation" WIDTH=121 HEIGHT=264
 CLASSID="CLSID:8BD21D20-EC42-11CE-9E0D-00AA006002F3">
    <PARAM NAME="ScrollBars" VALUE="3">
    <PARAM NAME="DisplayStyle" VALUE="2">
    <PARAM NAME="Size" VALUE="3210;6985">
    <PARAM NAME="MatchEntry" VALUE="0">
    <PARAM NAME="FontCharSet" VALUE="0">
    <PARAM NAME="FontPitchAndFamily" VALUE="2">
    <PARAM NAME="FontWeight" VALUE="0">
```

Skill 9

```
</OBJECT>
</TD> </TR>
</TABLE>
</BODY>
</HTML>
```

This HTML code creates an elongated ListBox that opens on the right side of the Web page.

Populating the ListBox

Now we have to populate the ListBox. As usual, you'll populate the ListBox with an OnLoad event. Go back to the Script Wizard and once again, select the Window OnLoad event. With the Wizard in Code View, select the ListBox's AddItem method in the Actions pane and double-click it. You're going to add quite a few items to the ListBox. Each one, in quotes, is the name of a gesture that the Agent can perform. Do the necessary clicking and typing to produce these lines of HTML:

```
call lstbxAnimation.AddItem("Acknowledge")
call lstbxAnimation.AddItem("Announce")
call lstbxAnimation.AddItem("Confused")
call lstbxAnimation.AddItem("Congratulate")
call lstbxAnimation.AddItem("Decline")
call lstbxAnimation.AddItem("DontRecognize")
call lstbxAnimation.AddItem("Explain")
call lstbxAnimation.AddItem("GestureDown")
call lstbxAnimation.AddItem("GestureLeft")
call lstbxAnimation.AddItem("GestureRight")
call lstbxAnimation.AddItem("GestureUp")
call lstbxAnimation.AddItem("GetAttention")
call lstbxAnimation.AddItem("GlanceDown")
call lstbxAnimation.AddItem("GlanceLeft")
call lstbxAnimation.AddItem("GlanceRight")
call lstbxAnimation.AddItem("GlanceUp")
call lstbxAnimation.AddItem("Greet")
call lstbxAnimation.AddItem("Pleased")
call lstbxAnimation.AddItem("Read")
call lstbxAnimation.AddItem("RestPose")
call lstbxAnimation.AddItem("Sad")
call lstbxAnimation.AddItem("Suggest")
call lstbxAnimation.AddItem("Surprised")
call lstbxAnimation.AddItem("Think")
call lstbxAnimation.AddItem("Uncertain")
```

NOTE   Type these lines so they follow the line you typed earlier that activates the Agent.

While you're in the neighborhood, open the Window OnUnload event and use it to deactivate the Agent when you close the Web page. Here's the script:

```
Sub window_onUnload()
agntControl.Active = False
```

Scripting the Change Event

One more chore, and we'll be finished with the Script Wizard for a while. We have to script the ListBox's Change event. In this event, we want to ensure that the Agent is active, and we want to ignore messy little errors that might result from inconsistencies such as type mismatches.

In the Event pane, select the ListBox Change event and in the Script pane, enter these lines of code:

```
Sub lstbxAnimation_Change()
If agntControl.Active = False Then
    agntControl.Active = True
End If
On Error Resume Next
call agntControl.Play(lstbxAnimation.Value, True)
```

The last line invokes the Agent's Play method, which you can bring into the Script pane by double-clicking on Play in the Actions pane. You'll find it by clicking on the + next to agntControl. This method, as its name implies, plays the animation that corresponds to the gesture named in its first argument. The second argument sets priorities. If its value is True, Play performs the animation immediately. If its value is False, the animation has to wait its turn in a queue of animations. As you'll soon see, the Agent moves quite a bit.

Close the Script Wizard making sure you save the code. In the Text Editor, keep the script in the upper part of the document (between <HEAD> and </HEAD>), the controls in the lower part—much like the arrangement in an ALX file. This will help you stay organized.

The Agent Web Page

If you open Agent.htm in IE, the ListBox appears and then, out of a puff of smoke, a blue-tinted genie adorns your screen! (You've probably already seen the genie at the Microsoft ActiveX Component Gallery.) Your screen will look like Figure 9.2.

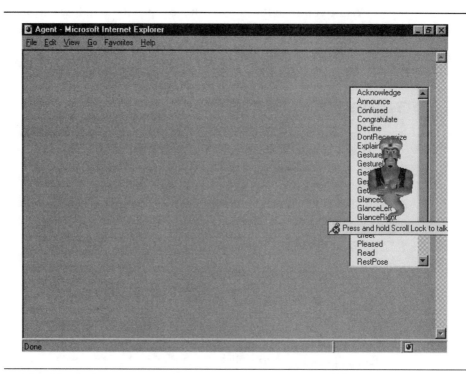

FIGURE 9.2: The Agent Web page, complete with Agent

You can use your mouse to drag the little guy to the center of the screen. Go through the ListBox and note the animations that correspond to each gesture. (My favorite is "Suggest." The Agent takes a little light bulb out of its pocket and holds it out.) Figure 9.3 shows the character at center-screen, caught in the middle of a "GestureRight."

Note the little box just under the Agent. It tells you to press the Scroll Lock key on your keyboard and the Agent will listen to you. If you have a microphone connected to your computer, give it a try. Hold the Scroll Lock key down (the caption in the box below the genie changes to *Listening…*), and into the microphone say "Genie." Chances are that the Agent will vocalize an extremely flattering reply, which is coordinated with the words appearing in a comic-style balloon. The speech recognition capability is good, and you don't have to worry about training the Agent to understand you. It was able to cope with my accent—a hybrid of Southeastern, Midwestern, and Brooklyn—with little difficulty.

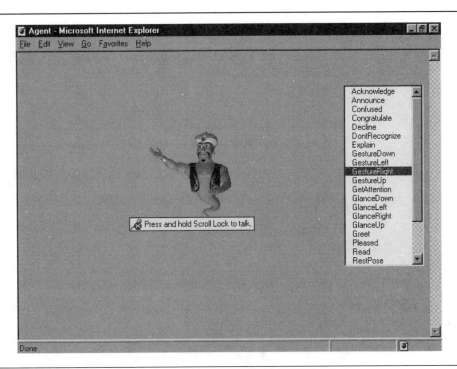

FIGURE 9.3: The Agent performing a gesture

The Agent also understands "Thanks," "Thank you," "Shut Up," and "Go Away." That last one makes the character disappear, but you can bring it back by saying "Genie." Admittedly, this isn't much as conversations go, but you'll add a little to the vocabulary before we're through.

You can change some of the Agent's properties right in the running Web page. Right-click on the character, and a pop-up menu appears. One of the options is to open the Agent's Properties sheet. If you choose this option, a set of tabbed Properties pages appears onscreen (see Figure 9.4). The Agent may have a few words to say as the Properties pages appear.

The Properties pages allow you to enter information about Input, Output, Speech Recognition, the Agent's character (a bit limited in the beta edition), and yourself. One change you can make immediately is in the page that's open in Figure 9.4. On the Input tab, you can click the first option button to change the mode of voice input. With that button selected, the Agent is constantly listening so you don't have to hold down the Scroll Lock key while you speak.

Skill 9

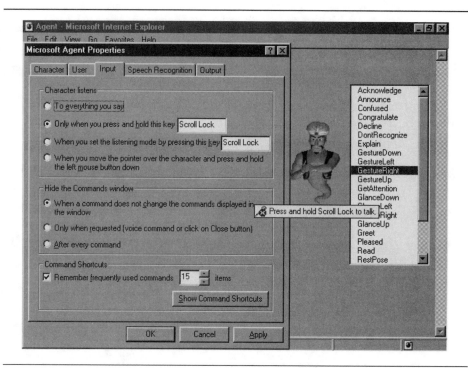

FIGURE 9.4: The tabbed Properties pages of the Microsoft Agent control

 TIP   Try to be careful about background noise when you speak to the genie. Background noise can degrade voice recognition performance.

Another option on the Agent's pop-up menu is Open Commands Window. If you choose that option, you'll see a very limited selection of commands. The Commands window turns out to be important later on when we discuss speech recognition (see "Harnessing Speech Recognition" for more information).

After you've gone through all the gestures a few times, spoken to the Agent, and examined the Properties pages, close the Web page and return to the Text Editor. Ordinarily, you would leave the Web page open when you go back to the ActiveX Control Pad, but this control is resource-intensive and you're better off shutting the page down while you work.

Adding Functionality to the Agent Web Page

As you've seen, you can drag the Agent to any location on the screen. Let's add a Command Button that does this programmatically, and let's make the Agent respond vocally to whatever we tell it to do.

Adding a Command Button

Back in the ActiveX Control Pad Text Editor, insert a Microsoft Forms 2.0 Command Button after the ListBox </OBJECT> tag. Change the Command Button's ID to **cmdbtnMove** and change its caption to **Move**. Make sure that the Command Button is between the ListBox and the </TABLE> tag (it should be just below the ListBox) so that the Command Button is part of the table. Put the Command Button in its own row and cell of the table by surrounding it with <TR> and <TD> tags.

The HTML for the two controls in the "table" should look like this:

```
<TABLE  ALIGN = RIGHT>
<TR> <TD>
<OBJECT ID="lstbxAnimation" WIDTH=121 HEIGHT=264
 CLASSID="CLSID:8BD21D20-EC42-11CE-9E0D-00AA006002F3">
    <PARAM NAME="ScrollBars" VALUE="3">
    <PARAM NAME="DisplayStyle" VALUE="2">
    <PARAM NAME="Size" VALUE="3210;6985">
    <PARAM NAME="MatchEntry" VALUE="0">
    <PARAM NAME="FontCharSet" VALUE="0">
    <PARAM NAME="FontPitchAndFamily" VALUE="2">
    <PARAM NAME="FontWeight" VALUE="0">
</OBJECT>
</TD></TR>
<TR> <TD>
<OBJECT ID="cmdbtnMove" WIDTH=111 HEIGHT=29
 CLASSID="CLSID:D7053240-CE69-11CD-A777-00DD01143C57">
    <PARAM NAME="Caption" VALUE="Move">
    <PARAM NAME="Size" VALUE="2928;776">
    <PARAM NAME="FontCharSet" VALUE="0">
    <PARAM NAME="FontPitchAndFamily" VALUE="2">
    <PARAM NAME="ParagraphAlign" VALUE="3">
    <PARAM NAME="FontWeight" VALUE="0">
</OBJECT>
</TD></TR>

</TABLE>
```

Skill 9

Scripting Agent Movement and Speech Production

A button-click will move the Agent, but rather than have it move to a set position, let's be adventurous and have it move to a random position each time. Also, let's have the Agent say something before it moves and something after it arrives at its destination.

How do we pick a random point? Each point onscreen corresponds to a pair of numbers. Thus, we have to randomly select two numbers—one for the left-to-right direction (in the Properties sheet, this is called Left) and one for the up-to-down direction (this is called Top).

To do the randomization, we use `rnd`, a procedure built into VBS. Left to its own devices, `rnd` will give you a random number between zero and one. The numbers we want, however, are much greater than one—numbers like 420, 230, and 350. The solution is to multiply the number that `rnd` gives us. To get a point in the left-to-right direction, we'll multiply that number by 500, and to get a point in the up-to-down direction we'll multiply the number by 400. Where do these numbers come from? Most screens are 640 in the left-to-right direction, 480 in the up-to-down. The two multipliers will be sure to keep the Agent in view.

One more challenge: Because `rnd` gives us numbers between zero and one, multiplying them will typically produce numbers with decimal places. The numbers we want are whole numbers. We solve this problem by using just the integer part of 500*`rnd` and the integer part of 400*`rnd`. We get the integer part by applying still another built-in VBS procedure, `int`. The bottom line? Our randomly selected point will correspond to this number pair: `int(500*rnd)`, `int(400*rnd)`.

To script the Agent's behavior, we have to come up with a series of gestures and vocalizations (making it almost literally a script). Let's script this sequence:

1. When the destination-point is calculated, the Agent gestures toward the point (turning toward the right, for example, if that's the intended direction of movement).

2. The Agent then makes a comment about moving.

3. The Agent moves.

4. The Agent makes a comment about having moved.

To get the Agent to gesture toward a particular point, we invoke the Agent's GestureAt method. This method takes three arguments. The first two are the two numbers that represent the point to gesture toward. The third, which can be either True or False, is like the third argument in the Play method (if True, the

Agent performs the gesture immediately; if False, the gesture waits in a queue). The name of this third argument is Now.

We make the Agent speak by using, appropriately enough, the Speak method. The first of the Speak method's two arguments is the text of what we want the Agent to say. The second argument is Now (using a True or False setting like the Play and GestureAt methods).

To prevent the Agent from always saying the same thing, you can specify a list of things for the Agent to say. For example, whenever you want an Agent to move from one spot to another, you might want it to say one of these three things:

- "You want me to schlepp all the way over *there*?"

- "I'm on my way."

- "If that's where you want me to go, that's where I'll go."

You can put the things you want the Agent to say in a list and separate them with a vertical line (|). Then, put a quote to the left of the first one and to the right of the last one.

Notice that the last word in the first bullet is in italics. The italic emphasizes that word, as a person might emphasize it when he or she says that line. You can have the Agent emphasize a word, too. To do this, put \Emp\ to the immediate left (no spaces) of the word to be emphasized.

The MoveTo method moves the Agent across the screen and takes four arguments. We've seen the first three—the two numbers that represent the destination and Now. The fourth is called Fast. If it's True, movement takes place without animation. If it's False, the Agent plays an animation that is appropriate for the movement.

Finally, have the Agent make a comment after arriving at the destination. Once again, use the Speak method, and make the first argument a list of possible comments. We'd like one of the possible comments to be "I made it all the way to" followed by the two numbers that represent the destination. This will require storing the randomly selected numbers in variables, and using the names of those variables in the comment. For this reason, use two variables x_coordinate and y_coordinate.

With all these considerations, we can now script the Command Button. In the Script Wizard, select the Command Button's Click event in the Event pane, and in the Script pane (in Code View) do the clicking and typing to produce:

```
Sub cmdbtnMove_Click()
If agntControl.Active = False Then
```

```
      agntControl.Active = True
End If
On Error Resume Next
x_coordinate = int(rnd*500)
y_coordinate = int(rnd*400)
call agntControl.GestureAt(x_coordinate, y_coordinate, True)
call agntControl.Speak("You want me to schlepp all the way over
➡\Emp\there?|I'm on my way|If that's where you want
➡me to go, that's where I'll go", False)
call agntControl.MoveTo(x_coordinate, y_coordinate, False, False)
call agntControl.Speak("Whew! | I made it all the way to " &
➡x_coordinate & "   " & y_coordinate, False)
```

Notice that, as in the ListBox's Change event script, everything is preceded with a check on whether the Agent is active, and the On Error Resume Next statement is included. Also, notice that we didn't declare the two variables x_coordinate and y_coordinate with Dim statements. VBS allows this: it's called the *implicit method* of variable creation.

In the HTML file, position this script right after the ListBox script, save your work, and open the Web page in IE. You should get comments, movements, and more comments in response to the button-click.

Tapping Into the Agent

If you open agntControl in the Script Wizard, you'll see it has a variety of properties, methods, and events. We can track some of these by adding another Command Button, scripting it to get the information, and displaying a Message Box with the data. We'll also have the Agent talk to us throughout the process. It's a good way to learn about the Agent and to hone your scripting skills.

Adding Two Controls

First, let's add the Command Button in the HTML file. If you use copy and paste techniques, you won't have to go into the Object Editor. Set the Command Button's ID property **cmdbtnInfo**, set its Caption property to **Info**, and make sure it's part of the "table" with its own row and cell. To do this, type **<TR> <TD>** on the line before cmdbtnInfo's <OBJECT> tag, and **</TD> <TR>** on the line after cmdbtnInfo's </OBJECT> tag. Make sure those last two tags precede </TABLE>.

Now we'll add still another control—a pop-up menu. The pop-up menu will be an intermediary between the Command Button and the information display. In the Object Editor, select a PopUp Menu control, and set its ID property to **ppmnuInfo**. Make sure it has a height of 0 and a width of 0. In the HTML file, position this control just after the </TABLE> tag.

We're going to track nine pieces of information, and these nine pieces fall neatly into three categories: Speech Input, Speech Output, and Location. When you click the Command Button, the PopUp Menu will display the three categories. Select a category and a Message Box will appear with the appropriate information.

Agent Data

In the Speech Input category, we'll track:

- Whether the Agent is listening (this information is in agntControl.Character.Listening).

- Whether the Speech Input capability is in effect (agntControl.Input.VoiceEnabled).

- The Speech Input mode, a number that indicates a user setting in the Input page of the tabbed Property pages. Figure 9.4 shows this page. The possible values (1–4) correspond to option button selections in the *Character Listens* group (agntControl.Input.Mode).

In Speech Output, we'll track:

- Whether the Agent is able to speak (agntControl.Output.AudioEnabled).

- The Volume of the Agent's voice (agntControl.Character.Volume).

- The Pitch of the Agent's voice (agntControl.Character.Volume).

- The Rate at which the Agent speaks (agntControl.Character.Volume).

In Location, we'll monitor:

- The onscreen position of the Agent's left edge (agntControl.Character.Left).

- The onscreen position of the Agent's top edge (agntControl.Character.Top).

Scripting the Button and the Menu

First things first. We have to populate the pop-up menu with the category choices for the information we're tracking. Add these three lines of code to the Window OnLoad event:

```
call ppmnuInfo.AddItem("Speech Input")
call ppmnuInfo.AddItem("Speech Output")
call ppmnuInfo.AddItem("Location")
```

In response to the cmdbtnInfo Click event, we want the Agent to gesture toward the PopUp Menu's location and make a comment such as, "Here's all the Info on Me," "What would you like to know?" or "Here's the story." Then we'll have the PopUp Menu appear. Here's the code for this sequence:

```
Sub cmdbtnInfo_Click()
If agntControl.Active = False Then
    agntControl.Active = True
End If
On Error Resume Next
call agntControl.GestureAt(300, 200, True)
call agntControl.Speak("Here's all the Info on Me | What
➥would you like to know? | Here's the story ", False)
call ppmnuInfo.PopUp(300, 200)
```

You can produce this code by typing and clicking in the Script Wizard, or you might find it just as easy to type it directly into Agent.htm.

The PopUp Menu's Click event script will depend on the Select Case structure we've used before (see Skill 4 for more information). This Click event has one argument—the selected item's position on the menu. Recall that the PopUp Menu is the array-type control that turned out to not start from zero. For the three-item PopUp Menu control, the value of the argument can be either 1, 2, or 3. In either case, we'll want the Agent to perform an animation, then say something, and then gesture toward the location of the Message Box. Then, the Message Box opens, providing the information we want. When we close the Message Box, we'll have the Agent make another comment.

In each Message Box, the information for each message will appear on a separate line. Each line will consist of some brief informative text that tells what the line represents, followed by the value.

You're now armed with enough information to produce the script for the PopUp Menu's Click Event. Here's my version. If you want the Agent to make different comments or play different animations, go ahead and make the necessary changes. Otherwise, in the Script pane create this script:

```
Sub ppmnuInfo_Click(item)
On Error Resume Next
Select Case item
    Case 1
    call agntControl.Play("GetAttention", True)
    call agntControl.Speak("So you want to know about Speech
    ➥Input", False)
    call agntControl.GestureAt(320,240, False)
    MsgBox "I'm Listening: " & agntControl.Character.Listening _
        & chr(13) & "Speech Input Enabled: " &
        ➥agntControl.Input.VoiceEnabled _
        & chr(13) & "Speech Input Mode: " & agntControl.Input.Mode, _
        64, "Speech Recognition Information"
    call agntControl.Speak("That's the scoop on speech", False)

    Case 2
    call agntControl.Play("Acknowledge", True)
    call agntControl.Speak("The Story on Speech Output", False)
    call agntControl.GestureAt(320,240, False)
    MsgBox "I Can Speak: " &
            agntControl.Output.AudioEnabled _
        & chr(13) & "The Volume of My Voice: " &
        ➥agntControl.Character.Volume _
        & chr(13) & "The Pitch of My Voice: " &
        ➥agntControl.Character.Pitch _
        & chr(13) & "The Speed of My Voice: " &
        ➥agntControl.Character.Speed, _
        64, "Voice Information"
    call agntControl.Speak("That's as much as I know about my voice",
    ➥False)

    Case 3
    call agntControl.Play("Suggest", True)
    call agntControl.Speak("Where \Emp\Am I?", False)
    call agntControl.GestureAt(320,220, False)
    MsgBox "My Left Edge At The Moment: " &
    ➥agntControl.Character.Left _
        & chr(13) & "My Top Edge At The Moment: " &
        ➥agntControl.Character.Top, _
        64, "Location Information"
    call agntControl.Speak("Does any of us know where we
    ➥\Emp\really are?", False)

End Select
```

Skill 9

Save your work and open the Web page in IE. Figure 9.5 shows what happens when you click on the Info button. Clicking on the pop-up menu displays a Message Box, and every action generates a comment from the talkative little Agent.

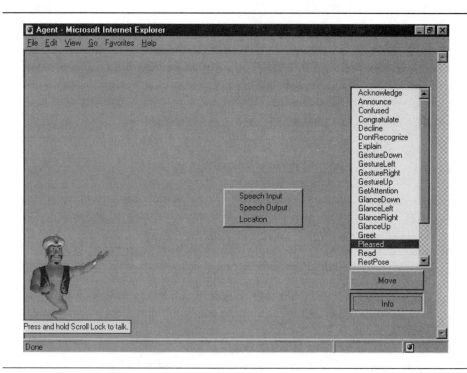

FIGURE 9.1: The updated Agent Web page. The Info button has been clicked.

Harnessing Speech Recognition

We finish this Skill by taking advantage of the Agent's most intriguing (and intelligent) facet—its capability for recognizing speech. Here's our game plan:

- We'll use the subroutines we've written for the Command Button Click events.

- We'll connect those subroutines with commands that we'll add to the Agent's Command menu. To open this menu, either left-click on the Agent, or right-click on the Agent and select Open Commands Window from the resulting pop-up menu.

- We'll take advantage of the connection between the Command menu and speech recognition: commands on the Command menu are accessible by voice as well as by mouse-click.

- When we finish, we'll be able to run the two Command Button Click event scripts via speech input (and via the Command menu, too).

Adding Commands

No additional controls are necessary, but some additional scripting is in order. To start, we have to add two commands to the Command menu. One will connect to cmdbtnMove's Click event script, the other to cmdbtnInfo's Click event script.

Open the Script Wizard, and put it in Code View. In the Actions pane, click on the + next to agntControl. Scroll down and you'll see Commands, the collection of commands available to the user. In this collection are the voice commands that the Agent understands at start-up. You can use the collection's Add method to put new commands on this list. The Add method takes three arguments. The first argument is a name for the command we're adding. The second is a caption that will appear on the Agent's Command menu. The third is the vocalization that we want the Agent to recognize in order to carry out the command.

It's best to start the process by setting the collection's Enabled property to False before adding new commands, and then finish by resetting Enabled to True. This ensures that commands don't fire before we want them to.

We proceed by coding a subroutine called `Start_The_Commands` in the Script Wizard. But where do we code it? It isn't a subroutine activated by an event in the Event pane; it's something we develop from scratch. To give ourselves a workspace in the Script Wizard, right-click on Procedures in the Actions pane, and select New Procedure. A workspace appears in the Script pane. Change the default name of the subroutine from `Sub Procedures1()` to `Sub Start_The_Commands()` and produce this code:

```
Sub Start_The_Commands()
agntControl.Commands.Enabled = False
agntControl.Commands.Add "MoveAgent","Move!","Move"
```

```
agntControl.Commands.Add "AgentInfo","Info...","Info"
agntControl.Commands.Enabled = True
end sub
```

In the Window OnLoad event, add the line

```
call Start_The_Commands().
```

Now we have to specify the action to take when one of the commands we added gets selected. The Agent's Command event is the event that will trigger the actions we specify. Find it in the Event pane and select it. In Code View, you'll see it has an argument called *UserInput*. UserInput holds a number of useful pieces of information, but the one that concerns us most is Name, the name of the command that a user selected to fire this event. We use Name as the test in a `Select Case` statement. The two names we supplied using the Commands.Add method were "MoveAgent" and "AgentInfo." Remember that our game-plan was to associate these commands with scripts we already wrote for the two buttons we embedded in `Agent.htm`. In one case, then, we'll call the command cmdbtnMove_Click, and in the other we'll call the command cmdbtnInfo_Click. In the Script Wizard, how do we invoke subroutines that we, ourselves, wrote? In the Procedures object that you right-clicked to get a New Procedure, click on the + . You'll see a list of subroutines that we've written. Double-click our Click event script names as necessary to produce:

```
Sub agntControl_Command(UserInput)

On Error Resume Next
Select Case UserInput.Name

    Case "MoveAgent"
        call cmdbtnMove_Click()
    Case "AgentInfo"
        call cmdbtnInfo_Click()
End Select

end sub
```

Save your work. Here is the Agent file in all its glory (`Agent.htm`).

Ⓒ Agent.htm

```
<HTML>
<HEAD>
<TITLE>Agent</TITLE>
```

```
    <SCRIPT LANGUAGE="VBScript">
<!--
Sub window_onLoad()
agntControl.Active = True
call lstbxAnimation.AddItem("Acknowledge")
call lstbxAnimation.AddItem("Announce")
call lstbxAnimation.AddItem("Confused")
call lstbxAnimation.AddItem("Congratulate")
call lstbxAnimation.AddItem("Decline")
call lstbxAnimation.AddItem("DontRecognize")
call lstbxAnimation.AddItem("Explain")
call lstbxAnimation.AddItem("GestureDown")
call lstbxAnimation.AddItem("GestureLeft")
call lstbxAnimation.AddItem("GestureRight")
call lstbxAnimation.AddItem("GestureUp")
call lstbxAnimation.AddItem("GetAttention")
call lstbxAnimation.AddItem("GlanceDown")
call lstbxAnimation.AddItem("GlanceLeft")
call lstbxAnimation.AddItem("GlanceRight")
call lstbxAnimation.AddItem("GlanceUp")
call lstbxAnimation.AddItem("Greet")
call lstbxAnimation.AddItem("Pleased")
call lstbxAnimation.AddItem("Read")
call lstbxAnimation.AddItem("RestPose")
call lstbxAnimation.AddItem("Sad")
call lstbxAnimation.AddItem("Suggest")
call lstbxAnimation.AddItem("Surprised")
call lstbxAnimation.AddItem("Think")
call lstbxAnimation.AddItem("Uncertain")
call ppmnuInfo.AddItem("Speech Input")
call ppmnuInfo.AddItem("Speech Output")
call ppmnuInfo.AddItem("Location")
call Start_The_Commands()
end sub

Sub window_onUnload()
agntControl.Active = False
end sub

-->
    </SCRIPT>
<SCRIPT LANGUAGE="VBScript">
<!--

Sub lstbxAnimation_Change()
If agntControl.Active = False Then
    agntControl.Active = True
End If
```

Skill 9

```
On Error Resume Next
call agntControl.Play(lstbxAnimation.Value, True)
end sub
-->
</SCRIPT>

<SCRIPT LANGUAGE="VBScript">
<!--
Sub cmdbtnMove_Click()
If agntControl.Active = False Then
    agntControl.Active = True
End If
On Error Resume Next
x_coordinate = int(rnd*500)
y_coordinate = int(rnd*400)
call agntControl.GestureAt(x_coordinate, y_coordinate, True)
call agntControl.Speak("You want me to schlepp all the way over
➥\Emp\there?|I'm on my way|If that's where you want me
➥to go, that's where I'll go", False)
call agntControl.MoveTo(x_coordinate, y_coordinate, False, False)
call agntControl.Speak("Whew! | I made it all the way to " &
➥ x_coordinate & "   " &y_coordinate, False)

end sub
-->
</SCRIPT>
<SCRIPT LANGUAGE="VBScript">
<!--
Sub cmdbtnInfo_Click()
If agntControl.Active = False Then
    agntControl.Active = True
End If
On Error Resume Next
call agntControl.GestureAt(300, 200, True)
call agntControl.Speak("Here's all the Info on Me | What
➥would you like to know? | Here's the story ", False)
call ppmnuInfo.PopUp(300, 200)

end sub
-->
</SCRIPT>
<SCRIPT LANGUAGE="VBScript">
<!--
Sub ppmnuInfo_Click(item)
On Error Resume Next
Select Case item
    Case 1
    call agntControl.Play("GetAttention", True)
```

```
        call agntControl.Speak("So you want to know about Speech Input", False)
        call agntControl.GestureAt(320,240, False)
        MsgBox "I'm Listening: " & agntControl.Character.Listening _
            & chr(13) & "Speech Input Enabled: " & agntControl.Input.VoiceEnabled _
            & chr(13) & "Speech Input Mode: " &
                agntControl.Input.Mode, _
            64, "Speech Recognition Information"
        call agntControl.Speak("That's the scoop on speech", False)

        Case 2
        call agntControl.Play("Acknowledge", True)
        call agntControl.Speak("The Story on Speech Output", False)
        call agntControl.GestureAt(320,240, False)
        MsgBox "I Can Speak: " & agntControl.Output.AudioEnabled _
            & chr(13) & "The Volume of My Voice: " & agntControl.Character.Volume _
            & chr(13) & "The Pitch of My Voice: " & agntControl.Character.Pitch _
            & chr(13) & "The Speed of My Voice: " & agntControl.Character.Speed, _
            64, "Voice Information"
        call agntControl.Speak("That's as much as I know about my voice", False)

        Case 3
        call agntControl.Play("Suggest", True)
        call agntControl.Speak("Where \Emp\Am I?", False)
        call agntControl.GestureAt(320,220, False)
        MsgBox "My Left Edge At The Moment: " & agntControl.Character.Left _
            & chr(13) & "My Top Edge At The Moment: " & agntControl.Character.Top, _
            64, "Location Information"
        call agntControl.Speak("Does any of us know where we
        ➥\Emp\really are?", False)

End Select

    end sub
-->
</SCRIPT>
<SCRIPT LANGUAGE="VBScript">
<!--
Sub Start_The_Commands()
agntControl.Commands.Enabled = False
agntControl.Commands.Add "MoveAgent","Move!","Move"
agntControl.Commands.Add "AgentInfo","Info...","Info"
agntControl.Commands.Enabled = True
end sub
-->
</SCRIPT>

<SCRIPT LANGUAGE="VBScript">
<!--
```

Skill 9

```
Sub agntControl_Command(UserInput)

On Error Resume Next
Select Case UserInput.Name

    Case "MoveAgent"
        call cmdbtnMove_Click()
    Case "AgentInfo"
        call cmdbtnInfo_Click()
End Select

end sub
-->
</SCRIPT>

</HEAD>

<BODY>

<OBJECT ID="agntControl" WIDTH=32 HEIGHT=32
 CLASSID="CLSID:855B244C-FC5B-11CF-91FE-00C04FD701A5">
    <PARAM NAME="_Version" VALUE="65536">
    <PARAM NAME="_ExtentX" VALUE="847">
    <PARAM NAME="_ExtentY" VALUE="847">
    <PARAM NAME="_StockProps" VALUE="0">
</OBJECT>

<TABLE  ALIGN = RIGHT>
<TR> <TD>
<OBJECT ID="lstbxAnimation" WIDTH=121 HEIGHT=264
 CLASSID="CLSID:8BD21D20-EC42-11CE-9E0D-00AA006002F3">
    <PARAM NAME="ScrollBars" VALUE="3">
    <PARAM NAME="DisplayStyle" VALUE="2">
    <PARAM NAME="Size" VALUE="3210;6985">
    <PARAM NAME="MatchEntry" VALUE="0">
    <PARAM NAME="FontCharSet" VALUE="0">
    <PARAM NAME="FontPitchAndFamily" VALUE="2">
    <PARAM NAME="FontWeight" VALUE="0">
</OBJECT>
</TD></TR>
<TR> <TD>
<OBJECT ID="cmdbtnMove" WIDTH=111 HEIGHT=29
 CLASSID="CLSID:D7053240-CE69-11CD-A777-00DD01143C57">
    <PARAM NAME="Caption" VALUE="Move">
    <PARAM NAME="Size" VALUE="2928;776">
    <PARAM NAME="FontCharSet" VALUE="0">
    <PARAM NAME="FontPitchAndFamily" VALUE="2">
    <PARAM NAME="ParagraphAlign" VALUE="3">
    <PARAM NAME="FontWeight" VALUE="0">
```

```
</OBJECT>
</TD></TR>
<TR> <TD>
<OBJECT ID="cmdbtnInfo" WIDTH=111 HEIGHT=29
 CLSID="CLSID:D7053240-CE69-11CD-A777-00DD01143C57">
    <PARAM NAME="Caption" VALUE="Info">
    <PARAM NAME="Size" VALUE="2928;776">
    <PARAM NAME="FontCharSet" VALUE="0">
    <PARAM NAME="FontPitchAndFamily" VALUE="2">
    <PARAM NAME="ParagraphAlign" VALUE="3">
    <PARAM NAME="FontWeight" VALUE="0">
</OBJECT>
</TD></TR>
</TABLE>
<OBJECT ID="ppmnuInfo" WIDTH=0 HEIGHT=0
 CLSID="CLSID:7823A620-9DD9-11CF-A662-00AA00C066D2">
    <PARAM NAME="_ExtentX" VALUE="0">
    <PARAM NAME="_ExtentY" VALUE="0">
</OBJECT>

</BODY>
</HTML>
```

Save your work and open the page in IE. You'll find that you've added a couple of words to the Agent's vocabulary, "Move" and "Info." The Agent responds to these two words with actions, not just talk, which is commendable in Agents and other beings. If the speech recognition is not as accurate as you'd like, try following the tabbed pages to the Training procedure, and train the Agent to understand your voice saying those two words. This will probably increase performance.

Summing Up

Agent technology is the probable wave of the future in computing. Just as object-oriented programming (which we'll discuss in Part II) has taken over today's application development efforts, don't be surprised if Agents work their way into prominence before too long. Once you get the hang of it, scripting behaviors for these little guys seems natural and fun. And when the Microsoft Agent control evolves from a beta version to an officially released control, you'll have a real eye-opener for your Web pages.

You've gone through a lot in Part I. From Command Buttons and Labels through scripts, graphics, multimedia, and Agents, you've pretty much run the gamut of ActiveX controls. Covering all of them would be impossible, since their

Skill 9

number grows every day. But by now you have a feel for many of them and how they work. You can easily learn the new ones that emerge.

The idea throughout Part I was to quickly get your hands dirty in the world of ActiveX. I informally introduced you to a number of concepts, particularly VBS concepts, as needed. In this way, you built a solid foundation for understanding more advanced concepts about VBS and about the tools you're using. You'll meet these concepts in Part II.

Are You Experienced?

Now you can...

- ☑ work with the Microsoft Agent control
- ☑ understand all of the Agent's animations, methods, and properties
- ☑ develop scripts for the Agent that use animation and speech output
- ☑ change the Agent's properties at runtime
- ☑ harness the power of speech recognition to generate behaviors in an Agent
- ☑ use subroutines you've written as callable parts of other subroutines

PART II

Exploring the Tools

In Part I, the objective was to get your hands dirty with ActiveX controls and give you a working knowledge of the tools and techniques that you use to embed these controls in Web pages. Now that you have a firsthand idea of what the tools are, what they can do, and why you use them, the Skills in Part II take you through ActvieX tools and technology in a more formal way. You'll examine VBS and its relationship with HTML, look into the nooks and crannies of the ActiveX Control Pad, and see where ActiveX came from by understanding the ideas behind it. You'll finish by looking at Internet Explorer and using its scripting object model.

Getting Into VBScript

- ❏ **General VBS concepts**
- ❏ **Variables**
- ❏ **Arrays**
- ❏ **VBS subtypes**
- ❏ **Operators**
- ❏ **Program flow**
- ❏ **Procedures**
- ❏ **Built-in functions**

Part I introduced you to a number of VBS concepts you needed to carry out exercises. The objective was to get you as comfortable as possible with the VBS language and the immediate application of its concepts before discussing the language in a more structured way.

Before we proceed, it will be helpful to review the VBS concepts you've already worked with. In Skill 2, you learned about the Script Wizard, and in Skill 3, you learned about functions, arguments, and methods. You also encountered Message Boxes and the string concatenation operator (&). Skill 4 showed you the Select Case statement and how to use a constant to update the value of a variable. In Skill 5 you saw these concepts: how a variable could update the value of another variable; the If...Then construct; the IsNumeric function; the Exit command; how to modify the appearance of Message Boxes; the Not statement; the Greater Than (>) and Less Than (<) operators. Skill 6 showed you how to use AddItem to populate a ListBox and taught you about global variables. Skill 7 introduced rows and columns, as well as the On Error Resume Next statement. Skill 8 instructed you on working with arrays, and on string concatenation in Label captions. In Skill 9 you used the rnd and int functions, and you learned how to write a procedure from scratch and then call it from another procedure.

As you can see, you already know quite a lot of VBS. If you feel the need to go back to the Skills in Part I and look at any of these concepts again, this would be a good time to do so.

The definitive reference for VBS is at http://www.microsoft.com/vbscript. You should download the HTML files that hold the documentation and install them in the folder that holds your ActiveX Control Pad. Then, you'll be able to access the documentation by selecting Help ➤ VBScript Reference from the Control Pad's menu bar. The documentation provides information on everything in VBS. It also offers a tutorial as well as a helpful list of features in VBA (Visual Basic for Applications—the Visual Basic that lives in Office 97) that VBS does not support.

Some General VBS Concepts

A *scripting language* such as VBScript is designed to operate inside another environment, such as an HTML document. Code written in a scripting language is *interpreted*, which means the code only works if the right interpreter is on hand to run it. Other programming languages generate *compiled* code, which runs by itself.

HTML can't run scripting language programs, but it can call on an interpreter to run them. The LANGUAGE attribute of the <SCRIPT> tag tells HTML which interpreter to call. In the Web pages you've built, HTML calls the VBScript interpreter that resides in IE.

As you saw in Part I, VBScript extends HTML by making ActiveX controls work inside HTML documents. This allows you to interact with the controls and have the controls respond to clicks, double-clicks, value changes, and other events. We link a control's events to actions and methods, and the result is a document full of controls that interact with users and with each other in meaningful ways. The scripting language and the language interpreter allow this interaction to happen on your machine and not on some server on the Web.

Variables

Throughout our discussion, we've talked about variables and we've used them to accomplish a number of objectives. In this section we discuss them in more detail.

Fundamentals

A variable is a placeholder for a value. As the word "variable" implies, this value can change. And one thing that a computer program often does is change the values in variables.

Although VBS is pretty flexible about variables (more so than most programming languages), here are some rules you must follow when you name them:

- The name must start with an alphabetic character. The rest of the name can contain any alphanumeric character, including the underscore ("_").

- A period can't be part of a variable's name.

- A variable's name can't be longer than 255 characters (you'll probably never have to worry about this one).

- You can't have two local variables with the same name within the same subroutine, or two identically named global variables in the same HTML document.

Creating Variables

You've already used the Script Wizard to create variables (see Skill 6) that were available to all the procedures in your script. When you right-clicked on Global Variables in the Script Wizard's Actions pane and selected New Variable... from the pop-up menu you brought up a dialog box asking you to supply a name for the new variable. After you supplied the name, closed the dialog box, and eventually closed the Script Wizard, you found a line somewhere in the VBS code that looked like this:

```
dim VariableName
```

The dim statement *declares* a variable. It tells the VBS interpreter to allocate space in your computer's memory to store that variable. You can use the dim statement to declare more than one variable at a time:

```
dim VariableName1, VariableName2, VariableName3
```

This way of creating variables is called *explicit*. Use the dim statement inside a subroutine or a function and you explicitly create a local variable. Use the dim statement outside a subroutine or a function (but still inside a <SCRIPT> </SCRIPT> pair) and you explicitly create a global variable.

VBS also has an *implicit* method for creating variables. In this method, you don't use dim to declare a variable before you use it for the first time in your script: you just go ahead and use the variable. The VBS interpreter is smart enough to know that you've created a variable. You did this in Skill 9 when you used x_coordinate and y_coordinate in the subroutine that moves the Agent. You never explicitly declared those variables, and everything worked fine.

You can force explicit declaration within a script. To do that, use this statement:

```
Option Explicit
```

and be sure to position this statement before any functions or subroutines. If you use Option Explicit, you have to declare every variable with a dim statement.

NOTE   If you use Option Explicit, you may find that it has no effect. You might have a version of VBS in which Option Explicit is not implemented. A quick way to check is to insert Option Explicit in Agent.htm (in skill 9). The VBS for this file has the two implicitly created variables in the Command Button procedure that moves the genie. If you don't get an error message when you try to run the program, you don't have Option Explicit implemented. If you do get an error message, explicitly declare the two variables x_coordinate and y_coordinate with dim statements.

Why would you want to make explicit declaration compulsory, when it's so easy to just create a variable as you need it? Suppose explicit declaration isn't compulsory. If you misspell an implicitly created variable name, the interpreter thinks you want to declare a new variable (whose name is the misspelled name), and your script continues merrily on with unpredictable results. Under the compulsory method, this can't happen (VBS would give you an error message).

Creating Arrays

Sometimes you want to be able to refer to a collection of items that are similar in some way, and you'd like to be able to refer to them as "the first one," "the second one," and so forth, without having to give them unique names. We did this in Skill 8, when we wanted to refer to file paths for the Interactive Music control. Instead of referring to each one uniquely, we put them in an array. Then we were able to refer to a specific file path by using the name of the array and the file path's position within the array (its *index*).

This was a real advantage. Whenever we selected the name of a music Style from the Styles ListBox, we looked up its file path by just going to the array of file paths and taking the one in the row that corresponded to the selected row in the ListBox. We didn't have to write a potentially long `Select Case` statement and invoke it every time we had to find a filename.

Simple Arrays

Suppose you have an array called `SportNames` that holds the names of sports in this order: "Baseball," "Basketball," "Bowling," "Football," "Hockey," "Soccer," and "Track." To help you understand the idea of an array, I've put this array into Table 10.1. As you can see, the index corresponds to the row, and we begin numbering indexes from 0 rather than from 1 (this is called *zero-based*).

T A B L E   1 0 . 1 : The *SportNames* Array

Index	Sport
0	"Baseball"
1	"Basketball"
2	"Bowling"
3	"Football"
4	"Hockey"

TABLE 10.1 CONTINUED: The *SportNames* Array

Index	Sport
5	"Soccer"
6	"Track"

We can use this array to refer to "Baseball" as SportNames(0), and to "Football" as SportNames(3). In VBS, we would create this array with the statement:

```
Dim SportNames(6)
```

In the context of ActiveX, we would put values in the array as part of a Window (or Layout) OnLoad Event with these statements:

```
SportNames(0) = "Baseball"
SportNames(1) = "Basketball"
SportNames(2) = "Bowling"
SportNames(3) = "Football"
SportNames(4) = "Hockey"
SportNames(5) = "Soccer"
SportNames(6) = "Track"
```

The values in ListBoxes are arranged in zero-based arrays. If we had populated a ListBox (let's call it lstbxSportNames) with the values in Table 10.1, we could refer to those values with the List property. In that case, the value of lstbxSport-Names.List(1) would be "Basketball".

Complex Arrays

Suppose we want to add a column to the table—a column that denotes whether the sport is in the Olympics. Table 10.2 shows the layout.

TABLE 10.2: Expanding the *SportNames* Table

Index	Sport	Olympic Sport?
0	"Baseball"	Yes
1	"Basketball"	Yes
2	"Bowling"	No
3	"Football"	No
4	"Hockey"	Yes
5	"Soccer"	Yes
6	"Track"	Yes

We can represent this kind of table in a *multidimensional* array. We would declare it in a `dim` statement by stating the number of rows minus one (as before) and the number of columns minus one (the number of columns is 2; the column that holds the index doesn't count):

```
dim Sportnames(6,1)
```

Now we would refer to `"Football"` as `SportNames(3,0)`. The information in the next column in this row—`SportNames(3,1)`—tells us whether Football is an Olympic sport.

We can have multicolumn ListBoxes whose values are in multidimensional arrays. Once again, the List property and the indexes give us the location of array items. If `lstbxSportNames` is structured like Table 10.2, then the value in `lstbxSportNames.List(4,0)` is `"Hockey"`.

Dynamic Arrays

VBS allows you to create an array even if you don't know how many items you're going to store in it when you get started. When you do this, you're creating a *dynamic array*. Events that take place in your script can then set the size.

Here's how you create a dynamic array:

```
dim SportNames()
```

Suppose a user let you know, via a TextBox or other selection mechanism, that he or she wanted to enter the names of 10 sports into the array. You would use the VBS `redim` statement to set the number of items:

```
redim SportNames(9)
```

One thing to be aware of when you use `redim`—it erases the existing contents of an array.

Subtypes

Different kinds of values can live in variables, and VBS is flexible in this regard. Its variable type, *variant*, can hold any kind of data. Since the variant is VBS' only data type, the different "kinds" of data are *subtypes*.

The up side of the flexibility that the variant provides is that you don't have to prepare a variable in advance to hold a particular subtype. On the other hand, as you saw in Skill 5, you often have to check the subtype in a variable to ensure that your script runs properly: End users are capable of all kinds of input errors, and some of these errors may result in the wrong kind of data in a variable.

Fortunately, VBS has a number of functions that help you check the type of data in a variable. One, VarType, takes the variable's name as its argument and returns a number which indicates the subtype of data currently stored in that variable. For example,

```
VarType(IntegerVariable)
```

returns 2.

Table 10.3 shows variant subtypes, describes each subtype, and presents the numerical value that VarType returns for each subtype.

TABLE 10.3: VBS Subtypes and the Value That VarType Returns for Each

Subtype	What It Is	VarType Returns:
Array	A collection of items named by a single variable and referred to by a numerical index	8192
Boolean	Either True (-1) or False (0)	11
Byte	An integer between 0 and 255	17
Date/Time	A date/time value. Permissible dates start at January 1, 100 and end at December 31, 9999	7
Double	A double precision floating-point number	5
Empty	Indicates an uninitialized variable or a string of zero length	0
Integer	An integer between -32768 and 32767	2
Long Integer	An integer between -2,147,483,648 and 2,147,483,647	3
Null	Indicates that a variable has been assigned a Null value (the variable contains no valid data)	1
Object	An instance of an object (like an ActiveX control)	9
Single	A single precision floating-point number	4
String	A string enclosed in quotes (e.g., "I'm a string")	8

NOTE   When its argument is an array, VarType always adds 8192 to another of its possible values to indicate the type of array. An array which holds integers, then, would return 8192 + 2, or 8194.

Remember when we trapped errors in Skill 5? We wanted to be sure that users enter numeric values and we used the `IsNumeric` function to test their entries. If the entry is a numerical value, `IsNumeric` returns True, otherwise it returns False.

VBS has similar functions which test for other subtypes. Table 10.4 lists these functions.

T A B L E 1 0 . 4 : VBS Functions That Test for Subtypes

Function	Returns True If Its Argument...
IsNumeric	Is a numerical value
IsDate	Is a valid date (2/31/97, for example, is not a valid date)
IsEmpty	Has never been assigned a value
IsNull	Has been assigned Null as its value. Assigning Null gets rid of the variable's contents without getting rid of the variable
IsObject	Is an object (like an ActiveX control)
IsArray	Is an array

Assigning Values to Variables

We've done this so often that it should be second nature by now. To assign a value to a variable, use an equal sign:

```
VariableName = Value
```

In VBS, we can update the value of a variable, as we did in Skill 3, by adding a number:

```
VariableName = VariableName + 30
```

We can also update a variable, as we did in Skill 4, by adding the value of another variable:

```
VariableName1 = VariableName1 + VariableName2
```

VBS has a special case regarding assignment. When the value you're assigning to a variable is an object (like an ActiveX control), VBS requires your assignment statement to look like this:

```
Set VariableName = cmdbtnControl
```

Skill 10

Testing Subtype Functions

Let's write a script that uses subtype functions to test the data type of a variable.

Open a new file in the ActiveX Control Pad and save it as Functions Test in skill 10. Insert a new layout called layout for Functions Test, and add five Command buttons and a Label control so it looks like Figure 10.1. Use the Command Buttons to insert predetermined values into a global variable. The value will show up in the Label. Each time you insert a value, you'll click the Test button. A Message Box will appear that shows the results of testing the data type of the variable using the IsNumeric, IsDate, IsEmpty, IsNull, and IsObject functions.

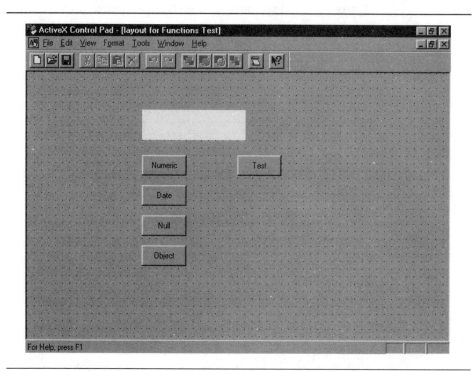

FIGURE 10.1: The *layout for Functions Test* includes a Label and five Command Buttons.

Set each Command Button's ID to cmdbtn + Caption so that, for example, the Command Button with the caption Numeric has the ID cmdbtnNumeric. Change the Label's ID to **lblTest**.

In the Script Wizard, create a global variable called TestVariable. Then, set each button's Click event in accordance with this code (layout for Function Tests.alx).

 layout for Function Tests.alx

```
<SCRIPT LANGUAGE="VBScript">
<!--
dim TestVariable

-->
</SCRIPT>
<SCRIPT LANGUAGE="VBScript">
<!--
Sub cmdbtnTest_Click()
MsgBox "IsNumeric: " & IsNumeric(TestVariable) _
    & chr(13) & "IsDate: " & IsDate(TestVariable) _
    & chr(13) & "IsEmpty: " & IsEmpty(TestVariable) _
    & chr(13) & "IsNull: " & IsNull(TestVariable) _
    & chr(13) & "IsObject: " & IsObject(TestVariable)
end sub
-->
</SCRIPT>
<SCRIPT LANGUAGE="VBScript">
<!--
Sub cmdbtnObject_Click()
set TestVariable = cmdbtnObject
lblTest.Caption = "cmdbtnObject"
end sub
-->
</SCRIPT>
<SCRIPT LANGUAGE="VBScript">
<!--
Sub cmdbtnNumeric_Click()
TestVariable = 90172
lblTest.Caption = TestVariable
end sub
-->
</SCRIPT>
<SCRIPT LANGUAGE="VBScript">
<!--
Sub cmdbtnNull_Click()
TestVariable = Null
lblTest.Caption = "Null"
end sub
-->
```

```
</SCRIPT>
<SCRIPT LANGUAGE="VBScript">
<!--
Sub cmdbtnDate_Click()
TestVariable = "9/01/72"
lblTest.Caption = TestVariable
end sub
-->
</SCRIPT>
```

I've left out the code for the <DIV> part of the layout. Note that in the Click event for inserting an Object and in the Click event for inserting Null, we put a string into the label to help us track what we've inserted. Note also the `set` statement in the Click event that inserts an Object.

Save the file, and open the Web page in IE. After you click each button, click the Test button to see a Message Box that shows the results of applying all the functions to TestVariable. Figure 10.2 shows the Web page in IE with the Message Box open after inserting a date.

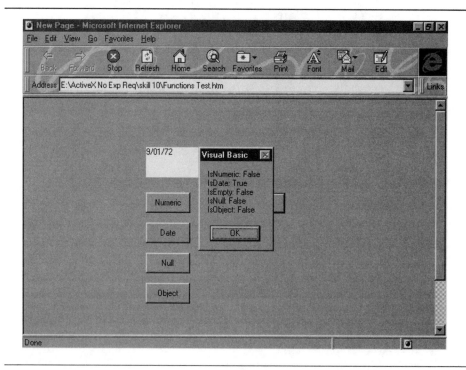

FIGURE 10.2: The Web page in IE after clicking the Date button and the Test button

Smooth Operators

VBS has a variety of operators—symbols that perform *operations* on other symbols. The plus sign (+) is an operator that adds two numbers together. As you've already seen, the ampersand sign (&) is an operator that concatenates two strings together.

VBS has three kinds of operators—comparison, logical, and arithmetic. The comparison operators appear in Table 10.5, the logical operators in Table 10.6, and the arithmetic operators in Table 10.7.

TABLE 10.5: The VBS Comparison Operators

Operator	Name
=	Equality
< >	Inequality
<	Less Than
>	Greater Than
<=	Less Than Or Equal To
=>	Greater Than Or Equal To
Is	Equivalence (do two variables refer to the same object)

TABLE 10.6: VBS Logical Operators

Operator	Name
Not	Negation
And	Conjunction
Or	Disjunction
XOr	Exclusion
Eqv	Equivalence
Imp	Implication

Skill 10

TABLE 10.7: VBS Arithmetic Operators

Operator	Name
^	Exponentiation
-	Negation
*	Multiplication
/	Division
\	Integer Division
Mod	Modulus
+	Addition
-	Subtraction
&	String Concatenation

Of the operators in Table 10.7, Mod might be the least familiar. This one handles *Modulus Arithmetic*, a term which might be even less familiar to you. All that this operator does is divide one integer by another and return the remainder. If the numbers aren't integers, it rounds them before dividing. So

```
Answer = 59 Mod 7.8
```

assigns 3 as the value for the variable Answer. (See Skill 14 for an application of the Mod operator.)

Program Flow

One of the hallmarks of any programming language is the ability to choose an alternative when a program comes to a decision point. VBS gives you several ways to do this, as you've already seen. Strictly speaking, each method is called a *control structure*. We won't emphasize that term, in order to avoid confusion with the use of the word "control" as in "ActiveX control."

In Skill 4, you first looked at Select Case, and in Skill 5 you first worked with If…Then. We'll go over them once more, and introduce you to If…Then's relative If…Then…Else.

Select Case

The Select Case statement enables your program to perform a test, and then based on the result, pick one of several possible paths (called *cases*). Within each path, you can have a number of lines of code. When the program finishes going through the code for that path, your program exits the `Select Case`. Imagine a variable called TestVariable with the possible values of 1, 2, 3, or 4. The `Select Case` would look like this:

```
Select Case TestVariable
    Case 1
        Statement 1
        Statement 2
        Statement 3
    Case 2
        Statement 1
        Statement 2
    Case 3
        Statement 1
        Statement 2
        Statement 3
        Statement 4
    Case 4
        Statement 1
Case Else
Statement 1
Statement 2
End Select
```

Note the final case, `Case Else`, which executes if TestVariable doesn't contain 1, 2, 3, or 4.

While the indents aren't necessary, they make the code easy to read. The `End Select` *is* necessary.

If...Then

When your program has to make a decision that doesn't have so many alternatives, If...Then is often appropriate. The format for If...Then is:

```
If condition = True Then
    Statement 1
    Statement 2
    Statement 3
        .
        .
        .
End If
```

As in the `Select Case`, the indents make the code easier to read, and the `End If` is necessary. It's also important to position Then at the end of the line that starts with `If`.

Another way to write the first line is:

```
If condition Then
```

VBS knows enough to check and see if the condition is True.

You can also have an If...Then start off with the condition being False:

```
If condition = False Then
    Statement 1
    Statement 2
    Statement 3
         .
         .
         .
End If
```

And the alternative way to write the first line is:

```
If Not condition = Then
```

If...Then...Else

The If...Then structure is simple and straightforward, but it leaves a bit to be desired. It tells the program what to do if a condition is True, but what if the condition is False? As we've seen, you could write a whole additional If...Then starting with the condition being False, but it seems inefficient to have to set up everything all over again.

Here's where If...Then...Else comes in handy. Its format is:

```
If condition Then
    Statement 1
    Statement 2
    Statement 3
Else
    Statement 4
    Statement 5
    Statement 6
    Statement 7
End If
```

Suppose you have a number of conditions to test. You can do this by extending the If...Then...Else structure to include ElseIf statements:

```
If condition1 Then
    Statement 1
    Statement 2
    Statement 3
ElseIf condition2 Then
    Statement 4
    Statement 5
```

```
        Statement 6
        Statement 7
ElseIf condition3 Then
        Statement 8
        Statement 9
        Statement 10
        Statement 11
ElseIf condition4 Then
        Statement 12
        Statement 13
            .
            .
            .
ElseIf conditionN Then
            .
            .
            .
End If
```

You can include as many ElseIf statements as you need to cover all your conditions.

Making Code Repeat

Another mainstay of programming languages is their ability to make portions of code execute repeatedly.

VBS has two ways of doing this:

- Do...Loop

- For...Next

Do...Loop

To repeat code, you can put it between a Do statement and a Loop statement.

```
Do
    Statement 1
    Statement 2
    Statement 3
Loop
```

The Do statement puts things into motion. The Loop statement sends the flow back to Do and everything begins again. But something's missing—how does this structure know when to stop?

Four possibilities to write a Do/Loop are available: two involve putting a condition on the line with the Do statement, two involve putting a condition on the line with the Loop statement. Let's start with the Do statement.

A Do While...Loop keeps repeating while a condition is True. Here's an example:

```
y = 14
Do While y < 30
    y = y + 2
Loop
```

A Do Until...Loop executes until a condition is True:

```
y = 14
Do Until y = 30
    y = y + 2
Loop
```

Now let's look at the Loop statement. You can put either While or Until on the same line as Loop. The Do...Loop While looks like this:

```
y = 14
Do
    y = y + 2
Loop While y < 30
```

The Do...Loop Until is:

```
y = 14
Do
    y = y + 2
Loop Until y = 30
```

You put While or Until on the line with Loop if you want to be sure that the code executes at least once. You put While or Until on the line with Do if you want to be sure that the code never gets to run if the condition is true.

For...Next

With the For...Next structure, you explicitly set the lower bound and the upper bound of a variable that counts the number of times the code repeats. When the counter gets to the upper bound, the code stops repeating:

```
For y = 1 to 30
    Statement 1
    Statement 2
    Statement 3
Next
```

In these lines of code, the counter increases by 1, each time the loop is completed. You can change that by using the Step statement. In the following example, the counter variable increases by 2 each time the loop completes:

```
For y = 1 to 30 Step 2
    Statement 1
    Statement 2
    Statement 3
Next
```

You can even make the counter go backward:

```
For y = 30 to 1 Step -3
    Statement 1
    Statement 2
    Statement 3
Next
```

Procedures

Procedures in VBS are either subroutines or functions. In addition to subroutines and functions that you design and build, VBS has a number of important functions built right into the language, which we examine in this section.

Subroutines

You've been writing subroutines throughout Part I. Whenever you used the Script Wizard to attach an event to an action or to a series of actions, your finished product was a subroutine. When you examined any of your subroutines in an HTML file or in an ALX file, you always found that it followed this format:

```
Sub Name(0 or more arguments)
    ...Code statements...
End Sub
```

A subroutine may have zero or more arguments inside parentheses that immediately follow its name. Each subroutine is a piece of code that you can call from anywhere in the script. Any subroutine that you wrote in the Script Wizard is a great example.

Functions

Unlike a subroutine, a function returns a value. Its format is

```
Function Name(0 or more arguments)
        Name = Code statements
End Sub
```

The important point here is that you must set a value for the name of the function before the function finishes.

You haven't written any functions yet, so here's an example. This function converts inches to centimeters:

```
Function In_to_Cm(Inches)
    In_to_Cm = 2.54 * Inches
End Function
```

This definition tells you that `In_to_Cm` does its computation on a numerical value for the argument `Inches`. Then, it stores the result of that computation in the name `Int_to_Cm`. This enables you to call `Int_to_Cm` in a script.

Within a script, you'd call `Int_to_Cm` like this:

```
sngLengthConvert = In_to_Cm(75)
```

When the function finishes its work, 190.5 is the value of `sngLengthConvert`.

Take a look at the variable name `sngLengthConvert`. I've used two important techniques in naming this variable. The first is to use both uppercase and lowercase letters to make the name readable. The second is to put a three-letter lowercase prefix at the beginning. This prefix tells you the subtype of the variable. (This one stands for *single-precision floating point*.) While it's true that the variant type allows all kinds of variables, you usually know how you'll use a variable in your script. To construct a prefix, use the first three consonants of the variable's subtype. If the variable will take more than one subtype as the script runs, the single letter v—for Variant—is a helpful prefix.

Writing a Function in the Script Wizard

Now let's write a function VBScript. This function will convert temperatures from Fahrenheit to Centigrade or from Centigrade to Fahrenheit. In the Active X Control Pad, start a new HTML file called `Temperatures` and save it in `skill 10`. Insert a new HTML Layout Control and save it in `skill 10` as `layout for Temperatures`. Insert a TextBox and three Option Buttons, and position them as shown in Figure 10.3 including captions. Make the IDs **txtbxTemperatures**,

optbtnFtoC, **optbtnCtoF**, and **optbtnClear**. In the Properties sheet for each Option Button, type **Temperature** as the value for the GroupName property.

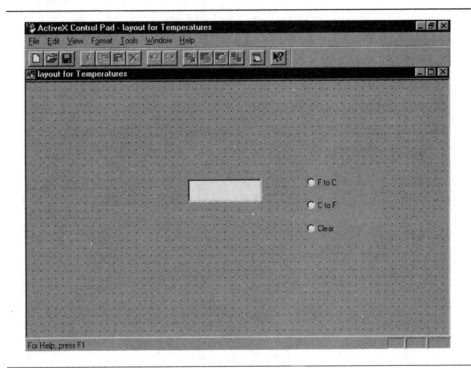

FIGURE 10.3: The layout for Temperatures

The user will enter a value in the TextBox, and click on an Option Button to do the conversion. Clicking on the Clear button will clear the TextBox.

In the Script Wizard Actions pane, right-click on Procedures and then click New Procedure and name your new procedure TempConvert. In the Script pane, type this code:

```
Function TempConvert(Temperature)
If optbtnCtoF.Value Then
    TempConvert = 9*(Temperature/5) + 32
Else
    TempConvert = 5*(Temperature - 32)/9
End If
```

Notice that you've changed Sub to Function in the first line. This code examines the value of one of the Option Buttons (the one for Centigrade-to-Fahrenheit conversion). If the value is True (meaning that this button has been clicked), Centigrade to Fahrenheit conversion proceeds. If not, Fahrnenheit to Centigrade conversion takes place. As you can see, we're careful to set a value for TempConvert in either case. TempConvert contains the value that the function returns.

Now for the Option Buttons. The Click event for optbtnCtoF should look like this:

```
Sub optbtnCtoF_Click()
On Error Resume Next
txtbxTemperature.Value = TempConvert(txtbxTemperature.Value)
```

The Click event for optbtnFtoC should look like this:

```
Sub optbtnFtoC_Click()
On Error Resume Next
txtbxTemperature.Value = TempConvert(txtbxTemperature.Value)
```

And, finally, the Click event for optbtnClear should look like this:

```
Sub optnbtnClear_Click()
txtbxTemperature.Value = " "
```

Each On Error Resume Next statement prevents errors resulting from clicking an Option Button before anything has been entered into the TextBox.

Open this page in IE, enter a value in the TextBox, click the Option Buttons and watch this script do its work. Although the page isn't very dynamic, the important aspect of this exercise is the format for writing and calling functions, and how to do that within ActiveX. The Click events for the first two Option Buttons show that you can use a control's property as a function's argument.

Built-in Functions

VBS has more than 80 built-in functions. You can use them as building-blocks in your scripts. We won't describe or even list them all here, but we will tell you about a few of the ones you might find most useful.

String Functions

VBS gives you a complete set of functions for working with strings. You can use them to take apart string input from a user, to reformat a string, and to manipulate output that you want a user to see. Table 10.8 gives you the string manipulation functions.

TABLE 10.8: VBS String Manipulation Functions

Function	What It Does...
Trim("String")	Removes all leading and trailing blank spaces from "String"
LTrim("String")	Removes all leading (leftmost) blank spaces
RTrim("String")	Removes all trailing (rightmost) blank spaces
Len("String")	Returns the number of characters in "String"
Left("String", x)	Returns the leftmost x characters
Right("String", x)	Returns the rightmost x characters
Mid("String", StartPosition, Length)	Returns Length characters, beginning with StartPosition
UCase("String")	Makes all the characters UPPERCASE
LCase("String")	Makes all the characters lowercase
InStr("String", Target)	Checks to see if Target is in "String". If it is, this function returns Target's position. If not, it returns 0

Another important related function is Chr(), which you've been using throughout most of the Skills. Back in Skill 3, we discussed the use of this function in connection with "keycodes." We didn't elaborate on what those keycodes were, except to say that each character has a numerical code. That code, called *ASCII*, assigns a unique number to every lowercase letter, uppercase letter, number, symbol, and for most keys on your keyboard.

The Chr() function was useful in dealing with keypresses because it takes an ASCII code as its argument and returns the corresponding character. VBS provides another function for going in the reverse direction: Asc() takes a character as its argument and returns the corresponding ASCII code.

Message Boxes

Still another important string-related function is MsgBox, which you've used frequently. As you know by now, a Message Box presents a message and waits for a user response. Here is a Message Box with three arguments:

```
MsgBox(prompt, buttons, title)
```

Wait a second! This doesn't look like the format that you've been using for MsgBox. Whenever we've used MsgBox we didn't include parentheses. What's the story?

You include the parentheses if you precede `MsgBox` with the word `call`. For example, in the subroutine for cmdbtnTest earlier in this Skill (see "Testing Subtype Functions"), you had this code:

```
Sub cmdbtnTest_Click()
MsgBox "IsNumeric: " & IsNumeric(TestVariable) _
    & chr(13) & "IsDate: " & IsDate(TestVariable) _
    & chr(13) & "IsEmpty: " & IsEmpty(TestVariable) _
    & chr(13) & "IsNull: " & IsNull(TestVariable) _
    & chr(13) & "IsObject: " & IsObject(TestVariable)
end sub
```

You could have written it as:

```
Sub cmdbtnTest_Click()
call MsgBox("IsNumeric: " & IsNumeric(TestVariable) _
    & chr(13) & "IsDate: " & IsDate(TestVariable) _
    & chr(13) & "IsEmpty: " & IsEmpty(TestVariable) _
    & chr(13) & "IsNull: " & IsNull(TestVariable) _
    & chr(13) & "IsObject: " & IsObject(TestVariable))
end sub
```

Both types of syntax (i.e., with and without parentheses) will work for any procedure (not just `MsgBox`) if you don't ask it to return a value. You can create some pretty elaborate Message Boxes because:

- `prompt` is the string expression that appears in the Message Box.

- `buttons` is a numeric expression that specifies the number and type of buttons in the display, the type of icons in the Message Box, which button is the default button, and the *modality* of the Message Box. ("Modality" indicates the extent of operations that are suspended until the user responds to the Message Box).

- `title` is the string expression that appears in the Message Box's title bar.

The buttons argument has a number of possibilities, some of which you've already seen in Skill 5. Table 10.9 shows what you can do.

TABLE 10.9: Message Box Button Settings

Value	What It Does...
0	Displays OK button only
1	Displays OK and Cancel
2	Displays Abort, Retry, and Ignore

TABLE 10.9 CONTINUED: Message Box Button Settings

Value	What It Does...
3	Displays Yes, No, and Cancel
4	Displays Yes and No buttons
5	Displays Retry and Cancel
16	Displays Critical Message icon
32	Displays Warning Query icon
48	Displays Warning Message icon
64	Displays Information Message icon
256	Makes second button the default
512	Makes third button the default
768	Makes fourth button the default
4096	Makes the modality system-wide; suspends all applications until the user responds to the Message Box

As you saw in Skill 5, you can use combinations of these values. For example, if you set MsgBox's second argument to 2 + 64 (don't add them together), you'll display a Message Box that has three buttons (Abort, Retry, and Ignore) and an information symbol.

The MsgBox function truly acts like a function when you ask it to return a value, and you do that when you're interested in which Message Box button a user clicked. Here's how you might code this:

```
intReturnCode = MsgBox("A three-button Message Box", 2)
```

When you have MsgBox return a value, you have to use the parentheses.

Since a variety of button-displays is possible, a variety of responses is possible. Table 10.10 shows the Message Box response settings.

TABLE 10.10: Message Box Response Settings

Value	Indicates That the User Pressed...
1	OK
2	Cancel
3	Abort
4	Retry

Skill 10

TABLE 10.10 CONTINUED: Message Box Response Settings

Value	Indicates That the User Pressed...
5	Ignore
6	Yes
7	No

Math Functions

Sometimes it's helpful to perform calculations on user input, or to be able to get date and time information. VBS helps you with a rich set of built-in mathematical functions, as Table 10.11 shows.

TABLE 10.11: VBS Built-in Math Functions

Function	What It Does...
Abs(number)	Returns the absolute value of number
Atn(number)	Returns the angle, in radians, whose Tangent is number
Cos(number)	Returns the cosine of an angle which is number radians
Date	Returns the current system date
Exp(number)	Returns e (the base of natural logarithms) raised to the power indicated by number
Fix(number)	Returns the integer part of number, and eliminates the fractional part. If number is negative, Fix returns the first integer greater than or equal to number
Hex(number)	Returns a string that represents the hexadecimal equivalent of number If number isn't a whole number, it's rounded off before Hex evaluates it
Int(number)	Returns the integer part of number, and eliminates the fractional part. If number is negative, Int returns the first integer less than or equal to number
Log(number)	Returns the natural logarithm of number.
Now	Returns the user's system's date and time setting
Oct(number)	Returns a string that represents the octal value of number. If number isn't a whole number, it's rounded off before Oct evaluates it

TABLE 10.11 CONTINUED: VBS Built-in Math Functions

Function	What It Does...
Rnd(number)	Returns a random number between 0 and 1. number is optional. If it's less than 0, Rnd uses the same *seed* (the number that starts the randomization process) each successive time you run it. If number is greater than 0 (or not supplied), Rnd uses the next random number as its seed. If number is 0, the seed is the most recently generated random number
Sgn(number)	Returns 1 if number is greater than 0; returns 0 if number is equal to 0, returns -1 if number is less than 0
Sin(number)	Returns the sine of an angle which is number radians
Sqr(number)	Returns the square root of number\. number must be greater than or equal to zero
Tan(number)	Returns the tangent of an angle which is number radians
Time	Returns a variant (whose subtype is date) that shows the current system time

If you don't have a specific use for any of these math functions at the moment, it might be difficult to see how and why you would use them. Just be aware of them. As you become more experienced with Web page design, you will undoubtedly discover uses for some of these functions.

One quick exercise is to use the Int function on our Temperature-Converter. Open the Script Wizard and change the Click event codes for the two conversion Option Buttons to:

```
txtbxTemperature.Value = Int(TempConvert(txtbxTemperature.Value))
```

Then convert a temperature from one system to the other and back again. You might not see the same value you started with! Keep going back and forth between the two buttons and you might see all sorts of changes. This results from the rounding that Int performs.

Summary

VBS is a very rich scripting language. It provides a wealth of control structures, operators, built-in functions, and flexibility. The best part is that you can apply all this capability to control the objects that bring a Web page to life.

Skill 10

Are You Experienced?

Now you can...

- ☑ understand the general concept of a scripting language

- ☑ understand the ideas behind VBS variables and subtypes

- ☑ work with arrays, including multidimensional arrays and dynamic arrays

- ☑ understand the connection between arrays and listboxes

- ☑ use VBS structures that control program flow and iteration

- ☑ understand how to create functions and be aware VBS built-in functions for string-manipulation and math

S K I L L

11

eleven

Putting VBS and HTML Together

- ❏ Using HTML form controls

- ❏ Combining HTML form controls and VBS

- ❏ Setting up frames

- ❏ Navigating frames with VBS

- ❏ Navigating frames with the ActiveX TabStrip control

Now that you're aware of the finer points of VBS, it's time to join VBS with HTML. In a number of exercises, this Skill builds on your knowledge of VBS and HTML and shows how they can work together to produce some powerful applications.

Using HTML Form Controls

Throughout our discussion, I've focused on ActiveX controls. HTML, however, also has its own controls that predate the advent of ActiveX. Referred to as *form controls*, they enable a user to enter text and make choices. While not as rich as ActiveX controls in either variety or functionality, form controls are still prevalent throughout the Web and probably will be for the foreseeable future. Because they're so widely used, this Skill shows you how to use VBS to script these controls. Then you'll have the appropriate techniques in your arsenal if you ever have to use them.

If you want to use these controls in an HTML document, you usually create <FORM> and </FORM> tags and put the HTML controls between them (although these controls can appear without <FORM> tags). A <FORM> </FORM> tag-pair has one purpose in life—to provide a home for form controls. The two tags are the boundaries of an HTML form. Inside the form, you use <INPUT> tags to indicate the controls. The TYPE attribute of the <INPUT> tag specifies the type of control.

HTML form controls include:

- Button, which is like an ActiveX Command Button

- Text, which resembles a one-line ActiveX TextBox control, displaying text as a user enters it

- Password, a text area that doesn't display text as a user enters it

- Checkbox, which is like an ActiveX CheckBox control

- Radio, which is the same as an ActiveX Option Button in a group of Option Buttons

Buttons, Checkboxes, and Radios have OnClick events that are similar to the Click events of ActiveX controls.

Two other types of controls hint at what Web-based interaction is like without ActiveX: Send is a button that transmits the values in a form's fields to a server on the Web. Reset is a button that resets the fields. The idea is that without VBS, button-clicks send data across the Web, and dynamic interaction takes place on the server, not the local machine (also called the *client*). The more interaction you can script in the client, the faster the interaction and the more enjoyable the Web experience for the user.

Combining Form Controls and VBS

We'll go through a couple of exercises to show you how VBS can activate form controls.

Buttons and Text

The form controls we'll start with are a Text control and two Button controls. The finished page will look like Figure 11.1.

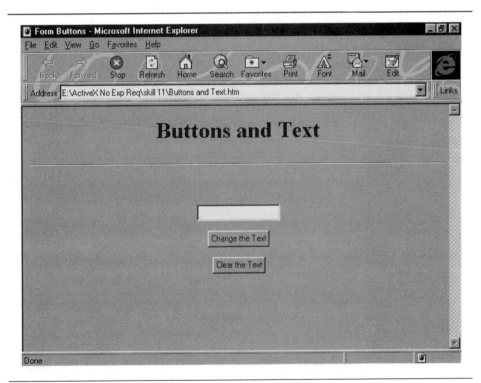

FIGURE 11.1: A Web page with three HTML form controls

Once we have created the form controls, we'll add VBS that enables one button's OnClick event to add text to the Text area, and the other button's OnClick event to remove it.

In your ActiveX Control Pad Text Editor, open a new HTML file and save it as Buttons and Text in skill 11. Enter **Form Buttons** as the title, and enter **Buttons and Text** as a centered <H1> heading followed by a horizontal line (which you create by typing **<HR>**). At this point, the Text Editor should look like this:

```
<HTML>
<HEAD>
<TITLE>Form Buttons</TITLE>
</HEAD>
<BODY>
<CENTER> <H1>Buttons and Text</H1> </CENTER> <HR>

</BODY>
</HTML>
```

Now let's create the form with the controls, and let's do it step-by-step:

1. To give ourselves some room, type **

** on the line after the heading.

2. On the next line, type **<CENTER>** to center the form we're about to create.

3. Go to the next line and type **<FORM NAME = "ScriptedForm">**. The NAME attribute will turn out to be important.

4. On the next line, type **<P>** to start a new paragraph. (We used this type of tag when we positioned text around graphics in Skill 4.) For positioning purposes, we'll use it to treat each form control as a separate paragraph in the form.

5. Put in the Text control by typing on the next line: **<INPUT TYPE = "text" NAME = "frmtxtArea" MAXLENGTH = 35>**. MAXLENGTH sets the upper limit on the number of characters a user can enter.

6. On the next line, set up a new paragraph for our first form control button. Type **<P>**.

7. Here's where we insert the first button. On the next line type **<INPUT TYPE = "button" NAME = "frmbtnChange" VALUE = "Change the Text">**. The VALUE attribute on a form control button is like an ActiveX Command Button's Caption property.

8. Go to a new line and complete the form by typing these lines:

\<P>
\<INPUT TYPE = "button" NAME = "frmbtnClear" VALUE = "Clear the Text">
\</FORM>
\</CENTER>

After all these steps, your file should look like this:

```
<HTML>
<HEAD>
<TITLE>Form Buttons</TITLE>
</HEAD>
<BODY>
<CENTER> <H1>Buttons and Text</H1> </CENTER> <HR>
<BR> <BR> <BR>
<CENTER>
<FORM NAME = "ScriptedForm">
<P>
<INPUT TYPE = "text" NAME = "frmtxtArea" MAXLENGTH = 35>
<P>
<INPUT TYPE = "button"  NAME = "frmbtnChange"
➥VALUE = "Change the Text">
<P>
<INPUT TYPE = "button"  NAME = "frmbtnClear"
➥VALUE = "Clear the Text">
</FORM>
</CENTER>

</BODY>
</HTML>
```

Opened in IE, this file looks like Figure 11.1. At this point, of course, the buttons don't do anything. We'll rectify that by adding a script.

To show you how smart the Script Wizard is, open it up and have a look at the Event pane. You'll see our form represented there, and if you click on the + to its left, you'll see our form controls. Figure 11.2 shows you how this looks. Even though we're not working with ActiveX controls, the Script Wizard recognizes these controls as objects.

We'll use the Script Wizard in a little while, but right now let's just type the code directly into the HTML document. Close the Script Wizard and we'll start writing.

Skill 11

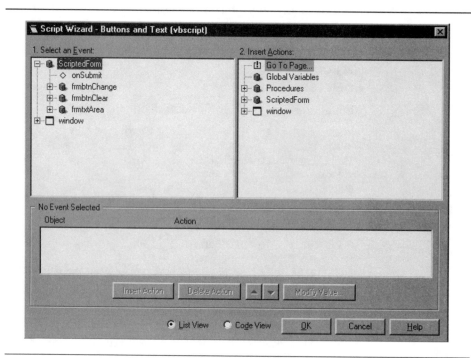

FIGURE 11.2: The Script Wizard shows the form and the form controls.

The important part of the script is this: The code has to know how to refer to the form controls. Fortunately, the NAME attributes have set this up for us. In the titles of the subroutines for the OnClick events, we use the names of the buttons: Sub frmbtnChange_OnClick and Sub frmbtnClear_OnClick. The underscore maintains the same format that we've always used to script events.

Within the script, we'll also require a way to refer to the text area and to its value, a property of that control. The area's name is frmtxtArea and it's an object in the form ScriptedForm. The logical way to refer to it, then, is ScriptedForm .frmtxtArea. Going one step further, the form is in our HTML document, which we can identify as Document. Thus, the full name of the Text area is Document .ScriptedForm.frmtxtArea.

Now for still another step: The text that appears in frmtxtArea is the Text area's value. It's a property of the Text area control, so we refer to it as Document.ScriptedForm.frmtxtArea.Value.

Next, we incorporate all this into a script. After the title and before </HEAD>, type

<SCRIPT LANGUAGE = "vbscript">
<!—

Then, type the code for the first Button's subroutine:

Sub frmbtnChange_OnClick
Document.ScriptedForm.frmtxtArea.Value = "I've changed!"
End Sub

This script sets things up so that clicking the button enters "I've changed!" in the text area. The next subroutine clears the text area:

Sub frmbtnClear_OnClick
Document.ScriptedForm.frmtxtArea.Value = " "
End Sub

Finish out the script with these lines:

—>
</SCRIPT>

Here's what the file (Buttons and Text.htm) should now look like.

Buttons and Text.htm

```
<HTML>
<HEAD>
<TITLE>Form Buttons</TITLE>
<SCRIPT LANGUAGE = "vbscript">
<!-
Sub frmbtnChange_OnClick
Document.ScriptedForm.frmtxtArea.Value = "I've changed!"
End Sub
Sub frmbtnClear_OnClick
Document.ScriptedForm.frmtxtArea.Value = ""
End Sub
->
</SCRIPT>
</HEAD>
<BODY>
<CENTER> <H1> Buttons and Text</H1> </CENTER> <HR>
<BR> <BR> <BR>
<CENTER>
<FORM NAME = "ScriptedForm">
```

Skill 11

```
<P>
<INPUT TYPE = "text" NAME = "frmtxtArea" MAXLENGTH = 35>
<P>
<INPUT TYPE = "button"  NAME = "frmbtnChange" VALUE = "Change the Text">
<P>
<INPUT TYPE = "button"  NAME = "frmbtnClear" VALUE = "Clear the Text">
</FORM>
</CENTER>
</BODY>
</HTML>
```

Save the file and open it in IE. Clicking the first button puts "I've changed" in the text area and clicking the second button clears the Text area. In fact, you can enter any text up to 35 characters in the text area, and clicking the second button clears it. Figure 11.3 shows the Web page's appearance after you've clicked the first button.

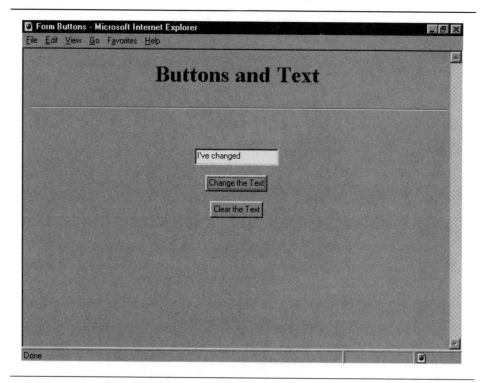

FIGURE 11.3: The Web page with three functional form controls. The first button has just been clicked.

NOTE   **We could have used a shorter version of** `frmtxtArea`**'s full name instead—** `ScriptedForm.frmtxtArea` **would have sufficed. I put you through the extra typing because I want you get some familiarity with** `Document`**, which we will discuss in Skill 14.**

Using the Script Wizard

We can also use the Script Wizard to write the code for our Command Buttons. The resulting code, while equivalent, comes out looking quite different, as you'll see.

Start by saving your file as `Script Wizard Buttons and Text` in `skill 11`. Change the title to **Script Wizard Form Buttons** and the heading to **Script Wizard Buttons and Text**. Then delete all the VBS code and both <SCRIPT> tags. Now you're ready for the Script Wizard.

Open the Script Wizard and in the Event pane click on the + next to Scripted-Form. Put the Script Wizard in Code View, and it will look like Figure 11.4.

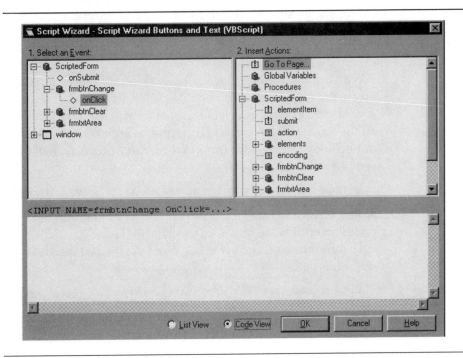

FIGURE 11.4: The Script Wizard for the Script Wizard *Form.htm* file

As you saw before, this reveals all the objects on the form. Click on each object and you'll see its events—you'll recognize the OnClick event. Notice that the set of events for a form control is not nearly as rich as the event-set for an ActiveX control. To see the methods and properties of the form controls, click the + next to ScriptedForm in the Actions pane (to make the controls visible), and then click the + next to each control.

We have to script the Command Buttons. We'll do this in the usual way, and it's instructive to keep the Wizard in Code View while we go through the steps.

The first thing to examine is the line just above the Script pane. It's different from the way it appears when we script ActiveX controls. If we were scripting a Command Button's Click event, the first line in the Script pane would be:

```
Sub cmdbtn_Click()
```

As Figure 11.4 shows, the line above the Script pane says:

```
<INPUT NAME=frmbtnChange OnClick=...>
```

The difference is related to where the Script Wizard will insert the finished code. When scripting ActiveX controls, the Script Wizard inserts the code in a subroutine inside <SCRIPT> tags. With HTML form controls, the Wizard inserts the code inside the tag that defines the control. In this case, the tag is:

```
<INPUT TYPE = "button"  NAME = "frmbtnChange" VALUE = "Change the Text">
```

With frmbtnChange's OnClick event selected, select frmtxtArea's Value property in the Actions pane and double-click it. (If you don't see this property, make sure you click on the + next to ScriptedForm in the Actions pane, and then click on the + next to frmtxtArea.) The term that appears in the Script pane is the full dot-notation identifier for frmtxtArea's Value property. Enter the text needed to complete this line of code:

```
Document.ScriptedForm.frmtxtArea.value = "I have changed"
```

Notice that we've changed "I've" to "I have". If you use "I've" the apostrophe causes an error when you open the page in IE.

To script frmbtnClear's OnClick event, do the clicking and the typing that produces this line:

```
Document.ScriptedForm.frmtxtArea.value = ""
```

Close the Script Wizard and examine the code in your HTML file (`Script Wizard Form.htm`). It should now look like this listing.

Script Wizard Form.htm

```
<HTML>
<HEAD>
<TITLE>Script Wizard Form Buttons</TITLE>
</HEAD>
<BODY>
<CENTER> <H1>Script Wizard Buttons and Text</H1> </CENTER> <HR>
<BR> <BR> <BR>
<CENTER>
    <FORM NAME="ScriptedForm">
<P>
        <INPUT TYPE=text NAME="frmtxtArea" MAXLENGTH = 35>
<P>
        <INPUT LANGUAGE="VBScript" TYPE=button VALUE="Change the Text"
    ➡ONCLICK="Document.ScriptedForm.frmtxtArea.value = &quot;
    ➡I have changed&quot;" NAME="frmbtnChange">
<P>
        <INPUT LANGUAGE="VBScript" TYPE=button VALUE="Clear the Text" ONCLICK=
    ➡"Document.ScriptedForm.frmtxtArea.value = &quot; &quot;"
    ➡NAME="frmbtnClear">
    </FORM>
</CENTER>
</BODY>
</HTML>
```

When scripting a control defined in an <INPUT> tag rather than in an <OBJECT> tag, the Script Wizard behaves differently. It inserts the code directly into the <INPUT> tags, along with the name of the language required to interpret the code. (Note also that each quotation mark you typed has become transformed to &quot, which is why you'll get an error message if you embed an apostrophe in the string.) Open the page in IE, and you'll see that it works exactly like the first version does.

Setting Up Frames

Frames add another dimension to your Web pages. They provide a way to split your screen into rows or columns, and each row or column can display a separate HTML document.

The frames do not all have to be the same size. In fact, it's often the case that Web site designers set up two frames, with one frame that is smaller than the

Skill 11

others and use the smaller frame to contain navigation controls. You use these controls to display Web pages in the other, larger frame.

In HTML documents, <FRAMESET> and </FRAMESET> set off the area in which you insert <FRAME> tags. The <FRAME> tags refer to documents that will appear in the frames.

To start our exploration of frames, open a new HTML file and save it as first in skill 11. This page won't hold much information—we'll just use it for experimental purposes. Edit the new file (first.htm) to look like this listing.

first.htm

```
<HTML>
<HEAD>
<TITLE>First</TITLE>
</HEAD>
<BODY>
<CENTER>
<B> This is the first page!
</CENTER>
</BODY>
</HTML>
```

Use this file as a template for two more files by saving it as second.htm and third.htm. Edit their titles and text appropriately and save them in skill 11.

Now open another new HTML file and save it as Frame Setup. This page will hold the <FRAMESET> and <FRAMES> tags. When you open it in IE, the pages you refer to in the <FRAMES> tags will appear. Here's the code for this file (Frame Setup.htm):

Frame Setup.htm

```
<HTML>
<HEAD>
<TITLE>Frame Setup</TITLE>
</HEAD>
<BODY>
<FRAMESET COLS=50%,50%>
<FRAME NAME = "leftframe" SRC = "first.htm">
<FRAME NAME = "rightframe" SRC = "second.htm">
</FRAMESET>
</BODY>
</HTML>
```

The <FRAMESET> tag's COLS attribute tells IE to divide the browser window into columns, and that each column will occupy half the window. Frames are flexible, however: after the column frames appear on-screen, you can adjust their widths. Save this file and double-click on its icon in skill 11. The window of your Web browser should look like the window shown in Figure 11.5.

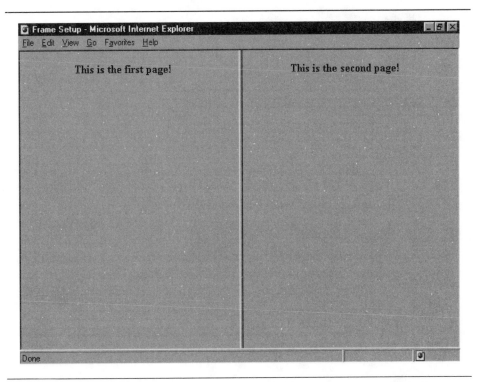

F I G U R E   1 1 . 5 : The appearance of your Web browser when you open *Frame Setup.htm*

Navigating Frames with VBS

The ability to present more than one document in a browser window presents a lot of possibilities. Things really take off, however, if one of the documents contains controls that allow you to specify the document that appears in the other frame.

To get this started, save Frame Setup.htm as Setup for Scripted Frames.htm in skill 11. Change it to look like this listing.

Setup for Scripted Frames.htm

```
<HTML>
<HEAD>
<TITLE>Setup for Scripted Frames</TITLE>
</HEAD>
<BODY>
<FRAMESET COLS=40%,60%>
<FRAME NAME = "navigation" SRC= "navigation.htm">
<FRAME NAME = "display" SRC= "first.htm">
</FRAMESET>
</BODY>
</HTML>
```

The <FRAMESET> tag sets up two column frames. One will contain navigation controls and occupy 40 percent of the screen. The other will display documents and occupy 60 percent. When the Setup for Scripted Frames.htm page first appears, navigation.htm frame will be in the frame on the left and first.htm will be in the frame on the right. Let's set up navigation.htm with three buttons. The first will bring first.htm into the display frame (on the right), the second will display second.htm, and the third will present third.htm.

Open a new HTML file and save it as navigation.htm in skill 11. Enter this code (navigation.htm).

navigation.htm

```
<HTML>
<HEAD>
<TITLE>Navigation</TITLE>
</HEAD>
<BODY>
     <BR> <BR> <BR>
     <CENTER>
<B>Navigation Buttons
     <FORM NAME = "NAVFORM">
     <P>
<INPUT TYPE = "button"  NAME = "frmbtnFirst" VALUE = "FIRST">
<P>
```

```
<INPUT TYPE = "button"  NAME = "frmbtnSecond" VALUE = "SECOND">
<P>
<INPUT TYPE = "button"  NAME = "frmbtnThird" VALUE = "THIRD">
     </FORM>
     </CENTER>
</BODY>
</HTML>
```

Now we must script the OnClick event for each button. The key point here is knowing how to identify the frame in which the three Web pages will appear. In the HTML file that sets up the frames, we referred to this frame as display. What is its full name in dot notation?

Before we work out what the name is, we have to understand a little about how the browser is organized. (We'll explore IE's organization in great detail in Skill 14.) Like an ActiveX control, the browser's window has properties, methods, and events. (You work with one of its events, OnLoad, whenever you populate a ListBox.) One of those properties, Top, identifies what's topmost on the window's list of what to display. (When you examine a Window menu from the menu bar in any application, such as Microsoft Word for Windows, you'll see one item checked. That's the one that's visible, or topmost.) In our example, the frame display is on top, so its full name is window.top.display.

Now that we know the name, we have to specify that what's in the frame will come from a particular file when we click a button. How do we do this? A frame is like a window, and it has the same properties, methods, and events as a window. One of those properties is Location, which provides the location of the file in the frame. Location, in turn, has a property called Href, which gives the URL of the file in the frame.

NOTE   We used Href in Skill 2 when we wanted to jump from one page to another. The principle is the same here: We use Href to jump to another page. This time the new page will show up in a frame, instead of in the entire browser window.

The bottom line is this: When we click a navigation button, we want to change the URL for the file in the display frame. In that way, we're directing the frame to display a different URL. When we click frmbtnFirst, for example, we want to set that URL to first.htm. Here's how we do it:

```
window.top.display.location.href = "first.htm"
```

That's the business end of the code for frmbtnFirst's OnClick event. We vary it as necessary for the other two buttons.

To keep things simple, we'll avoid the Script Wizard this time. In the Text Editor, do the typing that results in:

```
<HTML>
<HEAD>
<TITLE>Navigation</TITLE>
<SCRIPT LANGUAGE = "vbscript">
<!--
Sub frmbtnFirst_OnClick
window.top.display.location.href = "first.htm"
End Sub
Sub frmbtnSecond_OnClick
window.top.display.location.href = "second.htm"
End Sub
Sub frmbtnThird_OnClick
window.top.display.location.href = "third.htm"
End Sub
-->
</SCRIPT>
</HEAD>
<BODY>
<BR> <BR> <BR>
<CENTER>
<B>Navigation Buttons
<FORM NAME = "NAVFORM">
<P>
<INPUT TYPE = "button"  NAME = "frmbtnFirst" VALUE = "FIRST">
<P>
<INPUT TYPE = "button"  NAME = "frmbtnSecond" VALUE = "SECOND">
<P>
<INPUT TYPE = "button"  NAME = "frmbtnThird" VALUE = "THIRD">
</FORM>
</CENTER>
</BODY>
</HTML>
```

Save your work and open `Setup for Scripted Frames.htm` in IE. It should look like Figure 11.6. Click the buttons to display the indicated documents into the frame on the right. Clicking IE's Back button will bring back the last document that was in the frame on the right.

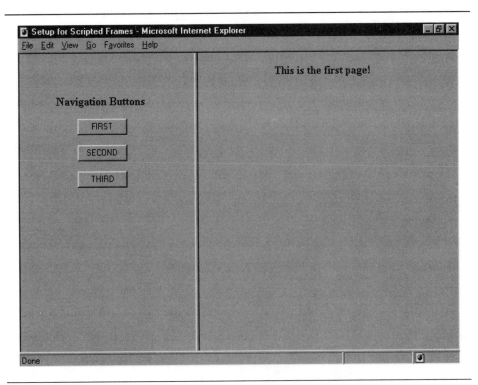

FIGURE 11.6: The display in IE when you open *Setup for Scripted Frames*

Keeping Tabs on Frames: The TabStrip Control

Now that we know about frames and how to navigate through them, we can be a bit more imaginative in our choice of navigation controls. With the rich world of ActiveX controls at our disposal, we're not confined to form control buttons or even to ActiveX Command Buttons.

Many of the most popular applications use tabbed pages to present information to users. (The Tools ➤ Customize… menu selection in Microsoft Word is one example.) We can easily do this with our Web pages, too. Here's how.

Remember that we're not confined to columns when we divide the browser window. We can also divide the window into rows. Like columns, the rows don't have to be equal in size. We can divide the screen into two row-frames so that the lower frame has the lion's share of the screen. In the (very small) upper frame, we'll put an ActiveX TabStrip control. Clicking the tabs will have the same effect as clicking the navigation buttons in the preceding section.

We've already done most of the work. We know how to set up the frames and we know how to refer to them. All we have to do is change our HTML setup file to specify rows instead of columns and change our script file to work with a TabStrip control instead of HTML form control buttons.

Begin by saving `Setup for Scripted Frames.htm` as `Setup for Tabbed Frames` in `skill 11`. Edit the file (`Setup for Tabbed Frames.htm`) so that it looks like this listing.

Setup for Tabbed Frames.htm

```
<HTML>
<HEAD>
<TITLE>Setup for Tabbed Frames</TITLE>
</HEAD>
<BODY>
<FRAMESET ROWS=10%,90%>
<FRAME NAME = "tabs" SRC= "tab_navigation.htm">
<FRAME NAME = "display" SRC= "first.htm">
</FRAMESET>
</BODY>
</HTML>
```

Now we have to create `tab_navigation.htm`. Open a new HTML file and save it under that name. Select Edit ➢ Insert ActiveX Control… and choose a Microsoft Forms 2.0 TabStrip. In the Object Editor, make the TabStrip's ID **tbstrpFrames** and its Font 12 pt Bold. Close the Object Editor.

The code in your Text Editor (`tab_navigation.htm`) now looks like this.

tab_navigation.htm

```
<HTML>
<HEAD>
<TITLE>Tab Navigation</TITLE>
</HEAD>
<BODY>

<OBJECT ID="tbstrpFrames" WIDTH=480 HEIGHT=25
 CLASSID="CLSID:EAE50EB0-4A62-11CE-BED6-00AA00611080">
    <PARAM NAME="ListIndex" VALUE="0">
```

```
        <PARAM NAME="Size" VALUE="16933;776">
        <PARAM NAME="Items" VALUE="Tab1;Tab2;">
        <PARAM NAME="TipStrings" VALUE=";;">
        <PARAM NAME="Names" VALUE="Tab1;Tab2;">
        <PARAM NAME="NewVersion" VALUE="-1">
        <PARAM NAME="TabsAllocated" VALUE="2">
        <PARAM NAME="Tags" VALUE=";;">
        <PARAM NAME="TabData" VALUE="2">
        <PARAM NAME="Accelerator" VALUE=";;">
        <PARAM NAME="FontEffects" VALUE="1073741825">
        <PARAM NAME="FontHeight" VALUE="240">
        <PARAM NAME="FontCharSet" VALUE="0">
        <PARAM NAME="FontPitchAndFamily" VALUE="2">
        <PARAM NAME="FontWeight" VALUE="700">
        <PARAM NAME="TabState" VALUE="3;3">
</OBJECT>

</BODY>
</HTML>
```

In the Text Editor, make the Width **480** and the Height **25** as I've done. We could open up the Script Wizard to programmatically add a third tab and to change the captions on all the tabs, but it's easier to just make the changes directly in the Text Editor. In order to allocate an additional tab (because we have three documents to tab to) change this line:

```
        <PARAM NAME="TabsAllocated" VALUE="2">
```

to

```
        <PARAM NAME="TabsAllocated" VALUE="3">
```

Each tab has to have a name, so change this line:

```
        <PARAM NAME="Names" VALUE="Tab1;Tab2;">
```

to

```
        <PARAM NAME="Names" VALUE="Tab1;Tab2;Tab3;">
```

Now let's address the captions on the tabs. Change this line:

```
        <PARAM NAME="Items" VALUE="Tab1;Tab2;">
```

to

```
        <PARAM NAME="Items" VALUE="FIRST;SECOND;THIRD;">
```

The script reuses most of what we've already done. In the Script Wizard, you can select tbstrpFrames' Click event and (in Code View) do some typing or you can do the typing directly into the Text Editor. This event works with one argument, the index of the clicked tab. The first tab's index is 0, the second tab's index is 1, and the third tab's index is 2. This sets up a Select Case based on the index. The script is:

```
<SCRIPT LANGUAGE = "VBSCRIPT">
<!--
Sub tbstrpFrames_Click(Index)
Select Case Index
Case 0
window.top.display.location.href = "first.htm"
Case 1
window.top.display.location.href = "second.htm"
Case 2
window.top.display.location.href = "third.htm"
End Select
end sub
-->
</SCRIPT>
```

Put the script before the <BODY> tag, save your work, and open Setup for Tabbed Frames.htm in IE. It will look like Figure 11.7.

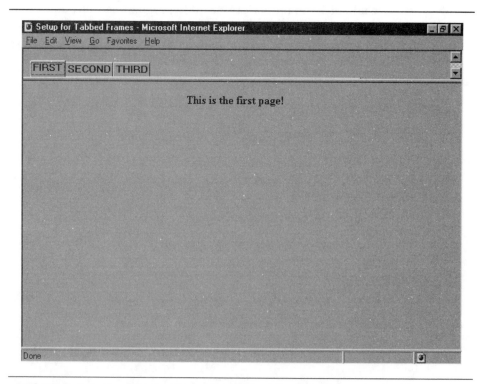

FIGURE 11.7: Opening *Setup for Tabbed Frames.htm* produces this display in IE.

Click the tabs to move from file to file. Navigation is the same as in the previous section but the look is more stylish and the display frame has a lot more space.

Summary

Now that you know more about VBS, you can join its strengths directly with the capabilities of HTML. You can use it to work with HTML forms, and more importantly, with frames. Frames allow you to divide a window into areas that display separate Web pages. VBS makes it easy to navigate among frames, once you know how to refer to them. Adding an ActiveX TabStrip control to the VBS-HTML mix results in a stylish frames navigation device.

Are You Experienced?

Now you can...

☑ **understand HTML form controls**

☑ **use VBS to script HTML form controls with and without the Script Wizard**

☑ **use HTML to set up frames that divide a browser window into segments that show different pages**

☑ **write VBS code that scripts HTML form controls to navigate among frames**

☑ **use VBS and the ActiveX TabStrip control to build a sharp-looking way of navigating among frames**

Skill 11

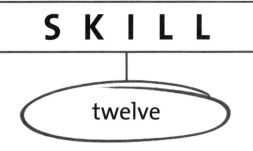

SKILL

twelve

12

Dissecting the ActiveX Control Pad

- ❏ **Exploring the Text Editor**

- ❏ **Tips and tricks for text editing**

- ❏ **Exploring the menus in the Script Wizard**

- ❏ **Discovering capabilities of the HTML Layout Control**

- ❏ **Understanding ALX files**

All our work in ActiveX is the result of a partnership—a partnership that includes VBS, HTML, and the ActiveX Control Pad. Thus far in Part II, you've put VBS under the microscope and put it to work directly with HTML. Now you get up close and personal with the ActiveX Control Pad.

You've worked with this tool so much that by now you've become familiar with many of its features on your own. Still, it's helpful to examine the Control Pad in a more formal way. Its components—the Text Editor, the Object Editor, the Script Wizard, and the HTML Layout Control have some features that you might not have encountered yet.

The Text Editor

The ActiveX Control Pad Text Editor, like the Windows Notepad, is a straightforward, plain vanilla text editor. Its only connection with HTML is the tags that appear when you use it to open a new HTML file, but it can work with HTML files written in tools designed specifically for creating and editing HTML

Perhaps the main drawback of the Text Editor is that it doesn't provide WYSIWYG editing. The way you type text into the editor is not necessarily the way it will appear when you view the file in IE.

Happily, the Text Editor does provide standard Cut, Copy, and Paste capabilities. In Skill 2 you put these to good use when you created ActiveX controls directly in the Text Editor. You cloned code you had already created and then made some adjustments to create new controls.

The Text Editor also lets you edit multiple documents at the same time. This is extremely useful when you want to copy code from one document to another.

In the course of our work, we've only had occasion to use a few of the choices from the Text Editor's menu bar. In case you haven't worked with the others on your own, we'll go over what they do. It's a good idea to open the Text Editor and follow along.

File Menu

Clicking File on the menu bar displays the menu shown in Figure 12.1. Another way to open this menu is to press Alt+F.

TIP   Another way to get to the File menu is to press F10. This keystroke takes you to the File menu but doesn't open it. You can then use the arrow keys to navigate through the File menu or the menu bar.

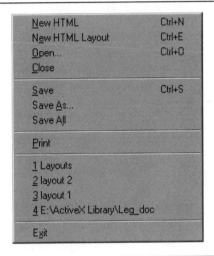

New HTML	Ctrl+N
New HTML Layout	Ctrl+E
Open...	Ctrl+O
Close	
Save	Ctrl+S
Save As...	
Save All	
Print	
1 Layouts	
2 layout 2	
3 layout 1	
4 E:\ActiveX Library\Leg_doc	
Exit	

FIGURE 12.1: The Text Editor's File menu

The first two choices in the File menu open new files. The first one opens a new HTML file, and the second opens a new ALX file. The third choice opens an existing HTML file, and the fourth closes the current file.

TIP   Ctrl+F4 is another way to close the current file.

Keystroke equivalents speed up your work, so it's a good idea to learn them. (They appear on menus next to the equivalent menu selections.)

One of the fundamental principles of good User Interface design is to give people several ways of invoking the same command. Notice that the File menu (and File menus in other applications) give you three ways to open a new file. With the menu visible, you can move the mouse to the first row or you can press N (or n). If the menu isn't open, you can press Ctrl+N. We can't always predict where our users' hands will be when they have to perform a particular operation. Giving them several alternatives covers most of the bases.

Skill 12

The next group of choices on the File menu offers standard options for saving the current file. Save As… is particularly useful for reusing a file by saving it under a new name. Save it under a different name, make necessary changes, and you've saved yourself some setup work.

The Print selection works as it does in other applications. The menu is missing the Ctrl+P keystroke combination that you find in other applications, but…it works. Ctrl+P will print the current file even though this combination doesn't appear on the menu.

The numbered items in the next group correspond to the files you've worked on most recently. Clicking one of them, or typing its number, opens the indicated file.

The Exit command closes the Control Pad.

 TIP   Alt+F4 is another way to close the Control Pad.

The Edit Menu

On the menu bar, click Edit (or press Alt+E) and you'll see the Edit menu shown in Figure 12.2. You'll work with this menu all the time, as it enables you to insert ActiveX controls and HTML layouts into your HTML documents.

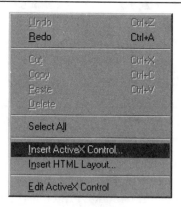

FIGURE 12.2: The Text Editor's Edit menu

The first two choices, Undo and Redo, are extremely important. The Undo capability has saved me more times than I care to admit! As its name implies, it undoes what you just did (and if you just did something catastrophic, you'll appreciate this selection as much as I do). Learn the Ctrl+Z keystroke combination, and it will bail you out of bad situations. It's also a good one to know if you happen to change your mind about an action you just took. Redo (Ctrl+A) is the opposite of Undo, as it "undoes" the Undo.

The next group of four choices handles typical editing operations within a file. The first, Cut, removes selected text from the file and places a copy of it on the clipboard, a temporary holding area for items that you've cut or copied. The keystroke combination Ctrl+X allows you to cut something without having to open the menu. The next choice, Copy (Ctrl+C) copies your selection onto the clipboard without removing it from the file you're working on.

The third choice in this group, Paste, takes the contents of the clipboard and inserts it into the current document at the cursor position. If you select Paste, what's on the clipboard replaces the current selection. (If you'd forgotten that you had selected a line or two of text and chose Paste, you'd have a nice opportunity to use Undo.) In addition to the menu selection, Ctrl+V also invokes the same command as Paste, as does Shift+Insert. The final choice in this group, Delete, deletes a selection without putting on the clipboard. It's like the Delete key (or like backspacing through the selection).

WARNING   The clipboard has a short memory. It only contains the last selection that you cut or copied.

When you have to select the entire file, the next menu choice, Select All, gets the job done. In many other applications, Ctrl+A is the equivalent keystroke combination, but that keystroke combination does not work in the ActiveX Control Pad.

You have two other ways to select everything. One way is to position the mouse at one end of the file and drag it all the way to the other. The other way is to position the cursor at one end of the file and then move the mouse (without dragging it) to the other end. When you get there, press the Shift key and click the mouse. You'll find that you've selected the entire contents of the file. The mouse can also help you make finer-grained selections: Double-clicking selects the entire current word, and triple-clicking selects the entire current line. Table 12.1 gives you some keystroke shortcuts for selecting text.

T A B L E 1 2 . 1 : Shortcuts for Selecting Text

Pressing...	Selects Everything from the Current Cursor Position to...
Ctrl+Shift+Home	The beginning of the file
Ctrl+Shift+End	The end of the file
Shift+Home	The beginning of the current line
Shift+End	The end of the current line
Shift+Right Arrow	One space to the right
Shift+Left Arrow	One space to the left
Shift+Up Arrow	The same position one line up
Shift+Down Arrow	The same position one line down
Ctrl+Shift+Right Arrow	The position just before the start of the next word
Ctrl+Shift+Left Arrow	The position just after the end of the previous word

The next two choices are the ones you've used most often. Insert ActiveX Control... (which appears highlighted in Figure 12.2) opens the list of ActiveX controls. Insert HTML Layout... opens a dialog box in which you enter the name of an ALX file. The dialog box lists folders and files in a default location, and you navigate to another location if necessary. If you enter the name of a new file, a message box asks you if you want this file created. Make a selection in this dialog box, close the box, and an <OBJECT> tag that refers to the selected layout appears in your HTML file at the current cursor location.

The final choice in this menu depends on the makeup of the HTML file and the position of the cursor. If you've inserted an ActiveX control and the cursor is positioned at the reference to the control, the choice appears as in Figure 12.2 (Edit ActiveX Control). If the cursor is positioned at a <SCRIPT> tag, or anywhere within the script, the final Edit menu choice is Edit Script. If the cursor is positioned at the reference to a layout, the choice is Edit HTML Layout. If none of these items is in the HTML file, the choice is disabled and appears as Edit Object.

The View Menu

The View menu (Alt+V) has two choices (shown here). You use the first to show or hide the toolbar (which is just below the menu bar). You use the second to show or hide the Status bar (which is at the bottom of the ActiveX Control Pad window).

The toolbar is a set of push button controls that correspond to frequently used menu options. They can save you an extra mouse-click or two. If you can't remember the command that a particular toolbar icon represents, two kinds of assistance are available: When you hover the mouse over a push button, balloon help tells you its name, and a message in the Status bar tells you what it does.

The Tools Menu

The Tools menu (Alt+T is the keyboard shortcut), shown here, has two choices.

The first choice opens the Script Wizard. The second, Options, opens a sub-menu (shown here).

The options in this submenu concern the appearance of the HTML Layout Control and the Script Wizard. Clicking the first option opens the dialog box shown in Figure 12.3.

FIGURE 12.3: Options for the HTML Layout Control

The first setting in the Grid Settings group allows you to specify or determine the vertical distance between the grid dots in the Layout Control, and the second allows you to specify or determine the horizontal distance between grid dots.

You use the first checkbox in the Defaults group to show or hide the grid when the HTML Layout Control opens. You use the second to specify whether an object in the HTML Layout Control automatically positions itself at the nearest grid point when you move it.

The second option on the Options submenu enables you to set up the appearance of the Script Wizard. Clicking that option brings up the dialog box shown in Figure 12.4. The upper group of radio buttons determines whether the Script Wizard opens in List View or Code View. The nearby Command Button opens a dialog box that you use to specify the font for the Script Wizard. The lower group of radio buttons determines whether the Wizard opens using VBS or JavaScript as the script language.

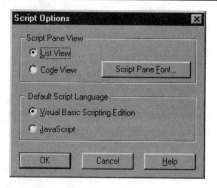

FIGURE 12.4: The dialog box for setting Script Wizard options

The Window Menu

The Window menu is shown here (Alt+W gets you there from the keyboard). The selections below the line show the currently open files.

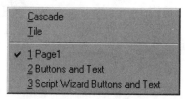

You open a file by clicking on its selection or by typing its number.

The first two selections determine the Control Pad window that appears when multiple files are open. Selecting Cascade gives you a display like the one in Figure 12.5, and Tile gives you a display like Figure 12.6.

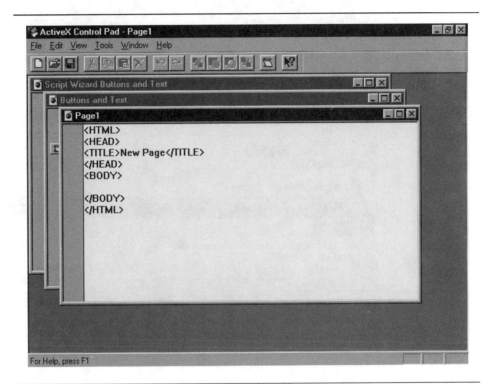

FIGURE 12.5: Selecting Cascade gives you this display.

In Figure 12.6 all the windows are visible, but Page 1 is still the topmost. If you open the Windows menu, you'll see that the checkmark is still next to Page 1. You can make one of the other windows topmost by clicking on it in the display.

 TIP   If several windows are open, you can quickly go from one to the other with Ctrl+F6.

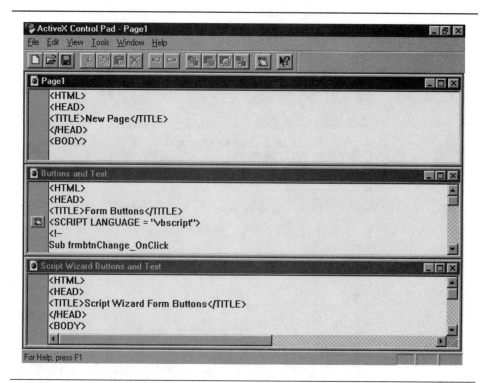

FIGURE 12.6: The display that results from selecting Tile

The Help Menu

The Help menu (Alt+H from the keyboard) appears here.

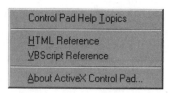

The first selection opens up a Help file containing topics pertaining to the ActiveX Control Pad and some of the ActiveX controls.

TIP   In the Text Editor, you can open the Help file by pressing F1. Pressing Shift+F1 turns the cursor into an arrow–question mark combination, which opens the Help file when you click the mouse.

The second and third choices bring up HTML files in IE. Both contain valuable information. The second choice brings up the reference material on HTML, and the third choice brings up the reference on VBS. If you haven't downloaded the VBScript reference, by all means head over to `http://www.microsoft.com/vbscript` and follow the instructions to install the files into the directory that holds your ActiveX Control Pad. The final selection in this menu gives you some information (like the version number) about the ActiveX Control Pad.

The Pop-up Menu

In addition to the menus on the menu bar, the Text Editor provides a pop-up menu (see Figure 12.7). You access this menu by right-clicking anywhere in the Text Editor window. Most of the choices on this menu are identical to the choices on the Edit menu. The one exception is the choice that displays the Script Wizard.

FIGURE 12.7: The Text Editor's pop-up menu

The Object Editor

You first encountered the Object Editor in Skill 1, when you inserted ActiveX controls into an HTML file. If you select Edit ➤ Insert ActiveX Control... from the Text Editor's menu bar, you open the scrollable list of ActiveX controls registered in your machine. Selecting a control brings up the Object Editor window and the selected control's Properties sheet.

In the Object Editor window, if you select the control and right-click, you open a pop-up menu with two entries. The first toggles the Properties sheet on and off. The second allows you to edit the control. (This choice is equivalent to double-clicking on the control.) Exactly what you can edit depends on the control. With a Command Button, for example, you can select Edit and then type the caption directly onto the Button.

The capabilities of the Object Editor window and the Properties sheet overlap to some extent. You can type the caption into the Caption property of the Properties sheet as well as entering it onto the Command Button. Also, you can use the sizing handles in the Object Editor to adjust the control's height and width, or you can enter those dimensions into the appropriate places in the Properties sheet.

As you've seen, closing the Object Editor inserts the control's HTML code directly into the HTML file.

The Script Wizard

The Script Wizard, our programming workhorse in Part I, has some features you should be aware of.

First, it's resizable. You can make it smaller so you can see other windows while you're using it. Also, you can resize the area that holds both the Event pane and the Actions pane. The tradeoff is that when you make those two panes bigger, you make the Script pane smaller, and vice versa.

The Script Wizard has three pop-up menus of its own, designed to make editing more convenient. You access each one by right-clicking inside one of the three panes in the Wizard.

The Event Pane's Pop-up Menu

The Event pane's pop-up menu has one item, Delete Event Handler. The term "Event Handler" refers to any subroutine that you create as a result of selecting an event in the Event pane and double-clicking a property or a method in the Actions pane. Use this menu to accomplish in one fell swoop a process that would take several editing steps in the Script pane.

The Actions Pane's Pop-up Menu

If you right-click in the Actions pane, you'll see the pop-up menu shown here. If you've selected a procedure, you'll see all the choices enabled, as they are here. The first choice allows you to create a new global variable (you've seen it open a dialog box for that purpose). You use the second choice to create a new procedure (the Script pane sets up a title for you). The third choice enables you to edit the selected procedure and the fourth choice to delete it.

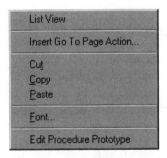

The Script Pane's Pop-up Menu

If the Script Wizard is in Code View, right-clicking in the Script pane gives you the pop-up menu that you see in here.

The first choice puts the Wizard in List View. Clicking the second choice is the equivalent of double-clicking the first item in the Actions pane: It puts a Go to Page statement in your procedure. This can be a great convenience if you have opened the methods and properties of a number of controls and you have to put that statement in your code. It saves you the trouble of taking the cursor out of the Script pane, scrolling to the top of the Actions pane, double-clicking, and going back to the Script pane to complete the statement.

The next three choices are the Cut, Copy, and Paste editing commands. The next-to-last choice, Font…, allows you to set the font for the Script pane. Clicking Edit Procedure Prototype… puts the cursor at the beginning of the title of the procedure currently in the Script pane so that you can edit that title.

With the Script Wizard in List View the first choice opens Code View, and the second choice (Insert Go to Page Action…) is the only other choice on the menu.

The Script Wizard's Command Buttons and Radio Buttons

At the bottom of the Script Wizard window, you'll find two Radio Buttons and three Command Buttons. The Radio Buttons put the Wizard in either List View or Code View. The OK Button saves your work and closes the Script Wizard. The Cancel Button closes the Wizard without saving your work. Clicking Help brings up a labeled diagram of the Script Wizard. Appropriately, the diagram for Code View differs from the diagram for List View.

When the Wizard is in List View, five additional Command Buttons are visible. One inserts an action into the Script pane, another deletes a selected action, and a third brings up a dialog box in which you edit a selected action. The two remaining buttons are an up-arrow and a down-arrow that take you through the rows in the Script pane.

The HTML Layout Control

If you haven't had much experience with HTML, it's a bit difficult to appreciate exactly what the HTML Layout Control does for you. In the HTML world, it isn't easy to place objects exactly where you want them in a Web page. You have to use tags to get the job done, and it's not always intuitive.

The idea behind the HTML Layout Control is to bring two-dimensional layout capabilities to HTML. Microsoft has been working with the World Wide Web Consortium to accomplish this. If you want to take a look at the Consortium's working draft, go to `http://www.w3.org/pub/WWW/TR/WD-layout.html`.

The HTML Layout Control is a preliminary implementation of W3's preliminary specification. If you uncover a few flaws as you work with it, remember that it's a "preliminary" of a "preliminary."

Let's dissect the control. The File and Edit menus are the same as in the Text Editor, with one exception. In the Layout Control's Edit menu, only one choice follows Select All. That choice, Group, operates when you select at least two controls on the Layout Control. If you click this choice, you treat the selected controls as a group rather than as individual controls. If you change a property of one of the group members you change that property of all of them. Dragging the sizing handles affects the size of all the controls in the group, for example. When controls are grouped, the menu choice toggles and becomes Ungroup.

The Tools, Window, and Help menus are the same as in the Text Editor.

The View Menu

Shown here, the View menu lets you set aspects of the Layout Control's appearance. You can turn the grid on or off, and you can show or hide the Toolbox, the toolbar (the strip of push buttons that activate frequently used menu choices) and the Status bar. Another choice shows the Properties sheet for the selected control.

The Format Menu

The Layout Control's Format menu provides some useful tools for laying out controls. This menu appears in Figure 12.8.

FIGURE 1 2 . 8 : The Format menu

Each of the first five choices on the format menu has a submenu. The Align submenu helps you line up a set of selected controls. Use this submenu to align their left edges, centers, right edges, tops, middles, or bottoms.

How does aligning by "centers" differ from aligning by "middles?" "Centers" puts selected controls into one column, with all the centers lining up. "Middles" puts them into one row so that they overlap. Figure 12.9 shows the difference. The four controls on the left have been aligned by Centers, the three controls on the right by Middles.

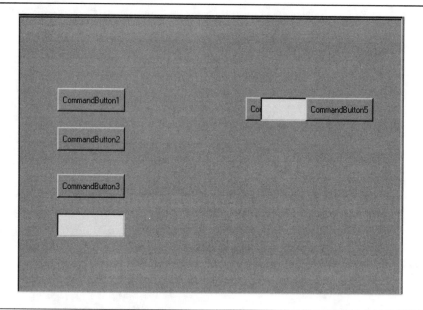

FIGURE 12.9: The difference between Align by Centers (left) and Align by Middles (right)

The submenu for Make Same Size allows you to match heights, widths, or both for selected controls.

The Size submenu lets you size a control to just fit its caption, or so that its boundaries coincide with the nearest grid points.

Horizontal Spacing's submenu has four choices:

- Make Equal
- Increase
- Decrease
- Remove

Use the first choice when you have three or more controls in a row. Select them, click Horizontal Spacing ➤ Make Equal, and you equalize the space from object to object. The other choices are straightforward. They allow you to increase, decrease, or remove the horizontal spacing between objects.

The Vertical Spacing submenu is just like the Horizontal Spacing's submenu, except in a vertical direction. Make Equal, for example requires that you select at least three objects in a column. This selection equalizes the space between objects.

The Snap to Grid menu option specifies what happens when you drag an object in the Layout Control. If it's checked, you must drag it at least grid point for it to move.

You use one of the last four menu choices come into play when objects overlap. The first choice puts a selected object all the way at the rear of a set of objects. The last choice brings it to the front. Move Backward moves the selected object one spot farther back in the set, and Move Forward moves the selection one spot closer to the front.

The Pop-up Menu

When you right-click within the HTML Layout Control, you open a pop-up menu that has some of the selections of the Text Editor Edit menu, and some new ones (see Figure 12.10).

FIGURE 12.10: The Layout Control's pop-up menu

The first four choices are standard Undo, Redo, Paste, and Select All. The fifth choice, Script Wizard…, opens the Script Wizard. The sixth choice, View Source Code, allows you to look at all the Source Code you wrote (in Windows Notepad), but this choice also saves your work and closes the Layout Control. The last choice, Properties, lets you work with the Layout Control's properties.

Skill 12

The Toolbox

The Toolbox, that collection of little tabbed pages that holds the controls you work with, has some helpful capabilities we haven't explored yet. When you right-click on a tab, you get a pop-up menu whose choices help you work with the tabbed page. You can add a new Toolbox page, delete the current page, rename the current page, or move the Toolbox. You can also import a page to the Toolbox (if you happen to have a Toolbox page in .PAG format lying around) or export the current page.

When you right-click on a control, you get a different pop-up menu. This one lets you add a new control, delete the current control, or customize the control. Selecting the Customize option brings up a dialog box that you use to change the appearance of the control's picture on the Toolbox.

The Add New Control… choice in this pop-up menu can be very helpful, even if you don't plan to add any controls. The scrollable list it brings up allows you to select from among any of the ActiveX controls registered on your computer. When you make a selection, the file path that locates the selected control appears on the bottom of the box that contains the list. It's a useful way to track down ActiveX controls in your computer.

One more Toolbox capability is good to know. Let's say you've selected a Command Button and you like the dimensions, caption, font, backcolor, and a host of other properties, and you'd like to save it and reuse it over and over again. In the Layout Control, select the Command Button you like and drag it back to the Toolbox. The Toolbox now holds this customized Command Button and you can use it as a template in future projects.

The ALX Files

As you've seen throughout our discussion, closing the HTML Layout Control puts an <OBJECT> </OBJECT> tag-pair into your HTML file. The information related to the layout sits between those tags, but you can't see any references to controls that you laid out or to script that you've written for controls in the layout. Instead, the HTML code refers to an ALX file which holds this information. One result of all this is that opening the Script Wizard from the Text Editor can't help you write scripts for the controls in the Layout Control. You have to access the Script Editor from within the HTML Layout Control directly.

In that file, script code appears at the beginning and control-related information is between the <DIV> and </DIV> tags.

One of the objectives in designing this tool was to extend the capabilities of the frame concept that you saw in Skill 11. A layout is supposed to be something like a frame. Just as you can have more than one frame on a Web page, you can have more than one layout. You might try experimenting with this. Keep in mind that your HTML file will refer to two separate ALX files. Make sure that their order in the HTML file reflects the order in which you want them to appear on the Web page. Keep in mind also that the controls in one layout can't interact with the controls in the other.

Opening ALX Files

If you want to look at ALX files, you have to go through a few gyrations. As you know, one way to see the code is via the pop-up menu in the Layout Control. The choice View Source… closes the Layout Control and opens the ALX file in Windows Notepad. You can make changes when you see the code, but it would be a lot smoother if you could just do that in the Text Editor.

Here's a way to make it a little easier to open an ALX file:

1. In your `C:\Windows` directory, find `Notepad.exe`.

2. Put a copy of `Notepad.exe` in your `ActiveX No Exp Req` folder.

3. Then, put a shortcut to this copy on your desktop. (You might want to rename the shortcut `ActiveX Notepad`.)

4. After you do this, you'll be able to double-click on the shortcut, select Open from the Notepad's File menu and immediately open up the `ActiveX No Exp Req` folder. You can then navigate through that folder to select the ALX file you want to open.

Want to make life even easier? Windows 95 provides a more sophisticated editor than Notepad. It's called Wordpad, and it might be worth your while to install Wordpad in `ActiveX No Exp Req` via the previous steps I outlined. You'll find `Wordpad.exe` in `C:\Program Files\Accessories`. If you use Wordpad to edit an ALX file (or to create one from an existing ALX file), remember to give it an .ALX extension and save it as a Text Only document.

In the not-too-distant future, all these gymnastics won't be necessary. After the Consortium finalizes its specification, the two-dimensional layout information will go directly in the HTML file, and we'll all be a lot happier.

Summary

That's the guided tour of the tool you've used so much. Now you know the ActiveX Control Pad inside out, and you can use your knowledge to increase your productivity. A saved keystroke here, a saved mouse-click there...pretty soon it adds up!

Are You Experienced?

Now you can...

- ☑ use all the menu choices in the Text Editor
- ☑ understand the Text Editor's strengths and limitations
- ☑ work with keystroke shortcuts to increase editing efficiency and productivity
- ☑ use the Script Wizard's pop-up menus to increase scripting productivity
- ☑ use the alignment and sizing menus and submenus in the Layout Control to properly align controls
- ☑ understand the ideas behind ALX files

S K I L L

thirteen

Digging Up the Roots
of ActiveX

- ❏ **Object orientation**

- ❏ **Object Linking and Embedding (OLE)**

- ❏ **The Component Object Model (COM)**

- ❏ **ActiveX out in the open**

Skills 10 through 12 explored the tools you use to implement ActiveX technology. In this Skill, you'll examine the ActiveX technology itself. What are the foundational concepts of ActiveX? How did it evolve? This Skill addresses these questions and more. Before you'll get to them, however, you'll have to step back and understand the basis of it all—object orientation. After that, you'll trace a little history as we show how ActiveX technology evolved.

Introducing Object Orientation

If you have any interest at all in programming—even a small interest—you've probably heard of Object-Oriented Programming (OOP). This method of developing software is part of almost everything related to software these days. For software developers, product managers, project managers, and just plain computer hobbyists, OOP is the answer.

But what, exactly, is the question?

The question, stated simply, is this: What's the best way to quickly develop reliable software—software that does what it's supposed to do—that we can use again and again in a variety of ways? Object orientation addresses this by departing from traditional approaches to software development that emphasize sequences of coding steps, or *procedures*. Object orientation, instead, focuses on the objects that operate on procedures and the objects that are operated on by procedures.

Once you have a reliable set of objects you're comfortable with, you can use them many times—you don't have to reinvent them over and over again. You might have to make a few adjustments to the objects when you reuse them, but if they're designed correctly, that should be easy to do.

Have you seen a set of software objects that you can use again and again, with a minor adjustment here and there? Of course you have: ActiveX controls. If not for object orientation, modern user interfaces (Web-based or not) would be extremely difficult to create. Command Buttons, Spin Buttons, TextBoxes, ListBoxes, and all other controls, are objects. You pick and choose the ones you want for each user interface you build, make adjustments in their Properties sheets, position them on an HTML Layout Control (another object) or in an HTML document, and you have the look of your user interface.

Traditional vs. Object-Oriented Development

The difference between traditional and object-oriented development has ripple effects throughout all the phases of a project. Here's one example: A traditional software engineer might start thinking about a project by trying to generate a flowchart of steps that will later become code in a programming language. An object-oriented software engineer might instead start the thought process by trying to picture the small piece of the world that the project pertains to, along with the entities in that world. The engineer might ask: What characteristics and properties do these entities have? How do those entities behave? How can we capture those properties and that behavior in our program? Do we have a set of ready-made objects that will act in the program like the entities do in the real world?

To traditional developers, writing a program is the creation of the most efficient sequence of steps to reach a goal (or a set of goals). To object-oriented developers, writing a program is nearly the same as building a model of that small piece of the world, and then making the elements of that model interact in appropriate ways.

By now, you've followed the object-oriented path many times. Each time you positioned an ActiveX control in an HTML Layout Control, or inserted one into an HTML document, you built a model of a Web page. Then, when you wrote a script, you specified the behaviors of those controls, making them interact with a user and with each other.

Points of View

Some commentators believe that object orientation has become popular because it closely reflects the way we think. According to this point of view, our thoughts typically focus on concrete things rather than on (possibly) abstract processes, so a development technique that does the same must naturally coincide with our mental machinery.

 NOTE   I'm not sure this is true. If object orientation matches the way we think, we might expect that object-oriented computer languages should be easy to learn, and this is typically not the case. Also, I'm not convinced that everyone's thought process operates the same way as everyone else's. Thus, one particular development methodology probably can't mimic the way *all* of us think.

Whether this point of view is accurate or not is probably irrelevant. It doesn't matter if it mirrors our minds as long as object orientation provides quick development of working software.

A tangible reason for object orientation's recent success is the explosion in hardware performance. High-performance machines provide the firepower that object-oriented applications need. From their debut in the 1960s (yes, OOP is an overnight success that took only 30 years to catch on), object-oriented applications shared one common trait: They were all very *slow*. Until the advent of high-performance CPUs, it just wasn't practical to use this methodology on real-world problems. Now that the hardware has caught up, we're reaping the rewards of object orientation: quicker product development, faster production of new versions, and reusable code.

Understanding Objects

To give you a feel for what objects and object orientation are all about, let's get away from the computer world for a while, and focus on real-world objects. Let's try and put the object-oriented framework around some everyday things.

Classes, Subclasses, Objects, and Properties

Look around you. You're probably near a bookcase. Each book on the bookcase has some properties in common with all the other books. Some of the common properties are:

- Title

- Author(s)

- Cover (hardcover or paper)

- Number of pages

- Language the book is written in

- Publisher

- Publication date

You can probably come up with a few more.

Think of each volume on your bookcase as a member of a category called, appropriately enough, Book. In the object-oriented jargon, we'd say that Book is a *class* (because of all the common features that its members share) and that each individual volume is an *object*. It's also the case that each object is an *instance* of its class. Your copy of *War and Peace*, then, is an object, and it's an instance of the class Book. Someone else's copy of *War and Peace* is a different instance.

Isn't Book a little too general? Don't we have fiction, nonfiction, and reference books? These kinds of categories within Book are *subclasses*, which have properties that may not be in another subclass of the same class. For example, a nonfiction book usually has an index, and a work of fiction does not. In other words, the Nonfiction subclass of the class Book has a property of Index, and the Fiction subclass does not.

Wait a second. Don't we also have magazines? Are they a whole different class? They can be, if you want to set things up that way. And if you decide to go up a level, you could say that Book and Magazine are subclasses of Reading Material. As an object-oriented analyst, you would determine which properties magazines have that books don't have, and vice versa. You would also determine the properties they have in common—in other words, the properties of the Reading Material class as shown in Figure 13.1. This figure also shows one form of notation for properties and one form for objects.

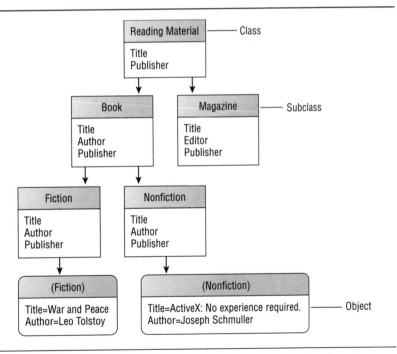

FIGURE 13.1: The Reading Material class and its subclasses, Book and Magazine. Instances appear at the bottom of the hierarchy.

What's the point of thinking about instances of classes (or of subclasses)? If I tell you that something is an instance of Nonfiction, you already know a lot about that instance without hearing anything else: You know it has the properties of the Nonfiction class. You know it has a publisher, a publication date, a number of pages, and more. You might not know the specific publisher, publication date, or number of pages (in other words, the *values* of those properties), but you know that the instance has those properties. An instance *inherits* properties from its class.

Operations and Methods

Classes, subclasses, and objects give you a start on drawing a picture of a small slice of reality. You make this slice come alive when you start thinking about things you can do with our objects. For example, you can:

1. Take a book from the bookcase.

2. Open the book.

3. Read the text.

4. Turn pages.

5. Look up a name.

You can undoubtedly think of more. The point is that you can apply these operations to a book, and each one consists of one or more steps. Another point is that the way you perform an operation could vary from subclass to subclass. To look up a name in a nonfiction book, you would:

1. Turn to the index.

2. Search for the name alphabetically.

3. Note the page that the index says contains the name.

4. Turn to that page.

In a work of fiction, the "look up a name" operation is different, because works of fiction have no index. You might have to start with page 1 and search successive pages until you find the name, or you might be able to narrow your search if you were familiar with the book. The operation is called "lookup" in both cases, but it involves different steps for the different objects. When an operation is different from class to class (or from subclass to subclass), it is said to be *polymorphic* (score big with that word the next time you play Scrabble).

The whole situation becomes much more interesting if you allow your imaginations a little leeway. Suppose you're living in a world where books are smart, and like the genie in Skill 9, they can understand spoken words. Let's further suppose that they can act on whatever you say, and that they know how to carry out operations like "look up a name" when you tell them to.

These operations are *methods*. The nonfiction books would have one kind of Lookup method (because each one has an index), while the fiction books would have another (because they don't have indexes). An instance would know how to perform its Lookup method because it inherits that method from its class. As an issuer of commands, you pretty much don't care how a book carries out its Lookup method: All you want the book to do is open itself up and show you the page(s) that a particular name is on.

Even Smarter Objects

Sometimes you're reading a book (let's call it Book 1) and you want a particular piece of information from another book (Book 2). One way that publishers do this for you is reprint the information from Book 2 in Book 1. You might say they *embed* that information in Book 1.

But let's suppose your books are *very* smart. Not only can they interact with you, but they can also interact with each other. If you need information from Book 2, Book 1 (in this very-smart-book world) can link up with Book 2 and get it for you. In fact, if you decide to buy a new, updated edition of Book 2 and put it on your bookcase, your exceptionally smart Book 1 knows how to link up with Book 2 to give you the updated information. Book 1 can do this with Book 3, Book 4, and all the other volumes on your shelf.

Where is this all headed? Let's get back to software. Suppose you could have that very-smart-book feature as part of documents that live in your computer. In other words, suppose documents were smart enough to link up with each other so that Document 1 could contain information from Document 2, and when the information in Document 2 changes, the related information in Document 1 changes automatically.

For people who use computers in their business operations, linked documents that understand (and work with) each other's updates would be a wonderful capability. What would you say if someone could set that up for you? If that kind of capability is extremely crucial to your business, you might be so enthusiastic that you just might say…OLE!

OLE: Linking and Embedding Objects

Let's add some reality. For many businesses—consulting, for example—the lifeblood of the enterprise is proposal writing. Consultants write a letter to a prospective client explaining the work they propose to do, break it down into individual tasks, and estimate the number of hours each task will take. The client, of course, is also interested in how much the whole deal will cost. Accordingly, as part of the proposal consultants include a table that shows the tasks, the hours, the hourly rate, and the totals.

Putting It All Together

If you had to put a proposal like this together, you'd probably use a word processor such as Microsoft Word for the letter, and perhaps a spreadsheet such as Excel for the table. The spreadsheet will do a lot of the work for you. It will multiply rates by hours, tally totals, and present the results in a table format. To make your proposal look really sharp, you'll want to put the table right into the letter instead of putting it on a separate sheet.

How can you do this? One way is to go into Excel, highlight the part that contains your table, copy it, and then paste it into the appropriate area of the Word document. Print the document, and you'll find that you have a professional piece of work.

Making Modifications

Is life always that simple? Your proposal will probably have to go through a corporate review process before you send it out, and reviewers always make comments such as:

- "In Task 3, you forgot to add in subtask 6."

- "Remember the last time we did something like this? Task 5 took 653 hours, not 17."

- "Oh, I forgot to tell you, our hourly rate for widget-makers went up by $10."

- "By the way, I hate your tie."

Except for the last one, comments like these necessitate an annoying amount of extra work.

Wouldn't it be wonderful if you could set up a spreadsheet-document connection that worked automatically? If you had to make a change to the spreadsheet wouldn't it just be great if the change reflected automatically in the letter? This wouldn't stop reviewers from making comments (they always will), but at least you'd be able to respond quickly and efficiently to what they say. Is such a thing possible? Again…OLE!

Working Together

Originally an acronym that stood for Object Linking and Embedding, OLE (now a standalone word) enables these capabilities. It lets an instance of one application (such as a Word document) work together with an instance of another (such as an Excel spreadsheet). Before OLE, applications didn't follow any standards, and you had to go through all kinds of gyrations to get them to team up (if it was even possible).

When Windows came along, it brought with it a feature called Dynamic Data Exchange (DDE). An ancestor of OLE, DDE allowed separate programs in Windows to link together and share data. It did its job, but it didn't quite live up to its name: Data was dynamic, but the exchange was only in one direction. It only went from the application that created the data (like the spreadsheet) to the application in which you wanted it to reside (the Word document).

DDE links weren't very strong, either. They often broke when you made a change to either end, and making those changes was no picnic. If you were in the word processor and you wanted to change the spreadsheet, you had to open the spreadsheet, do the edits, go back to the word processor, and do some updates.

OLE changed all that. As its original name indicates, you can have your applications team up either by *linking* or by *embedding*. The result is a *compound document*.

Linking two applications together means you don't really copy the spreadsheet table into the word-processing document. To the outside world reading the printed hardcopy, it looks like you copied it (which is why you did all this in the first place). When you link the letter with the spreadsheet, you establish a connection between the two, but the files are separate. Make a change in the spreadsheet and, because of the link, the change shows up in the letter.

Embedding actually puts a copy of the table into the letter. Figure 13.2 shows an example of a compound Word document with an embedded spreadsheet.

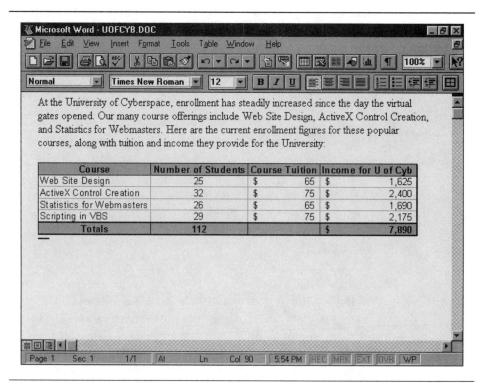

FIGURE 13.2: A compound Word document with an embedded spreadsheet

Embedding via OLE adds a wonderful convenience. If you're working on the file in Microsoft Word and you want to change the table, double-click on it and the Excel toolbar appears. You'll have all the capabilities of Excel at your disposal within Microsoft Word. This little trick, called *In-Place Editing*, is a real time-saver. You don't have to open Excel, edit, copy, delete the old table, and paste the new one into Word. In-Place Editing takes care of everything.

Figure 13.3 shows the compound document ready for In-Place Editing. The spreadsheet has been double-clicked, and the Excel toolbar is visible, even though Word is the application that you started out with.

Because the Word document can hold spreadsheets (and other objects) it is said to be a *container*. In the compound document, the spreadsheet is providing a *service* to the Word document, and for that reason it's called a *server*. The Word document is the recipient of the service and is called a *client*.

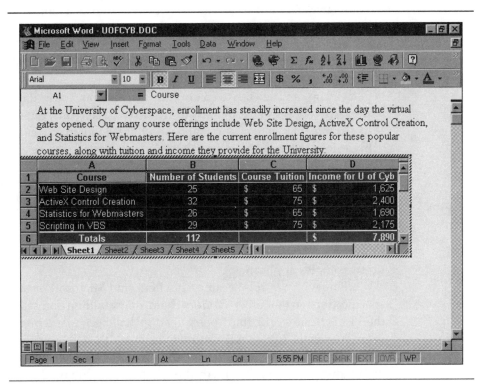

FIGURE 13.3: The compound document ready for In-Place Editing. The Excel toolbar is visible, even though this is a Word document.

Connections with ActiveX

"Well that's wonderful," you're probably saying, "the next time I have to write a compound document I'll be sure to use OLE, and I promise to keep clients, servers, and In-Place Editing in mind. In the meantime, why did you tell me all this in a book about ActiveX?"

I brought it up because OLE begat ActiveX. Perhaps some of this is beginning to sound familiar: We have one application (the spreadsheet) embedded in another (the Word document), and responding to a double-click. In many respects, this is the beginning of the technology that became ActiveX. After a little more about OLE, you'll see the connection more closely.

Your letter and your spreadsheet are objects. OLE is a kind of glue that holds objects like these together. It makes the objects work together and communicate with each other. OLE was intended as the spearhead of Microsoft's document-centric policy: The (compound) document you create should be the center of attention, not the application(s) that produced it.

In fact, you can use OLE to create your own custom application to do the job you have to do: Select a capability or two from Excel, some other ones from Word, put them together, and you have a hybrid tool that does your bidding.

In earlier versions of Microsoft Office, Visual Basic for some of Microsoft's applications (like Visual Basic for Access and Visual Basic for Excel) helped with this process. Subsumed now under the name Visual Basic for Applications, these development tools allowed you to add controls like Command Buttons, ListBoxes, and ComboBoxes. Visual Basic programmers used these kinds of controls all the time in their work. In previous versions of Visual Basic they were called VBXs (Visual Basic Extensions) and they became the components of some pretty complex applications.

Working with controls became a hot item, and Microsoft released a set of OLE specifications so that other vendors could start building and selling new ones. (In the Visual Basic world, third-party vendors had been marketing VBXs for several years.) Given the name OLE Control Extensions, their abbreviation (and filename extension) became OCX, and today, OCX controls are widespread. So widespread, in fact, that you've worked them already. In Skill 3 you used them when you tracked down the whereabouts of the controls you scripted. The files you looked for had OCX extensions.

As Microsoft software engineers began to design the second version of OLE—the one that spawned all the third-party OCXs—it dawned on them that they were on to something. Creating the glue for compound documents was just the tip of the iceberg. The main objective was to specify how software components in general could help each other. Thus the technology they built, the foundation for the new improved OLE, went far beyond compound documents.

 TIP   If you're starting to think of an HTML file with embedded ActiveX controls as analogous to the Word document with the embedded spreadsheet—you're on the right wavelength. That's the key to seeing how the Microsoft software engineers figured out that they had tackled something bigger than just letters and spreadsheets.

The notion of objects embedded in other objects and communicating with each other according to widely adopted standards has far-reaching importance. Some questions might be forming in your mind:

- "If I've used ActiveX controls, and they have OCX extensions, are OLE and ActiveX pretty much the same thing?"

- "I've seen MS Office 97. If you used to be able to add OLE controls into the applications in the previous Office, can you now add ActiveX Controls into this one?"

- "What's this technology that goes beyond compound documents?"

...And the answers are:

- yes

- yes

- the Component Object Model (COM).

COM: The Component Object Model

The Component Object Model (COM) is Microsoft's answer to the challenge of developing today's complex applications. Without object orientation, these applications would be extremely difficult to design and build. In fact, some of the applications you use today might not have been developed yet without OOP. And without COM, the objects in these applications wouldn't play well with others.

What It Is

In building the COM, Microsoft's vision was to accomplish for software development what the integrated circuit (IC) accomplished for hardware development in the 1970s. ICs are building blocks that enable hardware designers to conceive and create increasingly sophisticated chips.

COM sets the stage for developing software components that work the same way. In the ideal world, software developers should be able to buy a software component that performs a particular function for an application, instead of having to build it from scratch. The component should work with anything the developer plugs it into.

Microsoft anticipates that COM will benefit both individual users and corporations. Users will ultimately buy specialized components and plug them into their applications to increase productivity. In a similar vein, corporate software developers will buy components that fill a particular need and focus on developing the business-specific glue that holds these components together.

In a sense, that vision is already in place in the world of Web page development. Corporate Webmasters can build Web pages that consist of ActiveX controls wrapped around the corporate logo and information about the company. The ready-made controls free the Webmasters from having to create them.

 TIP   To apply the terminology from the previous section about OLE, the HTML document they embed these ready-made controls into is a *container*.

How It Works

Let's go back to your very-smart-books world, where books respond to verbal commands and to each other. Imagine that each book has a set of methods for taking itself off the shelf, for opening itself up, for turning pages, for looking up information, and more. For the books to be able to interact with one another, some channel of communication has to be in place—a channel that allows each book to have access to every other book's methods.

Let's say you were reading a novel by a particular author, and you wanted to know more about him or her. You could ask your very-smart-novel to find the information for you, and it would communicate with the very-smart-encyclopedia on the bookcase. Your novel would somehow have to have access to the encyclopedia's Lookup method.

The novel has to be able to take advantage of this method, but it doesn't really have to know how the method does its job. The novel just has to know that the encyclopedia has the method and what the method does.

The novel can get the encyclopedia to perform the Lookup method by establishing a "contract." The novel and the encyclopedia agree that the encyclopedia will deliver the requested information, and the novel won't bother the encyclopedia during the process. It can't look into the encyclopedia, look over its spine, or turn its pages. All it can do is wait for the information and trust the encyclopedia to deliver it.

This is a clever way to do this transaction. Why? Suppose an updated very-smart-encyclopedia appears on the market and you want to buy it and put it on

Skill 13

the shelf in place of the original. If the new encyclopedia has the ability to draw up a contract the same way the old one did, our really-smart-novels can access it the same way they accessed the old one, and not miss a beat. It won't matter if the new encyclopedia is from a different publisher than the old one, has a different number of pages, or even if its information isn't arranged alphabetically. As long as it has a Lookup method that can deliver information (and the Lookup method can be totally different from the old encyclopedia's Lookup method), your other books can access it and use its information.

COM specifies that software objects will interact this way, through contracts called *interfaces*. A client (like our novel) will never peek inside the methods of an object that provides a service. It manages its communication with that object through one or more interfaces. In COM, an object has functions that specify how the object will behave, and data that perform those functions. Each interface is something like a table of these functions for the server object.

In the COM world, an object is said to *expose* itself through its interfaces. The interfaces contribute to the interplay among objects. They let the client know the behavior it can expect from the server object. What kinds of behaviors are we talking about? Here are a few:

- The object displays itself.
- The object supports property pages.
- The object supports access to the information in its property pages.

Interfaces come ready-made, although programmers can create new ones when they create new controls. The most important of these interfaces supports a method that allows other objects to query it as to whether its control supports other particular interfaces (and hence, other methods). It's as if our very-smart-novel was able to ask our very-smart-encyclopedia to name the behaviors it (the encyclopedia) supports before deciding to use it. For example, the novel would want to be sure that the encyclopedia will present the requested information after finding it.

In addition to interfaces among objects, another important aspect of COM is the way it names classes. Each one has to be unique, so that an object knows which object it's interfacing with. With the potential for millions of classes of controls, this is quite a challenge. COM meets the challenge by assigning a 128-bit integer to each one. This integer is called a *GUID* (global unique identifier), and you see one every time you look at the CLSID for an object embedded in an HTML document or a layout. Won't we run out of GUIDs someday? Probably not: You could generate 10 million unique 32-digit hexadecimal GUIDs every second for the next 3,700 years!

ActiveX Out in the Open

COM is the foundation for ActiveX. When you think of all you've done with ActiveX controls so far, you'll realize an ActiveX control has to have particular COM features.

First, it must have interfaces that allow it to communicate with the HTML document or the HTML Layout Control it lives in, and it has to be able to respond to events from the outside world. This kind of In-Place Activation of embedded controls is a direct descendant of the In-Place Editing you can do with an embedded spreadsheet in a compound document.

As far as COM interfaces go, an ActiveX control has to have (at least) the one I described in the previous section. This is the one that enables other objects to ask it what it can do. This interface also has another capability. It can track how many ways the control is being used at any time, and when no other object is using it, it can go away. Because an ActiveX control only has to have this one interface (although it can have others), it differs somewhat from its forerunner, the OLE control (which had to have many more), and it's streamlined for Internet activity. This doesn't mean that ActiveX controls can only live in Web-based applications. Pretty soon you'll see them everywhere.

Summary

You might never have occasion to delve into the esoterica of COM. Still, it's good to know where ActiveX came from. At least a cursory understanding of COM will give you an idea of where the technology is heading.

Since ActiveX is expanding at such a rapid rate, it will be extremely difficult to keep track of the details of all the developments in the coming years. Knowing something about the foundational concepts, however, will keep you a step ahead of the game.

Are You Experienced?

Now you can...

- ☑ understand the fundamentals of object orientation
- ☑ comprehend the thought process behind OLE, ActiveX's immediate predecessor
- ☑ understand the relationship between OLE and ActiveX
- ☑ understand the Component Object Model, the basis for ActiveX
- ☑ look at ActiveX in the context of COM and understand the COM features it incorporates

Dissecting Internet Explorer

- ❏ The Microsoft Internet Explorer scripting object model
- ❏ Working with the scripting object model
- ❏ Writing to a document in IE
- ❏ Creating a frame on the fly
- ❏ Creating a frame with a scripted control

In previous Skills in Part II, you took a long hard look at the technology you've been using. You've explored VBScript, examined the VBS-HTML connection, dissected the ActiveX Control Pad, and investigated the roots of ActiveX. You finish your look at ActiveX technology by examining the Internet Explorer (IE) itself.

In this Skill, you'll learn how to use Visual Basic Script to manipulate the IE browser. As you work through this Skill, you'll apply your knowledge of object orientation from Skill 13 to help you understand the Internet Explorer scripting object model. This object model represents the structure of IE. It names IE's objects, methods, and properties so that your scripts can reference them (hence the name "scripting object model"). You'll see how to use the object model to write a script that manipulates IE.

Later in this Skill, you'll apply your knowledge of the scripting object model and your knowledge of frames from Skill 11. You'll create a frame that creates another frame "on the fly." You'll finish with a script that goes beyond simple on-the-fly frame creation: You'll set up a frame that creates a frame with its own fully functional scripted control.

The Internet Explorer Scripting Object Model

In order to manipulate IE, you have to delve into the object structure at its foundation. This structure is called the Internet Explorer scripting object model. You'll put the Skill 13 discussion about objects and classes to good use here.

In your book-objects world, each book has a cover. The cover itself is an object, as well as being a component of the book. So a component, like "Cover" can also be an object (and have components and properties of its own).

You can look at a book-object from another point of view. Each book can be part of a *collection*, a set of books grouped together in some way. The books on a bookshelf, for instance, form a collection. In ActiveX, the controls on a layout form a collection, too.

IE is an object and it has components that are also objects. The main object in IE is called *Window*, and it represents the browser window. The Window object has numerous components that are also objects, and it contains collections of objects as well (like a bookcase that contains shelves, and each shelf has a collection of books). The objects that Window contains have properties and methods, too.

The Window object contains these objects:

- Frames
- History
- Navigator
- Location
- Script
- Document

Where is the model? Can you see a picture of it? These are appropriate questions. In many applications, *object browsers* are usually available to help you visually examine the object hierarchy. They show which objects belong to which collections, and they display the properties and methods for each object.

You have a tool at your disposal that takes you through the objects of the Microsoft Internet Explorer scripting object model (IESOM). It's called the Script Wizard.

Picturing the Model

In addition to being a great tool for creating VBS code, the Script Wizard can also display the IESOM. Open a page in the ActiveX Control Pad Text Editor, and then open the Script Wizard. In the Actions pane, you'll see an entry for "Window." That's the Window object at the top of the IESOM.

You haven't worked with the Window's objects, properties, and methods yet, and for good reason. You've been concentrating on controls that reside in the browser window. You haven't had occasion, until now, to deal with the browser itself. You worked with the Window object's OnLoad event whenever you wrote a script to populate a Listbox control when the browser opens.

In Code View, enlarge the Script Wizard vertically, and then elongate the Event pane and the Actions pane. Click the + next to Window in the Actions pane and you'll see its objects, methods, and properties appear. What you're looking at is the IESOM (see Figure 14.1).

What the Objects Are

Window is the object that represents the browser and is at the top of the IESOM hierarchy. It represents the IE window and all of the Window objects, properties, and methods.

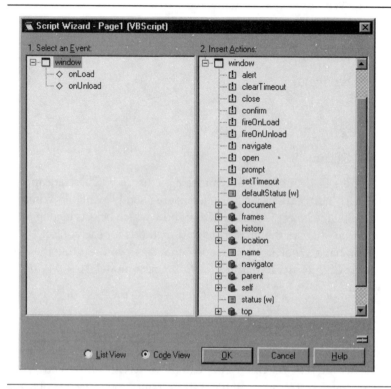

FIGURE 14.1: The Script Wizard displays the Internet Explorer scripting object model when you click the + next to Window in the Actions pane.

In addition to the objects I listed in the preceding section (frames, history, navigator, location, script, and document), a Window object has these properties and objects:

- Name (the name of the current window)

- Self (contains the Window object of the current window)

- Top (the topmost Window object; it's the window that contains all frames in the current browser)

- Parent (if a frame contains the window, the frame is the parent; if not, this property contains a reference to the current window)

- Status and DefaultStatus (each one puts text into the status bar at the bottom of a window)

The Window object's methods are:

- Alert (displays an Alert Message Box)
- Confirm (displays a Message Box with an OK button and a Cancel button)
- Prompt (displays a Message Box that prompts the user for input)
- Open (opens a new window with a specified URL)
- Close (closes a window)
- SetTimeout (sets a timer to call a function after a specified number of milliseconds)
- ClearTimeout (clears a timer using a specified ID)
- Navigate (takes the Window object to a new URL)

You can see these methods in the Actions pane. Some of the Window's objects are worthy of a closer look.

Frames

In Skill 11, you worked with frames—subdivisions of a window, each of which is a separate window with its own properties. In the IESOM, the Frames object is an array of the frames that reside in the Window object.

History

The History object accesses the browser's history list. This object has three methods, Forward (which jumps forward a specified number of items in the list), Back (which jumps back a specified number of items in the list), and Go (which takes a numerical argument and takes you to that numbered item in the history list). This object has a single property named Length. This property contains the number of items in the history list.

Navigator

The Navigator object contains information about the current browser. The Navigator object contains four properties, but no methods. The Navigator object's properties include the name of the application and the version number.

This object provides information to Web authors. Their scripts can access it to find out about the browser someone is using to look at their Web pages. Based on what they find out, they can send that browser to an appropriate version of the page (assuming that multiple versions are available).

If you want to see all the Navigator object's properties, set up an HTML page with one Command Button. Script the Command Button's Click event that presents the information in a Message Box. (The properties are called appCodeName, appName, appVersion, and userAgent.) Your code for the Click event should look like this:

```
<SCRIPT LANGUAGE="VBScript">
<!--
Sub cmdbtnNav_Click()
MsgBox "appCodeName: " & window.navigator.appCodeName & _
     chr(13) & "appName: " & window.navigator.appName & _
     chr(13) & "appVersion: " & window.navigator.appVersion & _
     chr(13) & "userAgent: " & _
      window.navigator.userAgent,,"Navigator Information"
end sub
-->
```

Open the page in IE, click the button, and note the values in the Message Box. This set of values contains important information about your browser. A good bit of this information refers to Netscape Navigator.

 NOTE

When you examine the values, you might think you wandered into the world of Netscape. The word "Mozilla," an important word in the Netscape lexicon, figures prominently in two of the property values. ("Mozilla" started out as sort of a Netscape in-house synonym for its browser application. It stems from Netscape's original name, Mosaic Communications.)

Why the Netscape references? And why call this object "Navigator" to begin with? IE does all this to maintain compatibility with Netscape Navigator. In Navigator, the object that contains information about the browser is also called the Navigator object. Accessing this object in either Microsoft Internet Explorer or in Netscape Navigator will let you find out all you have to know about the current browser.

ACTIVEX AND NETSCAPE NAVIGATOR

Netscape Navigator does not support ActiveX technology directly. You can add ActiveX capabilities to Netscape via ScriptActive, a third-party plug-in (a piece of software that augments the functionality of the main application). You can download ScriptActive from `http://www.ncompasslabs.com`.

If you have a fully licensed copy of Netscape Navigator and you want to give ScriptActive a try, here are some issues to be aware of:

- Neither VBS nor ActiveX controls will work directly in Netscape Navigator. You have to run your controls and scripts in the ScriptActive plug-in.
- To run an HTML file in the plug-in, you must have an <EMBED> tag for each <OBJECT> tag in the file, and you must compile your VBS into an additional file. The VBS's file also loads into the plug-in via an <EMBED> tag.
- A conversion utility included with ScriptActive handles the necessary changes.
- ScriptActive will work with the HTML Layout Control. Changes to the ALX file aren't necessary, but an <EMBED> tag still has to go into the associated HTML file.

Location

The Location object gives your script access to the browser's current URL. Thanks to this object, your script can look into IE's Address box (the little rectangle near the top of the IE window that holds the address of the page you're looking at). The Location object's properties contain different segments of the URL, from the href property (that contains the entire URL), to the protocol property (the URL's protocol—usually http), to the host property (like www.yourcompanyname.com), and a couple of others.

NOTE   The HTML Layout Control has access only to the href property of the Location object. To see this for yourself, open a ALX file in the ActiveX Control Pad and open the Script Wizard. In the Actions pane, click the + next to Window. You'll see only the Location object that exposes only the href property.

Document

The Document object represents the HTML document currently in the browser. It has properties that contain information about objects on the current page. For example, three of its properties deal with the color of links (parts of text that you click to jump to a new URL), while two other deal with color on the page:

- LinkColor is the current color of the links in the document.

- ALinkColor is the color of an active link (a link that you've positioned the cursor over, and pressed but not released the mouse button).

- VLinkColor is the color of visited links.

- BgColor and FgColor are background color and foreground color (we work with these two in the next section).

Three properties are arrays:

- The Anchors property is an array of anchors in the document (an anchor is an <A> </A> tag pair that surrounds a text link to a URL).

- The Links property contains an array of the hypertext links in the document.

- The Forms property contains an array of the forms contained in a document. (You used a form in Skill 11 to organize and position form controls that HTML provides.)

Other properties include Location (the Location object described earlier), LastModified (the most recent date that the Web page was modified), Title (the title of the document—the words that sit between <TITLE> and </TITLE>), and Referrer (the URL of the document that contained the link the user clicked to get to the current one).

The Document object has one other noteworthy property called Cookie. The Cookie property (a single string that's stored on a user's computer) contains information about a user and his or her interactions with a particular document (like personal preferences). This property represents the Cookie for the current document.

You'll be working with some of the Document object's methods, so this is a good place to introduce them. Write puts a string into the Document, WriteIn does the same thing, but with a new line character at the end. These two methods work with Open, Close, and Clear. As you may expect, Open opens the document so you can use the Write or WriteLn methods, Close closes it, and Clear closes the document and writes the information to the screen.

 NOTE   **For the definitive word on the IESOM, you can read Microsoft's documentation at** `http://www.microsoft.com/workshop/prog/sdk/docs/scriptom/`.

Working with the Scripting Object Model

Let's work with the IESOM by manipulating properties of the Document object. In your ActiveX Control Pad, open a new file and save it as IESOM1 in skill 14. Put this code into the file:

```
<HTML>
<HEAD>
<TITLE>Scripting the Properties of IE</TITLE>
</HEAD>
        <BODY>
<CENTER>
<H1> Scripting IE: Colors <H1> <HR>
</CENTER>
<BR> <BR>
<CENTER>


        </BODY>
        </HTML>
```

Now let's add some controls. Position the cursor in the blank line between <CENTER> and </BODY>. Start with a ListBox that enables you to change the Document's background color and its foreground color (the color of the text in the heading). Follow these steps:

1. Select Edit ➢ Insert ActiveX Control….

2. Select the Microsoft Forms 2.0 ListBox and click OK.

3. In the Object Editor, change the ListBox's ID to **lstbxColors**.

4. Close the Object Editor.

5. In the Text Editor, change the ListBox's Width to **70** and its Height to **150**.

Now insert a Command Button that opens a Message Box. The Message Box will track some of Document's properties. Follow these steps:

1. Select Edit ➤ Insert ActiveX Control….

2. Select the Microsoft Forms 2.0 CommandButton and click OK.

3. In the Object Editor, change the Command Button's ID to **cmdbtnDocument**.

4. Change its Caption to **Document Property Values** and make the Font property bold.

5. Close the Object Editor.

6. In the Text Editor, change the Command Button's Width to **165** and its Height to **30**.

7. Insert a </CENTER> tag after the Command Button.

Now for the script. You'll want your VBS code to:

- populate the ListBox with the color names that IE understands

- have the ListBox's Change event change the Document's background color and foreground color

- have the Command Button's Click event open a Message Box that displays values of some of the Document's properties

Open the Script Wizard and put it in Code View. Select the Window's OnLoad event and the ListBox's AddItem method. Produce these lines of code in the Script pane:

```
Sub window_onLoad()
call lstbxColors.AddItem("Aqua")
call lstbxColors.AddItem("Black")
call lstbxColors.AddItem("Blue")
call lstbxColors.AddItem("Fuchsia")
call lstbxColors.AddItem("Gray")
call lstbxColors.AddItem("Green")
call lstbxColors.AddItem("Lime")
call lstbxColors.AddItem("Maroon")
call lstbxColors.AddItem("Navy")
```

```
call lstbxColors.AddItem("Olive")
call lstbxColors.AddItem("Purple")
call lstbxColors.AddItem("Red")
call lstbxColors.AddItem("Silver")
call lstbxColors.AddItem("Teal")
call lstbxColors.AddItem("White")
call lstbxColors.AddItem("Yellow")
```

For the ListBox Change event, do the typing to make the first two lines of the Script pane read:

```
Sub lstbxColors_Change()
window.document.bgColor = lstbxColors.Value
```

Let's use some VBS concepts you haven't worked with before. So far, you've made the background color depend on the value selected in the ListBox. Let's set the foreground color in the same Change event. You don't want to make the foreground color the same as the background color, because then you'd never see the heading. Instead, you make the foreground color whatever color is seven rows down from the selected background color in the ListBox. (You could have chosen any number of rows. I happened to choose seven.)

To do this, you first have to reference the selected value's row. The ListBox's ListIndex property provides the row number of the selected row (starting at zero for the top row). Now you need a way to specify "seven rows down from the selected row." You can use the ListBox's List property along with indexing to reference any row in the ListBox. "Seven rows down from the selected row" is:

```
lstbxColors.List(lstbxColors.ListIndex + 7)
```

If you leave it that way, you'll have a problem. Once you get past row 8, you'll run out of rows, as the last row number is 15. You want the foreground color to start back at the beginning of the ListBox when that happens. In other words, when the selected row for the background color is 9, you want the row for the foreground color to be 0. When the selected row for the background color is 10, you want the row for the foreground color to be 1, and so forth.

How do you do that? Recall that the Mod operator (Skill 10) takes one numerical term, divides it by another, and returns only the remainder. So when you select a row, you'll add 7 to the row number of the selected row, divide the sum by 16 (because you have 16 rows), return the remainder, and that's the number of the row from which you'll take the foreground color. When the selected row is 9, 9 + 7 = 16, and dividing by 16 leaves a remainder of 0. When the selected row is 10, 10 + 7 = 17, and dividing by 16 leaves a remainder of 1.

The expression now looks like this:

```
lstbxColors.List((lstbxColors.ListIndex + 7) Mod 16)
```

Add this line to the lstbxColors Change event:

```
window.document.fgColor = lstbxColors.List((lstbxColors.ListIndex
➡+ 7) Mod 16)
```

Let's add one more line to the Change event. This one doesn't pertain to the Document object, but to the Window object. Let's put a message into the status bar at the bottom of the window and have it display the colors of the background and the foreground. The property that represents the status bar is `window` `.defaultStatus`. We'll set the defaultStatus property equal to the two values from the ListBox along with explanatory text:

```
window.defaultStatus = "BackgroundColor: " &  lstbxColors.Value _
          & "    Foreground Color: " & _
          lstbxColors.List((lstbxColors.ListIndex + 7) Mod 16)
```

Why did we use the ListBox values and not just the properties themselves here? As you'll see when we open the ListBox, those terms return hexadecimal RGB values and not color names. The whole Change event is:

```
Sub lstbxColors_Change()
window.document.bgColor = lstbxColors.Value
window.document.fgColor = lstbxColors.List((lstbxColors.ListIndex
➡+ 7) Mod 16)
window.defaultStatus = "BackgroundColor: " &  lstbxColors.Value _
          & "    Foreground Color: " & _
          lstbxColors.List((lstbxColors.ListIndex + 7) Mod 16)
```

The code for the Command Button's Click event is:

```
Sub cmdbtnDocument_Click()
MsgBox "Background RGB: " & window.document.bgColor _
              & chr(13) & "Foreground RGB: " _
              & window.document.fgColor _
              & chr(13) & "Document Title: " _
              & window.document.title, _
              64,"Document Property Values"
```

You're including the Document's Title in the Message Box just to track it.

NOTE   One important item to notice in all this code is the use of the dot notation. The Script Wizard handles it all for you, so sometimes it's easy to lose sight of what the notation signifies (and by now it's almost an afterthought). The dot notation tells you what belongs to what. In the expression `window.document.bgColor`, for example, you're referring to the bgcolor property of the Window object's Document object.

Click OK to close the Script Wizard. Save your work in the Text Editor, and open the page in IE. It will look like Figure 14.2.

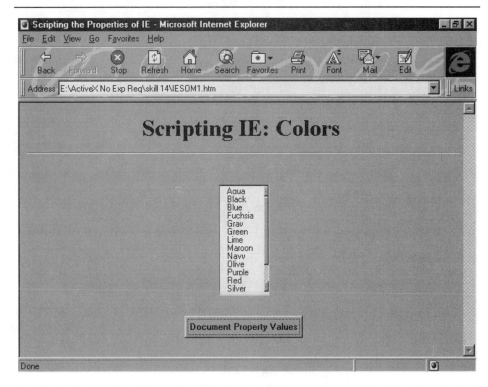

FIGURE 14.2: *IESOM1.htm* when it opens in IE

As you make some selections in the ListBox, you'll see the color of the document change dramatically, along with the color of the heading. Figure 14.3 shows the result of one particular selection. (I've also clicked the Command Button and dragged the Message Box to the right.)

In Figure 14.3, the browser's background is white, and the heading is now green. Notice the message in the status bar. Since we set the status bar message in the Listbox Change event, it changes whenever you make a selection in the ListBox. Also, take a look at the Message Box. It gives the RGB values for the background color and the foreground color, as well as the title of the document.

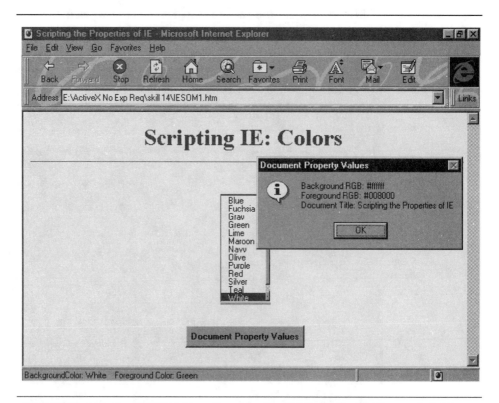

FIGURE 14.3: *IESOM1.htm* **after selecting White in the ListBox and clicking the Command Button.**

Writing in a Document

Let's explore the Document object a little further. We've looked at a couple of its properties, and now let's experiment with some of its methods.

The Document object's Write method takes a string as its argument and puts that string into the HTML document. Because the string goes directly into the document, you have to format it with HTML tags, just as if you were putting it into the ActiveX Control Pad Text Editor.

Before you write anything to the document, you use the Document object's Open method, and when you're finished, you use the Close method. Open, as I said earlier, opens the document for input. It also clears any existing information from the browser's copy of the document. The Close method updates the screen to display all the strings written after the last call to Open.

To see how this works, you'll create an HTML file with just a Command Button. When you click the Command Button, a heading and some text will appear in the document, and the Command Button will disappear.

Open a new file in the Text Editor and save it as IESOM2 in skill 14. Change its title to **Document Methods**. You won't bother with a heading or any text—you'll have the Write method do that for you. In the meantime, follow these steps:

1. Type five **
** tags.

2. Select Edit ➤ Insert ActiveX Control….

3. Select a Microsoft Forms 2.0 CommandButton control and then click OK.

4. In the Object Editor, change the Command Button's ID to **cmdbtnWrite** and its Caption to **Write** and make the caption Font bold.

5. Close the Object Editor.

6. Put a <CENTER> tag before the <OBJECT> tag and a </CENTER> tag after the </OBJECT> tag.

On to the script. Open the Script Wizard and select cmdbtnWrite's Click event. With the Script Wizard in Code View, got to the Actions pane and click the + next to window. Then click the + next to document. Select the document's Open method, and double click. Next, do the clicking (in the Actions pane) and the typing so the Script pane contains these lines of VBS code:

```
call window.document.open
call window.document.write("<CENTER> <H1> Here is a Heading <H1>
➥<HR> </CENTER>")
call window.document.write("<BR> <BR> <BR> <P>
➥<FONT FACE = Script SIZE = 7>")
call window.document.write("This is the start of some great text.
➥<BR>")
call window.document.write("... And here's another line!")
call window.document.close()
```

Take a close look at the four lines that call the Write method. Each one's argument is a single string, and each string is a line of HTML code. Three of those strings have at least one HTML tag.

The whole file (IESOM2.htm) should look like the following listing.

IESOM2.htm

```
</HEAD>
<BODY>
<BR> <BR> <BR> <BR> <BR>
<CENTER>
    <SCRIPT LANGUAGE="VBScript">
<!--
Sub cmdbtnWrite_Click()
call window.document.open
call window.document.write("<CENTER> <H1> Here is a Heading <H1> <HR> </CENTER>")
call window.document.write("<BR> <BR> <BR> <P> <FONT FACE = Script SIZE = 7>")
call window.document.write("This is the start of some great text.<BR>")
call window.document.write("... And here's another line!")
call window.document.close
end sub
-->
    </SCRIPT>
    <OBJECT ID="cmdbtnWrite" WIDTH=96 HEIGHT=32
     CLASSID="CLSID:D7053240-CE69-11CD-A777-00DD01143C57">
        <PARAM NAME="Caption" VALUE="Write">
        <PARAM NAME="Size" VALUE="2540;846">
        <PARAM NAME="FontEffects" VALUE="1073741825">
        <PARAM NAME="FontCharSet" VALUE="0">
        <PARAM NAME="FontPitchAndFamily" VALUE="2">
        <PARAM NAME="ParagraphAlign" VALUE="3">
        <PARAM NAME="FontWeight" VALUE="700">
    </OBJECT>
</CENTER>
</BODY>
</HTML>
```

Save the file and open it in IE. At first, you'll just see a Command Button. Click the Command Button, and the page looks like Figure 14.4. Notice that the Command Button is gone. The changes, of course, aren't permanent. You've written to the copy of the page in the browser, not to the original HTML file. You can see this in two ways. First, select View ➤ Source and you'll see the original code in Notepad. Next, click the Refresh button and you'll see the changes disappear and the Command Button reappear.

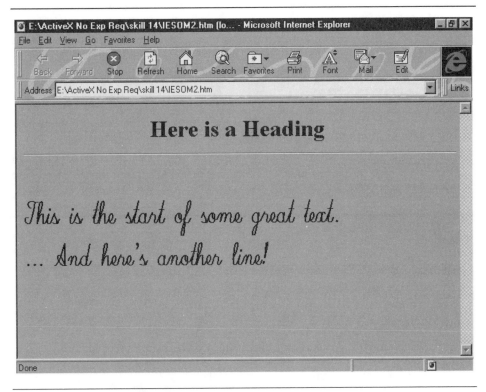

FIGURE 14.4: *IESOM2.html* after you click the Command Button and activate the document.write method.

Frames on the Fly

The previous exercise set you up for something really big. Using methods to programmatically create the content of a Web page is a great thing. If you know how to do that, you're not stuck with static content. Instead, you can respond to events and input, and you can create the content as the user interacts with a Web page.

You may have noticed one nagging problem with what you just did, however. Writing the new content into your document destroyed what was already there. When you started, you had a Command Button. When you finished, you didn't.

You'll get around that problem by using input from one page to write the content of another page. More specifically, you'll input some information into one frame and use it as the basis for creating the content of a document in a separate frame. And as you'll see, this is a terrific application of the IESOM.

Getting Started

Happily, you've already done some of the legwork. Some of your work from Skill 11 will get you going.

Open the skill 11 folder and copy Frame Setup.htm, first.htm, and second .htm to your skill 14 folder. The HTML in the file (Frame Setup.htm) looks like this:

 Frame Setup.htm

```
<HTML>
<HEAD>
<TITLE>Frame Setup</TITLE>
</HEAD>
<BODY>
<FRAMESET COLS=50%,50%>
<FRAME NAME = "leftframe" SRC= "first.htm">
<FRAME NAME = "rightframe" SRC= "second.htm">
</FRAMESET>
</BODY>
</HTML>
```

Just to refresh your memory, the <FRAMESET> tag lays out the page in columns (you also did an exercise in Skill 11 which laid out the page in rows), and the <FRAME> tags name the frames.

The HTML in first.htm is just:

```
<HTML>
<HEAD>
<TITLE>First</TITLE>
</HEAD>
<BODY>
<CENTER>
<B> This is the first page!
</CENTER>
</BODY>
</HTML>
```

And `second.htm` is no more than this listing.

 **second.htm**

```
<HTML>
<HEAD>
<TITLE>Second</TITLE>
</HEAD>
<BODY>
<CENTER>
<B> This is the second page!
</CENTER>
</BODY>
</HTML>
```

The `Frame Setup` file lays down the outline for the frame sizes and for the document that appears in each frame. We'll change `First` so it has the controls necessary to create the content of `Second.htm` in `rightframe`.

Moving Ahead

The strategy will be to put some TextBox controls into `First`, along with a Command Button. In the TextBoxes, you'll enter the new information for the document in `rightframe`, and clicking the Command Button will activate the Write methods that put that content into that document:

1. In `First.htm`, use Edit ➢ Insert ActiveX Control... to insert a TextBox, a ListBox, another TextBox, and a Command Button. You will have to enter the Object Editor each time you insert a new control.

2. For the second TextBox, be sure to set the MultiLine property to **True** and the WordWrap property to **True**.

3. Also in this TextBox, set the Font to 10 pt.

4. Give each control an appropriate ID. I used **txtbxHeading**, **lstbxFont**, **txtbxBody**, and **cmdbtnCreate**.

5. On the line before each box, enter some appropriate text as prompts. Before the txtbxHeading type **Enter a heading:**, before lstbxFont type **Select a font:**, and before txtbxBody type **Enter some snappy text:**.

6. Use <BR> and <P> tags to keep everything lined up correctly, and use <B> tags to make the prompts bold.

When you're finished, here's how the file (First.htm) should look:

First.htm

```
<HTML>
<HEAD>
<TITLE>First</TITLE>
</HEAD>
<BODY>
<P> <B> Enter a heading:
<P>
    <OBJECT ID="txtbxHeading" WIDTH=270 HEIGHT=35
     CLASSID="CLSID:8BD21D10-EC42-11CE-9E0D-00AA006002F3">
        <PARAM NAME="VariousPropertyBits" VALUE="746604571">
        <PARAM NAME="Size" VALUE="7112;900">
        <PARAM NAME="FontCharSet" VALUE="0">
        <PARAM NAME="FontPitchAndFamily" VALUE="2">
        <PARAM NAME="FontWeight" VALUE="0">
    </OBJECT>
<P> <B> Select a font for the heading:
<P>
    <OBJECT ID="lstbxFont" WIDTH=14 HEIGHT=30
     CLASSID="CLSID:8BD21D20-EC42-11CE-9E0D-00AA006002F3">
        <PARAM NAME="ScrollBars" VALUE="3">
        <PARAM NAME="DisplayStyle" VALUE="2">
        <PARAM NAME="Size" VALUE="2990;792">
        <PARAM NAME="MatchEntry" VALUE="0">
        <PARAM NAME="FontEffects" VALUE="1073741825">
        <PARAM NAME="FontCharSet" VALUE="0">
        <PARAM NAME="FontPitchAndFamily" VALUE="2">
        <PARAM NAME="FontWeight" VALUE="700">
    </OBJECT>
<P> <B> Enter some snappy text:
<P>
    <OBJECT ID="txtbxBody" WIDTH=200 HEIGHT=150
     CLASSID="CLSID:8BD21D10-EC42-11CE-9E0D-00AA006002F3">
        <PARAM NAME="VariousPropertyBits" VALUE="2894088219">
        <PARAM NAME="Size" VALUE="5292;3986">
        <PARAM NAME="FontHeight" VALUE="200">
        <PARAM NAME="FontCharSet" VALUE="0">
        <PARAM NAME="FontPitchAndFamily" VALUE="2">
        <PARAM NAME="FontWeight" VALUE="0">
    </OBJECT>
<P>
    <OBJECT ID="cmdbtnCreate" WIDTH=96 HEIGHT=32
     CLASSID="CLSID:D7053240-CE69-11CD-A777-00DD01143C57">
        <PARAM NAME="Caption" VALUE="Create">
```

```
            <PARAM NAME="Size" VALUE="2540;846">
            <PARAM NAME="FontEffects" VALUE="1073741825">
            <PARAM NAME="FontCharSet" VALUE="0">
            <PARAM NAME="FontPitchAndFamily" VALUE="2">
            <PARAM NAME="ParagraphAlign" VALUE="3">
            <PARAM NAME="FontWeight" VALUE="700">
        </OBJECT>
    </BODY>
</HTML>
```

To make sure you're on the right track with all this, open Frame Setup in IE. Your screen should look like Figure 14.5.

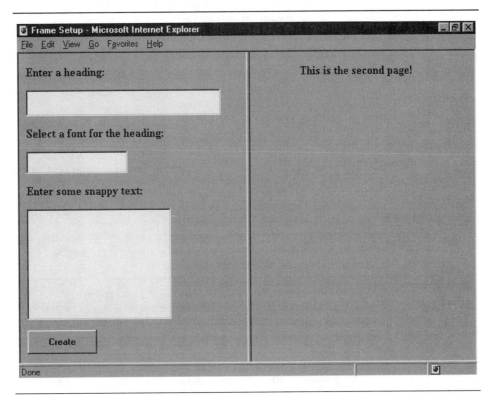

FIGURE 14.5: After you finish updating *First.htm*, here is what you should see when you open *Frame Setup.htm* in IE.

Remember: Frame Setup provides the skeleton for how the frames will appear onscreen. When you open Frame Setup, you see a document in each frame.

Setting the Stage for the Script

As you saw in Skill 11, the hardest part about writing the script is the reference to the frames. With your knowledge of the IESOM, however, that should be a snap. The goal is to refer to the frame on the right side of Figure 14.5, refer to its Document property, and then refer to the Document's Open, Write, and Close methods. You used those methods in the previous exercise, but you didn't use them in conjunction with a Frame object. Since a frame is a window, you'll just do what you did in the previous exercise, once you know how to refer to a frame.

Remember from IESOM that the Top property returns the "topmost" Window object, which contains all the frames in the current browser. Thus, the Top property will figure into the way you refer to a frame.

In fact, two ways to refer to a frame are possible. The first is based on the idea that the Top property is the Window object, which is the container of all the frames. Thus, you should be able to refer to a frame as

```
window.top.framename
```

and to the document in that frame as

```
window.top.framename.Document
```

The frame you're interested in is right frame, the frame on the right side of Figure 14.5. Thus,

```
window.top.rightframe.Document
```

will take you where you want to go—the document currently on display in the frame called `rightframe`. That document, you'll remember, is `Second.htm`.

 NOTE   You might remember that you used the Top property this way in Skill 11. You may want to go back to Skill 11 and review what you learned. It might be clearer now that you've examined the IESOM.

Another way to refer to a Frame object is through the Frames array. This is an array of frames in the current window. That window is Top, the window that holds all the frames. So

```
window.top.frames(1).Document
```

also takes us to `rightframe`. Why the "1" in the Frames array index? Back in `Frame Setup.htm` we defined `leftframe` first and `rightframe` second. That makes `rightframe` the second member of the array. Since array indexing starts at zero, the second frame has an index of 1.

> **TIP**   Another way to refer to rightframe is: `window.top.frames("right-frame").Document`.

Using the array-based referencing, when you want to access a document method from the document in `rightframe` the expression is:

```
window.top.frames(1).Document.method
```

Writing the Script

Now that the hard part is out of the way, let's backtrack and start the script with something easy. You have to populate your ListBox with a list of fonts, and you'll do it with ListBox's AddItem method. As you've done before, you'll code the AddItem method in the Window's `OnLoad` event. The entries in the ListBox will be the names of four fonts: Braggadocio, Haettenschweiler (what's a font list without those two?), Arial, and Desdemona.

In the Script Wizard, select the Window OnLoad event, put the Wizard in Code View, and produce these lines in the Script pane:

```
call lstbxFont.AddItem("Braggadocio")
call lstbxFont.AddItem("Haettenschweiler")
call lstbxFont.AddItem("Arial")
call lstbxFont.AddItem("Desdemona")
```

Now work on the frame-related code. The code will all be part of the script for the Command Button's Click event. Using the Script Wizard probably isn't that much of a convenience here. You might just as well type these lines directly into the Text Editor:

```
<SCRIPT LANGUAGE="VBScript">
<!--
Sub cmdbtnCreate_Click()
window.top.frames(1).Document.Open
window.top.frames(1).Document.Write "<HTML> <HEAD> </HEAD><TITLE>
➥A Brand New Page </TITLE>"
window.top.frames(1).Document.Write "<BODY>"
window.top.frames(1).Document.Write "<FONT FACE = "
➥& lstbxFont.Value & ">"
window.top.frames(1).Document.Write "<CENTER> <H1>"
➥& txtbxHeading.Value & "</H1> </CENTER> <HR>"
window.top.frames(1).Document.Write "</FONT>"
window.top.frames(1).Document.Write "<BR> <BR>"
window.top.frames(1).Document.Write "<P> <B>" & txtbxBody.Value
window.top.frames(1).Document.Write "</BODY> </HTML>"
```

```
window.top.frames(1).Document.Close
end sub
-->
    </SCRIPT>
```

 NOTE   In Skill 10, I explained that you could use the word `call` with any VBS procedure, and if you do, you must include parentheses. Compare this example with the last one and note the alternative forms of `Document.Write`. In the last example I used `call` and parentheses, in this one I didn't. If you use the Script Wizard for this example, instead of freehand typing, you'll have to use parentheses because the Wizard inserts `call` and the parentheses when you double-click on a method.

Let's now examine what you're doing. The first line opens the document in the second frame for input, and the last one closes it. All the lines in the middle write to the document in `rightframe`. In so doing, they create its content.

The first two instances of the Write method put HTML tags into the document in `rightframe`—tags that you would find at the beginning of any typical HTML file. The first `Write` creates the title `A Brand New Page` for the new HTML document. The last `Write` enters the closing tags to finish the new document.

In the third `Write`, you set up a string that includes the <FONT> tag and its FACE attribute. You join that string with the selected font from the ListBox, and then join with the closing angle-bracket. This will put the new heading in the selected font.

The fourth `Write` handles the heading. The <CENTER> and <H1> tags precede the content of the TextBox that holds the content of the new heading, and the closing tags follow the TextBox content, along with the tag that renders a horizontal line. The next two `Write`s provide tags that close off the <FONT> tag and provide line-breaks.

Now you're ready for the body of the new document. This is the product of the next `Write`, which puts a <P> tag and a <B> tag just before the contents of `txtbxBody`.

You now have the entire contents of `First.htm`. Open `Frame Setup` in IE. You'll see the two frames. In the frame on the left enter a heading, select a font for the heading, type in some text, and click the Create button. Right before your eyes, you'll see a document's contents created in the frame on the right!

Figure 14.6 shows one example. As you can see, the heading and the contents of the document in the frame on the right reflect the input from the document in the frame on the left. When you enter text into txtbxBody, you can include HTML tags and the browser will interpret them as it renders the new frame.

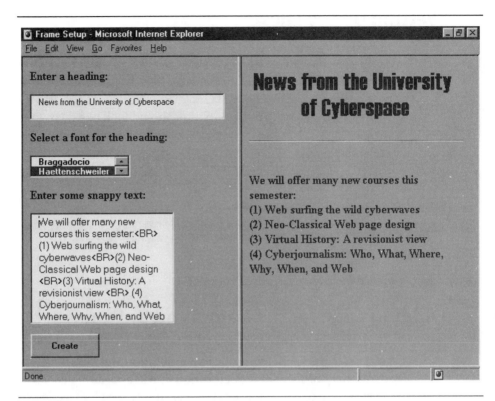

FIGURE 14.6: The heading and the contents of the frame on the right reflect the input from the frame on the left.

A Step Beyond

Creating a frame on the fly is a fine skill to add to your repertoire, even if the contents are static text, as in this example. Now, however, you'll go off into a new dimension and finish this Skill (and Part II) with a flourish: In this exercise, you'll create a frame that has a scripted, fully functional ActiveX control.

In some ways, this exercise is an extension of what you've already done. But from another point of view, you make a profound departure from the fundamental structure to build the foundation for on-the-fly creation of interactive Web pages.

Setting Up the Files

Let's start by reusing our files. Save First.htm as first control.htm in skill 14. Save Frame Setup.htm as Frame Control Setup.htm in skill 14.

In Frame Control Setup.htm change the title to **Frame Control Setup**. Also, change the first <FRAMENAME> tag to make first control.htm the source document for leftframe. Your Text Editor should look like this:

```
<HTML>
<HEAD>
<TITLE>Frame Control Setup</TITLE>
</HEAD>
<BODY>
<FRAMESET COLS=50%,50%>
<FRAME NAME = "leftframe" SRC= "first control.htm">
<FRAME NAME = "rightframe" SRC= "second.htm">
</FRAMESET>
</BODY>
</HTML>
```

Adding Code for the Command Button

Now let's open first control.htm. We're going to add a number of Document .Writes to the script for our Command Button and insert them before the statements that finish the new document that will appear in second.htm.

One group of Document.Writes will supply the HTML that defines an ActiveX control. The other group will supply the VBS for the control. We'll keep things simple. The control will be a Command Button, and the script will cause its Click event to display a Message Box that contains the title of the new document. Just to show that we understand IESOM, we'll have the Message Box reference the title in IESOM terms.

The HTML statements that specify an ActiveX control are rather involved, which is why we ordinarily use the Object Editor and the Layout Control to generate them. In this exercise, we're fortunate: We can use the existing statements for cmdbtnCreate to create our new ActiveX Command Button control. Select and copy (Ctrl + C) these statements from first.htm:

```
<OBJECT ID="cmdbtnCreate" WIDTH=96 HEIGHT=32
    CLASSID="CLSID:D7053240-CE69-11CD-A777-00DD01143C57">
        <PARAM NAME="Caption" VALUE="Create">
        <PARAM NAME="Size" VALUE="2540;846">
        <PARAM NAME="FontEffects" VALUE="1073741825">
        <PARAM NAME="FontCharSet" VALUE="0">
        <PARAM NAME="FontPitchAndFamily" VALUE="2">
```

```
            <PARAM NAME="ParagraphAlign" VALUE="3">
            <PARAM NAME="FontWeight" VALUE="700">
        </OBJECT>
```

You're going to paste them into the script for cmdbtnCreate in a specific place. In that script, create a blank line between

```
window.top.frames(1).Document.Write "<P> <B>" & txtbxBody.Value
```

and

```
window.top.frames(1).Document.Write "</BODY> </HTML>"
```

With your cursor positioned in that blank line, paste (Ctrl+V or Shift+Insert) the lines you selected and copied.

To the left of each of those lines, you have to have this statement:

```
window.top.frames(1).Document.WriteLn
```

You use the WriteLn method instead of the Write method because you want the Newline character inserted at the end of each line.

Once you've typed the Document.WriteLn statement, copy that statement and paste it to all the lines that define the Command Button. Pasting those statements tells VBS to send the specifications for the Command Button to the new document.

In each statement that you just put together, the statement that defines the Command Button has to be a string. So, surround each specification with double-quotes.

This creates another little challenge. Some of those statements already have double quotes inside them. With quotes around them, VBS will not know which quotes line up with which. We get around that by replacing double-quotes inside the statement with single-quotes.

After all the surgery, the new statements should look like this:

```
window.top.frames(1).Document.WriteLn
➥"<OBJECT ID= 'cmdbtnCreate'  WIDTH=96 HEIGHT=32"
window.top.frames(1).Document.WriteLn
➥"CLASSID='CLSID:D7053240-CE69-11CD-A777-00DD01143C57'>"
window.top.frames(1).Document.WriteLn
➥"<PARAM NAME='Caption' VALUE='Create'>"
window.top.frames(1).Document.WriteLn
➥"<PARAM NAME='Size' VALUE='2540;846'>"
window.top.frames(1).Document.WriteLn
➥"<PARAM NAME='FontEffects' VALUE='1073741825'>"
window.top.frames(1).Document.WriteLn
➥"<PARAM NAME='FontCharSet' VALUE='0'>"
window.top.frames(1).Document.WriteLn
➥"<PARAM NAME='FontPitchAndFamily' VALUE='2'>"
```

```
window.top.frames(1).Document.WriteLn
➡ "<PARAM NAME='ParagraphAlign' VALUE='3'>"
window.top.frames(1).Document.WriteLn
➡ "<PARAM NAME='FontWeight' VALUE='700'>"
window.top.frames(1).Document.WriteLn "</OBJECT>"
```

These statements will create a Command Button in the document in the new frame when we click the Create button in the first frame. But we want to position this Command Button several lines below the end of the new frame's text, and we want to center it. To accomplish this, we'll insert a line between these two statements:

```
window.top.frames(1).Document.Write "<P> <B>" & txtbxBody.Value
```

and

```
window.top.frames(1).Document.WriteLn
➡ "<OBJECT ID= 'cmdbtnInfo'  WIDTH=96 HEIGHT=32"
```

The line to insert is:

```
window.top.frames(1).Document.Write "<BR> <BR> <BR> <BR> <CENTER>"
```

To close off the <CENTER> tag, change the final specification statement from

```
window.top.frames(1).Document.WriteLn "</OBJECT>"
```

to

```
window.top.frames(1).Document.WriteLn "</OBJECT> </CENTER>"
```

Two more changes, and then we'll do the Document.Writes for the script. Let's change the ID and the Caption. Change this line:

```
window.top.frames(1).Document.WriteLn
➡ "<OBJECT ID= 'cmdbtnCreate'  WIDTH=96 HEIGHT=32"
```

to

```
window.top.frames(1).Document.WriteLn
➡ "<OBJECT ID= 'cmdbtnInfo'  WIDTH=96 HEIGHT=32"
```

and change this line

```
window.top.frames(1).Document.WriteLn
➡ "<PARAM NAME='Caption' VALUE='Create'>"
```

to

```
window.top.frames(1).Document.WriteLn
➡ "<PARAM NAME='Caption' VALUE='Info'>"
```

Adding Code for the Script

After the final specification statement, the one with </OBJECT> and </CENTER>, add these lines to have the new Command Button display a Message Box that shows the new document's title:

```
window.top.frames(1).Document.WriteLn "<SCRIPT LANGUAGE='VBScript'>"
window.top.frames(1).Document.WriteLn "<!-- "
window.top.frames(1).Document.WriteLn "Sub cmdbtnInfo_Click()"
window.top.frames(1).Document.WriteLn
➡"MsgBox ""The title of this  page is: ""
➡& self.document.title, 64, ""Brand New Message Box"" "
window.top.frames(1).Document.WriteLn "end sub"
window.top.frames(1).Document.WriteLn " -->"
window.top.frames(1).Document.WriteLn "</" & "SCRIPT>"
```

These lines should immediately precede this line:

```
window.top.frames(1).Document.Write "</BODY> </HTML>"
```

You'll notice a couple of things immediately. The first thing that stands out is the last line. Why didn't you just write the quoted string as "</SCRIPT>" instead of breaking it up into "</" & "SCRIPT>"? The reason is that VBS sees /SC as a special set of characters and generates an error message if you use them in a way that it doesn't expect.

The other attention-grabber is the line that contains the MsgBox statement. As you can see, you've put two double quotes around each term that usually takes a set of double quotes. So the message in the Message Box is ""The title of this page is: "" and the title of the Message Box is ""Brand New Message Box"". Single quotes just won't work in the arguments to Message Box. Notice the reference to the new document's title, which you set as A Brand New Web Page between <TITLE> and </TITLE>. Just as IESOM specifies, you use Self to reference the current document, and the document's Title property to retrieve the title.

Putting it all together, the script for cmdbtnCreate's Click event is:

```
</SCRIPT>
<SCRIPT LANGUAGE="VBScript">
<!--
Sub cmdbtnCreate_Click()
window.top.frames(1).Document.Open
window.top.frames(1).Document.Write
➡"<HTML> <HEAD> </HEAD><TITLE> A Brand New Page </TITLE>"
window.top.frames(1).Document.Write "<BODY>"
window.top.frames(1).Document.Write
➡"<FONT FACE = " & lstbxFont.Value & ">"
```

```
window.top.frames(1).Document.Write
➡"<CENTER> <H1>" & txtbxHeading.Value & "</H1> </CENTER> <HR>"
window.top.frames(1).Document.Write "</FONT>"
window.top.frames(1).Document.Write "<BR> <BR>"
window.top.frames(1).Document.Write "<P> <B>" & txtbxBody.Value
window.top.frames(1).Document.Write "<BR> <BR> <BR> <BR> <CENTER>"
window.top.frames(1).Document.WriteLn
➡"<OBJECT ID= 'cmdbtnInfo' WIDTH=96 HEIGHT=32"
window.top.frames(1).Document.WriteLn
➡"CLASSID='CLSID:D7053240-CE69-11CD-A777-00DD01143C57'>"
window.top.frames(1).Document.WriteLn
➡"<PARAM NAME='Caption' VALUE='Info'>"
window.top.frames(1).Document.WriteLn
➡"<PARAM NAME='Size' VALUE='2540;846'>"
window.top.frames(1).Document.WriteLn
➡"<PARAM NAME='FontEffects' VALUE='1073741825'>"
window.top.frames(1).Document.WriteLn
➡"<PARAM NAME='FontCharSet' VALUE='0'>"
window.top.frames(1).Document.WriteLn
➡"<PARAM NAME='FontPitchAndFamily' VALUE='2'>"
window.top.frames(1).Document.WriteLn
➡"<PARAM NAME='ParagraphAlign' VALUE='3'>"
window.top.frames(1).Document.WriteLn
➡"<PARAM NAME='FontWeight' VALUE='700'>"
window.top.frames(1).Document.WriteLn "</OBJECT> </CENTER>"
window.top.frames(1).Document.WriteLn "<SCRIPT LANGUAGE='VBScript'>"
window.top.frames(1).Document.WriteLn "<!-- "
window.top.frames(1).Document.WriteLn "Sub cmdbtnInfo_Click()"
window.top.frames(1).Document.WriteLn
➡"MsgBox ""The title of this page is: ""
➡& self.document.title, 64, ""Brand New Message Box"" "
window.top.frames(1).Document.WriteLn "end sub"
window.top.frames(1).Document.WriteLn " -->"
window.top.frames(1).Document.WriteLn "</" & "SCRIPT>"
window.top.frames(1).Document.Write "</BODY> </HTML>"
window.top.frames(1).Document.Close
end sub
-->
    </SCRIPT>
```

Save first.htm, and open Frame Control Setup.htm in IE. In the left frame, enter a heading, select a font, type in some text, and click the Create Button. As in the previous exercise, you'll see a Web page take shape. This one, however, has a scripted ActiveX Control created along with it. Click on the Command Button that was created in the new document. As Figure 14.7 shows, you'll see a Message Box that displays the title of the newly created document.

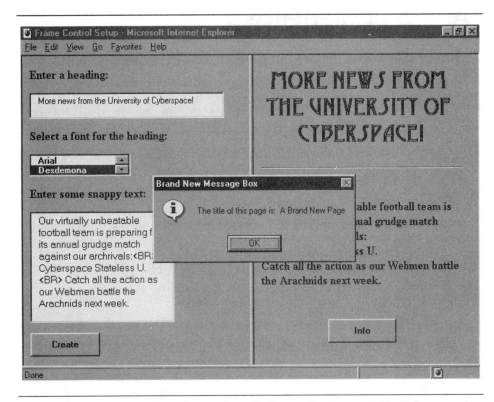

FIGURE 14.7: On-the-fly creation of a frame that has an ActiveX Command Button. The newly created Command Button is fully functional. Clicking it opens a Message Box that shows the new document's title.

Just as you used the Command Button information in the Document.WriteLn statements, you can copy information from other controls and use them (and script them) in on-the-fly Web pages. From here on, the only limit is your imagination.

Summary

Knowing the IESOM can take you a long way. With a little work, you'll be able to manipulate and extend IE in all kinds of useful ways. You can already build Web pages that build other Web pages on the fly. This capability can add zip to your creations and make them stand out from the crowd.

Are You Experienced?

Now you can...

- ☑ understand important aspects of the Microsoft Internet Explorer scripting object model

- ☑ use the scripting object model to change the look of Internet Explorer

- ☑ work with the VBS Mod operator

- ☑ use the Document.Write and Document.WriteLn methods to programatically enter information into a Web page

- ☑ create a Web page on the fly that has a heading, text, and a fully functional scripted ActiveX control

PART III

Building the Technology

Part I took you through a wide range of ActiveX controls. Part II explored the conceptual details of ActiveX technology. Now it's time to master the expanding world of ActiveX on your own. Part III will show you how to learn new controls, introduce you to Visual Basic 5 Control Creation Edition, and put you through the paces of developing new ActiveX controls. We'll finish up with a look at the future of ActiveX technology.

S K I L L

fifteen

Learning New Controls

- ❑ **A strategy for learning**
- ❑ **Scripting a card trick**
- ❑ **Dragging and dropping**
- ❑ **Getting more information**

You've already learned a lot about many ActiveX controls. All the controls you've seen, however, are just a drop in the ocean. And the ocean is getting bigger all the time. Vendors are turning out new controls at a blistering pace, so it's impossible for any book to cover all of them.

The best thing you can do is come up with a strategy for learning about new controls. Then, if you discover a potentially useful new control, you'll be able to learn about it quickly and efficiently.

A Strategy for Learning

All controls start from a common foundation. As objects in the ActiveX world, they all have events, methods, and properties. As an explorer in the ActiveX world, it's up to you to experiment with these controls and their features and ask questions about them. The questions will form the basis of your learning strategy.

Where do you start? If you understand where you've been, you'll always know where you're going. Use a new control in conjunction with controls you already know. Add it to your HTML Layout Control Toolbox, select it, and put it on a layout.

- Does it conflict with other controls?

- If the control doesn't work when you put it on the HTML Layout Control, does it work when you embed it directly into an HTML document?

- If it works in both a layout and in an HTML document, do you find any differences in behavior from one environment to the other?

As you answer these questions, you'll find differences between the control and others you've worked with. In this way, you'll learn its events, properties, and methods.

Events

Look closely at a new control's events in the Script Wizard's Event pane. Look for events that you already know and ask these questions:

- Does the control have a Click event? A Double-Click event? A Change event?

- What new events does it have that you've never seen before?

- How do these other events work? What are their arguments and what values can those arguments take?

Methods

You should also ask yourself questions about a control's methods:

- Does it have AddItem and DeleteItem methods? If so, is it similar to a ListBox or a ComboBox (or other controls with these methods)? If it indexes the items, what property gives you access to the index? Is the index zero-based?

- How many new methods does the control have?

- What are their arguments? What are the arguments' possible values?

- What effects do the methods have on the control?

Properties

Look for further clues in the control's properties:

- When you right-click on the control, does the pop-up menu present choices that you haven't seen before?

- If so, this probably indicates the control comes with Properties *pages*—an extremely valuable source of information on control-specific properties and on the values these properties can have.

- When you apply values to properties during designtime, do they visibly change the control?

Events We've Worked With

Since programming in the ActiveX world is event-driven, we'll focus our attention on events. Let's take a look at some of the events we've worked with.

We've written scripts that involve these events:

- Click (first in Skill 2 and then in most Skills thereafter)

- DblClick (Skill 2)

- MouseDown (Skill 2)

- MouseUp (Skill 2)

Skill 15

- MouseEnter (Skill 4)

- MouseExit (Skill 4)

- KeyDown (Skill 2)

- KeyPress (Skill 3)

- KeyUp (Skill 2)

- Change (first in Skill 2, more heavily in Skills 4 and 5)

Some Events We Haven't Worked With

I'll confine this group to the events that you find in many controls. This list, of course, is not exhaustive.

None of our scripts have incorporated:

- BeforeUpdate

- AfterUpdate

- Enter

- Exit

- BeforeDragOver

- BeforeDropOrPaste

- MouseMove

In the next section, you'll continue your education on frequently used events. You'll write a script that includes all of the events in the preceding list, and you'll work with a control you haven't seen before, the CardCtl Object. The script will include some useful tricks for learning about controls and events. You can use this experience with these events and controls as a foundation for learning new controls—the more events you know, the stronger your foundation for learning.

Scripting a Card Trick

As you read along in this section, note an important underlying theme—the use of multiple techniques to track events and turn the spotlight on what's happening.

The point is this: When you're learning about a new control, don't necessarily try to use it right away in a Web page. Treat your first effort as a rough draft.

Understand a new control by experimenting with its events, by using it in conjunction with other controls (some of which you might have no immediate use for), and by tracking what it does. This might take a little extra time, but in the long run you'll be a more knowledgeable and productive Web page designer.

To start this exercise, you have to do something that might be new for you. I want you to begin by wasting a little time. Of course, it will be time well-spent because something productive will come out of it (so I guess I can't call it "wasting time" after all). I'd like you to play Solitaire—not the Solitaire game that resides in your computer—but a Solitaire game on the Web. Go to this page: `http://www.microsoft.com/ie/most/howto/layout/solitaire/sol.htm` and play a round or two.

Why am I asking you to play a few games of Solitaire? First of all, it will take a few minutes to set the game up on your computer, but that's exactly the objective. In order for you to play this version of Solitaire, this Web page installs a particular ActiveX control. And we want that control—a deck of cards. It's called CardCtl Object and when you finish playing Solitaire and close IE, you'll have this control in your machine's `C:\Windows\Occache` directory (the filename is `card.ocx`).

The Object of the Trick

The objective is to produce a Web page that shows a playing card and enables a user to change the card's suit and its face value. You'll include these ActiveX controls in the page:

- a set of Option Buttons to change the card's suit
- a TextBox to enter the face value (Ace through King)
- a Label that appears when the mouse moves across the card and displays the card's face value and its suit

To change the card's face value you'll use a technique that you haven't used before—dragging and dropping. If you've worked with any recent version of Microsoft Word for Windows, you know what dragging and dropping is all about:

1. You select some text.
2. Press the left mouse button.
3. Keep the mouse button pressed.

4.   Drag the mouse to the desired location.

5.   Release the mouse button.

The result is that the text is inserted into the new location. During the process, a small indicator (a perforated box) lets you know that you're dragging the text. Dragging and dropping is a good capability to add to a Web page because so many people have grown accustomed to using it in their day-to-day activities.

To help you learn about dragging and dropping, you'll include two Labels on the page that track the arguments to the two events related to the drag-and-drop process—they're called BeforeDragOver and BeforeDropOrPaste.

Finally, you'll learn about the Enter, Exit, BeforeUpdate, and AfterUpdate events by scripting them for some of the controls.

The "trick" part of the card trick is this: You can't select a value and then drag and drop it on just any control. Like most controls, the CardCtl Object doesn't have the BeforeDragOver and BeforeDropOrPaste events. Therefore, it doesn't respond to a drag and drop. The trick, then, is to make it behave as though it does.

The Layout

In the ActiveX Control Pad, open a new file and save it as Card Trick in skill 15. We're not concerned with headings and text on this page, so leave it blank and select Edit ➤ Insert HTML Layout…. Save this layout as layout for card trick in skill 15. Open the HTML Layout Control, and start inserting controls:

1.   In the layout's Toolbox, click the Additional tab.

2.   Right-click on the Additional page and select Additional Controls… from the pop-up menu.

3.   When the list of controls appears, move through it and click the Checkbox next to CardCtl Object and click OK.

4.   You should now see a tiny icon of an Ace of Diamonds on your Toolbox page. Select this icon, and position the CardCtl Object in the upper-half of your layout, near the center.

Right-click on this control and you'll see that the pop-up menu's last choice is Card Properties. In your strategy for learning new controls, a menu choice like this is an important item. It tells you that information specific to the control is immediately available while you're designing the layout. Select Card Properties and you'll see the tabbed Properties page that appears in Figure 15.1.

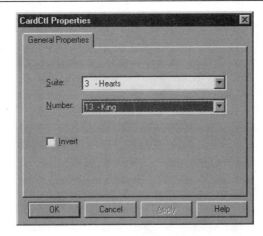

FIGURE 15.1: This tabbed Properties page gives control-specific information for the Card Control Object.

As you might imagine, the properties on this page—Suite and Number—have a lot to do with a playing card. This page is valuable because it tells you the exact values that the Suite and Number properties recognize, and it tells you what each value means. The Suite property includes positive numbers that correspond to suits:

    1 - Clubs

    2 - Spades

    3 - Hearts

    4 - Diamonds

and negative numbers that correspond to the design on the back of the cards. The Number property is a range of numbers that represent the card's face value (1=Ace, 11=Jack, 12=Queen, 13=King, and so on). To set up a starting value, select 3-Hearts from Suite and 13-King from Number and click OK.

In addition to CardCtl, we're going to use:

- a TextBox to enter the face value

- a set of Option Buttons to select the suit

- a Label that responds to the MouseMove event

Select the appropriate controls and position them as in Figure 15.2.

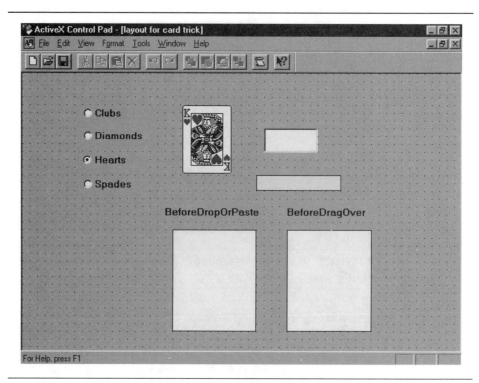

FIGURE 15.2: The layout for Card Trick

In Figure 15.2, all the rectangles are Microsoft Forms 2.0 Label controls except for the one to the immediate right of the card, which is a Microsoft Forms 2.0 TextBox control. As you can see, I've also put labels above the two large blank Labels that represent the BeforeDropOrPaste and BeforeDragOver events.

Enter these IDs for the controls. The playing card's ID is **crdTrick**. The Option Buttons are **optnbtnClubs**, **optnbtnDiamonds**, **optnbtnHearts**, and **optnbtn-Spades**. Set the GroupName property of each Option Button to **Suit**. The TextBox is **txtbxNumber** (because it holds the value that changes the Card's Number property), and the small label below it is **lblCard**. The two large labels are **lblMonitorBeforeDropOrPaste** (the one on the left) and **lblMonitorBefore-DragDrop**. The Labels that label these Labels (I can't believe I wrote that phrase!) are **lblBDP** (the one whose caption is "BeforeDropOrPaste") and **lblBDO** ("BeforeDragOver").

You can vary the properties that set the appearance of these controls any way you like. (I put solid borders around the labels, I gave lblCard a yellow background, and I tweaked the font a bit for the textbox and for the Option Button captions). It *is* absolutely necessary to set three particular properties, however:

1. Make sure all the Option Buttons have **Suit** as the value for their GroupName property.

2. For your work with the Enter and Exit events, set the TabIndex property of crdTrick to **3**.

3. Set the DragBehavior of txtbxNumber to 1-Enabled.

The Enter and Exit events are related to an object getting the focus and losing the focus. If you press the Tab key repeatedly, you move the focus from object to object on the layout. The TabIndex specifies the order in which objects receive the focus.

One more property value is not absolutely necessary, but it will add to the consistency of the layout. Because we set crdTrick to be the King of Hearts when we open the page in IE, click optnbtnHearts in the layout so that it opens in the clicked state.

Now for the trick: As I mentioned in the preceding section, CardCtl Object is one of the many ActiveX controls that doesn't have the drag-and-drop capability. One control that *does* have this capability is the Microsoft Forms 2.0 Label control. So here's the plan:

- Create a Label and carefully position it on top of the card.

- Make sure the Label is in front of the card.

- Make the Label's background transparent (this is *not* the same as making it invisible).

What do you accomplish? The user will be able to select a textbox entry, drag it over to the card, and drop it. The selection will drop onto the Label, not onto the CardCtl Object. Then you'll change the card's face depending on what you've dropped onto the Label.

Because you've made the Label control transparent, it looks like you've dragged and dropped some text onto the card and changed its value as a result.

Let's implement the plan. From the Toolbox, select another Microsoft Forms 2.0 Label control and follow these steps:

1. Drag the Label on top of crdTrick and make its size about equal to the size of the picture on the King of Hearts (if it's a bit smaller than the picture, that's OK).

2.   Open the Label control's Properties sheet and give it an ID of **lblNumber** (since this Label will hold the value of the card's Number property).

3.   Set its BackStyle property to 0-Transparent.

4.   Just to be sure lblNumber is in front of crdTrick, with the label selected choose Format ➤ Bring to Front from the menu bar.

The Script

Let's begin the script with the BeforeDragOver and BeforeDropOrPaste events. Then we'll script the MouseMove, Exit, and Enter events. We'll finish with the script for the BeforeUpdate and AfterUpdate events.

Dragging and Dropping

In the BeforeDragOver and BeforeDropOrPaste events, the word "Before" can be misleading. The name of the first event leads you to believe that something happens before you drag something. The name of the second event implies that something happens before you paste something. How *long* before? Two milliseconds? Three seconds? Nineteen years?

The problem is in the interpretation. The BeforeDragOver event really occurs *while* a drag-and-drop is taking place. "DuringDragOver" might have been a better name for this event.

The documentation on the BeforeDropOrPaste event (available from the ActiveX Control Pad by selecting Help ➤ Control Pad Topics) says this event occurs when the user is about to drop or paste data onto an object. What does "the user is about to" *really* mean? As you'll see, this event happens after you release the mouse button and before the dropped text gets picked up by the target. The documentation's Remarks section is closer to the mark. It says that "the system initiates this event prior to the drop or paste operation." I'll leave it to you to figure out a more intuitive name for "BeforeDropOrPaste."

The purpose of the two large labels (lblMonitorBeforeDropOrPaste and lblMonitorBeforeDragOver) is to help you understand the operation of these two drag-and-drop events. The idea is to get you to use Label controls this way when you have to learn something new. You wouldn't use them on a finished Web page, but for the rough draft, they're ideal.

In the Script Wizard Event pane, choose lblNumber (that's the transparent Label that sits on top of the card), click its + and select the BeforeDragOver event. Put the Wizard in Code View, and we'll start scripting.

The first line of the Script Wizard, as usual, gives you the name of this event's subroutine and the subroutine's arguments:

```
Sub lblNumber_BeforeDragOver(Cancel, Data, X, Y, DragState,
➥Effect, Shift)
```

The documentation on this event (also available in the ActiveX Control Pad by selecting Help ➤ Control Pad Topics) tells you that the first argument, `Cancel`, has two possible values, True and False. It also tells you that False means the control handles the event, and True means that the application handles the event. A little experimentation will reveal that your best bet is to set the value to True: Most controls don't support this event if Cancel's value is False. The first line of this subroutine, then, is:

```
Cancel.Value = True
```

The Effect argument can be equal to either 1, 2, or 3. It determines whether the operation *copies* the source information to the target control (1), *moves* it there (2), or is settable to one or the other (3) depending on values you provide for other arguments. We'll set this argument's value to 1:

```
Effect.Value = 1
```

We'll track the other arguments in lblMonitorBeforeDragOver. Before we do, the Data argument requires some explanation. This is the item that stores the selected text so that you can drag it across the screen and drop it on a target. It's a DataObject—something like the Clipboard, for holding cut or copied text. Because it's an object it has properties and methods. (If you didn't know this, and set something equal to "Data," you would generate an error message.) We're interested in one of those methods, GetText. We use the DataObject's GetText method to retrieve the data we selected. This is the method that allows us to set the Card's Number property.

The arguments x and y indicate the position of the cursor, and Shift indicates which Shift key was pressed when the event occurred (1=Shift, 2=Ctrl, 3=Shift+Ctrl, 4=Alt, 5=Alt+Shift, 6=Alt+Ctrl, 7=Alt+Shift+Ctrl). DragState provides the transition state of the dragged data (1=Outside Target Range, 2=Within Target Range).

The rest of the subroutine sets the caption for lblMonitorBeforeDragOver, and allows us to track this event and its arguments:

```
lblMonitorBeforeDragOver.Caption = "Cancel: " & Cancel & _
chr(13) & "Data: " & Data.GetText & _
chr(13) & "X: " & X & " Y: " & Y & _
chr(13) & "DragState: " & Dragstate & _
```

```
chr(13) & "Effect: " & Effect & _
chr(13) & "Shift: " & Shift
```

The script for the BeforeDropOrPaste event is somewhat more involved. First, you explicitly define a variable called strFace, which you'll need later in the subroutine when you set the value of the card's Number property. (Remember from Skill 10 to prefix a variable so that you know its subtype.)

```
Sub lblNumber_BeforeDropOrPaste(Cancel, Action, Data, X, Y,
➥Effect, Shift)
dim strFace
```

Before the drop takes place, the first part of the subroutine tests to see if the user has typed a valid entry:

```
If Not IsNumeric(txtbxNumber.Value) _
  And ucase(txtbxNumber.Value) <> "ACE" _
  And ucase(txtbxNumber.Value) <> "JACK" _
  And ucase(txtbxNumber.Value) <> "QUEEN" _
  And ucase(txtbxNumber.Value) <> "KING" Then
MsgBox "Please enter a number or Ace, Jack, Queen, or
➥King",,"Invalid Entry"
Exit Sub
End If
```

The If…Then statement checks whether the entry is not a numeric and not one of the admissible card names. Note the use of the ucase function. This function takes a string as its argument and returns the string transformed into all uppercase. Thus, a user can type **Ace**, **ACE**, **aCE**, or any combination of lowercase and uppercase letters that spell "Ace" for a valid entry (because you convert all the letters to uppercase before you evaluate the entry). If the entry isn't valid, an informative Message Box opens. When the user clicks the Message Box's OK button, the subroutine ends.

If the entry is valid, the subroutine continues to set values for the Cancel argument and the Effect argument. The two lines that do this are just like two of the lines in the previous subroutine, and they have the same meaning:

```
Cancel.Value = True
Effect.Value = 1
```

The entry might be a valid card name, and if it is, we have to convert it to a value that crdTrick understands. We'll do this with an If…Then…ElseIf statement and the variable strFace:

```
If ucase(Data.GetText) = "ACE" Then
strFace = "1"
```

```
ElseIf ucase(Data.GetText) = "JACK" Then
strFace = "11"
ElseIf ucase(Data.GetText) = "QUEEN" Then
strFace = "12"
ElseIf ucase(Data.GetText) = "KING" Then
strFace = "13"
Else strFace = Data.GetText
End If
```

Now you have to set the value of crdTrick's Number property:

```
crdTrick.Number = strFace
```

You finish the subroutine by setting the caption of lblMonitorBeforeDropOr-Paste so you can see what's happening with this event:

```
lblMonitorBeforeDropOrPaste.Caption = "Action: " & Action & _
chr(13) & "Data: " & Data.GetText & _
chr(13) & "X: " & X & "  Y: " & Y & _
chr(13) & "Effect: " & Effect & _
chr(13) & "Shift: " & Shift
```

Congratulate yourself! You've just scripted a very useful capability.

Before we move on, let's code two short subroutines that use Click events to clear the two labels. In the Script Wizard Event pane, select the Click event for lblMonitorBeforeDragover and in the Script pane, enter this code:

```
Sub lblMonitorBeforeDragOver_Click()
lblMonitorBeforeDragOver.Caption = " "
```

Then do the same for lblMonitorBeforeDropOrPaste:

```
Sub lblMonitorBeforeDropOrPaste_Click()
lblMonitorBeforeDropOrPaste.Caption = " "
```

MouseMove

You'll script the MouseMove event to make your Web page act like the applications that provide "balloon help." Many Windows programs do this: When you pass the cursor over a particular area, a small label—the so-called "balloon"—appears with a brief note. Usually, the note describes the area that the cursor is over. When the cursor moves out of the area, the label disappears.

NOTE   **The latest trend is to refer to balloon help as a "Tool Tip." (See Skill 16.)**

In the Event pane, click the + next to crdTrick to open its events, and select MouseMove. In the Script Wizard you'll see

```
Sub crdTrick_MouseMove(Button, Shift, x, y)
```

The first argument indicates which mouse button (if any) was pressed when the MouseMove event occurred (0=None,1=Left, 2=Right), and the second indicates which Shift key (if any) was pressed when the event occurred.

The first thing to do is explicitly define two variables. One variable will store the value of crdTrick's Number property and possibly convert it from a number to a name like "Jack." The other will convert the value of its Suite property (a number) to the name of a Suit (like "Hearts.") You'll need these for the balloon help. Since they're both going to be strings, let's call the first one strFaceValue (to distinguish it from strFace, which you used earlier) and the second one strSuit. The definition statements, then, are:

```
dim strFaceValue
dim strSuit
```

Next, you'll set up a condition based on the area of the card. If the mouse is in the area, the Label will be visible, and if it's not, the Label will be invisible. Since you're scripting this event for crdTrick, the area is defined in terms of that control (not in terms of the whole layout). In other words, for this subroutine, x is 0 and y is 0 at the upper-left corner of the area that holds the card. Notice that I said "area that holds the card." The card sits inside a slightly larger rectangular area, as you might recall from the layout. Some experimentation will give you useful x and y values for this subroutine. Here are the ones I used (yours might differ a bit, depending on how you sized the card's area in your layout):

```
If (x > 3 and x < 70) and (y > 1 and y < 104) Then
lblCard.Visible = True
Else
lblCard.Visible = False
End If
```

The control called lblCard is the little Label below the TextBox.

Now you have to convert the value of the card's Number property to a name (if necessary) and the value of its Suite property to the name of a suit. Two Select Case statements get this done:

```
Select Case crdTrick.Number
        Case "1"
                strFaceValue = "ACE"
        Case "11"
                strFaceValue = "JACK"
```

```
        Case "12"
                strFaceValue = "QUEEN"
        Case "13"
                strFaceValue = "KING"
        Case Else
                strFaceValue = crdTrick.Number
    End Select

    Select Case crdTrick.Suite
        Case "1"
                strSuit = "Clubs"
        Case "2"
                strSuit = "Spades"
        Case "3"
                strSuit = "Hearts"
        Case "4"
                strSuit = "Diamonds"
    End Select
```

Note the use of Case Else in the first Select Case.

Now you'll set the value for the lblCard's Caption:

```
lblCard.Caption = strFaceValue & " of " & strSuit
```

NOTE   When you open the Web page, you may find the MouseMove event a bit erratic. I've found that if I move the mouse too quickly, the x and y values sometimes don't register and the Label remains visible when the cursor is outside the card. This happens because the MouseMove event does not fire continuously as the mouse moves.

Enter and Exit

In an object's Enter and Exit events, it's the focus that does the entering and the exiting. You can change the focus by pressing the Tab key or clicking on a control. The TabIndex property determines which object gets the focus for each press of the Tab key.

You'll produce simple scripts for the CardCtl control's Enter and Exit events. The scripts will open Message Boxes that let you know what's happened.

Select crdTrick's Enter event in the Event pane and produce this in the Script pane:

```
Sub crdTrick_Enter()
MsgBox "The card just got the focus",,"Enter Event"
```

Select crdTrick's Exit event and code this in the Script pane:

```
Sub crdTrick_Exit(Cancel)
MsgBox "The card just lost the focus",, "Exit Event"
```

BeforeUpdate and AfterUpdate

The BeforeUpdate event occurs "before the data in a control is changed," and the AfterUpdate event occurs "after the data is changed through the user interface." The quotation marks indicate that I've taken those statements from the ActiveX Control Pad documentation on these events. Once again, we're faced with a troublesome "Before." What does it *really* mean?

Unless you go to the trouble of writing a script and watching it in action, you might not know. The meaning is this: When you change the value of a control, like clicking an Option Button, the BeforeUpdate event fires before the value changes. The AfterUpdate event fires after the change happens.

We'll script these events on one of the Option Buttons. In the Event pane, choose optnbtnClubs and its BeforeUpdate event. In the Script pane, produce this code:

```
Sub optbtnClubs_BeforeUpdate(Cancel)
MsgBox "Before Update Event!",,"Before Update"
```

Do the similar scripting for the AfterUpdate event:

```
Sub optbtnClubs_AfterUpdate()
MsgBox "After Update Event!",,"After Update"
```

The Option Buttons

Scripting the Option Buttons to change the card's suit is straightforward. Here are the scripts as they should appear in the Script Wizard:

```
Sub optbtnClubs_Click()
crdTrick.Suite = "1"

Sub optbtnDiamonds_Click()
crdTrick.Suite = "4"

Sub optnbtnHearts_Click()
crdTrick.Suite = "3"

Sub optnbtnSpades_Click()
crdTrick.Suite = "2"
```

The Whole Enchilada

In order for you to check your work, here's the listing (layout for card trick.alx).

 layout for card trick.alx

```vbscript
<SCRIPT LANGUAGE="VBScript">
<!--
Sub lblNumber_BeforeDropOrPaste(Cancel, Action, Data, X, Y, Effect, Shift)
dim strFace

If Not IsNumeric(txtbxNumber.Value) _
  And ucase(txtbxNumber.Value) <> "ACE" _
  And ucase(txtbxNumber.Value) <> "JACK" _
  And ucase(txtbxNumber.Value) <> "QUEEN" _
  And ucase(txtbxNumber.Value) <> "KING" Then
MsgBox "Please enter a number or Ace, Jack, Queen, or King",,"Invalid Entry"
Exit Sub
End If
Cancel.Value = True
Effect.Value = 1

If ucase(Data.GetText) = "ACE" Then
strFace = "1"
ElseIf ucase(Data.GetText) = "JACK" Then
strFace = "11"
ElseIf ucase(Data.GetText) = "QUEEN" Then
strFace = "12"
ElseIf ucase(Data.GetText) = "KING" Then
strFace = "13"
Else strFace = Data.GetText
End If

crdTrick.Number = strFace

lblMonitorBeforeDropOrPaste.Caption = "Action: " & Action & _
chr(13) & "Data: " & Data.GetText & _
chr(13) & "X: " & X & "  Y: " & Y & _
chr(13) & "Effect: " & Effect & _
chr(13) & "Shift: " & Shift
end sub

Sub lblNumber_BeforeDragOver(Cancel, Data, X, Y, DragState, Effect, Shift)
Cancel.Value = true
Effect.Value = 1
lblMonitorBeforeDragOver.Caption = "Cancel: " & Cancel & _
chr(13) & "Data: " & Data.GetText & _
```

```
chr(13) & "X: " & X & " Y: " & Y & _
chr(13) & "DragState: " & Dragstate & _
chr(13) & "Effect: " & Effect & _
chr(13) & "Shift: " & Shift
end sub
-->
</SCRIPT>
<SCRIPT LANGUAGE="VBScript">
<!--
Sub optnbtnSpades_Click()
crdTrick.Suite = "2"
end sub
-->
</SCRIPT>
<SCRIPT LANGUAGE="VBScript">
<!--
Sub optnbtnHearts_Click()
crdTrick.Suite = "3"
end sub
-->
</SCRIPT>
<SCRIPT LANGUAGE="VBScript">
<!--
Sub optbtnDiamonds_Click()
crdTrick.Suite = "4"
end sub
-->
</SCRIPT>
<SCRIPT LANGUAGE="VBScript">
<!--
Sub optbtnClubs_BeforeUpdate(Cancel)
MsgBox "Before Update Event!",,"Before Update"
end sub
Sub optbtnClubs_AfterUpdate()
MsgBox "After Update Event!",,"After Update"
end sub
Sub optbtnClubs_Click()
crdTrick.Suite = "1"
end sub
-->
</SCRIPT>
<SCRIPT LANGUAGE="VBScript">
<!--
Sub lblMonitorBeforeDragOver_Click()
lblMonitorBeforeDragOver.Caption = " "
end sub
-->
</SCRIPT>
```

```
<SCRIPT LANGUAGE="VBScript">
<!--
Sub lblMonitorBeforeDropOrPaste_Click()
lblMonitorBeforeDropOrPaste.Caption = " "
end sub
-->
</SCRIPT>
Sub crdTrick_Exit(Cancel)
MsgBox "Lost the Focus"
end sub
Sub crdTrick_Enter()
MsgBox "Card has the focus!"
end sub
-->
</SCRIPT>
<SCRIPT LANGUAGE="VBScript">
<!--
Sub crdTrick_Enter()
MsgBox "The card just got the focus",,"Enter Event"
end sub
Sub crdTrick_Exit(Cancel)
MsgBox "The card just lost the focus",, "Exit Event"
end sub
Sub crdTrick_MouseMove(Button, Shift, x, y)
dim strFaceValue
dim strSuitIf (x > 3 and x < 70) and (y > 1 and y < 104) Then
lblCard.Visible = True
Else
lblCard.Visible = False
End If

Select Case crdTrick.Number

    Case "1"
        strFaceValue = "ACE"
    Case "11"
        strFaceValue = "JACK"
    Case "12"
        strFaceValue = "QUEEN"
    Case "13"
        strFaceValue = "KING"
    Case Else
        strFaceValue = crdTrick.Number
End Select

Select Case crdTrick.Suite

    Case "1"
        strSuit = "Clubs"
```

Skill 15

```
      Case "2"
          strSuit = "Spades"
      Case "3"
          strSuit = "Hearts"
      Case "4"
          strSuit = "Diamonds"
End Select

lblCard.Caption = strFaceValue & " of " & strSuit
end sub
-->
</SCRIPT>
<DIV ID="layoutforcardtrick" STYLE="LAYOUT:FIXED;WIDTH:477pt;HEIGHT:293pt;">
    <OBJECT ID="crdTrick"
     CLASSID="CLSID:5A73F48A-B702-11CF-8498-00AA00BBF311"
     ➥STYLE="TOP:25pt;LEFT:173pt;WIDTH:58pt;HEIGHT:91pt;TABINDEX:3;ZINDEX:0;">
        <PARAM NAME="_ExtentX" VALUE="2037">
        <PARAM NAME="_ExtentY" VALUE="3201">
        <PARAM NAME="Number" VALUE="13">
        <PARAM NAME="Suite" VALUE="3">
    </OBJECT>
    <OBJECT ID="lblNumber"
     CLASSID="CLSID:978C9E23-D4B0-11CE-BF2D-00AA003F40D0"
     ➥STYLE="TOP:50pt;LEFT:190pt;WIDTH:25pt;HEIGHT:41pt;ZINDEX:1;">
        <PARAM NAME="ForeColor" VALUE="16777215">
        <PARAM NAME="BackColor" VALUE="16777215">
        <PARAM NAME="VariousPropertyBits" VALUE="8388627">
        <PARAM NAME="Size" VALUE="882;1446">
        <PARAM NAME="FontHeight" VALUE="0">
        <PARAM NAME="FontCharSet" VALUE="0">
        <PARAM NAME="FontPitchAndFamily" VALUE="2">
        <PARAM NAME="ParagraphAlign" VALUE="3">
    </OBJECT>
    <OBJECT ID="optbtnClubs"
     CLASSID="CLSID:8BD21D50-EC42-11CE-9E0D-00AA006002F3"
     ➥STYLE="TOP:34pt;LEFT:66pt;WIDTH:77pt;HEIGHT:17pt;TABINDEX:0;ZINDEX:2;">
        <PARAM NAME="BackColor" VALUE="2147483663">
        <PARAM NAME="ForeColor" VALUE="2147483666">
        <PARAM NAME="DisplayStyle" VALUE="5">
        <PARAM NAME="Size" VALUE="2716;600">
        <PARAM NAME="Value" VALUE="0">
        <PARAM NAME="Caption" VALUE="Clubs">
        <PARAM NAME="GroupName" VALUE="Suit">
        <PARAM NAME="FontEffects" VALUE="1073741825">
        <PARAM NAME="FontHeight" VALUE="200">
        <PARAM NAME="FontCharSet" VALUE="0">
        <PARAM NAME="FontPitchAndFamily" VALUE="2">
        <PARAM NAME="FontWeight" VALUE="700">
```

```
</OBJECT>
<OBJECT ID="optbtnDiamonds"
 CLASSID="CLSID:8BD21D50-EC42-11CE-9E0D-00AA006002F3"
➡STYLE="TOP:58pt;LEFT:66pt;WIDTH:77pt;HEIGHT:17pt;TABINDEX:2;ZINDEX:3;">
    <PARAM NAME="BackColor" VALUE="2147483663">
    <PARAM NAME="ForeColor" VALUE="2147483666">
    <PARAM NAME="DisplayStyle" VALUE="5">
    <PARAM NAME="Size" VALUE="2716;600">
    <PARAM NAME="Value" VALUE="0">
    <PARAM NAME="Caption" VALUE="Diamonds">
    <PARAM NAME="GroupName" VALUE="Suit">
    <PARAM NAME="FontEffects" VALUE="1073741825">
    <PARAM NAME="FontHeight" VALUE="200">
    <PARAM NAME="FontCharSet" VALUE="0">
    <PARAM NAME="FontPitchAndFamily" VALUE="2">
    <PARAM NAME="FontWeight" VALUE="700">
</OBJECT>
<OBJECT ID="optnbtnHearts"
 CLASSID="CLSID:8BD21D50-EC42-11CE-9E0D-00AA006002F3"
➡STYLE="TOP:83pt;LEFT:66pt;WIDTH:70pt;HEIGHT:17pt;TABINDEX:4;ZINDEX:4;">
    <PARAM NAME="BackColor" VALUE="2147483663">
    <PARAM NAME="ForeColor" VALUE="2147483666">
    <PARAM NAME="DisplayStyle" VALUE="5">
    <PARAM NAME="Size" VALUE="2469;600">
    <PARAM NAME="Value" VALUE="1">
    <PARAM NAME="Caption" VALUE="Hearts">
    <PARAM NAME="GroupName" VALUE="Suit">
    <PARAM NAME="FontEffects" VALUE="1073741825">
    <PARAM NAME="FontHeight" VALUE="200">
    <PARAM NAME="FontCharSet" VALUE="0">
    <PARAM NAME="FontPitchAndFamily" VALUE="2">
    <PARAM NAME="FontWeight" VALUE="700">
</OBJECT>
<OBJECT ID="optnbtnSpades"
 CLASSID="CLSID:8BD21D50-EC42-11CE-9E0D-00AA006002F3"
 STYLE="TOP:109pt;LEFT:66pt;WIDTH:70pt;HEIGHT:17pt;TABINDEX:5;ZINDEX:5;">
    <PARAM NAME="BackColor" VALUE="2147483663">
    <PARAM NAME="ForeColor" VALUE="2147483666">
    <PARAM NAME="DisplayStyle" VALUE="5">
    <PARAM NAME="Size" VALUE="2469;600">
    <PARAM NAME="Value" VALUE="0">
    <PARAM NAME="Caption" VALUE="Spades">
    <PARAM NAME="GroupName" VALUE="Suit">
    <PARAM NAME="FontEffects" VALUE="1073741825">
    <PARAM NAME="FontHeight" VALUE="200">
    <PARAM NAME="FontCharSet" VALUE="0">
    <PARAM NAME="FontPitchAndFamily" VALUE="2">
    <PARAM NAME="FontWeight" VALUE="700">
```

```
</OBJECT>
<OBJECT ID="txtbxNumber"
 CLASSID="CLSID:8BD21D10-EC42-11CE-9E0D-00AA006002F3"
 ➥STYLE="TOP:58pt;LEFT:264pt;WIDTH:58pt;HEIGHT:25pt;TABINDEX:6;ZINDEX:6;">
    <PARAM NAME="VariousPropertyBits" VALUE="747128859">
    <PARAM NAME="Size" VALUE="2046;882">
    <PARAM NAME="FontEffects" VALUE="1073741825">
    <PARAM NAME="FontHeight" VALUE="200">
    <PARAM NAME="FontCharSet" VALUE="0">
    <PARAM NAME="FontPitchAndFamily" VALUE="2">
    <PARAM NAME="FontWeight" VALUE="700">
</OBJECT>
<OBJECT ID="lblMonitorBeforeDragOver"
 CLASSID="CLSID:978C9E23-D4B0-11CE-BF2D-00AA003F40D0"
 ➥STYLE="TOP:165pt;LEFT:289pt;WIDTH:91pt;HEIGHT:107pt;ZINDEX:7;">
    <PARAM NAME="BackColor" VALUE="16777215">
    <PARAM NAME="Size" VALUE="3210;3775">
    <PARAM NAME="BorderStyle" VALUE="1">
    <PARAM NAME="FontHeight" VALUE="200">
    <PARAM NAME="FontCharSet" VALUE="0">
    <PARAM NAME="FontPitchAndFamily" VALUE="2">
    <PARAM NAME="FontWeight" VALUE="0">
</OBJECT>
<OBJECT ID="lblBDO"
 CLASSID="CLSID:978C9E23-D4B0-11CE-BF2D-00AA003F40D0"
 ➥STYLE="TOP:140pt;LEFT:289pt;WIDTH:91pt;HEIGHT:17pt;ZINDEX:8;">
    <PARAM NAME="Caption" VALUE="BeforeDragOver">
    <PARAM NAME="Size" VALUE="3210;600">
    <PARAM NAME="FontEffects" VALUE="1073741825">
    <PARAM NAME="FontHeight" VALUE="200">
    <PARAM NAME="FontCharSet" VALUE="0">
    <PARAM NAME="FontPitchAndFamily" VALUE="2">
    <PARAM NAME="FontWeight" VALUE="700">
</OBJECT>
<OBJECT ID="lblBDP"
 CLASSID="CLSID:978C9E23-D4B0-11CE-BF2D-00AA003F40D0"
 ➥STYLE="TOP:140pt;LEFT:157pt;WIDTH:107pt;HEIGHT:17pt;ZINDEX:9;">
    <PARAM NAME="Caption" VALUE="BeforeDropOrPaste">
    <PARAM NAME="Size" VALUE="3775;600">
    <PARAM NAME="FontEffects" VALUE="1073741825">
    <PARAM NAME="FontHeight" VALUE="200">
    <PARAM NAME="FontCharSet" VALUE="0">
    <PARAM NAME="FontPitchAndFamily" VALUE="2">
    <PARAM NAME="FontWeight" VALUE="700">
</OBJECT>
<OBJECT ID="lblMonitorBeforeDropOrPaste"
 CLASSID="CLSID:978C9E23-D4B0-11CE-BF2D-00AA003F40D0"
 ➥STYLE="TOP:165pt;LEFT:165pt;WIDTH:91pt;HEIGHT:107pt;ZINDEX:10;">
```

```
        <PARAM NAME="BackColor" VALUE="16777215">
        <PARAM NAME="Size" VALUE="3210;3775">
        <PARAM NAME="BorderColor" VALUE="0">
        <PARAM NAME="BorderStyle" VALUE="1">
        <PARAM NAME="FontHeight" VALUE="200">
        <PARAM NAME="FontCharSet" VALUE="0">
        <PARAM NAME="FontPitchAndFamily" VALUE="2">
        <PARAM NAME="FontWeight" VALUE="0">
    </OBJECT>
    <OBJECT ID="lblCard"
     CLASSID="CLSID:978C9E23-D4B0-11CE-BF2D-00AA003F40D0" STYLE
    ➡="TOP:107pt;LEFT:256pt;WIDTH:91pt;HEIGHT:17pt;DISPLAY:NONE;ZINDEX:11;">
        <PARAM NAME="BackColor" VALUE="8454143">
        <PARAM NAME="Size" VALUE="3210;600">
        <PARAM NAME="BorderColor" VALUE="4194368">
        <PARAM NAME="BorderStyle" VALUE="1">
        <PARAM NAME="FontCharSet" VALUE="0">
        <PARAM NAME="FontPitchAndFamily" VALUE="2">
        <PARAM NAME="ParagraphAlign" VALUE="3">
        <PARAM NAME="FontWeight" VALUE="0">
    </OBJECT>
</DIV>
```

KEEP YOUR EYES OPEN

As you write your own scripts, beware of weird behavior on the part of the Script Editor—particularly when you use the HTML Layout Control.

Here's one example: If your script causes a compilation error when you open a page in IE, you might find that the erroneous subroutine isn't there when you reopen the Script Wizard to correct it. After you retype your script, double-check to make sure you've fixed the error, and reopen the page in IE, you might get the same error message! Why? Because that erroneous original code didn't really vanish. It might still be lurking in the HTML document.

In a case like that, select View Source Code, find the erroneous code, and delete it.

Examining the Web Page

Save your work and open Card Trick.htm in IE. Figure 15.3 shows what the Web page looks like after you type **jACk** and drag and drop it on the card.

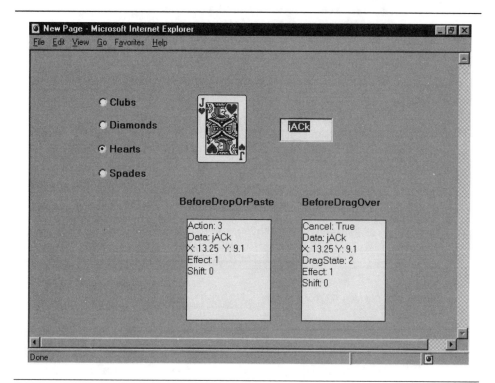

FIGURE 15.3: The card trick in IE

Try entering different values in the TextBox, dragging them to the card, and dropping them. Take note of the large Labels and what they tell you about the drag-and-drop events.

Note how the Card control handles decimal numbers, negative numbers, and numbers greater than 13. Press Tab repeatedly and watch what happens with the Message Boxes regarding the focus on the Card control. Select the Clubs Option button and see the behavior of BeforeUpdate and AfterUpdate by watching the Message Boxes. Move the mouse cursor through the card and watch the effect on the small label.

Above all, use the Labels and the Message Boxes to help you understand the events you scripted in this Skill.

Summarizing the Learning Techniques

Take note of what you've done in the card trick exercise. You've used Labels and Message Boxes to shed light on what happens during various events. The scripts that use them are usually pretty simple. All they do is print the names of arguments and their values, but sometimes that's all you need. This is a valuable technique for your learning strategy, and you should never hesitate to use it to learn about the events in new controls.

 **WARNING**   Be careful with Message Boxes. To monitor an event like BeforeDragOver, a Message Box is not a good idea. Why? BeforeDragOver occurs while an operation is in progress, and a Message Box stops an application and waits for a response. If you combine the two, the application stops, the process stops, and nothing gets going again, even after you click OK in the Message Box. In other words, your system freezes up.

Another useful technique is to script a Command Button's Click event or some other control's Change event to manipulate a control's property. This way you'll get to see the control in action on a running Web page.

Sometimes no amount of Labels and Message Boxes will get the job done, and you have to seek out documentation. Properties pages are a valuable source of information, but sometimes you just have to find documentation because some controls are complex and their arguments are nonintuitive. Newer controls from Microsoft tend to come with documentation, and reading it is often the only way to determine possible values of some of the arguments. The Microsoft Interactive Music control that you learned about in Skill 8, for example, is so rich with possibilities that reading documentation is an absolute must.

Acquiring New Controls and Information

The Web has a number of great sites for discovering new ActiveX controls, acquiring working samples, and gathering information.

The champion Web site for this is, of course, the Microsoft ActiveX Component Gallery, which I've mentioned a number of times. You can find it at `http://www.microsoft.com/activex/controls`. This site typically lists around 100 ActiveX controls from Microsoft and other vendors. You can see and download working demos of these controls. The Microsoft controls include instructive code samples.

Other Microsoft Web sites provide ActiveX-related information. Microsoft maintains a list of frequently asked questions on using ActiveX controls to develop Web sites. You can find this list at `http://www.microsoft.com/intdev/controls/ctrlfaq-f.htm`. If you don't feel like sifting through the questions online, you can download a zipped Word document of the questions and answers.

For introductory overview papers on ActiveX, have a look at `http://www.microsoft.com/activeplatform/actx-gen/actxovw.asp`.

A wide variety of information on the ActiveX Control Pad is at `http://www.microsoft.com/workshop/author/cpad/`, including frequently asked questions and the latest downloadable version of the Control Pad.

If you're looking for information on the HTML Layout Control, visit `http://www.microsoft.com/workshop/author/layout`. This site will point you to a white paper, sample pages, authoring tips, and more.

Microsoft isn't the only organization that devotes Web sites to ActiveX. For example, a grab bag of ActiveX delights awaits you at the ActiveXpress Control Room (`http://192.215.107.72/activexpress/control/control.html`). This site has a database on ActiveX controls in categories ranging from charts, games, and multimedia to document viewers, mapping, and developer tools. Up-to-date news and useful information round out this lively and engaging site.

Along these same lines, ActiveX.Com (`http://www.activex.com`) provides news, information, and a library of ActiveX controls that you can download and experiment with.

All these Web sites should get you started with new ActiveX controls and information, and they'll keep you busy for a long time.

Summary

The world of ActiveX is growing by leaps and bounds, and the end is nowhere in sight. We can't cover every ActiveX control in this book, but with some strategic thinking, questioning, and experimentation, it's easy to learn to work with new controls. Apply a few techniques, including using Label controls and Message Boxes, and you'll find that you can master a new control in a short time. A number of Web sites give you access to working demos of new controls that you can experiment with and keep you up-to-date on news in the ActiveX community.

Are You Experienced?

Now you can...

☑ develop and use a strategy for learning new ActiveX controls

☑ use Label controls and Message Box controls to track events and their arguments

☑ use the drag-and-drop technique in your Web pages

☑ Drag and drop onto controls that don't have this built-in capability

☑ have a stronger base for working with new controls because you understand the MouseMove, Exit, Enter, BeforeUpdate, and AfterUpdate events, in addition to the events you worked with in previous Skills

☑ access a variety of Web sites to download ActiveX controls, as well as find news and information on ActiveX

Introducing Visual Basic 5 Control Creation Edition

❏ Creating your own controls by combining existing ones

❏ Writing VB code for your controls

❏ Testing your controls

❏ The Visual Basic 5 Control Creation Edition Environment

Y ou've worked with a variety of ActiveX controls, you've dissected the technology, and you've discovered how you can learn about new controls. Now you're ready to move ahead.

One way to do this is to start contributing to the technology on your own by creating new ActiveX controls. Control creation used to be the province of high-powered C++ programmers, but Microsoft has expanded the playing field to include anyone interested in learning an easy-to-use version of Visual Basic.

With the Microsoft Visual Basic 5 Control Creation Edition (we'll call it VB5 CCE), you can create your own controls in several different ways:

- You can combine existing controls to produce a new one. (We'll focus on this method, which is called *aggregating* multiple controls into a *control assembly*.)

- You can customize a control to produce a new one (called *subclassing*).

- You can create a control from scratch.

To create controls, you use Visual Basic concepts that will probably be familiar to you from using VBS. Bear in mind that Visual Basic is a superset of VBS and contains features and concepts that you probably haven't seen yet. But most of the principles are the same, and VB5 CCE comes with some helpful tools that VBS doesn't have.

The VB5 CCE, while a fully functional package, is a specially tailored version of the commercially available Visual Basic 5. (If you've purchased Visual Basic 5, you already have VB5 CCE.) Although you can use VB5 CCE to create ActiveX controls, you can't use it to create standalone applications, as you can with Visual Basic 5. One of the best things about the VB5 CCE is its price: It's free. You'll need it to do the exercises in this Skill, so download it from `http://www.microsoft.com/vbasic/controls`.

 NOTE   With all the "VB"s around, you might be wondering what's what. VBS, the scripting language we've been using, is designed for applications that live in the HTML environment. VBA, Visual Basic for Applications, is designed for applications that live in the Office 97 environment. Visual Basic 5, the most advanced member of the family, is designed for building applications that stand alone. The Control Creation Edition of Visual Basic 5 (VB5 CCE) is strictly for designing and testing ActiveX controls.

In this Skill, you'll build and test two simple controls just to get the feel of how VB5 CCE works. Then, you'll explore the VB5 CCE environment. In the next Skill, you'll take one of these controls and set it up to work on a Web page. As you go along, you'll build on familiar concepts.

NOTE   As you go through VB5 CCE, you'll see the term "Tool Tip." It's that little label that appears when you hover your mouse over a particular area. In other contexts (and elsewhere in this book), it's called "Balloon Help." When we talk about the VB5 CCE environment, we'll use "Tool Tip" to refer to this feature.

Creating Your First Control

The controls you'll build in this Skill will get you acquainted with VB5 CCE very quickly.

The first control consists of components you've seen before and builds on an example from Skill 10—converting a number in a TextBox into either a Fahrenheit or a Centigrade temperature. We'll combine a TextBox, a Label, a Command Button, and two Option Buttons to create a single ActiveX control that performs the temperature conversion.

NOTE   I'll assume that you've downloaded VB5 CCE from `http://www.microsoft.com/vbasic/controls` and installed it on your machine. You can also download VB5 CCE Help files from this site as well as other useful documentation.

You can start VB5 CCE in any of several ways:

- One way is to select Windows 95 Start ➢ Programs ➢ Visual Basic 5.0 CCE ➢ Visual Basic 5.0 CCE.

- Another is to double-click on the VB5 CCE icon in the program group that the installation routine created.

- Still another way is to go to that icon and use it to create a shortcut icon for the desktop. Then you just double-click on the shortcut icon, and VB5 CCE springs into action.

Whichever way you decide to start VB5 CCE, an introductory screen identifies the application and then disappears. Figure 16.1 shows the New Project window that takes its place.

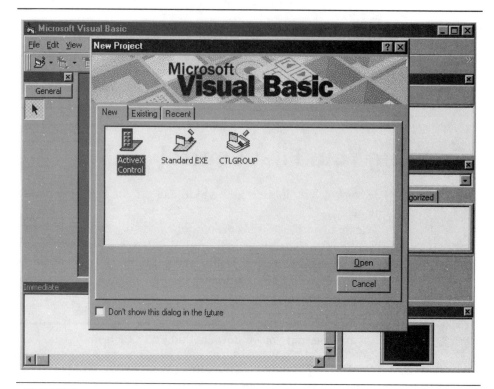

FIGURE 16.1: VB5 CCE's New Project dialog box

 NOTE   As Figure 16.1 shows, the New Project window presents an icon labeled "Standard EXE." Remember, however, that you cannot create standalone executables with the VB5 CCE. We do use this icon, as you'll see.

The first priority is to create a place to test the new ActiveX control that you'll create. This is somewhat analogous to creating an HTML file that contains ActiveX controls. In the VB5 CCE world, we create a *form* that serves as a *container* for

ActiveX controls. After you create a control, you put it in this container form so you can test it.

We also lay out a drawing board for creating our control. If the container is analogous to an HTML file, then the drawing board is analogous to the HTML Layout Control. In Visual Basic terminology, both the container and the drawing board are *projects*.

Creating the Container

To create the container form for our control, select Standard EXE and click the Open button. You'll see the display in Figure 16.2.

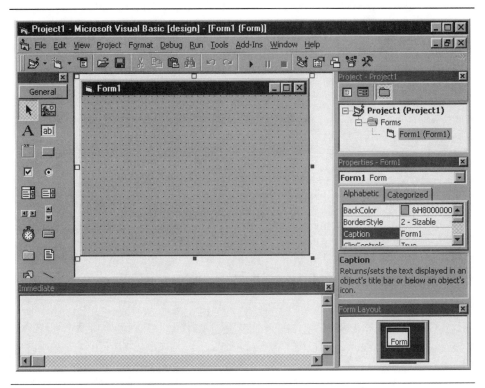

FIGURE 16.2: The display that appears when you select Standard EXE and click the Open button

NOTE   Depending on the size and resolution of your screen, your display might look slightly different.

If you haven't worked with Visual Basic before, you probably feel as if you've landed in a new world. In a way, you have. You'll examine all the parts of this display later in this Skill (see "The VB5 CCE Environment"), but for the moment you'll work with just a few.

The Form1 window holds the form which is our container. Now that you have our container, you'll follow these steps:

1. Set up the drawing board for putting the control assembly together.

2. Lay out the controls.

3. Add code to appropriate controls in the control assembly.

4. Close the drawing board that contains the control assembly.

5. Insert an instance of the assembly into the form in the Form1 window.

6. Test the instance of the assembly by running the code.

Setting Up the Drawing Board and Laying Out the Controls

The drawing board you'll set up is analogous to the HTML Layout Control because you can use it to insert multiple controls, move them around, and write code that determines each control's behavior. (In fact, the HTML Layout Control is an attempt to bring this two-dimensional style of development to the Web page design arena.)

To get a project started, select File ➢ Add Project…. Figure 16.3 shows the resulting Add Project dialog box.

Select ActiveX Control and, click the Open button. The User Control form appears. Select Window ➢ Cascade and your screen should look like Figure 16.4. To give yourself some room, you can also close the Immediate window (along the bottom of the screen) and the Form Layout window (in the lower-right corner).

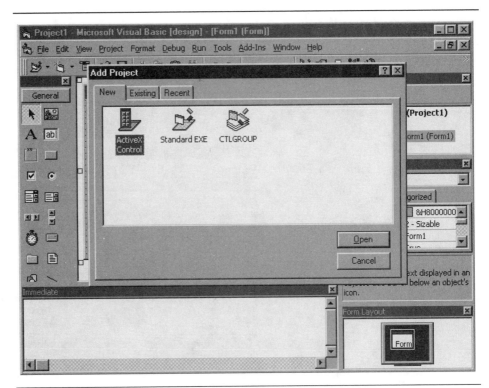

FIGURE 16.3: The display that results when you select File ≻ Add Project

Two windows in this display should look somewhat familiar. The long one on the left looks a lot like the Toolbox in the HTML Layout Control, and the lower window on the right resembles a Properties sheet in the ActiveX Control Pad Object Editor or in the HTML Layout Control. Let's take a closer look at each one.

Called the Properties window, the window on the right serves the same purpose as the Properties sheets you've worked with before. As you proceed, you'll see some differences between Properties windows and Properties sheets. For now, you'll use the Properties window to change the name of your control. In the first row of the Properties window, double-click the box to the right of the highlighted (Name) box, and type **TempControl**.

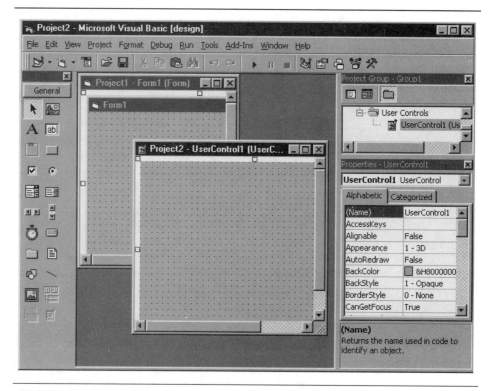

FIGURE 16.4: Selecting Window ➤ Cascade and closing some windows gives you this display.

The window on the left side, the Toolbox, holds a set of standard ActiveX controls, and just as in the HTML Layout Control's Toolbox, you can insert additional controls. You may notice a small and grayed out icon in the lower-right corner of the Toolbox. It represents the control we're about to build. When you're finished building your control, you'll be able to easily see this icon.

You're going to select controls from the Toolbox and lay them out on the gray grid in the newly named TempControl window (the window which also has "Project2" in its title bar). Remember that your custom ActiveX control assembly will consist of a TextBox, a Label, two Option Buttons, and a Command Button. Select these tools and lay them out as in Figure 16.5.

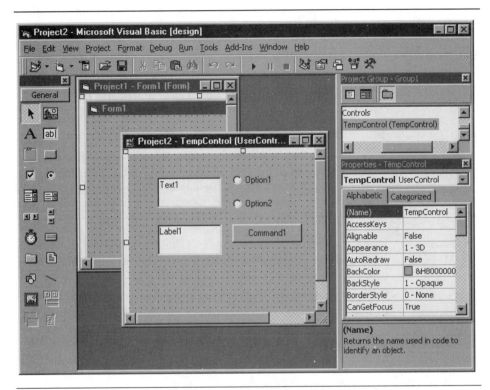

FIGURE 16.5: The layout of the controls for our TempControl assembly

I've left the original identifiers and captions in the controls so you can see where to position each one. Now you'll use the Properties window to change those identifiers. In the VBS world, we referred to these identifiers as IDs. In VB5 CCE, they're called *Names*. (We've already changed one Name property to TempControl.)

First, change the TextBox's name to txtbxInput. To do this, click on the TextBox control, and you should see its properties appear in the Properties window. Double-click on the Name property of the Properties window, type **txtbxInput**, and hit Enter. In the same way, change the Label's Name to **lblTemp**, the Command Button's Name to **cmdbtnTemp**, the first Option Button's Name to **optnbtnCtoF**, and the second Option Button's Name to **optnbtnFtoC**.

Change the appearance of the Label. Select the Label control and set its Back-Color property to white. You can do this on one of two tabbed pages that appear when you click the down-arrow in this property's row. Set the BorderStyle property to 1-Fixed Single.

Now let's make both the TextBox and the Label blank. Select the TextBox, and its Properties window, select the Text property and delete the current value, Text1. Select the Label, and in its Properties window select the Caption property and delete the current value, Label1.

 NOTE   In the ActiveX Control Pad, you can change a control's caption by double-clicking on that control and typing the caption. You can't do this in VB5 CCE. (In VB5 CCE, double-clicking on a control opens a window for writing VB code.)

Now you'll change the captions on the Option Buttons and the Command Button. In the Properties window for the first Option Button (optnbtnCtoF), set the Caption property to **C to F** and set the Font property to Bold. Do the same thing for the second Option Button (optnbtnFtoC), but enter **F to C**. Change the Command Button's caption to **Temperature** and set its Font property to Bold, as well.

Finish up by resizing the TempControl form to minimize wasted space and to minimize the control's size.

Coding the Control Assembly

Now you'll write the code for the controls in the assembly. After the user enters a number in txtbxInput and selects either optnbtnCtoF or optnbtnFtoC, clicking the Command Button should cause the appropriate calculation to take place. Thus, you have to code a subroutine for the Command Button's Click event. In this subroutine, you'll have to:

- Make sure a numeric value is in txtbxInput (and if not, display a Message Box, and exit the subroutine)

- Check to see which Option Button is selected

- Perform either a Centigrade to Fahrenheit conversion (if optnbtnCtoF is selected) or a Fahrenheit to Centigrade conversion (if optnbtnFtoC is selected)

VB5 CCE makes it easy to insert code for a control. Double-click on the control, and the Code window appears. It's ready for you to add code for one of that control's events. If the event it opens to is not be the event you want to code, select the event procedure you want from the Procedure combobox on the right and just below the Code window's title bar. The Object combobox on the left contains all the objects in your aggregate control. By selecting from each combobox, you can start the code for any object and any event in your project.

Most of the time the event you want is the one the Code window opens up to. For example, when you double-click on the Command Button, you'll see the Code window open to the control's Click event procedure as shown in Figure 16.6. (You may have to enlarge the window somewhat to get it to look like the one in the figure.)

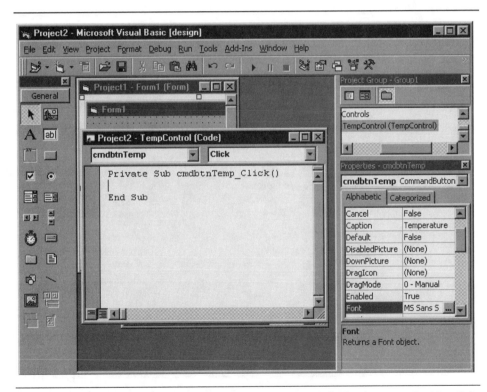

FIGURE 16.6: The Code window that opens by default when you double-click on a Command Button control

As you can see, the window is ready for you to enter code for the Click event. Start by typing these lines:

If Not IsNumeric(txtbxInput.Text) Then

MsgBox "Enter a Number", vbCritical, "Invalid Entry"

Exit Sub

End If

This code checks to see if a numerical value has been entered in the TextBox control. As you type, you'll notice some of VB5 CCE's helping hands start to appear. Figure 16.7 shows what happens when you're typing IsNumeric and you've gotten to txtbxInput followed by the dot.

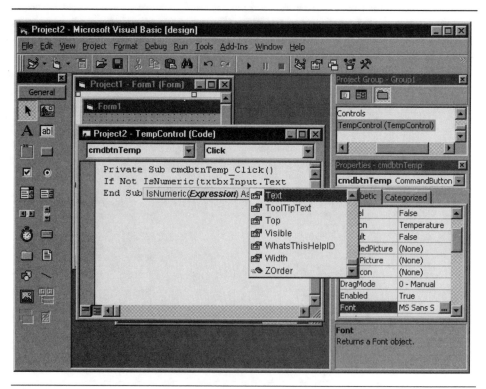

FIGURE 16.7: VB5 CCE helps you as you type code.

The first helping hand that you'll see is a Tool Tip that shows the syntax for the IsNumeric function. It appears when you enter the opening parenthesis of the `IsNumeric` function. When you get to the dot after `txtbxInput` you'll see a pop-up menu that contains the TextBox's properties and methods. You can double-click on a property to enter it into the code, rather than type it out, or you can just enter the first few characters of the property name and hit the Tab key when the property name you want appears highlighted. Figure 16.7 shows both the `IsNumeric` syntax Tool Tip and the Textbox's properties and methods drop-down.

The Tool Tip that appears when you type **MsgBox** is especially helpful. When you get to the second argument, it gives you all the possible values for the Message Box's appearance. Notice that you don't have to provide numbers or combinations of numbers for this argument, as VBS requires. (If you want combinations in your Message Box, you still have to provide combinations of the names that the Tool Tip lists for this argument.)

NOTE   Within the Tool Tip, arguments that appear in square brackets are optional.

The remaining code for the Command Button's Click event would ordinarily look like this:

```
If optnbtnCtoF.Value = True Then
lblTemp.Caption = 9 * (txtbxInput.Text / 5) + 32

& " degrees Fahrenheit"
End If

If optnbtnFtoC.Value = True Then
lblTemp.Caption = 5 * (txtbxInput.Text - 32) / 9 _
& " degrees Centigrade"
End If
```

You can do a little something extra to tidy up the display and quickly learn a helpful VB function in the process. If you leave the code as you have it, it's perfectly functional, but the display of the converted temperature might get a little messy: You leave yourself open to the possibility of many decimal places. To clean things up, you can use the VB `Format` function to limit the display of the converted number to two decimal places. Here's how you do it. In the first `If...Then`, edit the line that sets `lblTemp.Caption` and change it to:

```
lblTemp.Caption = Format((9 * (txtbxInput.Text / 5) + 32), "###0.00") __
& " degrees Fahrenheit"
```

In the second `If...Then`, edit the line that sets `lblTemp.Caption` and change it to:

```
lblTemp.Caption = Format((5 * (txtbxInput.Text - 32) / 9), "###0.00") _
& " degrees Centigrade"
```

Format, as you can see, takes two arguments. The first is the expression you want to format, the second is the format in which you want it to appear.

Testing the Control Assembly

Close the Code window by clicking the X in the upper-right corner, and close the window that holds the control assembly. The icon that represents our newly created aggregate control in the Toolbox should no longer be grayed out. It should be visible as the last icon in the last row (to the right of an icon that says "OLE"). If you hover your mouse over this icon, TempControl appears in a Tool Tip label.

Click on this icon, and move your mouse cursor to the Form1 window. When you get it there, drag the mouse to insert the control you've created onto Form1. Resize it to open the assembly and display all the component controls. Your screen should now look like Figure 16.8.

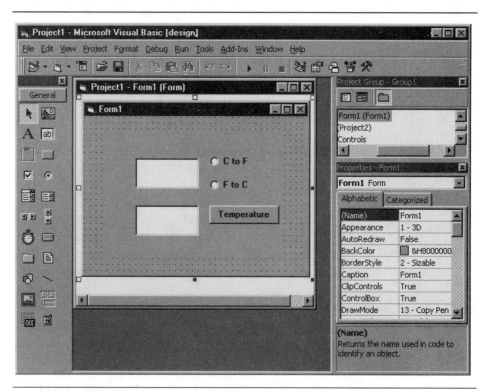

FIGURE 16.8: Your screen's appearance after you drag the aggregate control's icon to the Form1 window and resize it so all the component controls are visible

Now run the code and test the assembly. Press F5 and the form appears, ready for you to enter a temperature into the TextBox. Enter a number, select an Option Button, and click the Command Button. You should see a temperature appear in the label. Enter a non-numeric value and watch the Message Box open, complete with the "Critical" icon we specified in the MsgBox statement's second argument.

 TIP   You can run the code in two other ways. You can select Run ➤ Start from the menu bar, or you can click the right-pointing triangle on the toolbar (just below the menu bar).

When you finish testing the control assembly, end the test run by selecting Run ➤ End or by clicking the End button on the toolbar.

Saving Your Work

Let's proceed by taking the control off the form and saving the project. This way you'll have a blank Form1 that you can use to test the next control you build. In the Form1 window, click anywhere in the aggregate control to select it. Then delete it by pressing Del. To make the project visible once again, you have to use the window on the right side of the screen—the one just above the Properties window. This is called the Project Explorer, and it represents a hierarchical view of the objects contained in our projects.

Click on Project2 in the Project Explorer and set its only property, Name, to **Temperature**. You'll see the name change take effect immediately in the Project Explorer. Right-click on Temperature and select Save Project from the resulting pop-up menu.

Save the project in your \ActiveX No Exp Req\skill 16 folder.

You'll be prompted to save another file. Save that file, named Temperature .vbp, in skill 16, too. The names of the files you saved (Temperature.vbp and TempControl.ctl) now appear in parentheses in the VB5 CCE Project Explorer window. Still in the Project Explorer window, right-click on Temperature.vbp and select Remove Project from the resulting pop-up menu. A prompt informs you that this project is referenced in another project and asks if you want to proceed with the removal. Click Yes. (The other project is the Form we created to test the control.) If you're prompted about whether to save changes to the project, click Yes.

Coloring a Label

Another control example will help you learn a few more VB5 CCE principles. In this example, we'll use a ListBox and two Command Buttons to change the BackColor and the ForeColor of a Label. The ListBox will contain the names of the colors you can choose from. One Command Button will apply the selected color to the Label's BackColor property setting, the other Command Button will apply the selected color to the ForeColor property setting:

1. Select File ➢ Add Project….

2. In the Add Project window, select the ActiveX Control icon and then click the Open Command Button.

3. Next, in the Project Explorer window, click on Project2 (Project2) to bring up the project's Name property in the Properties window.

4. Change the Name property to **LabelColors**.

5. Again in the Project Explorer window, click on the UserControl1 icon in the LabelColors project.

6. In the Properties window, change its Name property to ColorLabel.

Laying It Out

On the grid in the LabelColors - ColorLabel(UserControl) window, lay out a Label, a ListBox, and two Command Buttons as in Figure 16.9.

Once again, I've left the original Names and Captions so you can see where to position the controls. Note that I've set the Label's BackColor to white, its BorderStyle to 1-Fixed Single, and its Appearance to 0-Flat. Use the Label's Properties window to make these changes to the Label in your display.

Change the Label's Caption property to **A Sample Caption** and set its Font property to 10 pt bold. Set the Name properties of the controls to **lblColor**, **lstbxChoices**, **cmdbtnBack**, and **cmdbtnFore**. Change cmdbtnBack's caption to **BackColor** and cmdbtn's Caption to **ForeColor**.

Now you come to a great convenience that isn't available in the ActiveX Control Pad. In VB5 CCE, you can populate a ListBox during the design phase. Here's how to do it: Click on the ListBox to view its properties in the Properties window.

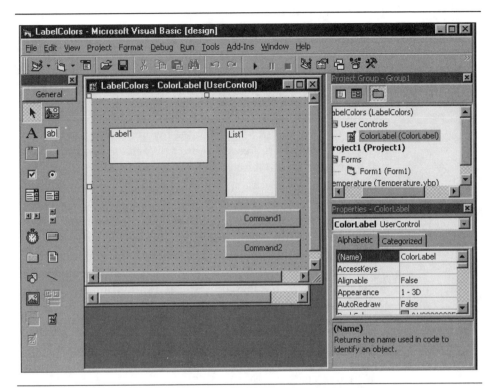

FIGURE 16.9: The layout for the aggregate ColorLabel Control

Scroll down until you find its List property. Click in the List property's row, and then click on the resulting down-arrow on the right side of the row. You'll see a drop-down area you can use to enter items into the ListBox. Type an item and then press Ctrl+Enter to move to the next line. When you're done, press Enter and you'll find all your items in the ListBox. In lstbxChoices' List property, type these values: **Black**, **Blue**, **Green**, **Cyan**, **Red**, **Magenta**, **Yellow**, and **White** and follow each one with Ctrl+Enter. When you're finished, press Enter and you'll see all the color names in the ListBox.

Writing the Code

Double-click on lstbxChoices to open its Code window to the control's Click event procedure. Before we add code to this event, we have to set up a global variable called glblColorChoice (the "glbl" prefix indicates that the variable is

global). This variable will hold the name of the color selected from lstbxChoices
so the Command Buttons will be able to use it. Click the Object combobox and
select (General). This will put you in the General Declarations section of the
code module associated with the LabelColors form. Type **Dim glblColorChoice
as Variant** to create the global variable. Now go back to the lstbxChoices' Click
event so we can enter the code associated with that event procedure.

In the Click event procedure, you'll have a `Select Case` examine the choice
that the user clicked (it's stored in the ListBox's Text property). Because VB uses
numerical values to represent colors, you need a mechanism to supply the appropriate numerical value for each choice in the ListBox. The VB RGB function is the
mechanism to use. For each choice in the ListBox (in other words, for each `Case`
in the `Select Case`), you'll use the VB RGB function to assign the appropriate
numerical value for the color name. RGB takes three arguments, referred to as
Red, Green, and Blue, and returns a number which represents a color (consisting
of the three color components). Each argument is a number from 0 to 255 indicating that color component's contribution to the whole color. Black, for example, is
RGB(0, 0, 0), Green is RGB(0, 255, 0), and White is RGB(255, 255, 255). Your
code for lstbxChoices' Click event, then, should look like this:

```
Private Sub lstbxChoices_Click()

Select Case lstbxChoices.Text
Case "Black"
glblColorChoice = RGB(0, 0, 0)
Case "Blue"
glblColorChoice = RGB(0, 0, 255)
Case "Green"
glblColorChoice = RGB(0, 255, 0)
Case "Cyan"
glblColorChoice = RGB(0, 255, 255)
Case "Red"
glblColorChoice = RGB(255, 0, 0)
Case "Magenta"
glblColorChoice = RGB(255, 0, 255)
Case "Yellow"
glblColorChoice = RGB(255, 255, 0)
Case "White"
glblColorChoice = RGB(255, 255, 255)
End Select
End Sub
```

Notice that we refer to the selected ListBox item as `lstbxChoices.Text`. This is
another departure from VBS. In VBS, the selected item would be `lstbxChoices
.Value`.

The code for the two Command Buttons is:

```
Private Sub cmdbtnBack_Click()
lblColor.BackColor = glblColorChoice
End Sub

Private Sub cmdbtnFore_Click()
lblColor.ForeColor = glblColorChoice
End Sub
```

Testing and Saving

Close the Code window and the Project window (with the component controls), and you'll see the aggregate control's icon at the bottom of the Toolbox. Select this icon, draw out the control assembly on Form1, and hit F5 to start running the code.

You should be able to select a color in the ListBox control and use the Command Buttons to apply that color to the Label control's BackColor property or the ForeColor property. Figure 16.10 shows the Label with Black selected for the BackColor and White for the ForeColor.

Skill 16

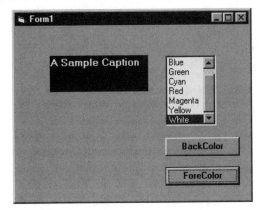

FIGURE 16.10: The ColorLabel control in action

When you're done testing, click the solid box in the toolbar or select Run ➢ Stop. Delete the control assembly from Form1 and right-click on the LabelColors project in the Project Explorer window and save the project in skill 16.

In the Project Explorer window, right-click on the LabelColors project and select Remove Project from the pop-up menu. If you're prompted about saving changes to the project, click Yes. Right-click on the Project1 project (the one that contains the form we used to test our controls) and select Remove Project from the pop-up menu. When you're prompted about saving changes to this project, click No.

The VB5 CCE Environment

As you've already seen, the VB5 CCE environment is rich with features. When you first start VB5 CCE and see the display shown in Figure 16.1, tabbed pages give you the choice of starting a new project, selecting an existing project, or browsing through recent projects to make a selection. Once you've decided on your selection, you're in VB5 CCE's *Integrated Development Environment* (IDE), so named because it integrates layout, design, editing, and a number of other functions.

Let's step back a moment and look at the IDE's main components. When the IDE first appears, you typically see:

- The menu bar
- The Standard toolbar
- The Toolbox
- The Project Explorer window
- The Properties window
- The Form Layout window

Except for the Form Layout window, you've already worked with these components (see Figure 16.2).

You often have occasion to make additional components visible as you work within the IDE:

- Pop-up context menus
- Object Browser
- Debugging windows
- Toolbars for editing, form design, and debugging

Let's take a closer look at each of these features.

Menu Bar

The menu bar has the standard menus: File, Edit, View, Window, and Help. It also has menus with special features for VB5: Project, Format, Debug, Run, Tools, and Add-Ins. Most of the choices on these menus are accessible via keystroke combinations and toolbar buttons. Some are accessible via pop-up menu choices. You can open each menu by pressing Alt+the key underlined on the menu bar.

The commands on the File menu allow you to work with projects and forms when you build and test a control. You add, remove, save, and open projects with these commands. You also use File menu commands to save forms. Other commands on this menu allow you to print your work, to set up the printer, and to exit VB5 CCE.

The Edit menu holds the commands you work with when you create code. When you write lengthy programs, the Find… and Replace… choices are particularly helpful. Cut, Copy, and Paste capabilities are also available on this menu.

The View menu's choices enable you to show or hide each of VB5 CCE's windows.

With the Project menu, you add items to—or remove items from—the project you're working on. Project ➤ Components (also available on a pop-up menu in the Toolbox) is like the Additional Controls… choice on the HTML Layout Control's Toolbox pop-up menu. You use it to decide which controls appear on the Toolbox.

The Format menu closely resembles the HTML Layout Control's menu of the same name. Its selections help you size and position the controls in your current project.

You use the Debug menu and the Run menu when you test your controls. The choices in the Run menu allow you to run your code and to stop it (as you did when you placed your controls in Form1, ran your code, and stopped it). The Debug menu's selections allow you to manipulate the way your code runs so you can track down errors.

The Tools menu gives you the ability to add or modify a procedure in your code, to create a custom menu for your application, and to specify your IDE's appearance.

The choices in the Add-Ins menu give you access to VB5 CCE's Wizards. One of the two available wizards allows you to add Property pages to your control, and the other allows you to specify properties, methods, and events for your control.

NOTE   You've seen Property pages before. The Interactive Music control (Skill 8), the Agent control (Skill 9), and the Card control (Skill 15) provide Property pages that allow you to set values for their properties and, in some cases, inform you as to what the possible values are.

As in most other Windows applications, the Window menu enables you to tile windows and to cascade them, and to access available windows that may be hidden from view.

If you've installed the VB5 CCE Help files (and you should), the Help menu gives you access to them. The Help files provide information about all of VB's built-in functions, menu-choices, toolbars, windows, and more.

Standard Toolbar

The Standard toolbar typically appears when you open VB5 CCE (see Figure 16.11). Partitioned into six groups, the buttons on the Standard toolbar give you quick access to frequently used menu choices.

FIGURE 16.11: VB5 CCE's Standard toolbar

Right-clicking on either the menu bar or the Standard toolbar pops up a context menu that enables you to display the toolbars for editing, form design, or debugging. The buttons on these toolbars give you access to menu choices that encompass these operations. The buttons on the Form Design toolbar, for example, are shortcuts to selections on the Format menu. Another choice on this context menu, Customize..., enables you to change aspects of your menus and toolbars.

The Toolbox

You've worked with the Toolbox to select the components for your aggregate controls and to place your aggregate control on a form so you can test it. Similar to the Toolbox in the HTML Layout Control, you can decide which controls should appear on the Toolbox.

You can do this with either Project ➢ Components or Components... from the pop-up menu that appears when you right-click in the Toolbox. Either technique displays the Components dialog box that contains a list of available controls for the Toolbox.

One more choice on the context menu enables you to toggle *dockability* on and off for the Toolbox, meaning that you can determine whether or not you can drag the Toolbox and reposition it in the IDE. In the docked state, the Toolbox is anchored ("docked") to a corner of the IDE window and you can't move it. Toggle dockability off and you can move the Toolbox around.

The Project Explorer Window

The Project Explorer window presents a hierarchy of the projects you've opened and added, along with all the items in each project. Figure 16.12 shows the Project Explorer window with the LabelColors project and the Temperature project.

FIGURE 16.12: The Project Explorer window, showing the LabelColors project and the Temperature project

The three buttons on the Project Explorer window's toolbar are called (left to right) View Code, View Object, and Toggle Folders. They allow you to open the Code window for the selected object, open the selected object's Object window (the window in which you designed your aggregate control), and hide/show the folders but still display the objects they hold.

The pop-up menus for this window depend on what's selected when you right-click. With a Project selected, right-clicking in this window opens a pop-up menu whose choice (Set as Start Up) makes the selected project run when you press F5 or select Start from the Standard toolbar. The second choice opens a set of tabbed pages that constitute a Properties dialog box for the project. (You use this dialog box to set numerous properties such as Project Name, Version Number, and Version Information.) The next two choices enable you to Save the project and to Remove it. Another selection (Add) brings up a group of choices that are the same as selections in the Project menu. The remaining commands on this menu allow you to print your work, to toggle the Project Explorer window's docked state, and to Hide the window.

With an object selected (in other words, a CTL file), the pop-up menu's first two choices are identical to the View Code button and the View Object button in the window's toolbar. The next choice opens the Properties window for the selected object if the object's User Control window is open. The third choice (Add) has the same function as in the Project Explorer's other pop-up menu—it brings up choices that are the same as selections in the Project menu. The next three choices allow you to Save the object, Save it under a different name, and Remove the object. The final three choices (Print, Dockable, and Hide) are the same as in the Project Explorer's other pop-up menu.

The Properties Window

Like the Properties sheet in the ActiveX Control Pad, the Properties window lists the current settings of a selected object's properties and enables you to set the values of those properties.

The Properties window is different from the ActiveX Control Pad's Properties sheet because the window has tabbed pages. The Alphabetic tab presents the selected object's properties in alphabetical order. The Categorized tab orders the properties within seven categories—Appearance, Behavior, Font, List, Miscellaneous, Position, and Scale.

The pop-up menu for the Properties window contains three choice: Description is a toggle that shows/hides a Description pane (for displaying information about a selected property), Dockability toggles the window's docked state, and Hide hides the property sheet.

The Form Layout Window

The Form Layout window presents a picture of a computer screen. This screen picture shows how your form will look and where it will appear when it comes onscreen in run mode.

If you right-click on this window, the pop-up menu presents selections that allow you to show resolution guides (dotted lines that show the right and lower borders of standard resolutions, they're not available in 640 by 480), set the form's startup position, toggle the window's dockability, and hide the window.

The Object Browser

The Object Browser, shown in Figure 16.13, shows all *type libraries* (collections of objects you can use in Visual Basic), their objects and related properties, methods, and events. You can filter the type libraries and search for a particular member (in other words, a property, method, or event).

After you find the item you're looking for, you might want to use it in your code. If so, you don't have to type it into the Code window: You can select the result of your search, and then a Copy capability allows you to copy and paste it into your code. A Details pane at the bottom of the Object Browser provides details on your selection. The figure shows the ComboBox object selected in the Browser's Classes pane.

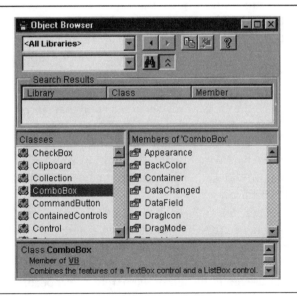

FIGURE 16.13: The Object Browser

Right-clicking in the Object Browser brings up a pop-up menu that provides the Copy command, some search-related commands, the Show Hidden Members command (a toggle that shows and hides the *hidden* members in the Object Browser for each class), a choice called References…(that makes objects from another application available for your code), a choice for toggling the Object Browser's dockability (it's called Dockability), and a command (Hide) that hides this window.

 NOTE   Not usually visible in the Object Browser, a hidden member is a member that a programmer is not able to use. When you select Show Hidden Members to toggle them on, they appear in the Object Browser as grayed text.

Debugging Windows

The three debugging windows help you track down errors in your code. For example, you can use the Immediate window to test functions, and to see the values of variables, properties, and objects. Or, sometimes when you're debugging code, it's helpful to be able to examine the values of the declared variables in a procedure. The Locals window displays this information. Also, a helpful debugging technique is to monitor what a particular variable or expression does during execution. You can designate such expressions to monitor—they're called *watch expressions*—and the Watch window appears automatically to show these expressions during test runs.

The Immediate window's pop-up menu has editing commands, a selection that opens the Object Browser, a selection that starts the code, another that ends it, and commands for dockability and hiding. Another selection provides a *definition*: It opens the Code window and displays the expression under the cursor in the Immediate window. If the definition appears in a referenced type library (a file that provides information about an object), this selection shows it to you in the Object Browser.

When you right-click the Locals window, you'll see a pop-up menu whose selections are editing commands, commands that start and end code, and commands for docking and hiding the window. Another selection, Collapse Parent, shortens a hierarchical list in the window by shrinking it to its parent item: the minus sign to the left of the parent object becomes a plus sign.

The pop-up menu for the Watch window has editing commands, commands for adding, editing, and deleting watch expressions, commands for starting and ending the code, a definition selection, Collapse Parent, and the usual dockability and hide selections.

Summary

The VB5 CCE is rich with features, and no single chapter can do it justice. The best we can do is dive right in and start using it, getting our hands dirty with as many of its capabilities as possible. Then, it's easier to understand the environment when we start dissecting its high points. If you need further information on any of the aspects of the IDE, select Help ➤ Microsoft Visual Basic Help Topics or Help ➤ Search Reference Index. You're certain to find what you're looking for.

To help you learn about VB5 CCE and its environment, we built a couple of simple aggregate control assemblies based on our earlier work. We laid them out, coded them, and tested them. We did not, however, turn them into controls that we can use in our Web development work.

How do we use the IDE to create controls that we can put in our Web pages? By the end of the next Skill, you'll know.

Are You Experienced?

Now you can...

- ☑ use the VB5 CCE to design an aggregate control

- ☑ write Visual Basic code for controls, including a global variable, a *Select Case*, and the *RGB* function

- ☑ run and test the code

- ☑ understand the main features of VB5 CCE's Integrated Development Environment (IDE)

Creating and Using Controls

- ❑ Working with the controls you created in the previous Skill

- ❑ Creating an OCX file

- ❑ The ActiveX Control Interface Wizard

- ❑ Using your new control in a Web page

In Skill 16, you learned the fundamentals of the VB5 CCE, and you used its Integrated Development Environment (IDE) to create two aggregate ActiveX controls. In this Skill, you'll learn how to dress up those controls. You'll take a control and set its properties, methods, and events. Best of all, you'll learn how to package your controls so you can use them in the ActiveX Control Pad, script them with Visual Basic Script, and see them appear on a Web page.

Let's get started.

Working with the Controls You Created

The controls you put together in Skill 16 carry out simple tasks. The LabelColors control changes the background color and the foreground color of a Label, and the Temperature control converts a number into either a Fahrenheit or a Centigrade temperature.

You tested these aggregate controls within the VB5 CCE environment by placing each control on another project's form, and running the code. At this point, however, these controls aren't functional outside VB5 CCE. As you'll recall from Skill 3 and Skill 12, functional controls are OCX files. In order to make your aggregate controls functional, then, you have to somehow use them to create OCX files. Fortunately, VB5 CCE makes this process as easy as selecting from a menu.

 NOTE   You'll be working within your skill 17 folder, with files you created in Skill 16. Thus, you'll begin by copying files from your skill 16 folder to your skill 17 folder. Instead of just copying them as you normally would copy files from one folder to another, you'll do the copying within VB5 CCE. This will give you the opportunity to learn some useful VB5 techniques, and gain firsthand experience with some of the VB5 CCE windows.

Opening the LabelColors Control

Let's work with the LabelColors control:

1. In the VB5 CCE, select File ➤ Open Project….

2. Click the Recent tab.

3. Open the LabelColors project from skill 16.

Open your Project Explorer window and you should see a display corresponding to the LabelColors project. Click the + next to User Control, and your display will look like Figure 17.1.

FIGURE 17.1: The Project Explorer window after you open the LabelColors project and click the + next to User Control

Copying the Control

To open the control in a design window, double-click on ColorLabel(ColorLabel .ctl). You'll see the window in Figure 17.2.

Then, follow these steps:

1. Select File ➤ Add Project....

2. In the resulting dialog box, select the ActiveX Control icon and click Open. You'll see a blank grid in a window entitled Project 1- User Control (UserControl). Drag this window slightly so you can see the window in Figure 17.2.

3. Click on the window entitled LabelColors - ColorLabel (UserControl).

4. To select all the controls in the aggregate, press Ctrl+A.

5. Make a copy of your selection by pressing Ctrl+C.

6. Click on the Project 1 - User Control (UserControl) window.

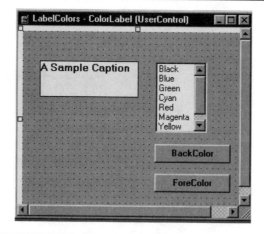

FIGURE 17.2: The ColorLabel control in a design window

7. Press Ctrl+V (or Shift+Ins) to paste the copied controls onto this window. On the grid in this window, center the group of pasted controls. Then deselect the copied controls by clicking anywhere on the grid.

8. Close both the Project 1 - User Control (User Control) window and the LabelColors - ColorLabel (User Control) window.

You've now copied all the aggregated controls to a new project, but you have not yet copied the underlying code to make those controls function. The next task is to copy this code.

Copying the Code

You can click the symbol in the upper-left corner of the Project Explorer window to display the VB code for the selected object. (If you hover your mouse over this symbol, you'll see a Tool Tip that says "View Code.") To copy the code, follow these steps:

1. In the Project Explorer window, select ColorLabel(ColorLabel.ctl).

2. Click on the View Code button in the Project Explorer window's toolbar. A Code window entitled LabelColors - ColorLabel (Code) opens.

3. Now you'll repeat the process for the other project. In the Project Explorer window, select User Control1 (UserControl1).

4. Click on the View Code button in the tool bar of the Project Explorer window. Another Code window opens, entitled Project1 - User Control1 (Code). Unlike the first Code window, this window is blank.

5. Click on the LabelColors - ColorLabel (Code) window.

6. In the Code window for LabelColors, press Ctrl+A. This will highlight all the code.

7. Copy the code by pressing Ctrl+C.

8. Click on the Project1 - User Control1 (Code) window.

9. Paste your copied code into this window by pressing Ctrl+V (or Shift+Ins).

10. Close both Code windows.

 NOTE   Here's a new Visual Basic term that you'll encounter as you deal with VB code: *module*. A module is a set of declarations (like Dim statements that define variables) followed by procedures. Each Code window displays a module.

Saving the New Files

Now that you've copied the controls and the underlying code to a new project, you no longer need the original LabelColors project from skill 16. In the Project Explorer window, select LabelColors (LabelColors.vbp) and right-click. From the resulting pop-up menu, select Remove Project.

At this point, Project1 (Project1) should be the only project remaining in the Project Explorer window. Now you have to rename the project and the control before you save them.

Renaming the Project

First, rename the project:

1. Select Project1 (Project1) and right-click.

2. On the pop-up menu that opens, select Project1 Properties... (or select Project ➤ Project1 Properties... from the menu bar). You'll see the Project Properties dialog box that appears in Figure 17.3.

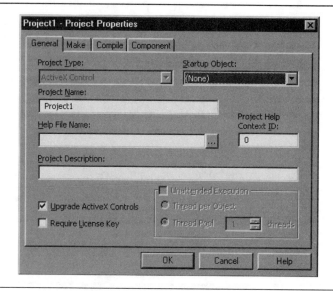

FIGURE 17.3: The Project Properties dialog box for Project1

3. The Project Name: textbox shows `Project1`. Delete this name and type **LabelChange** into that textbox.

4. Click OK to close the Project Properties dialog box. The top line in the Project Explorer window should now be LabelChange (LabelChange).

Renaming the Control

Now let's rename the control:

1. Select User Control1 (User Control1).

2. Double-click on User Control1 (User Control1).

3. Right-click in the resulting LabelChange - User Control1 (UserControl) window.

4. In the pop-up menu that appears, select Properties. The Properties window opens.

5. In the Properties window, the line at the top provides the control's name. It's currently UserControl1. Change the name to **LabelColor** and press Enter.

6. The Properties window moves behind the Project window. The title of the Project window is now LabelChange - LabelColor (User Control). Close this window and close the Properties window. You'll see that the new names now appear in the Project Explorer window.

Giving the Project a Home

I'm assuming you've already created a `skill 17` folder. Now it's time to put the project into that folder:

1. In the Project Explorer window, select LabelChange (LabelChange).

2. Right-click and on the pop-up menu, select Save Project (or, with the project selected, in the menu bar select File ➤ Save LabelChange).

3. The Save File As dialog box appears. Navigate through this dialog box until you find your `skill 17` folder.

4. Open the `skill 17` folder.

5. Click the Save button.

6. The dialog box then prompts you to save `LabelChange.vbp`. Click the Save button again.

You should now have these files in your `skill 17` folder: `LabelColor` (a Visual Basic Project file), `LabelChange.ctl`, and `LabelChange.ctx`.

Creating an OCX File

You've set the stage for creating a control that you can insert into an ActiveX Control Pad HTML file (or into an HTML Layout Control), script in the Script Wizard, and then see in a Web page.

A Rough Draft

As a learning experience, you'll now create a bare-bones version of the OCX file. To create the file, select File ➤ Make LabelChange.ocx… from the menu bar. This opens the Make Project dialog box. In the File Name textbox, you'll see the file path that will put this OCX file into the `skill 17` folder. Click OK.

If you look at your `skill 17` folder, you'll see `LabelChange.ocx`.

Equally important, this process has registered the LabelChange control on your computer. To verify this, run Regedit to open the Registry. (Select Windows 95 Start ➤ Run, type **Regedit** in the resulting dialog box, and click OK.) When the Registry Editor window appears, click on the + next to HKEY_CLASSES_ROOT in the left pane. Scroll down until you find LabelChange.LabelColor. Click on the + to its left to display the CLSID folder, and then click on that folder. In the right pane, you'll see this control's 32-digit CLSID. This means that LabelChange .LabelColor is fully registered on your machine. You can almost start using it in Web pages—the operative word being "almost." Close the Registry Editor and we'll proceed.

 WARNING As I pointed out in Skill 3, when it comes to the Registry, look but don't touch! If you change anything you might seriously impair your computer's functioning (or it might not work at all).

Examining the Control

Minimize VB5 CCE (don't close it). Getting back to familiar territory, this next exercise will help you understand the nature of the tasks still ahead of you. You'll embed your "almost-ready" new control in an HTML document and watch what happens when you try to script it:

1. Open the ActiveX Control Pad.

2. Select Edit ➤ Insert ActiveX Control….

3. On the resulting list of controls, scroll down until you find the newly created LabelChange.LabelColor. Select this control and click OK.

When the Object Editor opens, take note of the Properties sheet, as shown in Figure 17.4.

As you can see, the control in its present form has very few properties. Close the Object Editor. In the Text Editor, you'll see code that looks like this:

```
<OBJECT ID="LabelColor1" WIDTH=320 HEIGHT=240
 CLASSID="CLSID:0B95445A-B8B4-11D0-9421-444553540000">
    <PARAM NAME="_ExtentX" VALUE="8467">
    <PARAM NAME="_ExtentY" VALUE="6350">
</OBJECT>
```

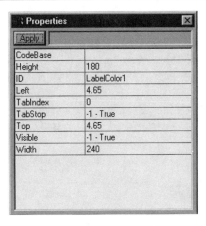

FIGURE 17.4: The Properties sheet of the LabelChange.LabelColor control

 NOTE   The code won't match up exactly because your CLASSID will most likely be different from mine.

If you look at the Script Wizard, you'll see that not much is happening there, either. The new control doesn't display any events, properties, or methods. Close the Script Wizard.

You could put this control on a Web page, and it would work. (Before the page opens, you'd get a warning that the control is not known to be safe, but in fact it is.) It's fully functional in that you could make selections in the ListBox, click the Command Buttons, and watch the changes take effect in the Label. The problem is that it presents no events, properties, or methods to interface with other controls.

Don't bother saving this file. Close the ActiveX Control Pad; you obviously still have some work to do on the control itself.

The Code in the Rough Draft

Alt + Tab back to the LabelChange project in the VB5 CCE. Your objective is to give the new control some properties, events, and methods—the collection of these items is called the control's *interface*. The interface allows you to work with the control and script it to work with other controls. We're going to make a number of changes to the code in this control, so let's first look at the code in its present state:

```
Dim glblColorChoice As Variant

Private Sub cmdbtnBack_Click()
lblColor.BackColor = glblColorChoice
End Sub

Private Sub cmdbtnFore_Click()
lblColor.ForeColor = glblColorChoice
End Sub

Private Sub lstbxChoices_Click()

Select Case lstbxChoices.Text
Case "Black"
glblColorChoice = RGB(0, 0, 0)
Case "Blue"
glblColorChoice = RGB(0, 0, 255)
Case "Green"
glblColorChoice = RGB(0, 255, 0)
Case "Cyan"
glblColorChoice = RGB(0, 255, 255)
Case "Red"
glblColorChoice = RGB(255, 0, 0)
Case "Magenta"
glblColorChoice = RGB(255, 0, 255)
Case "Yellow"
glblColorChoice = RGB(255, 255, 0)
Case "White"
glblColorChoice = RGB(255, 255, 255)
End Select
End Sub
```

This is the code you wrote in Skill 16. It includes the declaration of the global variable and code for the component controls.

The ActiveX Control Interface Wizard

The VB5 CCE provides an ActiveX Control Interface Wizard that sets up the interface.

In the Project Explorer window, select LabelColor (`LabelColor.ctl`) and double-click on it to open its Project window. In the menu bar, select Add-Ins ➤ ActiveX Control Interface Wizard…. You'll see the wizard's introductory screen (see Figure 17.5).

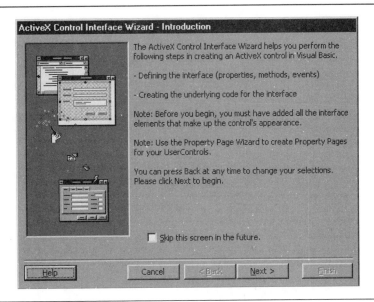

FIGURE 17.5: The ActiveX Control Interface Wizard's introductory screen

Click the Next button to open the Select Interface Members window. In this window, you select the properties, methods, and events that you want in your control (see Figure 17.6).

The ListBox on the left contains the available properties, methods, and events, and the ListBox on the right contains the selected items. You select an item from the ListBox on the left and click the button with the right-pointing arrowhead to move into the ListBox on the right. If you change your mind and decide to deselect an item, click on that item in the right ListBox, and click the button with the left-pointing arrowhead to move the item back into the ListBox on the left. Clicking a button with two arrowheads causes all the items in a ListBox to move in the indicated direction.

The window opens with a number of properties, events, and a method already in the ListBox on the right. These items are common to many controls and have been selected for you as the default set of properties, events, and methods for your new control.

Changing the Mindset

What should you select? Ideally, you would make this decision when you design the control. Since this control does a simple task, however, it should be easy to make the appropriate selections.

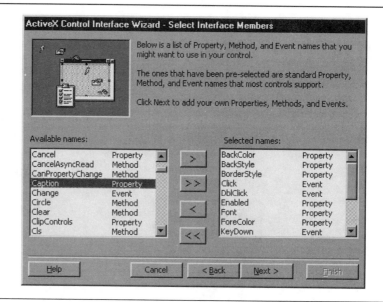

FIGURE 17.6: The Select Interface Members window of the ActiveX Control Interface Wizard. You use this window to select the properties, methods, and events you want in your control.

You must ask yourself what a developer would need in the interface in order to script the control. This is a different mindset from the one you've been operating under. Previously, when you laid out controls and scripted the interaction among them, your target was the person *looking* at a Web page. Now, you're aiming your efforts at the person *developing* a Web page. What events should the developer be able to script? What properties should he or she be able to set? What methods should you empower the developer to invoke?

Making Choices

Let's start with individual components of our aggregate control. A Label is part of the aggregate control and it's what the control is designed to work with, so you ought to allow the developer to address properties of a Label. The obvious property to include is Caption, which Figure 17.6 shows selected in the left ListBox. Another useful Label property is Alignment, which sets up how text aligns in a Label's caption. Still another is Font. Select these properties in the left ListBox and move them to the right ListBox.

The ListBox component, lstbxChoices, will remain unchanged in terms of its composition, but you can select a property that will alter its appearance. If you make sure that ForeColor is selected, a developer can use that property to change the color of the words inside the ListBox.

So far, you've worked with two of the individual components. You can also consider the entire aggregate control. It might be useful to be able to show the entire control and hide it programmatically, so let's also select the Show and Hide events. And you might want to empower a developer to change the appearance along the aggregate control's boundary, so select Appearance.

After you've made all these selections, click on Next. The window that appears asks you for Custom Interface members (properties and events that you design yourself). You won't have any for this control, so click this window's Next button.

Mapping

The window now on your screen enables you to attach (in other words, to *map*) each of your property, method, and event selections to a specific component control within your aggregate control, or to the entire aggregate control itself. This window is called the Set Mapping window (see Figure 17.7).

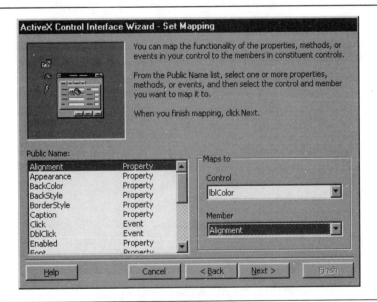

FIGURE 17.7: The ActiveX Control Interface Setup Wizard's Set Mapping window. You use it to map properties, methods, and events to components of your aggregate control, or to the entire aggregate.

The idea is to select an item from the ListBox on the left and then select a component control from the Control combobox on the right. In the Member combobox, you select the member of that control that your selection should map to.

For example, if you select Alignment in the box on the left, and lblColor (the Label in our aggregate) from the upper drop-down menu, you'll probably (but not necessarily) select the Label's Alignment property in the Member combobox. The wizard automatically selects this property for you in the Member combobox. Make these selections, so that you map Alignment to lblColor's Alignment property.

We should also map Caption and Font to lblColor so someone adding this control to a Web page can set these properties for the Label component. Map ForeColor to lstbxChoices, in order to make the color of the ListBox's choices settable.

Map everything else (including BackColor) to the entire aggregate control, which is represented in the Control combobox by the choice UserControl.

When you're done with all the mapping, click Next. The resulting window tells you that you're finished, and asks you if you want to see a summary report. Click the View Summary Report checkbox and you'll see that report (a to-do list of tasks for proceeding further) when you click the Finish button. You can either save this report (by clicking Save) or discard it (by clicking Close). Although we won't refer to it in this exercise, the Summary Report is a useful reminder of tasks that remain in order to finish up the control.

 WARNING   **When you feel the need for more information about any of the wizards, select Help ➤ Microsoft Visual Basic Help Topics. In the tabbed page that appears, double-click on Interface Reference and then double-click on Wizards.**

The Code Revisited

All these selections and mappings have had a profound effect on your control's code. It now looks like this:

```
Dim glblColorChoice As Variant
'Event Declarations:
Event Click() 'MappingInfo=UserControl,UserControl,-1,Click
Event DblClick() 'MappingInfo=UserControl,UserControl,-1,DblClick
Event KeyDown(KeyCode As Integer, Shift As Integer)
➥'MappingInfo=UserControl,UserControl,-1,KeyDown
Event KeyPress(KeyAscii As Integer)
'MappingInfo=UserControl,UserControl,-
➥1,KeyPress
Event KeyUp(KeyCode As Integer, Shift As Integer)
➥'MappingInfo=UserControl,UserControl,-1,KeyUp
```

```
Event MouseDown(Button As Integer, Shift As Integer, X As Single, Y As
➥Single) 'MappingInfo=UserControl,UserControl,-1,MouseDown
Event MouseMove(Button As Integer, Shift As Integer, X As Single, Y As
➥Single) 'MappingInfo=UserControl,UserControl,-1,MouseMove
Event MouseUp(Button As Integer, Shift As Integer, X As Single, Y As
➥Single) 'MappingInfo=UserControl,UserControl,-1,MouseUp
Event Show() 'MappingInfo=UserControl,UserControl,-1,Show
Event Hide() 'MappingInfo=UserControl,UserControl,-1,Hide

Private Sub cmdbtnBack_Click()
lblColor.BackColor = glblColorChoice
End Sub

Private Sub cmdbtnFore_Click()
lblColor.ForeColor = glblColorChoice
End Sub

Private Sub lstbxChoices_Click()

Select Case lstbxChoices.Text
Case "Black"
glblColorChoice = RGB(0, 0, 0)
Case "Blue"
glblColorChoice = RGB(0, 0, 255)
Case "Green"
glblColorChoice = RGB(0, 255, 0)
Case "Cyan"
glblColorChoice = RGB(0, 255, 255)
Case "Red"
glblColorChoice = RGB(255, 0, 0)
Case "Magenta"
glblColorChoice = RGB(255, 0, 255)
Case "Yellow"
glblColorChoice = RGB(255, 255, 0)
Case "White"
glblColorChoice = RGB(255, 255, 255)
End Select
End Sub

'WARNING! DO NOT REMOVE OR MODIFY THE FOLLOWING COMMENTED LINES!
'MappingInfo=UserControl,UserControl,-1,BackColor
Public Property Get BackColor() As OLE_COLOR
    BackColor = UserControl.BackColor
End Property

Public Property Let BackColor(ByVal New_BackColor As OLE_COLOR)
    UserControl.BackColor() = New_BackColor
    PropertyChanged "BackColor"
End Property

'WARNING! DO NOT REMOVE OR MODIFY THE FOLLOWING COMMENTED LINES!
'MappingInfo=lstbxChoices,lstbxChoices,-1,ForeColor
```

Skill 17

```
Public Property Get ForeColor() As OLE_COLOR
    ForeColor = lstbxChoices.ForeColor
End Property

Public Property Let ForeColor(ByVal New_ForeColor As OLE_COLOR)
    lstbxChoices.ForeColor() = New_ForeColor
    PropertyChanged "ForeColor"
End Property

'WARNING! DO NOT REMOVE OR MODIFY THE FOLLOWING COMMENTED LINES!
'MappingInfo=UserControl,UserControl,-1,Enabled
Public Property Get Enabled() As Boolean
    Enabled = UserControl.Enabled
End Property

Public Property Let Enabled(ByVal New_Enabled As Boolean)
    UserControl.Enabled() = New_Enabled
    PropertyChanged "Enabled"
End Property

'WARNING! DO NOT REMOVE OR MODIFY THE FOLLOWING COMMENTED LINES!
'MappingInfo=lblColor,lblColor,-1,Font
Public Property Get Font() As Font
    Set Font = lblColor.Font
End Property

Public Property Set Font(ByVal New_Font As Font)
    Set lblColor.Font = New_Font
    PropertyChanged "Font"
End Property

'WARNING! DO NOT REMOVE OR MODIFY THE FOLLOWING COMMENTED LINES!
'MappingInfo=UserControl,UserControl,-1,BackStyle
Public Property Get BackStyle() As Integer
    BackStyle = UserControl.BackStyle
End Property

Public Property Let BackStyle(ByVal New_BackStyle As Integer)
    UserControl.BackStyle() = New_BackStyle
    PropertyChanged "BackStyle"
End Property

'WARNING! DO NOT REMOVE OR MODIFY THE FOLLOWING COMMENTED LINES!
'MappingInfo=UserControl,UserControl,-1,BorderStyle
Public Property Get BorderStyle() As Integer
    BorderStyle = UserControl.BorderStyle
End Property

Public Property Let BorderStyle(ByVal New_BorderStyle As Integer)
    UserControl.BorderStyle() = New_BorderStyle
    PropertyChanged "BorderStyle"
```

```
End Property

'WARNING! DO NOT REMOVE OR MODIFY THE FOLLOWING COMMENTED LINES!
'MappingInfo=UserControl,UserControl,-1,Refresh
Public Sub Refresh()
    UserControl.Refresh
End Sub

Private Sub UserControl_Click()
    RaiseEvent Click
End Sub

Private Sub UserControl_DblClick()
    RaiseEvent DblClick
End Sub

Private Sub UserControl_KeyDown(KeyCode As Integer, Shift As Integer)
    RaiseEvent KeyDown(KeyCode, Shift)
End Sub

Private Sub UserControl_KeyPress(KeyAscii As Integer)
    RaiseEvent KeyPress(KeyAscii)
End Sub

Private Sub UserControl_KeyUp(KeyCode As Integer, Shift As Integer)
    RaiseEvent KeyUp(KeyCode, Shift)
End Sub

Private Sub UserControl_MouseDown(Button As Integer, Shift As Integer,
➡X As Single, Y As Single)
    RaiseEvent MouseDown(Button, Shift, X, Y)
End Sub

Private Sub UserControl_MouseMove(Button As Integer, Shift As Integer,
➡X As Single, Y As Single)
    RaiseEvent MouseMove(Button, Shift, X, Y)
End Sub

Private Sub UserControl_MouseUp(Button As Integer, Shift As Integer,
➡X As Single, Y As Single)
    RaiseEvent MouseUp(Button, Shift, X, Y)
End Sub

'WARNING! DO NOT REMOVE OR MODIFY THE FOLLOWING COMMENTED LINES!
'MappingInfo=lblColor,lblColor,-1,Caption
Public Property Get Caption() As String
    Caption = lblColor.Caption
End Property

Public Property Let Caption(ByVal New_Caption As String)
    lblColor.Caption() = New_Caption
```

Skill 17

```
        PropertyChanged "Caption"
End Property

Private Sub UserControl_Show()
    RaiseEvent Show
End Sub

Private Sub UserControl_Hide()
    RaiseEvent Hide
End Sub

'WARNING! DO NOT REMOVE OR MODIFY THE FOLLOWING COMMENTED LINES!
'MappingInfo=lblColor,lblColor,-1,Alignment
Public Property Get Alignment() As Integer
    Alignment = lblColor.Alignment
End Property

Public Property Let Alignment(ByVal New_Alignment As Integer)
    lblColor.Alignment() = New_Alignment
    PropertyChanged "Alignment"
End Property

'WARNING! DO NOT REMOVE OR MODIFY THE FOLLOWING COMMENTED LINES!
'MappingInfo=UserControl,UserControl,-1,Appearance
Public Property Get Appearance() As Integer
    Appearance = UserControl.Appearance
End Property

'Load property values from storage
Private Sub UserControl_ReadProperties(PropBag As PropertyBag)

    UserControl.BackColor = PropBag.ReadProperty("BackColor",
➥&H8000000F)
    lstbxChoices.ForeColor = PropBag.ReadProperty("ForeColor",
➥&H80000008)
    UserControl.Enabled = PropBag.ReadProperty("Enabled", True)
    Set Font = PropBag.ReadProperty("Font", Ambient.Font)
    UserControl.BackStyle = PropBag.ReadProperty("BackStyle", 1)
    UserControl.BorderStyle = PropBag.ReadProperty("BorderStyle", 0)
    lblColor.Caption = PropBag.ReadProperty("Caption", "A Sample Caption")
    lblColor.Alignment = PropBag.ReadProperty("Alignment", 0)
End Sub

'Write property values to storage
Private Sub UserControl_WriteProperties(PropBag As PropertyBag)

    Call PropBag.WriteProperty("BackColor", UserControl.BackColor,
➥&H8000000F)
    Call PropBag.WriteProperty("ForeColor", lstbxChoices.ForeColor,
➥&H80000008)
    Call PropBag.WriteProperty("Enabled", UserControl.Enabled, True)
    Call PropBag.WriteProperty("Font", Font, Ambient.Font)
```

```
        Call PropBag.WriteProperty("BackStyle", UserControl.BackStyle, 1)
        Call PropBag.WriteProperty("BorderStyle", UserControl.BorderStyle, 0)
        Call PropBag.WriteProperty("Caption", lblColor.Caption, "A Sample
        ➥Caption")
        Call PropBag.WriteProperty("Alignment", lblColor.Alignment, 0)
    End Sub
```

The wizard inserted all the comments and warnings, as well as all the new subroutines and objects. If you compare this listing to the original one (see "The Code in the Rough Draft"), you'll see that this wizard, like the Script Wizard in the ActiveX Control Pad, does an amazing amount of work for you. Although the code looks complicated, breaking the code down into sections shows that it's pretty straightforward.

The first section comes right after you declare the global variable ColorChoice. The wizard has added a set of event declarations, and you'll note they're all associated with UserControl (just as you specified). The original three subroutines immediately follow, and then everything else relates to properties, events, and their mapping to component controls or to the aggregate control. The Property Get procedure gets the current value of a property. The Property Let procedure assigns a new value to a property. Each subroutine that involves RaiseEvent activates the indicated event.

The final two subroutines are very important, and you have to modify them slightly in order to ensure your control works correctly when you use it in the ActiveX Control Pad. The first, UserControl_ReadProperties, reads values that you saved about any of the properties during design time. UserControl _WriteProperties activates whenever you have to save the control. For your purposes, this occurs when you have inserted the control in an HTML Layout and you want to open the Script Wizard. All the property values that you've set in the Layout Control have to be saved, and this event signals the control to save them so they can reappear when necessary (when you exit the Script Wizard, for example), meaning that UserControl_ReadProperties can read them.

Both use PropertyBag, an object that holds information about a control, and has methods that enable you to read (ReadProperty) and write (WriteProperty) that information. Each time you move between designing a control and running it, or between the HTML Layout Control and the Script Wizard, you destroy the instance of the control you worked with, and when you redisplay the control, you create another instance. The PropertyBag preserves the necessary information across all the "destroys" and "creates."

You'll also see the word Ambient in these subroutines. An ambient value is a "suggested" value (suggested by the system)—for example, a suggested font for a label or a suggested color for a background.

Skill 17

We modify these last two subroutines by inserting On Error Resume Next as the first line in each one. The two subroutines should read:

```
'Load property values from storage
Private Sub UserControl_ReadProperties(PropBag As PropertyBag)
    On Error Resume Next
    UserControl.BackColor = PropBag.ReadProperty
    ➥("BackColor", &H8000000F)
    lstbxChoices.ForeColor = PropBag.ReadProperty
    ➥("ForeColor", &H80000008)
    UserControl.Enabled = PropBag.ReadProperty("Enabled", True)
    Set Font = PropBag.ReadProperty("Font", Ambient.Font)
    UserControl.BackStyle = PropBag.ReadProperty("BackStyle", 1)
    UserControl.BorderStyle = PropBag.ReadProperty("BorderStyle", 0)
    lblColor.Caption = PropBag.ReadProperty
    ➥("Caption", "A Sample Caption")
    lblColor.Alignment = PropBag.ReadProperty("Alignment", 0)
End Sub

'Write property values to storage
Private Sub UserControl_WriteProperties(PropBag As PropertyBag)
    On Error Resume Next
    Call PropBag.WriteProperty("BackColor", UserControl.BackColor,
    ➥&H8000000F)
    Call PropBag.WriteProperty("ForeColor", lstbxChoices.ForeColor,
    ➥&H80000008)
    Call PropBag.WriteProperty("Enabled", UserControl.Enabled, True)
    Call PropBag.WriteProperty("Font", Font, Ambient.Font)
    Call PropBag.WriteProperty("BackStyle", UserControl.BackStyle, 1)
    Call PropBag.WriteProperty("BorderStyle",
    ➥UserControl.BorderStyle, 0)
    Call PropBag.WriteProperty("Caption", lblColor.Caption, "A Sample
    ➥Caption")
    Call PropBag.WriteProperty("Alignment", lblColor.Alignment, 0)
End Sub
```

In the ReadProperties subroutine, On Error Resume Next protects against users' entering erroneous values from a Text Editor. (We used the ActiveX Control Pad Text Editor to enter property values for a TabStrip control in Skill 11.)

In WriteProperties, On Error Resume Next protects against writing the values incorrectly when you're working with the control in an HTML Layout or in an HTML document. Without this statement in WriteProperties, here's what can happen:

1. You insert your control into an HTML Layout Control.

2. You use the Properties sheet to set some property values.

3. Try to open the Script Wizard and error message appears.

4. Click on the error message, and diagonal lines appear on the control.

5. The Script Wizard opens.

6. After you finish with the Script Wizard, you close it to return to the HTML Layout Control.

7. Those diagonal lines are still on the control. Right-click on the control and select Properties.

8. The Properties sheet opens and…all the properties are gone! Not just the values you set, but the properties, too.

The Real LabelChange Control

At last we're ready to make a real control. Select File ➢ Make LabelChange.ocx…. The Make Project dialog box appears, opened to the folder with the existing version of `LabelChange.ocx`. Click OK, and when the Message Box appears asking if you want to replace the existing file, click Yes. After a few minutes (how many depends on your system), your new OCX file is registered, rested, and ready.

You're now in business.

Using Your New Control

Now you're going to use the control you created by embedding it into a Web page. You're going to set property values, write VBS, and make it interact with other controls, just like a control from a commercial ActiveX control vendor.

Here you go:

1. Close the Project Explorer window and close the VB5 CCE.

2. Answer No to the dialog box question about saving a VBG file.

3. Open the ActiveX Control Pad. In the Text Editor, save the file as `NewControl.htm` in your `skill 17` folder.

4. Select Edit ➢ Insert HTML Layout… and create a new Layout Control called `layout for NewControl`.

5. Save this layout in `skill 17`.

The Layout

Open the new Layout Control. Right-click in the Toolbox and select Additional Controls…. In the list of available controls, scroll down until you find your newly created control, LabelChange.LabelColor. Select this control, and you'll see its file path (which includes ski11 17) at the bottom of the list. Click its checkbox to put your new control on the Toolbox, and then click OK to close the list. On the Toolbox, you should now see the same icon that the VB5 CCE generates when you're finished creating a control. If you hover the mouse over this icon, you'll see the name of your new control in a Tool Tip. You're ready to use the new control in a layout.

Maximize the Control Pad and the layout. Select your new control, and draw it out on the layout so all the component controls are visible. First, right-click on the control and select Properties. The Properties sheet (see Figure 17.8) quickly shows you the results of your handiwork with the ActiveX Control Interface Wizard. It's a far cry from the Properties sheet in Figure 17.4.

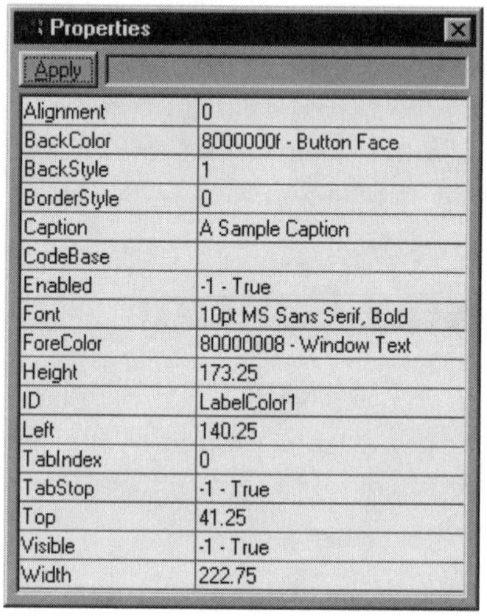

Properties	
Alignment	0
BackColor	8000000f - Button Face
BackStyle	1
BorderStyle	0
Caption	A Sample Caption
CodeBase	
Enabled	-1 - True
Font	10pt MS Sans Serif, Bold
ForeColor	80000008 - Window Text
Height	173.25
ID	LabelColor1
Left	140.25
TabIndex	0
TabStop	-1 - True
Top	41.25
Visible	-1 - True
Width	222.75

FIGURE 17.8: The Properties sheet of your new control shows the results of working with the ActiveX Control Interface Wizard.

In the Properties sheet, change the ID to **lblchngrNewControl**. If you feel like changing the Caption, Font, BackStyle, BorderStyle, and ForeColor, go right ahead. You'll work with the BackColor and the Caption in the script you're about to write.

Before you get to the script, insert a few more controls, two Command Buttons and a TextBox. The objective is to have a Web page on which:

• one Command Button shows the new control

• the other Command Button hides the new control

- the user can type into the TextBox and the typing appears as the caption of the new control's label

- clicking on the new control changes its background color

- double-clicking on the control resets its background to the original color

Insert two Command Buttons to the immediate right of lblchngrNewControl, one above the other. Change the upper button's ID to cmdbtnShow and its Caption to **Show**. Change the lower button's ID to cmdbtnHide and its Caption to **Hide**. Make both Captions bold.

Just below the Command Buttons, insert a TextBox and make it approximately the size of the Label in the new control. Change its ID to **txtbxCaption**. Your layout should look like Figure 17.9.

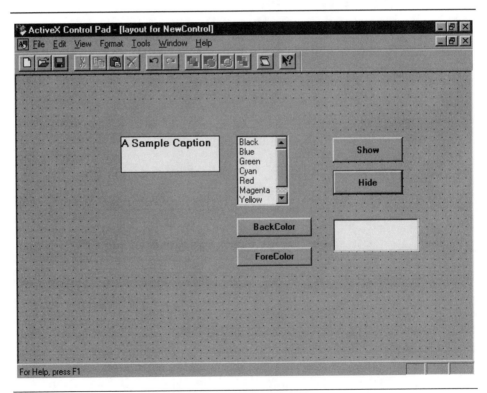

FIGURE 17.9: The *layout for NewControl* includes your newly created control, two Command Buttons, and a TextBox.

The Script

Open the Script Wizard and examine lblchngrNewControl. In the Event pane, click on the + to its left to display all the events. Do the same in the Actions pane to see all its methods and properties. In both cases it's a pretty full list, thanks again to the ActiveX Control Interface Wizard in the VB5 CCE.

The Command Buttons

Put the Script Wizard in Code View, and let's start with cmdbtnHide. Follow these steps:

1. In the Event pane, click the + to its left.

2. Select the Click event.

3. In the Actions pane, click the + to the left of lblchngrNewControl.

4. Double-click on lblchngrNewControl's Hide Control method.

5. The Script pane should display:

    ```
    Sub cmdbtnHide_Click()
    lblchngrNewControl.Visible = False
    ```

Now follow a similar agenda for cmdbtnShow:

1. In the Event pane, click the + to the left of cmdbtnShow.

2. Select the Click event.

3. In the Actions pane, click the + to the left of lblchngrNewControl.

4. Double-click on lblchngrNewControl's Show Control method.

5. The Script pane should look like this:

    ```
    Sub cmdbtnShow_Click()
    lblchngrNewControl.Visible = True
    ```

The New Control

Put the Script Wizard back into List View. We're going to associate some lblchngrNewControl events with color changes and List View allows us to work with a color palette:

1. In the Event pane, display the events of lblchngrNewControl by clicking its +.

2. Select the Click event.

3. In the Actions pane, select lblchngrNewControl's BackColor property, and double-click it.

4. In the resulting dialog box click the Color… button and then select any color (except the original gray) for the BackColor property. (I selected light blue.)

5. Click the OK button on the color palette to close the palette and return to the Script Wizard.

6. In the Event pane, select lblchngrNewControl's DblClick event.

7. In the Actions pane, double-click once again on lblchngrNewControl's BackColor property.

8. This time, select the original gray from the resulting color palette.

The TextBox

Let's finish things off by scripting the TextBox's Change event. The objective, remember, was to provide a TextBox so users can enter new captions for the Label in the aggregate control. Here are the steps to follow:

1. Return the Script Wizard to Code View.

2. In the Event pane, click txtbxCaption's + to display its events.

3. Select the Change event.

4. In the Actions pane, select lblchngrNewControl's Caption and double-click it.

5. In the Script pane, do the typing and clicking that produces:

```
Sub txtbxCaption_Change()
lblchngrNewControl.Caption = txtbxCaption.Value
```

To save your work and close the Script Wizard, click OK. Save your work in the Layout and select Window ➢ 1 New Control to go back to the Text Editor.

The HTML File

In the HTML document, change the Title to New Control, and in the line after <BODY> type **<H1> Under Control! </H1> <HR>**. The HTML document now looks like this:

```
<HTML>
<HEAD>
<TITLE>New Control</TITLE>
```

```
</HEAD>
<BODY>
<H1> Under Control! </H1> <HR>
<OBJECT CLASSID="CLSID:812AE312-8B8E-11CF-93C8-00AA00C08FDF"
ID="layoutforNewControl_alx" STYLE="LEFT:0;TOP:0">
<PARAM NAME="ALXPATH" REF VALUE="layout for NewControl.alx">
 </OBJECT>


</BODY>
</HTML>
```

Save your work. For one last time, we present VBS code in its entirety so that you can match it with what you've done. Here's the code for the layout (layout for NewControl.alx):

 layout for NewControl.alx

```
<SCRIPT LANGUAGE="VBScript">
<!--
Sub txtbxCaption_Change()
lblchngrNewControl.Caption = txtbxCaption.Value
end sub
-->
</SCRIPT>
<SCRIPT LANGUAGE="VBScript">
<!--
Sub cmdbtnShow_Click()
lblchngrNewControl.Visible = True
end sub
-->
</SCRIPT>
<SCRIPT LANGUAGE="VBScript">
<!--
Sub lblchngrNewControl_Click()
lblchngrNewControl.BackColor = &H00FFFF00
end sub
Sub lblchngrNewControl_DblClick()
lblchngrNewControl.BackColor = &H00C0C0C0
end sub
-->
</SCRIPT>
<SCRIPT LANGUAGE="VBScript">
<!--
```

```
Sub cmdbtnHide_Click()
lblchngrNewControl.Visible = False
end sub
-->
</SCRIPT>
<DIV ID="layoutforNewControl" STYLE="LAYOUT:FIXED;WIDTH:477pt;HEIGHT:293pt;">
    <OBJECT ID="lblchngrNewControl"
    CLASSID="CLSID:8A835314-B8EF-11D0-9421-444553540000"
    DATA="DATA:application/x-oleobject;
    ➥BASE64,FFODiu+40BGUIURFU1QAAJOyAACEAAAAAwAIAAvyVOcgAAAAXwBlAHgAdABl
    ➥AG4AdAB4ALIeAAADAAgACvJXRyAAAABfAGUAeAB0AGUAbgB0AHkA4BcAAA0A
    ➥BAB18w28wP///2YAbwBuAHQAA1LjC5GPzhGd4wCqAEu4UQEAAAC8Atx8AQAN
    ➥TVMgU2FucyBTZXJpZg== "
     STYLE="TOP:33pt;LEFT:91pt;WIDTH:223pt;HEIGHT:173pt;TABINDEX:0;
    ➥ZINDEX:0;">
    </OBJECT>
    <OBJECT ID="cmdbtnShow"
    CLASSID="CLSID:D7053240-CE69-11CD-A777-00DD01143C57"
    ➥STYLE="TOP:66pt;LEFT:330pt;WIDTH:74pt;HEIGHT:25pt;TABINDEX:1;
    ➥ZINDEX:1;">
        <PARAM NAME="Caption" VALUE="Show">
        <PARAM NAME="Size" VALUE="2619;873">
        <PARAM NAME="FontEffects" VALUE="1073741825">
        <PARAM NAME="FontCharSet" VALUE="0">
        <PARAM NAME="FontPitchAndFamily" VALUE="2">
        <PARAM NAME="ParagraphAlign" VALUE="3">
        <PARAM NAME="FontWeight" VALUE="700">
    </OBJECT>
    <OBJECT ID="cmdbtnHide"
    CLASSID="CLSID:D7053240-CE69-11CD-A777-00DD01143C57"
    ➥STYLE="TOP:99pt;LEFT:330pt;WIDTH:74pt;HEIGHT:25pt;TABINDEX:2;
    ➥ZINDEX:2;">
        <PARAM NAME="Caption" VALUE="Hide">
        <PARAM NAME="Size" VALUE="2619;873">
        <PARAM NAME="FontEffects" VALUE="1073741825">
        <PARAM NAME="FontCharSet" VALUE="0">
        <PARAM NAME="FontPitchAndFamily" VALUE="2">
        <PARAM NAME="ParagraphAlign" VALUE="3">
        <PARAM NAME="FontWeight" VALUE="700">
    </OBJECT>
    <OBJECT ID="txtbxCaption"
    CLASSID="CLSID:8BD21D10-EC42-11CE-9E0D-00AA006002F3"
    ➥STYLE="TOP:149pt;LEFT:330pt;WIDTH:91pt;HEIGHT:33pt;TABINDEX:3;
    ➥ZINDEX:3;">
        <PARAM NAME="VariousPropertyBits" VALUE="746604571">
```

Skill 17

```
        <PARAM NAME="Size" VALUE="3201;1164">
        <PARAM NAME="FontCharSet" VALUE="0">
        <PARAM NAME="FontPitchAndFamily" VALUE="2">
        <PARAM NAME="FontWeight" VALUE="0">
    </OBJECT>
</DIV>
```

Note that your VBS for lblchngrNewControl may not look exactly like this listing if you didn't choose exactly the same color I did. Even if you chose light blue, you might still see a discrepancy. The color palette offers two light blues, and although they look alike they have slightly different parameters.

Take a moment to study the code that specifies your new control. The DATA attribute stores a wealth of information about property settings and mappings in ways that HTML can understand. Compare this code with the earlier listing (in "The Code in the Rough Draft"), and you'll see major differences. The first listing, of course, has no DATA attribute because the control contained no property information. Notice the change in the CLASSID attribute because of the recompile (in other words, creating the OCX for the second time).

The Web Page

You're ready for your big moment: your first Web page featuring a control you created!

Open NewControl.htm in IE. Just before the page opens, you'll see a Message Box advising you of security considerations and advising you to proceed only if you're sure it's safe to do so. Click Yes (after all, this is one control you can vouch for) and after a few seconds you'll see your newly created aggregate control flanked on the right by two Command Buttons and a TextBox. Click on the new control to change its background color, and double-click to bring it back to gray. Manipulate the ListBox and the two component buttons to alter the colors in the Label. Use the Show and Hide buttons to make the control invisible and then visible again, and use the TextBox to change the Label's caption.

Figure 17.10 shows the Web page after manipulating the Label's colors, clicking the aggregate control, and supplying a new caption.

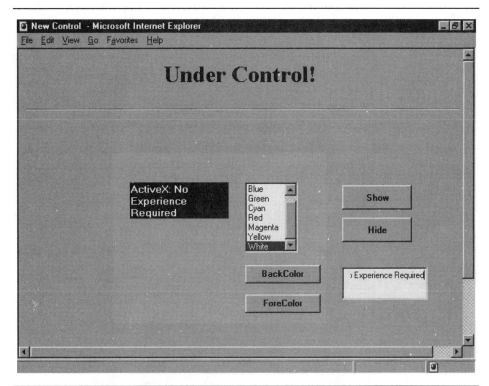

FIGURE 17.10: The New Control page in IE. The aggregate control has been clicked, the Label's colors selected, and a new caption provided.

Where to Go from Here

At this point, you can follow several different paths. One will take you farther with the control you just created. We've exposed a lot of properties, methods, and events for our aggregate and we've only scripted a few. You can try scripting a few more and inserting new controls for your control to work with. You might even put two instances of the new control on one page and have their events influence each other. Another possibility is to experiment with the Property Pages Wizard and create tabbed Properties pages for Web page designers to work with.

Still another possibility in this path hinges on distributing this control. The one you've put together will only work on your machine. If you want to distribute it to other Web designers, you have to create a setup program and a number of other files to go along with it. The VB5 CCE includes an Application Setup Wizard to help you through this process. It's not accessible from within the VB5 CCE application itself. You activate this Wizard by selecting Start ➤ Programs ➤ Visual Basic 5.0 CCE ➤ Application Setup Wizard.

You can take another path: You can solidify your knowledge by going through the tasks in this Skill once more with a different aggregate control. As you'll recall, you also created a temperature converter in Skill 16 and you haven't worked with that one yet. Try your hand at turning that aggregate into a working ActiveX control.

The best path of all? Start creating your own controls and watch them work on Web pages. As you create stunning effects with the controls and techniques you've already learned, you'll find that this path ends only at the edges of your imagination.

Summary

In the 1940s, hobbyists and GIs took great pleasure in fashioning radios out of wire, safety pins, and razor blades (aggregate controls of an earlier era?). Nothing, they said, could approach the feeling you get when a makeshift radio you assembled starts pulling in broadcast signals.

Fifty years later, we may have just duplicated that feeling: Imagine your delight when you've fashioned your own ActiveX control and developers can use it to reach tens of millions of people over the Internet.

In this Skill and the preceding one, you've learned the fundamentals about using components to build ActiveX technology. In the final Skill, you'll see where the technology is heading.

Are You Experienced?

Now you can...

- ☑ use many of the features of the VB5 CCE

- ☑ create your own aggregate ActiveX controls

- ☑ map properties, methods, and events to components of these aggregate controls

- ☑ understand what the VB5 CCE ActiveX Control Interface Wizard adds to your VB code

- ☑ script your own controls to interact with other controls on Web pages

Skill 17

Scoping Out the Future of ActiveX

- ❑ The evolution of Internet Explorer and HTML

- ❑ ActiveX and Office 97

- ❑ The future of ActiveX in business, academia, and entertainment

ActiveX technology is one of the cornerstones of Microsoft's vision for the Internet. The vision is that the Internet, like your hard drive or your local area network, is just one more resource you can access from your desktop. To make this vision a reality, the tools and controls you use to access and manipulate information on the Web should be the same ones you use to manipulate information on your local computer or computer network. The net effect (pardon the pun) of this vision should be a seamless connection between your computer and information, no matter where that information resides. ActiveX technology is one of the major building blocks that will make this vision a reality.

As the Web grows and develops, ActiveX technology will evolve along with it. As a result, the investment you've made in learning the ActiveX technology will reap increasing dividends. This Skill looks at the future of the ActiveX technologies and examines of ActiveX controls in Microsoft Office 97. It concludes with some speculation on how ActiveX controls can play an ever-expanding role in business, academia, and entertainment.

ActiveX Technologies

The controls you've learned about and created in this book are just one piece of the ActiveX puzzle, and that puzzle gets bigger and more complex every day. It consists of a number of technologies, and ActiveX is the glue that holds them together.

The full set of ActiveX technologies is:

- ActiveX controls

- ActiveX scripting

- The Java Virtual Machine

- Active Documents

- ActiveX Server Framework

The first two technologies are, of course, the subject of this book. The Java Virtual Machine is software that enables Internet Explorer (IE) to run small Java programs called *applets* and to integrate those applets with ActiveX controls. The

Active Documents technology allows you to use IE to view non-HTML documents, such as Microsoft Word documents or Microsoft PowerPoint presentations. (See "ActiveX and Office 97" for more information.) The ActiveX Server Framework technology offers functions such as security and database access for Web servers.

Originally designed for Windows, Microsoft is working to bring ActiveX to the Macintosh and to UNIX machines. When these efforts are complete, the ActiveX-based Web pages you create will be available to every computer user regardless of the kind of computer they use.

The Evolution of IE

ActiveX is tied closely to IE (and rumor has it that Netscape will build ActiveX capability into future versions of its browser). As IE evolves, its use of ActiveX will also continue to grow.

IE 4.*x*, for example, promises tighter integration between the browser and the Windows interface. In fact, the "browser" as you have come to know it will ultimately disappear and its capabilities will migrate directly into the operating system. A key element of this integration is the *ActiveX Control Viewer*, which makes it much easier to manage all the ActiveX controls you create and use.

Each time you visit the Microsoft ActiveX Component Gallery (or one of the other control repository sites mentioned in Skill 15), you're probably going to encounter a new control or two that you'll want to download. Each time you download a new control it gets installed to the 0ccache directory. After a while, the number of controls on your machine can mount up. Getting rid of the ones you don't need can be a real chore.

IE 4.*x*'s ActiveX Control Viewer changes all that. A directory that lives in the Windows folder, the Control Viewer will display icons for all the ActiveX controls on your machine. Right-clicking on a control's icon will produce a pop-up menu with choices that include Uninstall and Properties. The Properties choice opens a dialog box containing information on the company that produced the control, the last time you accessed it, its CLSID, and more. The Uninstall choice smoothly deletes the control from your hard drive.

The Evolution of HTML

In IE 4.*x* developers will create and use ActiveX controls in an environment called *Dynamic HTML*. You can think of Dynamic HTML as HTML on steroids—it's

Skill 18

based on an object model that turns everything on a Web page—not just controls—into programmable objects. With Dynamic HTML, you'll will be able to easily build Web pages that modify themselves in response to interactions with users (something like the on-the-fly page we created in Skill 14). Web page authors also will be able to quickly create rich multimedia effects (like animated objects, animated areas of text and color, and screen transition effects like the ones in PowerPoint).

The implications for ActiveX controls will be significant. For instance, some of the tasks that ActiveX controls currently handle will migrate to Dynamic HTML. As this happens, the ActiveX controls will take over more sophisticated tasks that extend Dynamic HTML's capabilities. They will become "smarter," more complex, and increasingly customizeable, fitted to the requirements of individual developers. Time spent learning a control development environment like VB5 CCE will pay off handsomely because customized ActiveX controls will play a more important role in Web page development.

Microsoft promises that Dynamic HTML will be the foundation for the next generation of User Interface design. The next generation of ActiveX controls will have to keep pace. In fact, we can already see the evolution in ActiveX controls. Philadelphia-based Speech Solutions, Inc. has recently released a suite of ActiveX controls that add speech recognition capabilities to applications. Check out information on these controls at `http://www.speechsolutions.com`.

 NOTE   You don't have to wait until ActiveX controls evolve to see some creative examples of their use. Take a look at `http://www.msn.com`.

ActiveX and Office 97

The popularity of the Web may expand greatly with the release of Microsoft Office 97. Millions of users are familiar with the tools in this suite of applications, and with the Internet-related tools and capabilities built-in to Office 97, they will easily make the transition to using those tools for creating Web-based products. But with Office 97, you can also use ActiveX controls on local documents that will never see the Web.

ActiveX controls make your Office documents interactive in the same manner that they make Web pages interactive. You can use ActiveX controls to documents you create in Word, slideshows you put together in PowerPoint, databases you build in Access, and spreadsheets you create in Excel.

The controls you add make your applications more powerful by providing additional information, functionality, or alternative pathways through an application. Figure 18.1 shows a Word document with a Command Button. Clicking the Command Button opens the informational Message Box in Figure 18.2. In a PowerPoint slideshow, Command Buttons could take the user through different sequences of slide presentations, based on the user's individual preferences.

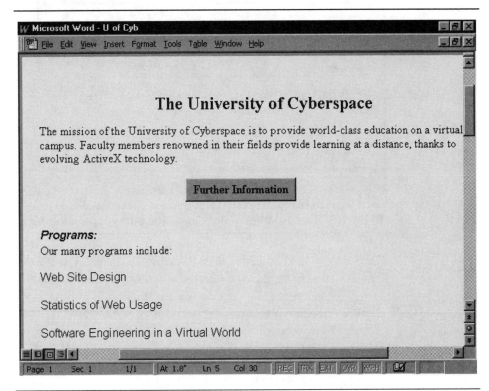

FIGURE 18.1: A Word 97 document with an embedded Command Button control

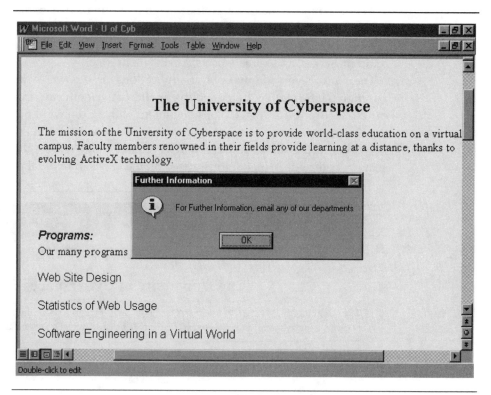

FIGURE 18.2: Clicking the Command Button opens this Message Box.

You can use IE to open an Office 97 document in its original format. This is the Active Document technology referred to in the previous section "ActiveX Technologies." The University of Cyberspace document in Figure 18.3 shows an example of a Word document that has not been converted to HTML.

Office 97 also lets you save a document in HTML format and then build on the HTML version the same way you would with any other HTML document. To give you an idea of how much work Word does when you save a document in HTML, here is the HTML code that Word generates for the University of Cyberspace document:

```
<HTML>
<HEAD>
<META HTTP-EQUIV="Content-Type" CONTENT="text/html;
➥charset=windows-1252">
<META NAME="Generator" CONTENT="Microsoft Word 97">
<TITLE>The University of Cyberspace</TITLE>
</HEAD>
<BODY>
```

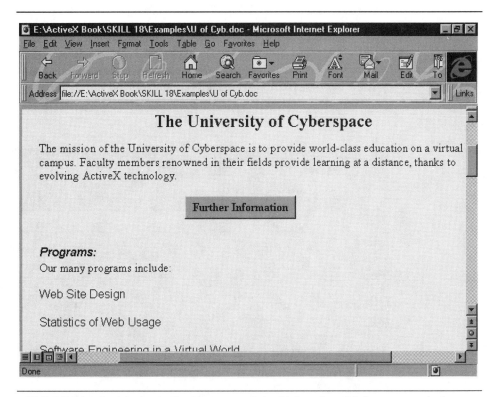

FIGURE 18.3: An Active Document—the University of Cyberspace mission statement in its original Word document format, opened in IE.

```
<B><FONT FACE="Courier PS" SIZE=5><P ALIGN="CENTER">
➡The University of Cyberspace</P>
</B></FONT><FONT FACE="Courier PS" SIZE=2><P> </P>
</FONT><P>The mission of the University of Cyberspace is to
➡provide world-class education on a virtual campus. Faculty
➡members renowned in their fields provide learning at a
➡distance, thanks to evolving ActiveX technology.</P>
<P></P>
<B><I><FONT FACE="Arial"><P>Programs:</P>
</B></I></FONT><P>Our many programs include:</P>
<FONT FACE="Arial"><P>Web Site Design</P>
<P>Statistics of Web Usage</P>
<P>Software Engineering in a Virtual World</P>
</FONT><P> </P>
<P> </P></BODY>
</HTML>
```

Notice that saving in HTML has eliminated the Command Button, but other styles and formats are intact. Figure 18.4 shows how this HTML document looks in IE.

 NOTE   The HTML <META> tag stores application-specific information.

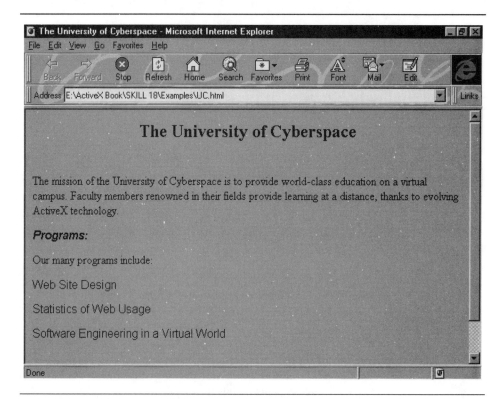

FIGURE 18.4: The University of Cyberspace HTML document opened in IE

You could use the ActiveX Control Pad's Text Editor to add a background and the Object Editor to embed some controls, building this document into an attractive Web page. The point is that people can now use tools they're familiar with to kick off their Web development efforts. Whether in local documents, intranet documents, or documents produced for the Web, ActiveX is sure to play a major role.

Business Applications

In order to discuss the use of ActiveX technologies in a business setting, it's helpful to list the functions that are critical for any business. Those functions are:

- Marketing
- Commerce
- Research
- Communications
- Customer service
- Product distribution
- Organization development

How can ActiveX technologies help with each of these function? Put another way, how can ActiveX controls embedded in a Web page on the company's Web site help the company perform a particular function? In the subsections that follow, we define each function and explore the possibilities.

Marketing

Marketing positions a company and its products and services, advertises that company's capabilities, and prospects for new leads.

A company could use ActiveX technologies to produce a multimedia marketing presentation, making it viewable at the company's Web site via the ActiveMovie control. A multimedia presentation like this would enable the company to present an informative, engaging, and entertaining look at what the company does.

Another possibility is to use ActiveX technologies to present a catalog of the company's goods and services. Each HTML page could contain an image of a product and a description, along with an audio-based pitch about the product.

Music via the Interactive Music control could provide another Web-based dimension to a company's image. While it offers no new information, the music would enhance the user's experience with the Web page and make it a more memorable one.

Agent technology offers a potentially useful tool to marketing departments. An intelligent agent control could go out on the Web and find potential new customers. This is different from the types of tasks that we gave the Agent in Skill 9, but it's representative of the jobs that most people give Agents.

IBM, a leader in research on Intelligent Agents, maintains a Web page devoted to its efforts in this field. You can find it at `http://www.networking.ibm.com/iag/iaghome.html`. This page provides information on IBM Intelligent Agent projects, technical white papers, and links to other research centers doing work in this field. You can find still more on Intelligent Agents at `http://botspot.com`, a Web site that connects to Agents (also known as "bots") from a variety of sources. You can use these Agents to seek out information for you on the Web. This site also provides links to many other Web sites that will enlighten you about Intelligent Agents.

Commerce

Commerce involves responding to a customer's order and receiving payment for products and services.

A major part of responding to an order is the process of *product configuration*. In this process, components are put together to make a product that meets the customer's requirements. ActiveX controls (like the previously mentioned catalog) that show the components and help the user combine them would facilitate this process. The controls would have to be intelligent enough to know which other components they can work with, as not every component can successfully combine with every other component.

Some Web sites feature "shopping carts" that enable a user to add items to an order until he or she is finished. The "cookie," a document property that we mentioned in Skill 14, is a string stored on a user's computer that contains information about a user and his or her interactions with a document. Cookies are ideal for implementing shopping carts, and an ActiveX ListBox control should provide an ideal interface between the user and the cookie.

VBS that calculates costs and inserts the costs into a Label control (to let the user know the final tally) will help with the payment process. Other controls, like TextBoxes, acquire the user's credit card information and submit it (along with the cost) to the company's server.

Research

A company's research efforts are geared toward finding out about its markets, competitors, relevant technology, legislative and regulatory changes, and materials it needs to do business.

Corporate researchers could have Agent constantly search the Web to provide the appropriate information and to watch for changes that affect the company's business.

Communications

In every corporation, efficient, timely communication is a must. Corporate employees must stay in touch with fast-breaking corporate developments. Many corporations are multinational, which adds to the challenge.

Corporate intranets can meet this challenge. Companies could use them to present corporate information (perhaps in multimedia format) to employees, and ActiveX controls would help the employees navigate through the information.

In many of today's organizations, a paper-based newsletter keeps employees informed of corporate developments at scheduled intervals. *Push technology* (thought by many to be the Next Big Thing in the Internet world) can change that. This technology sends news items to computers as events occur. It's called "push" to distinguish it from the standard method of information retrieval from the Web, in which users "pull" the information they need when they need it.

ActiveX controls can mediate person-to-person communication. For example, one control enables an application to send e-mail and another retrieves e-mail from a mail server. Embedding these in Web pages is a natural: A picture of an employee could be made clickable and the result of clicking the picture could be a window that allows a user to e-mail that employee.

Another ActiveX development called *NetMeeting* will find increasing application in the corporation of the future, particularly with respect to organizational communication. NetMeeting, a set of conferencing tools, enables users to hold virtual "meetings" with one another in a number of ways. They can communicate by voice in real-time, "chat" by typing messages in a window that all users can see, draw pictures in a window available to all users (as on a whiteboard in a real face-to-face meeting), transfer files to one another, and share applications.

Still another development, *NetShow*, enables the communication of audio and video from a Windows NT server machine to other computers. Ideal for organizational communication, NetShow could ultimately become the standard corporate vehicle for in-house multimedia presentations.

Skill 18

Customer Service

The customer service function deals with problem resolution. If a customer has a problem with a company's product or service, this is the corporate function that solves it.

Customer service is the business function that might produce the greatest evolutionary changes in ActiveX controls. Recent developments in the field of Artificial Intelligence (AI) could produce ActiveX controls that have the knowledge to solve most customer problems. The AI developments that spring most readily to mind are *expert systems*, *case-based reasoning*, and *neural networks*.

 NOTE   Artificial Intelligence is a branch of computer science. Its goal is to produce computer programs whose accomplishments, like playing chess, writing novels, solving real-world problems, make them seem to function at the level of human intelligence.

An expert system contains the knowledge of a human expert—a customer service representative or a field service engineer, for example—and can use this knowledge to solve problems. A case-based reasoning system contains an encyclopedia of problems and associated solutions: Its "intelligence" is the ability to recognize that a user's problem is similar to a problem already in its encyclopedia, even if it's worded differently. A neural network—so named because its processes are said to resemble the inner workings in a biological nervous system—is a piece of software that can be trained to recognize patterns (like the patterns of symptoms in frequently occurring problems).

ActiveX controls that incorporate these types of systems might be ideal for the Customer Service function: The user enters the symptoms, and the control recognizes and solves the problem.

 NOTE   Just as AI might provide the impetus for intelligent customer service, ActiveX and the customer service function might provide the impetus for an evolutionary change in AI. Why? Customer service applications have to be fast as well as accurate, and ActiveX controls have to be thin enough to download and install quickly on a user's machine. Many AI applications will have to change to meet these requirements.

Once a customer's problem has been recognized, ActiveX controls could pave the way for creative methods of walking the customer through the solution. Multimedia presentations (like an ActiveMovie) could show, step by step, how to implement the recommendations. Another possibility is that the system that solves the problem (whether AI-based or not) could create a Web page on the fly, based on interactions with the customer, and the newly created Web page could present the solution.

Still another possibility is that the whole customer service interaction could be handled by an agent similar to the one you worked with in Skill 9. With sufficient speech recognition capabilities, and sufficient knowledge of problems and solutions, an agent can make the whole customer service experience a pleasant one.

The idea of a customer service agent could blaze new trails in this area. Instead of waiting for problems to occur and responding to them, an agent included with a product could provide a tutorial on how that product works. If the product is a software package, the Microsoft agent model implemented in Office 97 would be a great one to follow.

Product Distribution

This is the process of delivering goods and services to the customer. The software industry is the likeliest candidate to utilize the Web for this business function. Web pages containing ActiveX controls that configure a software package and download it to the customer's machine are likely to increase in popularity.

Skill 18

Organization Development

The organization development function is concerned with upgrading a company's capabilities, from recruiting to training.

Many people in search of jobs put their résumés out on the Web. A corporate human resources department could send an intelligent agent out to search for these résumés and bring back a list of qualified candidates. The agent could maintain this list so that when a person takes a position with another company, the agent removes that individual from the list. Agents can keep track of existing employees as well, notifying them of training opportunities and positions within the company.

Companies could use ActiveX-based intranet pages to deliver training. Multimedia controls could present an entire training course in a new skill or corporate process, and they could be available whenever an employee wanted them. Via NetMeeting, corporate mentors could always be available, even to employees at remote locations.

An organization can also use its intranet to maintain a reference library of important corporate documents. One way to present these documents is in HTML format to take advantage of evolving ActiveX controls that could liven them up. Another way is to present them in PDF (Portable Document Format) through a control like the Adobe Acrobat Reader, in order to maintain their original corporate look, combined with some navigational capabilities.

Academic Applications

Just as we mapped out critical functions for businesses, we can conceptualize critical functions for the academic world. Some possible functions are:

- Teaching

- Research

- Institutional communication

- Scholarly communication

ActiveX technologies can provide assistance for each of these functions.

Teaching

Expect numerous institutions of higher education to implement "learning at a distance," a style of course presentation that eliminates the necessity to be on campus to take courses. Instead, course delivery can proceed via the Web. Multimedia presentation via ActiveX controls will be a prime vehicle for presenting the information in the future.

Some coursework can proceed through simulation. A student could learn how engines work, for example, by working with an engine simulator.

Hand-in-hand with course instruction is a methodology for Web-based student testing. Similar to product configuration, a student taking an exam has to decide on alternatives and submit them. Multiple choice exams could involve question presentation and option buttons that represent the choices. Grading could be instantaneous, providing immediate feedback for the student.

The idea of immediate feedback opens up another possibility for instruction, but probably not at the level of higher education. Coursework could be presented via "programmed instruction." The student reads some material about a topic and then immediately answers a question about the material. The answer determines where the course goes next. If the answer is correct, the next phase in the topic appears on the screen. If not, the coursework moves in a remedial direction. This would seem to be a natural technique to implement in Web pages, with ActiveX controls providing the navigation through the course.

Research

Computer-based data acquisition and data analysis form the basis for many areas of scientific research. In experiments in the field of cognitive psychology (the study of mental processes), for example, the computer presents stimuli onscreen, captures a person's keyboard response, times that response in milliseconds, and stores that information for statistical analysis. This could all be done using Web pages with ActiveX controls handling the stimulus presentation and the data acquisition.

 NOTE   Response timing in studies like these demands millisecond accuracy. Although we've thrown the term "milliseconds" around with wreckless abandon (particularly in Skills 4–6), the fact is that our Timer controls don't really perform at that level. The system checks the clock 18 times each second, not a thousand. For the purposes of the applications we developed earlier, that accuracy level is sufficient. For studies in cognitive psychology, it's not. This doesn't present a major problem, it just necessitates additional software (and perhaps hardware, depending on how one chooses to address the issue).

The advantage to having Web pages be the containers for data gathering is that they're easily modified for later studies and easy to communicate to others. It's often easier to show someone information than to describe it. Putting a computer-based experiment on a Web page makes it accessible to anyone in the scientific community that has access to the Web.

Skill 18

Scholarly Communication

Communicating the results of research is a hallmark of the academic world. At present, this is mostly the province of peer-reviewed, paper-based academic journals and conference proceedings.

Just as "e-zines," Web-based electronic magazines, are becoming increasingly prevalent, we might also expect to see "e-nals"—Web-based peer-reviewed academic journals. (Some text-based ones are already online.)

An e-nal (a term I just invented, as far as I know) would have advantages over a traditional academic publication. ActiveX controls could provide multimedia presentations that show exactly how a researcher carried out a study, and animated graphs could present the results in a lively and comprehensible way. The graphs could be an important consideration. A study often encompasses more variables than a two-dimensional graph can portray on a piece of paper. Animation and rotating graphs could easily address this problem.

The text in an e-nal would be comprehensible to a wide range of readers, thanks to hypertext. Authors could be required to include hypertexted explanations of keywords, phrases, and jargon. Novices could click on text they didn't understand and an explanation would appear onscreen box. Experts could just keep reading.

Web-based academic publishing would have another important advantage— easy access to referenced material. At present, if you're reading a research article and the author cites a previous study that piques your interest, you have to go the library to find the reference. In the best of all possible worlds, one would click on the reference to view it.

Before we get too carried away with the idea of e-nals, let's remember that archiving is an important aspect of academic research, and this brings a potential downside. How long should an e-nal remain on a server? What should we do with it when its time on the server has passed? How do we ensure permanence so future generations of researchers will have access to results that originally appeared in an e-nal? The research community has to address these questions before scholarly communication migrates from paper to the Web.

Entertainment

Dissecting this category is easy. The primary forms of entertainment are:

- Radio
- Television
- Movies

Multimedia controls, of course, will do the majority of the work in this area. Intelligent agents could also prove useful, finding appropriate types of entertainment for people who dispatch them onto the Web.

Radio

The RealAudio control you worked with in Skill 8 enables users to listen to live radio broadcasts over the Internet. Local broadcasts can now reach the whole world via streaming audio. Web sites for radio stations and radio networks will become more prevalent, and these Web sites will have to feature streaming audio. Archived audio is also important, enabling you to listen to radio broadcasts (or parts of broadcasts) at times convenient for you.

NOTE Head over to `http://1on1sports.com` and you'll see (and hear) an example of what I mean. That's the Web site of the One-on-One Sports Network, which archives clips from its call-in sports shows.

Television

With the advent of streaming audio and streaming video, can an ActiveX control for streaming television be far behind? If it's not available by the time you read this, somebody is sure to be on the verge of developing an ActiveX control that sits inside a Web page and tunes an onscreen "television" to pick up live TV broadcasts. Several organizations are working toward converging the television and the PC, so a control like this will likely become a reality sooner rather than later.

Web sites for major TV networks will probably start featuring streaming television so when you visit these sites you can watch whatever TV show is in progress on that network. Local TV stations will probably follow suit on their own Web sites. Archived TV shows will enable us to watch our favorite programs at times that are convenient for us. If we download and store those shows for later viewing, will we see the end of the VCR?

Movies

Web sites for major studios show previews for upcoming movies. If you want to design sites like these, multimedia controls like ActiveMovie are a necessity. Expect to see an ActiveX control of Progressive Networks' recently released streaming video player (RealVideo), which will also be indispensable to sites that send video your way.

As computer hardware becomes more sophisticated, perhaps you'll be able to watch entire movies on computers at your leisure. ActiveX controls can play a role in this by displaying the movies and allowing you to advance, replay, and archive them. Another potential death-knell for the VCR?

The Web opens up an additional avenue for entertainment: Coming soon (perhaps) to a computer near you: entertainment produced specifically for the Web. To check out a company that's starting to work in this area, go to the Web site of

Skill 18

California-based Digital Planet (`http://www.digiplanet.com/showcase.html`). You'll get a sense of the way Web-based entertainment is shaping up.

Will we one day see movies and TV shows that reside not in theaters or on TV stations, but entirely on the Web? Will the computer be our major source of entertainment as well as information and communication? Will we be able to use the Web to personalize our entertainment schedules?

Stay tuned.

Summary

As you can see from all these possibilities, the future of ActiveX is an extremely bright one. (With all the potential academic applications, maybe someday we really *will* see a University of Cyberspace.) If you know how to work with multimedia controls and agent controls, you'll surely be able to stay on top of the expanding Web.

Keep in mind that the possibilities outlined in this Skill are just one person's ideas of the way the future will unfold—additional possibilities undoubtedly abound in the minds of others. After you've developed some applications, you'll see the potential of ActiveX technology, and you'll bring that potential to fruition in your own way.

You've taken your first steps in a great adventure. Exactly how great the adventure is depends on you.

Are You Experienced?

Now you can...

- ☑ **understand the larger picture of ActiveX technologies**
- ☑ **see how ActiveX controls can work within Microsoft Office 97**
- ☑ **understand how ActiveX can help businesses with their critical functions**
- ☑ **comprehend the potential of ActiveX in the academic world**
- ☑ **understand how ActiveX can work in entertainment applications**

GLOSSARY

G

Glossary

a

accelerator key

A keyboard shortcut for an onscreen control. Pressing Alt+the accelerator key gives the focus to the control and activates one or more of its events. The activated events vary with the type of control.

ActiveX Control Pad

A development environment that enables you to quickly and easily put ActiveX objects (called *controls*) into your Web pages. The ActiveX Control Pad has four major components. See also *Text Editor*, *Object Editor*, *HTML Layout Control*, and *Script Wizard*.

ActiveX Control Viewer

A key element in IE 4.*x*, the ActiveX Control Viewer is a folder that makes it easy to manage the ActiveX controls you download and use. The ActiveX Control Viewer presents an icon of each control. You use the icon to retrieve information about the control or to uninstall the control.

agent

A form of intelligent software that carries out a well-defined task such as seeking out information on the World Wide Web or helping you work with an application. Some agents watch users and learn to anticipate their needs.

aggregating

The process of combining existing ActiveX controls to produce a new control.

ALX

The file extension for files you create via the HTML Layout Control.

applet

A small Java program embedded into a Web page.

argument

A variable that a subroutine or function has to have in order to execute.

array

A collection of items tied together because they're similar in some way. You can refer to them by the name of the array and the index number. If this makes you think of a table and its rows (where the table is the array, and the row numbers are indexes), you've pretty much got it.

attributes

Parameters that provide a browser with information on exactly how to implement an HTML tag. See also *tag*.

AVI

An acronym for Audio/Video Interleaved. See also *interleaving*.

b

bitmap

A graphics format with the .BMP extension that takes up a lot of space, even for simple drawings. Although you may be accustomed to working with bitmap files, they're typically too cumbersome for Web applications. See also *GIF*, *JPEG*.

c

class

A group of objects that have the same attributes and behaviors.

COM

An acronym for Component Object Model, Microsoft's specification for building reusable software components.

compiled code

Code that runs by itself, without an interpreter. See also *interpreted code*, *scripting language*.

control assembly

An ActiveX control formed by combining existing controls.

control

A User Interface component such as a command button, list box, or text box.

d

dockability

In VB5 CCE, a feature that enables you to determine whether you can drag a window, such as the Toolbox, and reposition it in the IDE.

dynamic array

An array whose size is undeclared and is set programmatically (in other words, while the program runs).

dynamic HTML

A form of HTML featured in IE 4.x, it's based on an object model that turns everything on a Web page—not just controls—into programmable objects.

e

event

An occurrence—like a click, a double-click, or a value change—which causes an object to respond.

Event Handler

A procedure activated by a specific event.

f

focus

The ability of an object to take input (for example, keystroke input or mouse-clicks). The application or the user can determine which object has the focus, as only one object can have the focus at a time. A highlighted caption or title bar indicates the object that has the focus.

form controls

HTML's controls that predate the advent of ActiveX. They enable a user to enter text and make choices. While not as rich as ActiveX controls in either variety or functionality, form controls are still prevalent throughout the Web and probably will be for the foreseeable future.

frame
A subdivision of a browser window. A frame is itself a window and has its own properties.

function
A procedure that returns a value.

g

GIF
Acronym for Graphic Interchange Format, a format CompuServe created to combat long transmission times for graphics on the Web. Each pixel in a GIF image can store up to eight bits. This means that a GIF image can have up to 256 colors.

global variable
A variable that all the subroutines and functions in a script can work with. (By contrast, a *local* variable can only live and work in one subroutine or function.)

GUID
Acronym for Global Unique Identifier, a 128-bit integer that COM assigns to an object. You can see one every time you look at the CLSID for an object embedded in an HTML document or a layout. See also *COM*.

h

HTML Layout Control
Part of the ActiveX Control Pad, a two-dimensional visual tool to edit HTML files in WYSIWYG fashion. See also *ActiveX Control Pad*.

Hot Spot
An invisible ActiveX control that delineates an area that responds to mouse events.

HyperText Markup Language (HTML)
A language used for creating documents on the World Wide Web, HTML uses tags (indicated by surrounding angle-brackets) to mark the structural parts of a document.

i

image map
In HTML, a way for a user to interact with a graphic. An image map links part of an image to a URL. Point-and-click maps are a typical application of this feature.

index
An item's position in an array. In a zero-based array, the top position is zero, the bottom position is one less than the number of items in a ListBox.

inheritance
The feature of object-oriented programming that endows an instance of a class with the same properties as all the other instances of the same class.

Integrated Development Environment (IDE)
VB5 CCE's visual environment that integrates layout, design, editing, and a number of other functions.

interleaving
Combining video and audio into one signal. See also *AVI*.

interpreted code

Code that only works if the right interpreter is on hand to run it. See also *compiled code, scripting language*.

j

JPEG

An acronym for Joint Photographic Experts Group, it's the name of the format this group derived for transmitting complex images such as photographs. JPEG (pronounced "JAY-peg") stores 24 bits in each pixel. As a result, an image in this format can have more than 16 million colors. Although 16 million colors sounds like a lot, a JPEG image, when decompressed, isn't exactly the same as the precompressed original image. See also *lossy*.

l

lossy

A loss of information that occurs in JPEG files due to compression. The information is typically imperceptible to the human eye, however. Lossiness is adjustable: If you decrease the degree of compression, you increase the image quality and lower the lossiness. See also *JPEG*.

m

marquee

An HTML feature that allows text in a Web page to move across the screen.

method

A behavior built into a control, a method is a procedure that a control knows how to follow automatically.

module

A set of declarations (like Dim statements that define variables) followed by procedures. Each Code window displays a module.

n

NetMeeting

A set of conferencing tools that enables users to hold virtual "meetings" with one another in a number of ways. They can communicate by voice in real-time, "chat" by typing messages in a window that all users can see, draw pictures in a window available to all users (as on a whiteboard in a real face-to-face meeting), transfer files to one another, and share applications.

NetShow

A technology that enables the communication of audio and video from a Windows NT server machine to other computers. Ideal for organizational communication, NetShow could ultimately become the standard corporate vehicle for in-house multimedia presentations.

o

object

An instance of a class. An ActiveX object has properties, events, and methods. See also *class*.

Object Editor

Part of the ActiveX Control Pad, used for setting values for properties of ActiveX controls and inserting those controls into an HTML document.

object orientation

A kind of programming that focuses on objects that perform procedures and on procedures that operate on objects, rather than on sequences of programming steps. See also *procedure*.

p

polymorphic

A object-oriented term that indicates an operation is different from class to class (or from subclass to subclass).

pop-up menu

A menu that appears when you right-click inside a window or a Web page.

procedure

A function or a subroutine.

Properties sheet

A window that lists the properties of an object and allows you to set the values of those properties.

property

An attribute of an object; you set its value to determine a characteristic of the object or an aspect of the object's behavior.

push technology

A technology that sends news to computers as events occur. It's called "push" to distinguish it from the standard method of information retrieval from the Web, in which users "pull" the information they need when they need it.

r

radio buttons

A group of option buttons set up so the user can select only one—just like using a button on a radio to select a station.

Registry

The Windows 95 central repository of information on how you've configured software and hardware on your computer.

s

script

A program written in a scripting language such as VBS. In ActiveX, a script can specify how ActiveX controls will work with one another and with the user.

Script Wizard

An ActiveX Control Pad tool that guides you as you build VBScript. See also *ActiveX Control Pad*.

scripting language

A language such as Visual Basic Scripting Edition, designed to operate inside another environment (for example, an HTML document). Code written in a scripting language is interpreted. See also *interpreted code, compiled code*.

Setting Box

The rectangular area at the top of a Properties sheet, into which you enter values for a control's properties.

sizing handles

Little squares that appear on the boundaries of a control at designtime. Sizing handles enable you to use the mouse to adjust the size of a control.

start tag

In HTML, the first of a pair of tags that marks a structure within a document. For example, <TITLE> marks the beginning of a document's title.

stop tag (or end tag)

In HTML, the second of a pair of tags that marks a structure within a document. For example, </TITLE> marks the end of a document's title.

subclassing

Customizing an ActiveX control to produce a new one. For example, you could subclass a TextBox control to accept only integers.

subroutine

A procedure that does not return a value.

t

tag

The angle-bracketed element in HTML that marks the structures in a document.

Text Editor

A component of the ActiveX Control Pad for creating pages in HyperText Markup Language (HTML). See also *ActiveX Control Pad*.

TextBox

An ActiveX control into which a user can type new text as well as copy, cut, and paste existing text.

u

URL

An acronym for Uniform Resource Locator, the address of a document or other resource on the Internet.

Index

Note to the Reader: First level entries are in **bold**. Page numbers in **bold** indicate the principal discussion of a topic or the definition of a term. Page numbers in italic indicate illustrations.

Symbols

A

F

G

H

I

N

O

P

W

X

Z

The ActiveX Control Pad

Text Editor   HTML Layout Control

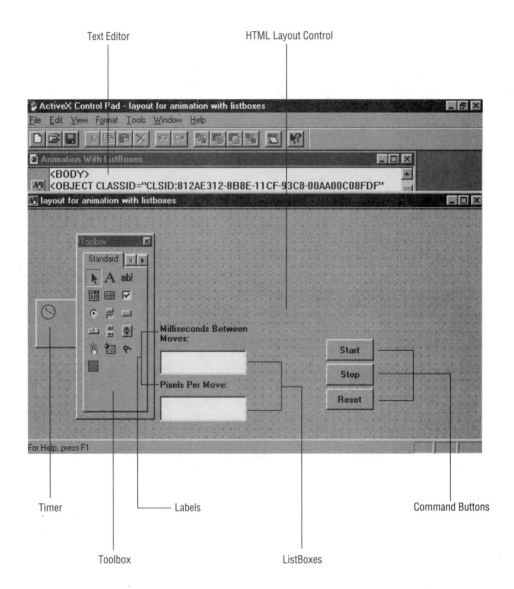

Timer   Labels   Command Buttons

Toolbox   ListBoxes